HUMAN GROWTH AND
DEVELOPMENT IN A

Theoretical and Practice P

Edited by
Jonathan Parker and Sara Ashencaen Crabtree

P

First published in Great Britain in 2020 by

Policy Press
University of Bristol
1-9 Old Park Hill
Bristol
BS2 8BB
UK
t: +44 (0)117 954 5940
pp-info@bristol.ac.uk
www.policypress.co.uk

North America office:
Policy Press
c/o The University of Chicago Press
1427 East 60th Street
Chicago, IL 60637, USA
t: +1 773 702 7700
f: +1 773-702-9756
sales@press.uchicago.edu
www.press.uchicago.edu

British Library Cataloguing in Publication Data
A catalogue record for this book is available from the British Library

Library of Congress Cataloging-in-Publication Data
A catalog record for this book has been requested

ISBN 978-1-4473-3737-9 paperback
ISBN 978-1-4473-3738-6 ePdf
ISBN 978-1-4473-3739-3 ePub

The right of Jonathan Parker and Sara Ashencaen Crabtree to be identified as editors of this work has been asserted by them in accordance with the Copyright, Designs and Patents Act 1988.

The statements and opinions contained within this publication are solely those of the editors and contributors and not of the University of Bristol or Policy Press. The University of Bristol and Policy Press disclaim responsibility for any injury to persons or property resulting from any material published in this publication.

Policy Press works to counter discrimination on grounds of gender, race, disability, age and sexuality.

Cover design by blu inc
Front cover image: Stocksy/Ruth Black
Printed and bound in Great Britain by CMP, Poole
Policy Press uses environmentally responsible print partners

Contents

List of figures, tables and boxes

Figures

Tables

Boxes

Notes on contributors

Sara Ashencaen Crabtree is Professor of Social and Cultural Diversity and co-convener of the Women's Academic Network at Bournemouth University. She is the author of the first European book on *Islam and Social Work* (2008).

Elena Cabiati is Lecturer and Researcher in Social Work at the Catholic University of Milan and Brescia. She teaches Methodology of Social Work and Intercultural Social Work. Her main research interests are intercultural social work and social work education. She has worked as social worker and middle manager in child protection services.

Valentina Calcaterra is Lecturer and Researcher in Social Work at the Catholic University of Milan. She teaches Methodology of Social Work and Participatory Methods in Social Work. She has interests in community work, child protection and relational social work. She has worked as a social worker and independent advocate.

Julie Christie is the International Service Manager for the Dementia Centre, Hammond Care, an established international centre for research and education. She is Visiting Research Fellow at the University of Edinburgh and Adjunct Lecturer at the University of New South Wales, Australia.

Mastoureh Fathi is a Marie Skłodowska-Curie fellow at the Institute for Social Science in the 21st Century at University College Cork, Ireland. Her research revolves around everyday experiences of migration with a focus on intersectionality, gender and class in migration processes, identity, home-making and belonging in diaspora and the importance of objects in displacement.

Fabio Folgheraiter is Professor of Social Work at the Catholic University of Milan and Brescia where he is manager of the Bachelor's, Master's and PhD programmes in Social Work. He is the founder of the relational social work method, coordinator of the Relational Social Work Research Centre and editor of the journal *Relational Social Work*. He has published widely and internationally on relational social work.

Rachel Fyson is Professor of Social Work and Director of the Centre for Social Work at the University of Nottingham. She has researched widely in the area of intellectual disability policy and practice.

Vanessa Heaslip is Associate Professor of Nursing at Bournemouth University. She has researched peoples marginalised in society, especially the Roma population.

Richard Heslop teaches Criminology at Bournemouth University and the Open University. He served for 28 years as a police officer in West Yorkshire Police before joining academia.

Maggie Hutchings is Associate Professor of Transformative Education in the Department of Social Sciences and Social Work at Bournemouth University. Her research interests focus on practice-based education, interprofessional learning and widening participation with care leavers and other disadvantaged groups.

Hyun-Joo Lim is Senior Lecturer in Sociology at Bournemouth University. She has an interest in transnational families and migrant mothers.

Jonathan Parker is Professor of Society and Social Welfare at Bournemouth University. He is author of the best-selling book *Social Work Practice* (Sage, 2017).

Margarete Parrish is Senior Lecturer in Social Work at Bournemouth University.

Bridget Penhale is Reader in Mental Health and Older People at the University of East Anglia. With a professional qualification in social work, she had an extensive career in social work and social work management. In her subsequent academic career she has developed research expertise in elder abuse and adult safeguarding.

Sam Porter is Professor of Nursing Sociology at Bournemouth University. He has research interests in critical realism, palliative care nursing and social theories.

Gabriele Schäfer is Professor in the School of Social Work at the University of Applied Sciences in Bremen/Germany. She is trained as a psychologist and family therapist and has worked in several therapeutic institutions in Auckland, New Zealand.

Peter Szto is Professor of Social Work at the Grace Abbott School of Social Work, University of Nebraska at Omaha. His current research and area of publication focuses on documentary photography as a tool of social research, social welfare development in China, and international social work.

Steve Tee is Professor and Executive Dean of the Faculty of Health and Social Sciences at Bournemouth University. He is a nurse by professional background.

Acknowledgements

This book would not have been possible without the past contributions, patience and kindness of our teachers and guides, our social work and other professional colleagues over the years and, most of all, those people with whom we have worked as social workers. Our thanks go to you all. In relation to compiling the current volume we would like to give special thanks to Catherine Gray who first discussed the idea with us in the early spring of 2016 and worked alongside us encouragingly as we strived to bring our authors together. We would also like to thank Helen Carter, the marvellous development editor, who brought us expertly and swiftly to get to the production stage, passing us into the capable hands of production editor, Vaarunika Dharmapala. Of course, our gratitude must also go to the authors of chapters who put up with our demands and requests, often in the face of very tight timescales, with good humour and fortitude. There are always too many people to thank personally in a project like this and for this we humbly apologise. You are remembered; without you all, this book would not have been possible.

Introduction

Jonathan Parker and Sara Ashencaen Crabtree

Introduction to this textbook

This book forms the second of a two-volume edited set which offers readers a comprehensive collection of authored chapters covering theories and models of human growth and development in their contemporary application to social work practice with adults. A critical discussion is offered throughout that seeks to challenge assumed, taken-for-granted normative wisdom, such as that human development follows given stages and those being normally linear. If we take time to reflect on these assumptions based on our own life experiences to-date, or those people that we know, we will soon come across examples which contradict these ideas of normative patterns to realise that human growth and development is much more fluid and diverse than theories often suggest. This runs as a counter to the traditional kinds of approaches to human growth and development that have been criticised for privileging hegemonic concepts from Western science and medicine and ignoring difference and diversity. Psychoanalytic models, learning theories and biological development theories are explored and discussed, but this is done within an integrated framework that understands the influence of the socio-cultural worlds inhabited by people at all stages in their lives.

The book brings together the wide and sometimes contrasting or competing discussions of growth and development. Human life, at whatever stage one currently finds oneself, is complex and messy and cannot be fitted neatly into theoretical boxes. Thus, we present growth and development in adulthood as mutable and adaptable, something dependent on a variety of bio–psycho–social–spiritual factors and an individual's response to them from the perspective of their own ecology. Readers are offered understandings that can be applied to social work, health and social care, education, nursing and midwifery practice with adults of all ages in ways that allows adaptation of that knowledge to individual circumstances.

The two volumes share similar formats and are divided into three parts. In the first part of the book, there will be a critical examination of key models and theories of human growth and development. Following this, the book will present and discuss how these concepts relate to common issues and events in human life including physical and emotional development, as an individual adult or member of a family, and in work and leisure environments, in developing external relationships, losses in adulthood, continuing education and learning, health, (dis)ability, sexuality, the impact of socio–cultural and structural factors, and transitions throughout the life course. These areas of life will be considered from the perspective of social work professional practice and cognate disciplines and how they might exert and impact on people using human services, organisations and social work professionals themselves.

As a student of social work, this textbook will equip you with the tools:

- to comprehend key theories and concepts in human growth and development;
- to reflect on your journey of development and those of people that you know well in terms of human growth and development and how this compares or contrasts with the theories and concepts discussed here;
- to recognise how difference and diversity found in people and communities may influence such patterns and stages in human life;
- to be able to apply your understanding in relevant situations in practice contexts.

Who should use this textbook?

The main audiences for this book are:

1. social worker students, practitioners and academics;
2. human service professionals in cognate and allied disciplines;
3. other students studying health and social care, psychology, nursing and education may also benefit from developing a deeper understanding of theoretical and conceptual frameworks that form essential information for good professional practice with people.

How to use this textbook

This textbook seeks to enhance your learning as part of your introductory social work course, it will enable you to set into a wider theoretical context many of the concepts that relate to human behaviour and need that you will meet during your studies. It is essential reading to understand the integral and enmeshed domains of the physical, the psychological, the cultural, the generational and the spiritual that construct what we understand by a 'person'. The *case studies* and *examples* used throughout the volume are designed to help the reader to make links between theory, concept and realistic life scenarios. Each chapter periodically has *reflection points*, encouraging you to stop and think deeply about the issues covered before moving on. Accordingly, this book will also help you to develop the reflective skills that are essential to critical social work in thinking about how what you have learned, what thoughts it elicits, how what you have read relates or not to your own life and relationships – and why that might be; and in particular how you can use and adapt these ideas to create your own 'best' practice.

A note on terminology

While both volumes in this two-part edited collection are primarily targeted at a social work audience, we are also aware of and welcome a potentially wider readership. In recognition of this we frequently use the term 'human services' to denote the range of allied professions that come under the general idea of the 'helping professions'. Social work, as well as the work of these other professions, is not a neutral activity: it is passionate, engaged and committed in its ethos and its practice, where often sights of deprivation, unfairness and hardship will shake our equilibrium and belief in a fair and just world order. People are both the same, in their basic needs, as Maslow's (1943) Hierarchy of Need indicates – and very different as well in so many ways. Consequently, we need to bring a sharply critical lens to bear on the theoretical and conceptual ideas discussed here, along with the humility and intellectual curiosity to perceive the fascinating and often inspiring differences of people, that are referred to in this volume, but more importantly still, through our professional practice. For this reason, we have preferred to avoid the term 'lifespan development' in the title of these books as too suggestive of some predictable and linear process that will affect all people at more or less the same time, whoever they are or wherever they may be. In preference our chosen titles of 'human growth and development' acknowledges human life as full of intriguing and unpredictable potential that questions the very nature of what is growth in human life? What do we mean by human development? Such questions we invite the reader to keep in mind and to reflect on throughout.

Textbook outline

This book is presented in the following three parts:

- Part I: Theories and models of human growth and development in adults
- Part II: Specific developmental issues
- Part III: Professional practice

Detailed overview of this textbook

Part I: Theories and models of human growth and development in adults

Each of the following chapters will continue to explore the fluidity of the line between childhood and youth and moving into adulthood whilst developing notions of development, growth and change throughout adult life. The complex concept of transitions will form part of this discussion bridging this volume and its companion.

Each chapter in Part I will follow a similar format allowing also for individual authors to stamp their positions and qualities on them. Each chapter, with some individual, creative variation, will include an:

- Introduction
- History and development of the theories and models
- Key thinkers and theories
- Place within contemporary human service practice
- Critical perspectives and thinking

Chapter 1 will set the scene for considering practice and other models. We outline the more traditional theories including bio-physical approaches to growth and development in adults, psychodynamic approaches and social learning theories. This allows us to move through the book considering ways in which these models and theories can be adapted and shaped and where new understandings can add to our knowledge, and therefore enhance our practice.

Chapter 2 builds upon the first chapter by moving into the amalgam of psychosocial and social learning theory perspectives to consider the ways in which cognitive theories of development add a fresh perspective that includes the importance of internal mechanisms and emotions. From this we move into **Chapter 3** that explores moral, spiritual and existential development. The re-emergence of spiritual and existential aspects of our human selves has added another dimension to consider in the holistic development of through the life course. These concepts have often been associated exclusively with religion and, to a large extent, erroneously avoided as a result. However, in cultural terms the belief systems and faiths of individuals, families and communities represent important reference points in growth and development, sometimes marked by physical and/or psycho-social ritual, and religion cannot be avoided. Equally so, spirituality and the things that people find most meaningful in life are powerful forces endorsing or questioning 'right' development within particular social contexts and in terms of the individual's sense of place within his or her world. This chapter will explore how spirituality and beliefs systems have been 're-discovered' and present an excursus into their importance in the lives of people as they move through life. A critical perspective will be taken that questions 'givens' and indicates something of the fluidity of belief systems and its place within the growth and development of all people of all ages.

Chapter 4 explores the potential of relational approaches to social work in working with the emotions and range of ways of being in contemporary environments. Whilst, finally, in Part I of this volume, **Chapter 5** considers critical perspectives on human growth and development. The ways in which the world is experienced in multiple ways and dependent on a range of social and structural positions, alongside the influence of individual social actors on the world around them and the world on their development, will be examined and questioned in this chapter. The malleability and cultural specificity of models and theories of human growth and development will be discussed, and a critical perspective will be offered as a way of ensuring that models and theories are not applied in a prescriptive way but seen within a wider ecological context in which individual experiences and characteristics are part of the mix influencing growth and development for individuals.

Part II: Specific developmental issues

The second part of the book introduces specific issues that are commonly considered in traditional discussions of human growth and development. Each chapter will question the application of the models and understandings whilst seeking to inculcate a critical edge.

Chapter 6 explores the socio-historical development of research concerning adult attachment, bonding and relationships in adult life. The complex socio-political context of Bowlby's and Ainsworth's early discussions of attachment theory in respect of children and young people and attachment models will be revisited as social, historical and spatial contexts develop and change. A critique of the political and economic impacts of attachment as well as those having an impact on intra-psychic and interpersonal well-being will also be considered.

Chapter 7 examines relationship development in diverse cultures building on the exploration of relationship development in the companion volume to this work. It introduces perspectives that are often ignored by the Westernised focus of much social work and human professions thinking and academic work. We follow this in **Chapter 8** by debunking the myths that education stops at the end of childhood. Schooling in childhood and youth represents a formative and formal experience for the majority but it is not something that ends with the transition to adulthood. With increased educational expectations post-compulsory schooling and expectations of continuing education and learning in most occupations it is important to consider education and learning throughout adult life. This goes further than education serving the instrumental purposes of work and career and also involves learning for pleasure and leisure, something exemplified by the burgeoning of the University of the Third Age over recent decades.

Chapter 9 looks again at life course criminology, this time from the perspective of adults. Relationship development and social mores have a great impact on the ways in which norms are established and rules governing social behaviour are accepted. Relationships with peers and within families exert a significant impact on the social development and behaviour of individuals, the opportunities they get in society and their subsequent development. The role of environment and relationships in instilling values and codes of behaviour are recognised as central to each adult's development as a social being as well as in developing skills and competence that can be put to 'good or ill'.

Chapter 10 explores how the health and/or (dis)ability statuses of adults affects their potential for engagement with other people and organisations just as it does with children and young people. It is written by a nurse academic demonstrating how important multidisciplinary knowledge is when practising in this area. An understanding of the ways in which social and medical models of health and disability are employed and assumed by both human service professionals and people using services themselves will be explored critically forming a backdrop to chapters in the professional practice section. This chapter leads into an exploration of the historical and particular understandings of death and dying that influence the ways we approach it in Western society in **Chapter 11**. Adult experiences of loss and bereavement are wide ranging and the coping strategies and rituals surrounding them are equally broad and culturally diverse at macro and micro levels. Loss of jobs, relationships, health and security feature prominently across different groups and bereavement and impending death affect all adults especially as they age. The profound and often lasting influence of experiencing various forms of loss and bereavement require understanding of the context of the adult social world which is constantly changing and complex. This chapter bridges the second and third parts of the volume by reflecting on some of the applications of the core knowledge in professional practice.

Chapter 12 discusses ways of working with people with disabilities. The social and historical contexts of working with physical and learning disabilities in adults will be described and critiqued as socially constructed and associated with particular cultural and social mores. Professional and policy responses reflect valorised assumptions of how people with disabilities and their families should behave and interact with wider society and prescribe behaviours which construct social and cultural definitions of disability that may reflect power positions that exclude or include certain group within society. Concepts of social role valorisation and the campaign 'nothing about us without us' represent important critiques for professional practice in these areas across different cultures.

Part III: Professional practice

Closely allied to working with disabilities is **Chapter 13**, which explores mental health and ill-health in adults. The ways in which adults experience the world and are affected by life changes will be considered especially in respect of developing reactive mental health problems and considering the cultural and gendered nuances that are often marginalised. A consideration of organic and endogenous causes of mental ill-health will also be presented. The ways in which these concepts are understood and applied in a human professional context will be subject to critical analysis and tools for the questioning practitioner will be explored.

In **Chapter 14** we consider adults at risk of abuse. 'Safeguarding is everybody's business', as guidance on the Care Act 2014 states. This chapter examines the impact that experiencing abuse and witnessing the abuse of others may have on people in social and professional settings. An historical excursus into adult protection, including elder abuse and domestic abuse will be offered showing the development through social problem construction. In this vein moves towards the concept of 'safeguarding' in the UK will also be analysed. This will be further critiqued through the lens of cultural and social diversity leading to a range of questions professional workers should ask when working in these complex and often emotionally challenging areas.

A significant part of many adults lives is related to parenting offspring and, increasingly, looking after grandchildren and **Chapter 15** focuses on this. This can be further compounded by care-giving responsibilities for ageing parents and/or partners and by the increase in transnational families. This demanding and nurturing support draws on the learned resources of adults and creates opportunities for new learning and behaviours. It can also be associated with multiple losses and the need for human service professional involvement may be indicated. This chapter will explore when that help and support may be necessary, what forms it may take and what questions should be asked by professionals.

Our final chapter in this volume, **Chapter 16** examines dementia: care practices, complexities and mythologies. The increasing longevity of people across the world has seen a concomitant increase in the numbers of people living with dementia which exerts new and changing demands on social and health care services and on families and people living with dementia who must adapt to novel situations. This chapter explores how dementia may have an impact on those involved and what human service professionals may do within those contexts. It offers a new model based on resilience.

The book brings together the wide and sometimes contrasting or competing discussions of growth and development. Human life, at whatever stage one is at, is complex and messy and cannot be fitted neatly into theoretical boxes. Thus, we present growth and development in adulthood as mutable and adaptable, something dependent on a variety of bio-psycho-social-spiritual factors and an individual's response to them from the perspective of their own ecology. Readers are offered understandings that can be applied to education, social work, health and social care, nursing and midwifery practice with adults of all ages in ways that allows adaptation of that knowledge to individual circumstances.

PART I

Theories and models of human growth and development in adults

The first part of this book is devoted to exploring some core theoretical models of human growth and development, or lifespan or life course development as it is sometimes known. This section of the book will include a consideration of traditional approaches, which will form a backdrop from which one can see social work in the wider context of human or helping professions, and to understand the various perspectives that other professionals may work from.

The approaches covered will include biophysical development, psychoanalytic, social learning theory (Chapter 1) and cognitive theory approaches (Chapter 2). Subsequently, we will explore spirituality in Chapter 3, looking at ways in which existential matters (those things that matter to the core of the person) may affect development. This chapter is written by a US social work academic; it provides a novel and important insight that also has resonance in other countries, including the UK. In Chapter 4 we turn to consider relationships and relational social work as practised in an Italian context. Relationships form the bedrock of social work practice across the world and it is useful to gain these comparative perspectives to develop UK practice and understanding. International perspectives expand our approach to these matters and demonstrate the range of different approaches that may be taken in social work. The final chapter in this section of the book brings together traditional and innovative theoretical approaches to human growth and development by taking a particular critical perspective, something that, again, is key to social work practice and understanding.

Part I objectives

- develop notions of development, growth and change throughout adult life;

- explore the fluidity of the line between childhood and youth and moving into adulthood;

- show diversity in thinking and form, which is something that is important to develop in your approach to the complexity of issues in social work practice.

1

Introduction and history: approaches to human growth and development in adults

Jonathan Parker and Sara Ashencaen Crabtree

Introduction

Social work, a highly adaptable and porous helping profession, borrows widely from a range of theoretical perspectives within the social sciences and psychology, to name but two areas of expertise. Human growth and development is an immensely important area within social work, which enables practitioners to understand the individual within a psychosocial framework of the biological, sociological and psychological domains of human existence that create what we understand as the 'person'. However, this is not to suggest that theories regarding human growth and development are fully accepted and thus incontestable models or paradigms. Social work interventions that use these theories are likely to come across examples of poor 'fit', particularly if we assume that all peoples, in all cultures, experience the same general pattern of growth and development. This may not be the case at all. Even within more familiar, 'known' cultures, there is a wide variation in how people function and respond to bio–physical changes. We also need to be aware that these models have not remained static but have shifted in acceptability and importance through history and these shifts are often associated with parallel shifts in the social and political climate of societies.

Social work thought in the 1980s was beginning to consider development throughout the life course; however, there remained an unspoken assumption that human growth and development was associated with children and young people, as though there was an invisible point after which theories of development were no longer relevant.

> Social and structural conditions were predominantly ignored, and the inevitable decline towards disengagement and death was simply assumed. (Cumming and Henry, 1961)

However, the notion that in fact adults are still going undergoing the transitions of 'development', and that in fact this process does not cease until the last breath of life, was one that was not properly considered outside of counselling psychology and theology. Yet this idea does not represent such a contradiction to social work in fact, which is premised upon the principle of self-actualising personhood, which implies growth, although here we would think more in terms of psychological/ emotional, interpersonal and spiritual growth, rather than that associated with the radical physical metamorphoses of childhood and adolescence.

Chapter objectives

- provide an overview of bio-physical, social learning theory and psychodynamic aspects of human growth and development in the context of adults (including older people);

- present and critique some current thinking and thinkers;

- explore how bio-physical, social learning theory and psychoanalytic models of human growth and development may still be relevant to and important in professional social work practice today.

REFLECTION POINT 1.1

What are your thoughts about growth and development in adulthood? Have you ever thought about it or have you considered this to be more concerned with children and young people? Have your thoughts changed as you have become a student?

The following discussions will take you through elements of growth and development in adulthood and paint a picture of continual change – which makes life both interesting and exciting or challenging!

Biomedical approaches to ageing

Biological and medical approaches to ageing in developed countries have assumed a level of credence given the increased longevity people enjoy and advances in reducing infant and maternal mortality, leading to a reduction in the birth rate and, subsequently, monumental changes in demography. In the Western world, theories of ageing from bio-medical perspectives also reflect anxieties concerning individual mortality and its association with the physical and overt processes of ageing. However, one can immediately identify some of the discourses that underpin these theories given the focus on old age, decline and the inevitability of death.

The study of biological and physical ageing can be further separated into specific areas such as cellular ageing, genetic and evolutionary theories, stochastic theories that concern the build up of physical, environmental and life-style insults over time. (Sauvain-Dugerdil et al, 2006)

In social work circles, there has been an almost universal rejection of a purely bio-medical approach to ageing, partly because of a tendency to associate the older person solely with physical and mental decline as described earlier, or, as Simon Biggs (1993) described it, 'biological reductionism'. Something else we must not forget is that social workers too express discourses or a 'tribal identity' that shows preference for social models. There are problems, however, in rejecting biological perspectives because of a misplaced emphasis on and uncritical acceptance of social models. The experiences and problems associated with disease, illness and physical decline in old age, in particular, should not be minimised or dismissed. Also, there are clear social work needs arising from these situations. For instance, the older person who falls at night may not only be at risk of injury and broken bones but may risk losing the ability to cook, shop or even remain in their own home, therefore demanding an integrated, rather than tribal response from services, that is centred around the person's needs. Biological, decremental approaches to ageing are not necessarily the predominant ones for social workers who would not wish to define older people simply in terms of illness and disease categories. There is a need, however, to have a sound understanding of bio-physiological changes, such as age-related sensory change, and indeed expected psychological changes such as in cognitive processes, in order to distinguish between those aspects of ageing that one may expect and those that require further investigation and/or assistance, which might include social work.

What must also be remembered is that there are changes throughout adulthood and before old age that also require adjustment or may have a profound impact on people's lives. These may include becoming a parent that involves biology and for the woman significant bio-physical change and development over the course of the pregnancy. Other hormonal changes can cause severe disruption in adult life, as shown in Case Study 1.1. While having an accident or serious health condition may also exert a degree of influence that changes the direction of one's life, prevents one from working or pursuing the career trajectory of choice. All these changes, have psycho-social elements, and demand a knowledge of bio-physical change and development. Social workers should be open to the full range of theoretical positions.

CASE STUDY 1.1

Julia is 56 years old, married, with teenage children living at home, the main bread-winner and at the peak of her legal career as a lawyer. An energetic and authoritative individual Julia has found herself struggling since last year to maintain her usual high-intensity work patterns, with insomnia leaving her physically exhausted and seemingly unable to remember the important details crucial to her court work.

Although she would normally characterise herself as an upbeat and optimistic person Julia feels increasingly low in spirit, anxious and tearful with morbid and suicidal thoughts invading her usually clear thinking. These suicidal ideations (thoughts) frighten Julia considerably who believes she has gone insane.

Questions
1. How would you describe the issues Julia is currently facing in terms of physical, emotional, social, family and cultural issues?
2. How can Julia best be helped to manage these different domains?
3. How might her position in society affect her reactions?

Discussion
It may be that Julia is more able to consider how these changes are part of her biological make-up and, from her position as a lawyer, to campaign on her own behalf to ensure work, family and friends understood what was happening and how she was feeling. However, the tremendous impact of hormonal changes in middle age can exert significant pressures on people whoever they are. For many years, as we know, these issues have been either brushed aside or dismissed as mere women's things. So, we must take into account the social and structural impacts on people as well as considering their biology.

Psychodynamic approaches

Psychodynamic therapies are a strongly established and well-recognised form of treatment for mental health issues that are not solely managed by pharmacology (medication), although can be used in conjunction. The prevalence of mental health problems in society is recognised as great (see Chapter 13) and the services available to manage these are currently serious outweighed by the need, which seems to be particularly acute among children and young people. Social workers are therefore very likely to encounter this in the general public on numerous occasions in their work, even if not directly associated with such specialisms. Some background knowledge of psychodynamics will provide a useful context for those working in the broad areas of human growth and development.

Changes after the First World War

New psychological developments for treating mental distress emerged from the massive trauma of the First World War, leading, for example, to the founding of the famous centre for psychological therapies, the Tavistock Clinic in London (Pilgrim, 1990), which continues its innovative work up the present time (for more details please see https://tavistockandportman.nhs.uk/about-us/who-we-are/history/). Moreover, London, prior to and during the Second World War, became the home for the famous founders of psychoanalysis, from which psychodynamics would draw, along with other psychological approaches. Arriving in London as refugees in 1938, Dr Sigmund Freud and his daughter, Anna (a well-known psychoanalyst in her own right) fled the Nazi Anschluss (annexation) of Austria (Smith, 1996); a highly necessary exile owing to the persecution of Jews, including even the Freuds, in Hitler's Third Reich. Melanie Klein, a psychoanalytic colleague of the Freuds, had already established herself in London several years before, forming the 'English' School of psychoanalysis in contrast to that of the 'Viennese' School as established by Freud and his legacy (Cooper, 1996). This concentration of such celebrated psychoanalysts helped to consolidate a strong tradition of therapy in the UK.

Psychoanalysis, however, is not a single model, despite the debt owed to Freud, but embraces a number of different theorisations, as developed by its various disciples including Melanie Klein and Carl Jung, to name but two. However, the key features relating to psychoanalysis examine the development of the mind and the connection between unconscious drivers in the mind and the manifestations of anxiety and other psychological states of distress in the individual.

Freud's views

Freud viewed the mind as composed of three main domains, the Id, the Ego and the Superego. The Id ('it') is innate and manifests itself at birth (and no doubt prior as well). The Id is an unformed and uncritical appetite for food, care and security, which demands gratification, as any new parent of a screaming baby is soon made aware. The motivation of the Id is moderated by the ego, which forms somewhat later in the child's life. It arises through the socialisation of childrearing, whereby the child becomes conscious of family and societal values. Accordingly, the child becomes aware that demands of the Id may have to be modified to the realities of the situation occasionally, and therefore gratification may need to be delayed to a more appropriate time. Through the internationalisation of these learned values the superego is formed. One could construe it as the development of conscience, just as the ego is a development of consciousness of the self in the lived world. The superego polices the self, rewarding behaviour internalised as good, and punishing that deemed bad. Thus, the moral agency of the individual, essential to normal functioning in society, is developed.

The overarching principles of psychoanalysis, relating to theorisation of the mind and the causations of mental distress/dysfunction, provided the development of psychodynamic approaches, which during the post-war period, would become the basis of so-called 'talking therapies' as part of the newly established British National Health Service.

Klein's focus

Klein's work focused on the development of the psyche in infancy and early childhood, where the baby is governed by two raw impulses: love and hate, both of which are directed towards the primary caregiver and relate to the baby's terrifying nascent awareness of its helplessness and dependency upon that care. The infant psychologically splits these experiences as good (e.g. warm milk upon demand, company and comfort) and bad (e.g. hunger, wanting comforting cuddles not immediately given, soiled, uncomfortable nappy/diaper). Love, in Kleinian thinking, therefore relates roughly to the life force: the zest/appetite for life. Hatred, and its corollaries, destructiveness and envy, are 'emanations of the death drive' (Cooper, 1990, p 43). These Kleinian concepts have entered everyday language and understanding, such as when we describe someone who seems to take very opportunity to worsen their position in life as 'self-destructive'.

Human service staff, particularly social workers, were regularly well versed in at least a basic working knowledge of counselling skills for application in their interventions; this soon formed an integral part of their professional education. Counselling skills and theory were often inspired by psychodynamic principles based on classic psychoanalytical concepts, incorporating the perspectives of British therapists, such as Donald Winnicott and his work on the importance of play among children (1971), and Carl Rogers in the US and his famous, non-judgemental person–centred approach (1967). Today, and arguably, highly regrettably, there is less emphasis on therapeutic skills for those working in the broader human science disciplines, in favour of less theoretical interventionist training focusing now on interpersonal skills. Psychodynamic expertise is now confined to the remit of counsellors and psychotherapists, rather than, as it once was for instance, shared with social workers.

Shifting political perceptions

The changes in education relate to shifting political perceptions of what kind of function and role human services should carry in British society. These have had a huge impact on both practice and professional training. Of course, such changes purely relate to the situation in the UK, whereas, for example, in the US, social workers may carry a caseload that is much more psychodynamic/psychoanalytic in practice; and in northern Europe, counterparts may regard their work as more closely allied to educational intervention with individuals and families in keeping with social pedagogic perspectives. The range of diversity of expertise as defined and enacted in, for instance, social work globally, is strongly recognised and articulated by the International Federation of Social Work (IFSW).

To return to the theoretical underpinnings of psychoanalysis and psychodynamics, the defences of the individual erected as a psychological defence mechanism are explored by the therapist, given the understanding that these can rebound to give rise later to quite serious problems for the individual. Yet, at the same time, this is not always the case. For example, among the 11 forms of defence Freud identifies (Smith, 1990), the defence of 'ideal' (a concept that has entered everyday language) often come to the fore, as we know, upon receiving some bad news. It acts as an essential buffer against a possibly overwhelming reality that enables the person to come to terms with upsetting information more slowly over time. This is an entirely normal and healthy process of self-protection. However, defence mechanisms that cause the individual to repress them too deeply in the psyche may then not be accessible for the individual to process them in a better way. Nor can the cause of original distress now be dismissed, but like the monster in the dark under the bed, is ever there, manifesting itself in dreams and dysfunctional thinking and behaviour that gives rise to high levels of anxiety and mounting mental distress requiring therapeutic intervention (Malan, 1990). Freud's famous aim was to convert unalleviated mental distress into normal human unhappiness, which individuals can at least attempt to personally rectify. The hidden feelings within the mind (psycho) and the mental mechanisms resulting (dynamics) must be revealed to the client through the process of engaging with therapy and accordingly explains why Carl Rogers emphasises that clients must be genuinely motivated to work through what can be very difficult and painful issues in therapy. For Freud was at first very hopeful that revelations discovered in the therapeutic encounter would liberate his patients from their neuroses with rapidity. He learned that unfortunately 'patient' (client) enlightenment could again be fogged by opaque confusion and suffering, such is the complexity of the mind and the powerful impulse towards self-protection through defence.

Psychodynamics has in turn fertilised other theoretical positions. One of the best known to social work, despite its ethnocentric basis, is that of Erik Erikson's eight stages of development (1959). This proposes that each stage of human life, from the earliest, contains its own specific crisis that must be overcome for successful cognitive-behavioural development (Gibson and Gibson, 2016). The stages are:

- birth to one year: trust versus mistrust (this relates to aspects of Klein's theorisation);
- one to three years: autonomy versus shame/doubt;
- three to six years: initiative versus guilt;
- six to eleven years: industry versus inferiority;
- adolescence: identity versus role confusion;
- young adulthood: 20s–30s, intimacy versus isolation;
- middle adulthood: 40s–60s, generativity versus stagnation;
- late adulthood: ego integrity versus despair.

For a more detailed explanation of the stages, see Janet Walker (2017).

Although most social workers are unlikely to be working directly with psychodynamics in their interventions, a good working knowledge of key concepts remains important to good practice generally and is important for multidisciplinary liaison to other professional services. This may well involve work with mental health specialists, psychologists and counsellors, although many would argue that the therapeutic element of social needs to continue to be seen as an important part of the social work armoury for best practice. Accordingly, basic familiarity with psychodynamic principles remains important to social workers to inform their own understandings of the psychological and emotional states of mind of service users, their families and indeed all people. They are subject to, as well as need to reflectively understand their own responses to others and reactions to events that will arise in social work practice. The following case study (1.2) describes how one person evasively but unconsciously responds to unwanted probes into some unresolved issues in their life.

> ## CASE STUDY 1.2
>
> A social worker was acting as the practice educator of a particular student, who seemed to have a difficult and chaotic home life and would regularly arrive late and disorganised to the placement setting as well as often audibly quarrelling with someone on his mobile phone. Concerned about the student's progress and general attitude the practice teacher sought to address this concern on numerous occasions, but although the student seemed animated and interested during supervision sessions when discussing the caseload he held, as soon as the conversation moved to his personal life the student started yawning widely and looking very sleepy, making it difficult to continue supervision. The practice educator noticed this recurring pattern and started to gently draw the student's attention to this behaviour.
>
> ## Questions
> 1. What do you think are the unconscious dynamics at work here?
> 2. What might the student or practice educator do at this point?
> 3. How might psychoanalytic thought help you understand the situation?
>
> ## Discussion
> It is important that as broad an understanding as possible is sought. It could, of course, be the case that the student is simply tired, has been out late or is not feeling physically well. A broader understanding using psychoanalytic thought might see this as displacement activity, moving their discomfort with the situation, whatever that may be, to expressing a physical tiredness, something that means the actual situation does not need to be faced.

French psychoanalysis

In France, psychoanalytic approaches remain commonplace and greatly valued within psychiatric practice and it is helpful to have some understanding of this (Botbol and Gourbil, 2018). The specific place of French psychoanalytic theory and practice began with the most famous French psychoanalyst, Jacques Lacan (Nobus, 2000). Lacanian psychoanalysis is recognised as controversial in suggesting resistance to American ego-psychology (such as that emphasised by Erikson previously), and a return to Freudian theory; indeed, Lacan and his form of psychoanalysis were expelled from the International Association of Psychoanalysis in the 1960s after he had formed a specific association to further his thinking and practice (Birksted-Breen et al, 2009). His call for a return to Freudian approaches is underpinned by both structuralism and Marxism, which gives it a unique perspective. Thus, Lacanian psychoanalysis is complex and deeply theoretical, but it does allow for a recognition that structural–environmental factors exert a powerful force on individuals as does the relationship between service users or clients and those social workers, counsellors and psychotherapists helping them (Botbol and Lehembre, 2008; also see Chapter 5 in this volume). The acceptance of structural influences and interpretation add a rounded psychosocial understanding that is important in social work, given the holistic approach taken to the person in their environment (see Germain, 1981; Gitterman et al, 2013).

Lacanian psychoanalysis considers the symbolic, linguistic world, based on speech, alongside an imaginary register which structures individuals' perceptions of their ecological environment (Lacan, 2018). Part of the way sense is made of the world is through the use of signifiers, mental representations of verbalised sounds or how words are imagined when spoken or heard. The representations provide meaning for that which is signified. However, speech always leaves something unsaid and in people there remains a desire to be understood which often finds expression in other speech (Lacan, 2019).

Lacanian thought also uses Freud's notion of transference. Lacan imparts a symbolic element to transference which becomes imaginary, part of that mental representation, and is seen as a desire to communicate deeper desires through signifiers. This means that psychoanalysis considers the uncovering of what imagination lies behind the signifiers will expose deep desires of the person and thus help them to get in touch with symbolic, imaginary and real aspects of themselves (Nobus, 2000).

The influence of psychoanalytic thinking stems from France's unique culture in respect of secularism and the societal respect afforded to public intellectuals. This gave rise to the right social conditions for this complex set of theories to be accepted as part of mainstream thought (Birksted-Breen et al, 2009).

French psychoanalytic thinking is complex, and an example may help understand how this might apply to social work practice. We have mentioned previously that it provides a holistic approach that sees the individual as part of an array of wider systems – interpersonal (person-to-person), organisational (relationships with organisations and broader groups) and social systems (the interactions one has with society as a whole – its legislation, policy and unspoken contexts for living). Read Case Study 1.3 in the light of this brief introduction to French psychoanalytic theory.

CASE STUDY 1.3

Jennifer, a 52-year-old Welsh woman, told her social worker that she was feeling 'trapped' in her current relationship with Alwyn, a mechanic and long-time family friend. She had lived with Alwyn for two years. Her husband, Ted, had died four years ago. He had been the senior gamekeeper on the local estate. The social workers wanted to explore more deeply her 'imagined world' (the one she constructed mentally) that was signified by the use of the word (signifier) 'trapped'.

Jennifer brought aspects of her relationship with Alwyn, which had become controlling and psychological abusive, to the social worker whom she saw as a 'gamekeeper', who was understanding and able to help her from her current plight.

In exploring the difficulties in her current relationship, she told the story of her husband releasing a small muntjac (deer) caught in an old leg-hold spring trap (something that has been illegal throughout the European Union since 1995). She said her husband had been clearing these traps for a number of years and 'hated them'. Ted, her husband, had brought the injured deer back to their house where their looked after it, nurturing it back to health before releasing it once more into the estate.

Discussion with the social workers centred on the signifier and signified and Jennifer realised she felt as though she was the deer needing nurture and release. It also transpired that she saw the social worker as her 'gamekeeper' husband expecting to be nurtured and set free. The social worker was able to work with this understanding to encourage and enable Jennifer to formulate her own plan to set herself free from her 'trap'.

Questions

1. Given what you know about contemporary social work practice, can you think of ways in which you might use this type of thinking in your own social work practice?
2. If it is not something you can use directly in your practice might this way of thinking help in understanding and working with your colleagues?
3. How might you work with transference?

Discussion

As we have noted, psychoanalytic thinking, especially French concepts, are complex and to practise using them requires significant study and practice at an advanced level. So, you are not going to be a psychoanalyst just by qualifying as a social worker. However, the thinking provides a range of important theoretical concepts that aid understanding of the person in the contexts you find them.

You are likely to come across transference in your work when a service user or client unconsciously puts feelings about another person, themselves or situation on to you and being aware of this will help you explore, in depth, with people you are working with to ensure they are telling you what they want to. It is important, however, that you recognise that as a social worker you may transfer your unconscious feeling and thoughts on to those people with whom you work. It is therefore important you are aware of the way some of these psychoanalytic notions work to guard against making assumptions in your practice and ensuring you are critical in your approach (see Chapter 5).

Behavioural and social learning theories

Behavioural and social learning theories (SLT) refer to the ways in which our interactions with other people and world around us increases, decreases or maintains the behaviours we engage in. SLT seek to understand human behaviour in its social context (see also Gitterman et al, 2013). A basic presupposition is that change and development depend on our experiences and context. This is something that has been well researched in respect of children and adolescents and has developed into different therapeutic approaches to alter and manipulate behaviours. However, its application to adults especially in the fields of anger management, learning disabilities and mental health have also developed, although they are combined more often with cognitive approaches today (see Chapter 2).

The key theories that have developed are the same as those applied to ways in which children and young people grow and develop. They include the following approaches, which are interconnected but underpinned by different theoretical paradigms:

- respondent or classical conditioning;
- operant or instrumental conditioning;
- modelling, imitative or vicarious learning (social learning theory).

A more detailed outline of these models and theories can be found in Chapter 1 in the companion volume.

Respondent or classical conditioning

Respondent or classical conditioning suggests that an automatic or unconditioned response may be repeated if its trigger or stimulus is paired with another event or stimulus. This 'conditioned stimulus' or trigger event may also be paired with another event to produce the original response, and so on (Watson, 1925; Pavlov, 1927).

An example may help here. For our protagonist, Kelvin, smoking a cigarette (an unconditioned stimulus) triggers a desire to drink alcohol (an unconditioned response). Kelvin smokes his cigarettes in the garden which is accompanied by a large scotch (a conditioned response). Over time, being in a garden (a conditioned stimulus) makes Kelvin want to have a drink (conditioned response).

In this model, behaviours are prompted by association with a certain event or stimulus. The same response may occur when the initial prompt is associated with a second event or stimulus. Respondent conditioning is so-called because the behaviour is considered to be a response to the initial stimulus.

If the conditioned stimulus continues to be repeated without the corresponding appearance of the unconditioned stimulus or trigger, it eventually loses its potency, so over time Kevin's desire to have a drink in the garden may not last if he was stop smoking. Having said this, however, it must be noted that well-established phobic responses do become very resistant to change. Respondent learning theory has been helpful in explaining the development of fear reactions or phobic responses (Watson and Raynor, 1920; Sheldon and Macdonald, 2009). For instance, the pairing of an experience that provokes fear, such as being stung by a bee, with something associated with it, such as pruning the buddleia bushes in the garden, may reinforce that fear reaction over time, and one's seemingly irrational fear of buddleia becomes established.

On the other hand, if, through experience, a person learns that there is no reliable connection between a stimulus event and a behaviour, this can lead to apathy, and a lack of motivation or 'learned helplessness' (Maier and Seligman, 1976). An example will help here. Anielka came to England from Poland in 2005 to study and stayed after gaining a job in marketing. She worked as much overtime as she could, completed her work on time, with a view to gaining promotion. After applying for more senior positions on over 15 occasions but always losing out to a less experienced male colleague, she 'learned' that working hard and being good at her job was not at all important in getting promotion and simply did her job and worked the hours she was contracted for without expectation. Learned helplessness assists in understanding behaviour it also, as we can see here, requires an understanding of the socio-political aspects of the environment in which learning takes place (see Chapter 5). However, in social work, respondent conditioning can be used to foster a reassertion of control over one's environment. In this sense, the behavioural approach using respondent conditioning seeks to empower people and increase their choices in living.

Operant or instrumental conditioning

Operant learning theory is slightly different, stating that behaviours are learnt and repeated because of the consequences immediately following their expression. The strength, frequency and type of these consequences greatly influence any future expression of the preceding behaviour.

Specific stimuli do not automatically elicit operant behaviour; however, events and social contexts are important as they provide cues for the kind of behaviour that is appropriate. These cues are referred to as antecedent stimuli. Social cues can often indicate when reinforcement may be available for the expression of a particular form of behaviour.

So, using this learning theory, we may be able to interpret the development of some behaviours in adults. Chantal likes to dance and enjoy her nights out. She finds that taking ecstasy helps give her a sense of euphoria and being able to dance the whole night through. Thus, the antecedent stimulus of dancing and going out does not elicit her drug use but provides the conditions for it. It is the feeling and experience she gets after taking ecstasy that reinforces the likelihood of her taking it again. Using perhaps a more positive example, when Derek became increasingly confused and his behaviour more demanding and erratic, his wife Linda was able to soothe him by singing to him. It was not his behaviour that provoked the singing but the knowledge that this was likely to calm and soothe him and thereby make things easier for her to cope with.

Modelling, vicarious or imitative learning

The first two approaches to social learning are taken from traditional behavioural psychology. However, more recently it has been recognised that many of our behaviours are learned through socialisation or through interaction and social imitation – observing the behaviour of other people we admire and copying these, so they become part of our own behavioural repertoires. An example may help here. One of us (Parker) grew up in the North of England and had developed a clear, if not thick, northern accent by the age of 18. This changed partly when attending university and working in a different part of the country because of association with people around him. However, the northern aspects remained, until it appeared important to modify the accent as well as when moving in different circumstances, and Parker changed his accent to fit more in the environments he was working in at the time. To a lesser or greater extent we all learn in this form. It is also important to remember that the ways we use our interpersonal skills differs from culture to culture. We only need to look at how funeral rites are conducted and expected in the subdued, low key traditional British funeral – a stiff upper-lip approach – compared with, say, a burial taking place for the victims of a rocket attack in Gaza, where the raw emotion and grief is allowed and encouraged to come to the fore. How to act appropriately in social situations and settings can also be explained by reference to this form of learning; it provides us with environmental cues. So, this form of SLT provides social workers with a means of understanding social situations and how these might have developed, which, of course, also offers social workers a means of understanding (by careful and skilled assessment) what and how a situation may be changed.

Modelling is composed of the following elements:

- a person sees another person performing a behaviour and observes their actions;
- the observer forms an opinion about how this behaviour is done;
- they note the situation in which the behaviour was performed, and the consequences for the person behaving in a certain way;
- the observer reproduces the behaviour according to his or her perception of it (Parker and Penhale, 1998).

It is necessary for the model to be attractive in some way to the observer to have an effect and is more likely to be imitated if the behaviour is rewarded. The opportunity to practise it and to experience positive reinforcement for doing so is needed. The success of modelling is dependent on the degree to which it creates or strengthens feelings of self-efficacy through successful accomplishment or performance.

Watching the environment in which people live gives us an opportunity to understand why people may have learned to behave in certain ways, what maintains it, and what other opportunities there might be for changing and adapting and to learning new ways of being. The adages about teaching dogs new tricks and leopards and their spots are tested when using social learning theories. They suggest that adults learn and adapt to their wider environment and their understandings or experiences of it. This is useful in seeing that adults are flexible and mutable rather than set on a trajectory of slow but inevitable decline.

REFLECTION POINT 1.2

Thinking of the three traditional ways of understanding growth and development in adults, can you identify some of the benefits of the thinking and also some of the drawbacks? No theory or model will ever explain everything, and you may have thought that combining these understandings might pay some dividends. To an extent, this is what social workers will do in practice. However, you need to be mindful of potential contradictions between theories and models and to reflect on these.

Conclusion

Human beings grow and develop throughout their lives. This does not stop and, as a social worker, it is important to recognise this and not to assume a person is set in their ways after a certain age. This is quite a positive way of viewing ageing across the life span. In this chapter we have seen how changes of a physical nature take place at various points in a person's life. Of course, we must see this ageing process in the context of power relations and assumptions, as we will come to in Chapter 5, as popular views of certain ages are valued more highly than others and these assumptions can be seen to underpin social policies, organisational and even social work approaches to different adult groups. We have also considered psychoanalytic approaches to understand the adult drawing on a range of traditional, US and French approaches to understanding the influence of unconscious thinking, desires and drives on the ways in which we live and behave. This led us also to review how adults continue to learn, grow and develop through social learning – looking at the triggers, consequences and observations of admired figures. This provides a backdrop to move on to Chapter 2 and to consider cognitive approaches to development.

Reflective questions

1 Consider what you know about traditional approaches to human growth and development and think about these in respect of your own development as an adult. How do they fit? What do they fail to do?

2 How might you adapt human growth and development approaches in your practice?

3 Which ideas have you found most useful in this chapter? How would you explain them to an interested, non-social worker, friend or relative?

Further reading

• Rogers, C. (1967) *On Becoming a Person*. London: Constable & Robinson Ltd.
This classic work introduces person-centred practice which has become such a focus of Western social work. It remains an important text for social work students to read.

• Malan, D.H. (1990) *Individual Psychotherapy and the Sciences of Psychodynamics*. London: Butterworths.
Familiarising yourself with psychoanalytic and psychodynamic thinking is important if you are to apply it to your practice. You will not have the time to work psychoanalytically, but you may be guided by the thinking and this book offers a solid foundation.

• Walker, J. (2017) *Social Work and Human Development* (5th edn). London: Sage.
Janet Walker's introductory text is useful in covering the life course as a whole and in introducing models and theories that relate specifically to adults.

References

Biggs, S. (1993) *Understanding Ageing*. Buckingham: Open University Press.

Birksted-Breen, D., Flanders, S. and Gibeault, A. (eds) (2009) *Reading French Psychoanalysis*. London: Routledge.

Botbol, M. and Lehembre, D. (2008) French perspectives on psychiatry as a therapeutic discipline, *Die Psychiatrie*, 5: 12–13.

Botbol, M. and Gourbil, A. (2018) The place of psychoanalysis, 1 French psychiatry, *BJPsych International*, 15(1): 3–5.

Cooper, C. (1990) Psychodynamic therapy: the Kleinian approach. In W. Dryden (ed.), *Individual Therapy: A Handbook*. Milton Keynes: Open University, pp 39–68.

Cumming, E. and Henry, W. (1961) *Growing Old: The Process of Disengagement*. New York: Basic Books.

Erikson, E. (1959) *Identity and the Life Cycle, Psychological Issues* (Monograph 1). New York: International Universities Press.

Germain, C.B. (1981) The ecological approach to people-environment transactions, *Social Casework*, 62(6): 323–331.

Gibson, A. and Gibson, N. (2016) *Human Growth, Behaviour and Development*. London: Sage.

Gitterman, A., Germain, C.B. and Knight, C. (2013) Ecological framework. *Encyclopaedia of Social Work*. National Association of Social Workers Press/Oxford University Press. Available from: https://oxfordre.com/socialwork/view/10.1093/acrefore/9780199975839.001.0001/acrefore-9780199975839-e-118

Lacan, J. (2018) *The Four Fundamental Concepts of Psychoanalysis*. Abingdon: Routledge.

Lacan, J. (2019) *Desire and its Interpretation: The Seminars of Jacques Lacan*. Cambridge: Polity Press.

Maier, S.F. and Seligman, M. (1976) Learned helplessness: Theory and evidence, *Journal of Experimental Psychology: General*, 105(1): 3–46.

Malan, D.H. (1990) *Individual Psychotherapy and the Sciences of Psychodynamics*. London: Butterworths.

Nobus, D. (2000) *Jacques Lacan and the Freudian Practice of Psychoanalysis*. London: Routledge.

Parker, J. and Penhale, B. (1998) *Forgotten People: Positive Approaches to People with Dementia*. Aldershot: Ashgate.

Pavlov, I.P. (1927) *Conditioned Reflexes*. London: Oxford University Press.

Pilgrim, D. (1990) British psychotherapy in context. In: W. Dryden (ed.), *Individual Therapy: A Handbook*. Milton Keynes: Open University Press, pp 1–17.

Rogers, C. (1967) *On Becoming a Person*. London: Constable & Robinson Ltd.

Sauvain-Dugerdil, C., Leridon, H. and Mascie-Taylor, N. (eds) (2006) *Human Clocks: The Bio-Cultural Meanings of Age*. Bern: Peter Lang AG.

Sheldon, B. and Macdonald, G. (2009) *A Textbook of Social Work*. London: Routledge.

Smith, D.L. (1990) Psychodynamic therapy: the Freudian approach. In: W. Dryden (ed.), *Individual Therapy: A Handbook*. Milton Keynes: Open University, pp 18–38.

Walker, J. (2017) *Social work and Human Development* (5th edn). London: Sage/Learning Matters.

Watson, J.B. (1925) *Behaviorism*, New York: W.W. Norton.

Watson, J.B. and Raynor, R. (1920) Conditioned emotional reactions, *Journal of Experimental Psychology*, 3(1): 1–14.

Winnicott, D.W. (1971) *Playing and Reality*. London: Tavistock Publications Ltd.

2

Cognitive theories and cognitive development relevant to adults

Margarete Parrish

Introduction

Cognitive theories and the concept of cognitive development are associated with how and what people think and believe. In respect of development across the life course, cognitive development and theory is concerned with how those thoughts and beliefs may change and develop over time and across circumstances. When considering adults, this is very wide-ranging because of the duration and multiple changes that take place in adult life. Cognitive factors play a large part in understanding possible explanations and solutions to problems across the lifespan, and it is important to note this continues throughout adulthood. It is this that is central to social work practice using cognitive theories.

It is worth reiterating that a great deal of cognition is conscious or intentional but there is much that occurs outside the realm of conscious awareness. However, cognitive theories are more oriented to the present, especially as they relate to thoughts, beliefs and how people interpret the world around them in that particular context, environment and time. Psychoanalytic theories emphasise unconscious drives and conflicts (see Chapter 1), and relate back to earlier experiences rather than the here and now. Across the lifespan, cognitive factors include such features as memory, judgement, intelligence, problem-solving skills and mental capacity. Social work with adults often entails addressing the ways in which people understand their circumstances, and their interpretation of events, which makes cognitive concepts particularly relevant to social work practice.

The inherent optimism in cognitive theories (i.e. that change can happen) readily lends itself to applying them to social work practice across the lifespan, whether working with young adults, people in middle age or at the end of life or, indeed, in different circumstances. When working with adults experiencing difficulties or distress, the ability to consider ways in which their responses have been learned over time is readily linked with re-learning new, more effective responses in the here and now.

Chapter objectives

- provide an overview of key contributors to cognitive theories as they relate to adults, see Piaget, Vygotsky, Kelly, Bandura, Seligman, Ellis and Beck;

- explore key concepts associated with cognitive theories such as self-efficacy, learned helplessness, attribution theory, 'A–B–C' principle, theories of intelligence;

- understand linkages between cognitive theory and current adult social work practice.

History and development of the theories and models

The historical development of cognitive theories, from the early 20th century onwards, indicates that they have played a major role in influencing the ways in which practitioners and theorists alike have understood and assessed people's circumstances and difficulties. Links with behavioural theorists and practitioners have sometimes resulted in an amalgam with more cognitively focused practitioners, and thus cognitive and behavioural theories are often considered in tandem with one another as was briefly considered in Chapter 1. For the purposes of this discussion, however, emphasis will be placed on Cognitive Theories, with particular emphasis being placed on *Social Learning Theory* (see Parrish, 2014).

Key thinkers and theories

In this section, we introduce some of the key thinkers, many of whom we have dealt with at length in the companion volume. However, it is important to review and repeat some of the ideas as these are also important when considering various facets of adult development.

Jean Piaget

Interestingly, it is important to begin our discussion of adults with the work of *Jean Piaget* (1896–1980) who is often viewed as the earliest contributor to understanding childhood cognitive development. However, his thinking applies also to adults throughout the life course. Piaget gained his doctorate in Biology at the University of Neuchatel in Switzerland at age 22. He worked with Carl Jung, and others before pursuing further studies at the Sorbonne, where Piaget contributed to the development of standardised reasoning tests in the laboratory of Alfred Binet in Paris. These studies focused on variations in intelligence and reasoning and sparked Piaget's interest in understanding how people learn, and the logic of their conclusions (Vourlekis, 2009). Thus, it is clear that Piaget had a broad education and cannot be simply labelled as relevant to children and young people but also to the different times in an adults life.

Piaget's theory of cognitive development provided a fundamental basis of subsequent cognitive theories, and despite being a key figure in child development, moral development in childhood and learning, he considered his theories had wider reach concerning the development of abstract thought, and biological and environmental influences on it. Thus, while his initial emphasis was primarily on children's understandings, his concepts are also relevant to adult cognitions.

Piaget challenged conventional thinking that suggested children were simply miniature adults and that their thought patterns and ways of interpreting the world simply followed the adult world albeit in miniature. Looking at the ways in which children and young people learn, although he considered children to be naturally curious, with clear intentions to interpret their observations and experiences in an increasingly systematic and (at least to themselves) logical way, he recognised that this was building understandings of the world that prepare the ground for the development of the adult in the world.

Using the moral development of the child as a focus, Piaget proposed that learning is essentially experiential. Learning happens in the process of constructing individuals' cognitive realities and understandings of their environment when they experiment with it and test assumptions of what may happen if one acts and behaves in a certain way in a certain context. Hence, Piaget's concepts are considered to be *constructivist* which simply means that humans construct meaning of the world around them through their experiences of it. He regarded development as an ongoing, lifelong, dynamic process stemming from the ability to adapt thinking and form new ideas in response to the demands of a changing environment (see Case Study 2.1).

Piaget's theories were built into stages that demand individuals progress from one stage to the next through physical and mental maturation. He identified four factors that influenced the developmental process:

- physical maturation of the brain, resulting in new capacities (we now know that the brain's development follows a much longer course and changes throughout life and according to experiences);
- experiences that resulted in developing knowledge (experiential learning is, again, a lifelong process);
- social transmission of knowledge (education);
- equilibration or equilibrium.

These factors can be considered as being mutually interactive and though they are produced to explain child development they have resonance with adults moving through life. For example, an adult may have a mature brain and cerebral function but needs to have real life experiences in order to grow and develop and internalise that knowledge. Take the example of a woman of 35 who has been in the army since university. She is now seeking a career in teaching. Without exposure to the classroom and to children in a learning environment, she is likely to apply her learning and experience from the army to the tasks she is given which are likely to be somewhat inappropriate for teaching. Case Study 2.1 provides a further example of these interactions for you to reflect upon.

CASE STUDY 2.1

Dyffed was a police officer of 25 years' experience. He had always been a staunch supporter of zero tolerance for misdemeanours and believed punishment of offenders was the best way of preventing future crime and protecting communities. However, over the last few months he had begun to doubt his long-standing conviction. He had seen an increasing number of people whose social situations were distressing and had shown increased sympathy to their plight rather than arresting them for minor crimes committed.

Questions

1. What do you think might be happening in Dyffed's development here?
2. How does an understanding of Piagetian development help you comprehend the change?
3. What might this mean for you as a social worker?

Discussion

The experiences that Dyffed had accumulated over time and allowed him to develop a changed perspective. It is important as a social worker to bear in mind the changeable aspects of people's thinking and behaviour and to understand it is contextual.

According to Piaget, knowledge results from the simultaneous and corresponding mental processes he called *assimilation and accommodation*. Assimilation involves the way new information is absorbed into the existing intellectual organisation. Accommodation refers to the modifications required to deal with the new material. According to Piaget (1970, p 8), *there is no accommodation without assimilation*.

A further example of assimilation and accommodation would be a case involving an adult's immigration to a new country, in which they were faced with the necessity of learning a new language, culture and potentially work-related skills. Simultaneously, they would also be required to accommodate such new information within their existing frames of reference.

Lev Vygotsky

The landmark work of Russian psychologist *Lev Vygotsky* (1896–1934) was approximately contemporary with that of Piaget. His approach to learning and development helps to underpin many contemporary ways of developing activities and work within organisations and communities of learning. A combination of political suppression during the Stalin era, alongside the lack of sufficient translations, delayed his work becoming familiar to most Western readers until the 1970s (Passer et al, 2009). Vygotsky's work provides a fascinating combination of Marxist ideas of tensions involving wider society and the social relations within it with psychological concepts of human developmental processes.

Vygotsky stated that cognition is a social function, which means that it operates within a social and interactive environment. He suggested this because learning and social activities interact and are moulded by environment and culture; context is all important (Joravsky, 1979). Vygotsky is especially known for his concept of the '*Zone of Proximal Development*'. This refers to how people learn through their associations with (or 'proximity' to) others, again indicating the social aspect. This is tempered by culture and context. His ideas on learning apply to adults as much as children and young people. Take, for example, your own learning to be a social worker. There are some skills that you bring as an independent human begin to the role. However, there are a range of things including knowledge, experience, personal qualities and values for which you will benefit from formal learning, suggesting, as Vygotsky emphasised, that collaborative efforts represent an essential component of problem-solving behaviours. A further example of this may be found with instructors functioning as facilitators of adult learning, or with group projects.

Vygotsky's contribution is to recognise that learners' interactions with their surrounding culture and social environment (presumably at any age) are essential aspects of their intellectual and continued development (Luria, 2004). In Chapter 8 we see the importance of continued learning and education throughout life. Vygotsky's promising career was tragically brief; he died of tuberculosis at age 37. However, he remains important to adult learning.

George Kelly

American psychologist *George Kelly* (1905–1966) is considered by some to be the 'father' of cognitive clinical psychology (the interesting gendered appellation may say something about those who have contributed to developing these theories; they're all men!). According to Kelly, people function as individual researchers, perpetually engaged in interactions with the world, based on hypotheses that both anticipate and predict future outcomes or responses to their own actions. This has very practical consequences and is exemplified clearly in the idea that drivers anticipate other drives following the rules and therefore drive according to the shared assumed rules for driving in the confidence that accidents will not happen.

Kelly's *Personal Construct Theory* suggested a constant, daily engagement of people with their surrounding world/environments in order to construct explanatory theories of the ways the world works. This is fundamentally contextual. He suggested that we test our hypotheses against what we envisage to be an external reality, and we revise and refine those hypotheses according to their predictive accuracy (Kelly, 1963). An individual's schemata or personal constructions of the world are subject to this continual experimentation and revision. This helps the individual to negotiate the world and to predict consequences, while adapting when these consequences are proven wrong (Ewen, 2010). Take, for instance, the 60-year-old man with a broken leg, crutches and cast who waits for a bus. He anticipates that he will be able to mount the bus because they are all accessible in his town and drop to allow people to board. He also thinks that he will be able to get a seat because his experience has been that people are polite when they see his difficulties and offer him a seat if there are none available. He may have to revise his personal constructs should he not be offered a seat or, worse still, if he is jostled and pushed by other travellers.

Taking the previous example, Kelly would suggest that individuals are capable of revising their constructs as a means of adapting to testing and experience. This kind of social adaptation links to an extent with the earlier evolutionary theories of development that began in bio-physical developmental areas (see Kelly, 1963; Chapter 1 in the companion volume). Although he also argued, in respect of child psychological development, that children had the capacity to test and anticipate in reliable and productive ways, starting from infancy (e.g. 'If I cry, someone will come and comfort me'), he also developed this anticipatory thinking for adults. He proposed that parenting extremes (such as overindulgence, inconsistency and maltreatment) were potentially detrimental to children's otherwise healthy development of personal constructs (Kelly, 1963). Such extremes during childhood have clear implications for adult functioning, which can be recognised in cases where an adult has been either over-indulged or deprived during childhood, and continues to expect similar treatment throughout life.

Attribution Theory relates to the ways in which people explain perceptions and how they assess the causes of their experiences and observations. Attribution theory refers to a collection of theorists' work (including Kelley, 1971; and Weiner, 1986), rather than a single theorist. It relates strongly to how adults interpret the causation of behaviours and experiences.

By attributing causes to explain observations or experiences, people can avoid the risk of bad things happening randomly or uncontrollably. Patterns of attribution tend to be either internal (such as inherent traits or genetics) or external (such as environment or even supernatural). According to Weiner's (1986) concepts of attributional structure, causation can be located along several dimensions, among which the internal/external dichotomy is often used to explain attributions. Internal, personal attributions infer that people's individual characteristics determine their behaviour or experiences. An example would be: "My A on the test resulted from my hard work", or "I got a C because I didn't study hard enough". External or situational attributions infer that external influences determine people's behaviour or experiences. An example would be: "My 90% on the test came from the test being so easy", or "I failed the test because the lecturer is so boring".

The idea that causation can be attributed either to the person's inherent characteristics or outside forces (or a combination of both) is a key component of the theoretical construct known as locus of control. The person's attribution of causation to their own inherent factors would relate to internal locus of control (see Chapter 1), whereas the attribution of causation to outside influences beyond the individual's control would relate to external locus of control. The locus of control typically serves to shape whether an individual perceives a situation or difficulty as something within or beyond their control (Passer et al, 2009).

Examples of internal attributes associated with causation include:

- genetic or inherited characteristics;
- inherent traits or features;
- honesty;
- preparation;
- intelligence;
- adherence to prescribed treatment.

Examples of external attributes associated with causation include:

- environment;
- peers;
- supernatural factors (God, angels, spirits of deceased loved ones);
- chance (luck, fate, magic, 'on the cards').

Attributions may be culturally relevant, particularly when people's culture is either more individually or collectively focused. Attributions provide hypotheses or frameworks to help explain why or how things happen. They may or may not be accurate. *Misattribution* entails the inaccurate perception of a sequence of events in which causation is attributed incorrectly. Sometimes attributions reflect a mental shortcut, and lack analysis. This can result in what is called an attributional bias, which is associated with misattribution.

Attributions and misattributions can play vital roles in shaping behaviours and expectations or hypotheses about experiences. Using an 'If ___ then ___' formula to understand the attribution process, most of us are very familiar with ways in which we seek explanations for events, feelings and circumstances that we otherwise find threatening, overwhelming or unjust. In some cases, a pattern of self-attribution consistently contributes to an excessive level of self-blame or internalised pejorative self-regard or labelling. Examples of this can be seen in cases where people regard themselves as 'losers', 'useless' or consistently along the hopeless–helpless continuum.

Howard Gardner

Howard Gardner (1943–present), an American cognitive psychologist, has influenced educators, social and care workers and parents to consider the different forms that intelligence can take. His theory of *multiple intelligences* resulted from his questions about the dominance of psychometric testing to measure intelligence.

Gardner questioned the idea of intelligence comprising a single (inherited) entity, or being measurable by a standardised test. He argues that the question of 'How smart are you?' is less relevant than exploring 'How are you smart?' (Chen and Gardner, 2005).

According to Gardner, intelligence is actually an array of factors better referred to as plural 'intelligences'. He challenges Piaget's sequential model of development, arguing that intelligences are more about people's different capacities than stages of progression. Gardner proposes that there are at least eight distinct intellectual abilities or intelligences, as noted in the next section (Gardner, 1983). He also notes that, of these, only the first two or three are generally valued in traditional Euro-American schooling.

1. Linguistic intelligence
   - language skills, written and spoken;
   - ability to learn new languages, expressive use of words;
   - linked with: teachers, speakers, authors, poets.
2. Logical–mathematical intelligence
   - abstract thinking;
   - fluency with numbers;
   - analytical skills;
   - scientific investigation of problems, deductive reasoning;
   - linked with: mathematicians, computer scientists.
3. Musical intelligence
   - acute sensitivity to sound patterns;
   - ability to perform, compose and appreciate musical patterns; recognition of pitches and rhythms;
   - linked with: musicians, conductors, disc jockeys.
4. Spatial intelligence
   - recognition and use of patterns of space and proportions;
   - ability to draw, design, decorate, sculpt;
   - linked with: architects, artists, interior decorators, clothes designers, tailors, engineers.

5. Bodily-kinaesthetic intelligence
   - skilful use of the body to solve problems or create new objects;
   - ability to coordinate mental and physical activities;
   - linked with: craftsmen, repair workers, dancers, surgeons, athletes.
6. Interpersonal intelligence
   - understanding of others' emotions and intentions;
   - ability to work well with others through a well-developed sense of self and others;
   - linked with: educators, salespeople, religious and political leaders.
7. Intrapersonal intelligence
   - capacity to understand one's own emotions and intentions;
   - ability to use one's own self-knowledge for self-regulation and effective relations with others;
   - linked with: carers, parents and mentors often exhibit such traits.
8. Naturalistic intelligence
   - expertise in the natural world of plants and animals;
   - capacity to recognise, grow and tend animals, plants, gardens;
   - linked with: animal trainers, gardeners.

Gardner emphasises the complex nature of intelligences. Unlike Piaget's developmental premise, Gardner proposes that different intelligences have distinctly different developmental paths. For example, musicians and artists often demonstrate their talents during childhood, whereas logical-mathematical talents typically emerge at later stages. This consideration can be particularly important when working with people whose intellectual skills may have gone unappreciated during their school experience.

Albert Bandura

Perhaps the most prominent among the learning theorists, *Albert Bandura* (1925–present) is a Canadian-born psychologist. His innovative work, which he originally referred to as 'social cognitive theory', challenges the operant conditioning premise promoted by Skinner of controlling external environments in order to shape behaviour (see Chapter 1). A pioneer in the area of *social learning* and *self-efficacy*, Bandura has been on the psychology faculty of Stanford University in California since 1953.

Bandura's *social learning theory* places a strong emphasis on understanding the importance of observed models of behaviour providing a frame of reference for anticipating consequences (or the lack thereof). Through his concepts of *observational learning*, Bandura proposed that people's behaviour changes through the replication or interpretation of observing other people's behaviour – these other people are known as 'models'. The process of behavioural imitation allows a person to develop and increase their repertoire of behavioural responses to their environment. For example, if we look back to 1960s and 1970s popular music we can note the numerous affected North American accents adopted by British singers. This was done because the model was in some way attractive and to emulate them provided the learner with rewards that would not be otherwise gained. You may think of a range of other examples in respect of the ways in which people dress, walk, wear their hair and so on. Unlike traditional behaviourist ideas which rely on rewards from the environment, social learning also demands that the individual has paid close attention to what has been observed and is able to construct a method of repetition in the future so they can reproduce those modelled behaviours (Bandura, 1969).

Social learning theory emphasises contextual and environmental influences on people's behaviour. Although social learning theory can explain why behaviour develops and occurs, it is also useful in social work to understand how behaviour may be changed by altering environmental influences and introducing alternative models.

One of Bandura's main contributions to cognitive theories concerns self-efficacy – how people's self-appraisal and confidence to act amounted to a belief system about themselves that enhanced this or prevented it. Bandura (1977, 1986) introduced the term self-efficacy to refer to individuals' perceptions of their own capacity to succeed at a given task or effort. Self-efficacy beliefs can shape behaviour by encouraging or preventing a person's willingness to try new behaviours. A high self-efficacy belief entails an expectation of competence, and a capacity to succeed at a given task (Vourlekis, 2009). It can also determine the level of persistence someone is willing or able to devote to practising unfamiliar or difficult tasks. For instance, if you think you have the right interpersonal skills as a student social worker to engage with people and make a working agreement with them you are more likely to stick at it, even if at first you do not live up to your own expectations. However, should you believe that you have not got the skills to achieve this, despite knowing what those skills are, you may simply believe you are proven right when an interview does not go as planned and resign yourself to not being very good at this. Your levels of self-efficacy can allow you to identify where you need help and support, however, and this is very useful when working with people as a social worker.

By demonstrating how exposure to violence is significantly linked with replicating violence, Bandura has contributed immensely to the appreciation of observational learning in the transmission of aggression. Although his initial work was with children, this has immediate relevance to working with adults and shows, again, the connections between theoretical constructs developed for or in different points of the life course.

Martin Seligman

Often considered alongside Bandura's concepts of self-efficacy, *Martin Seligman* (1942–present) is credited with introducing the concept of *'learned helplessness'*. Seligman's work indicates that if someone experiences no connection between their actions and influencing an outcome, they become resigned to the inevitability of outcomes being outside their control and therefore unlikely to try ways of managing their life and environment (Seligman, 1979). Seligman's contributions to the understanding of 'learned helplessness' is particularly relevant to the understanding of how some interpretations and expectations become 'foregone conclusions' or 'self-fulfilling prophecies', especially when linked with negative outcomes. As you may note in the vignette provided in Case Study 2.2, Stan's expectations (based on his school experiences) are potentially relevant to his experiences following an injury.

Seligman was influenced by his admiration for Aaron Beck and has developed a 'positive psychology' which focuses on the characteristic strengths that contribute to resilience and well-being (Peterson and Seligman, 2004). Although recognising the subjectivity of resilience, he also considers the ways that people make meaning of the world to be important. Seligman highlights strengths perspectives, well-being, wisdom, humanity, courage and temperance. Thus, it is the positive features of living that are emphasised, rather than the detriments.

REFLECTION POINT 2.2

Consider the thinkers and theorists we have considered so far. How do you think their work can be used when working as a social worker with adults? Reflect, especially, on those who began their studies with children and young people. What does this say about the connections and differences between adults and children and young people?

Two people most commonly associated with cognitive-behavioural approaches to mental ill-health, particularly depression, are North Americans *Albert Ellis* and *Aaron Beck*.

Albert Ellis

Albert Ellis (1913–2007) originally trained in psychoanalytic psychology, but moved during the 1950s, and came to refer to himself as a 'rational psychologist'. This is best exemplified in Ellis's development of rational–emotive therapy (RET) which represents an important and interesting application of cognitive theory. Ellis emphasised 'irrational thinking' as the source of much unnecessary emotional suffering – thinking such as 'I am no good', 'I am fat', 'I am unworthy'. His rational-emotive therapy is based on the premise that negative emotions, especially depression, and problematic relationship patterns such as avoidance or submission, develop from inaccurate interpretations of experiences, rather than from the experiences per se (Passer et al, 2009). For example, a woman who was insulted by a group of teenagers while out shopping might interpret the experience as the unpleasantness and stupidity of a group of teenagers or may internalise what they said, believing it about herself and forming negative opinions about herself in her next encounter with the world. Ellis is particularly associated with the '*A-B-C principle of problematic belief*'. Ellis used this concept to explain how flawed interpretations of *Antecedents* (or *Activating Events*) influenced problematic *Behaviours or Beliefs*, thus leading to negative or distressing *Consequences*. So, our example of the woman who was insulted when out shopping interpreted the antecedent (A) as a true representation of herself, which made going shopping difficult and frightening (B) and thus led her to believe she was no good and useless (C).

Aaron Beck

Aaron Beck (1921–present) also trained as a psychiatrist and psychoanalyst but began to focus more intently on people's conscious belief systems, rather than their unconscious conflicts as he became disenchanted with psychoanalysis. Similarly to Ellis, Beck came to consider that dysfunctional thinking resulted in problematic or unwanted behaviours, and that underlying beliefs were the source of dysfunctional thinking. There is a positive aspect to this model, since according to Beck, changes in symptoms result from changes in thinking (Fenichel, 2000). Thus, if thinking can be changed to more positive thoughts, it can alleviate distressing symptomatology. As a social worker, you are not going to be involved in cognitive working at this level, though you may progress towards it over time and you do need to know the ways in which a person's thinking changes their behaviour.

Using theories in practice

As we have seen, Bandura's concept of self-efficacy is important for working with people in ways that facilitate positive change by identifying two sets of expectations – outcome expectations (those things that need to be done to achieve a certain outcome) and efficacy expectations (self-beliefs in one's ability to achieve those outcomes) – social workers can help people to take small steps towards increasing beliefs in one's ability to change things.

An example could be a student social worker who has experienced success in a challenging practice learning setting might feel more inclined to encourage or even mentor a younger student – who might lack confidence – to choose a more challenging placement than they would have otherwise chosen. Similarly, students who perceive themselves as successful with academic tasks are potentially more likely to attempt additional academic challenges than their classmates who lack confidence in their own academic capacities. Bandura saw the role of *mentoring* as a means of providing pro-social examples of behaviour.

Seligman's theory of learned helplessness has important implications for working with people across the lifecycle. For students who have come to perceive themselves as being incapable of academic success, the expectation of failure, regardless of effort or practice, can prove a powerful disincentive to persistence, sometimes amounting to a self-fulfilling prophecy as we have seen. Helping people to identify their positions and beliefs allows you to work with them to form alternative goals and ways of living. From this it is possible to change the embedded beliefs by small steps towards achievement.

Ellis's 'A–B–C' principle is particularly applicable to working with people following trauma or struggling with difficulties linked with consequences of problematic behaviours (including, but not limited to, substance use). It is clear how this model relates to adults. It provides a useful and fairly easy way of beginning to challenge ways in which people interpret their circumstances and experiences, how this relates to behaviour and ways that may be changed.

Antecedents are those factors that trigger or exacerbate problematic behaviours. Those triggers may be expectations of positive or negative consequences. An example may help here. Consider a woman who witnessed the violent abuse of her mother by her father over many years who comes to think that it is normal for a man to act violently. However, when in a violent relationship herself she noted that her partner was arrested and charged by the police for his violence towards her. This may suggest that the trigger and the accepting behaviour are challenged because of this reaction replacing her original ABC (violence, compliant/accepting behaviour/dominance and submission) by a new one of violence/reporting behaviour/taking charge. Charges that this kind of approach may lead to some victim blaming in working with the abused person to alter their response may have some legitimacy and it is crucial that great care is taken that this does not happen. Also, in cases where the aggressor perceives their problematic behaviour as having been triggered or provoked by others, Ellis's A–B–C model provides a means of reinterpreting the consequences of responding to that provocation (see Case Study 2.2).

CASE STUDY 2.2

Stan, aged 30, is employed as a postman for the Royal Mail. He enjoys his work, as it involves being out and about, interacting with a variety of people, and doesn't require that he spends much time sitting at a desk. He is well-liked by his colleagues and his employers, as a hard-working, reliable member of staff.

While he has always been intellectually above average, Stan was not academically inclined; he did not enjoy school and left at 16 with minimal qualifications. Stan states that he felt 'stupid' at school, and he still struggles with concentration when reading. He has a long-term relationship with Emma, and they became engaged last year.

While making a delivery on a busy neighbourhood street, Stan was struck by a hit-and-run driver. He was thrown onto the pavement, sustaining serious head injuries. Thanks to the very prompt arrival of an ambulance and immediate surgery, Stan has survived his injuries without paralysis. He has, however, sustained injuries that impair his memory and judgement.

Stan cannot recall the details of his injury, but can remember most of what he has been told about it. His short-term memory is problematic. When his physiotherapist gives him exercises to practice between sessions, Stan struggles to remember what is expected, and is easily bored with repetitive activities.

Stan's behaviour tends to be more impulsive than before, and he becomes very frustrated when he doesn't remember details being discussed. Sometimes his frustration leads to aggressive outbursts. He becomes angry when discussing the fact that the driver of the other vehicle did not stop and has not been found. Stan's future employability is uncertain, given the cognitive implications of his injuries.

Questions

1. What would you consider the primary cognitive aspect of Stan's situation?
2. How might Bandura's concepts of self-efficacy be applied to working with Stan?
3. How might Seligman's concepts of learned helplessness be applied to understanding Stan?
4. How might Ellis's 'A-B-C' model be applied to working with Stan?

Discussion

There needs to be consideration, of course, of the physical impacts of the injury on Stan's functioning. However, the cognitive theories we have reviewed may provide indications of the environments in which memory and cognition affect recall, performance and so on. In terms of self-efficacy, we would want to know whether Stan can identify what it is that needs to be done to complete a task and whether or not he believed he had the wherewithal to do so. This links to the concept of learned helplessness, especially if he does not see any outcome for his actions and has 'learned' that whatever he does it changes nothing. So, if together you determine that the main thing to work on is his aggression, you may wish to assess what the activating events are that create the thoughts and beliefs that underpin the consequence – his anger and aggression – and seek to work with those beliefs and to modify them to something less destructive.

Critical perspectives and thinking

There has been a great increase in the use and popularity of cognitive and cognitive-behavioural approaches in the last few decades. However, that does not mean that these approaches are not subject to criticism. In respect of cognitive theory applications, a key criticism levelled at Piaget's work is its cultural and gender bias. This is something that can be considered in relation to most research, however, as all research is time, context and culture specific and this can cause difficulties when trying to replicate the research or employ models of intervention that are drawn from that work. Using Piaget's work with adults rather than children may also run in to some degree of criticism because of its explicit relationship to child development stages in his sample. Here it is the importance of the general concepts, outlined previously, that we should keep in mind.

Conclusion

Cognitive-Behavioural Therapy (CBT) provides a very popular and well-supported approach to helping people with an array of problems especially in respect of mental health and substance use issues. However, its structured and natural science/psychology-based approach tends to put off many British social workers. If we look in greater detail, we can see that CBT is a relatively short-term intervention, and therefore popular with cash-strapped services and managers, but can also be congruent with collaborative, person-centred approaches because of its focus on perception and experience which, necessarily, remains subjective. CBT is primarily focused on the present, rather than underlying problems or past experiences that may be contributing to the person's current difficulties. Of course, one criticism levelled against CBT by more critically oriented practitioners is that it is generally focused on individual work, rather than on social or environmental factors, which may entail elements such as oppression, racism, discrimination, or poverty, which may play essential roles in people's difficulties. It is important that we, as social workers, take these structural factors into account when using CBT in our work.

Reflective questions

1 What are some of the ways in which previous experiences of unhealthy relationships could influence partners' expectations of their new relationship with each other?

2 What are some of the ways in which successful early experiences of school, sports or music could influence adults' expectations and confidence when trying something new?

3 How might cultural or religious norms influence people's understanding and expectation when immigrating to a new and different country?

Further reading

• Musson, P. (2017) *Making Sense of Theory and its Application to Social Work Practice*. St. Albans: Critical Publishing.
  Musson's book seeks to make some of the complex theories used in social work more understandable and cognitive theories are covered in an accessible way.

- Parrish, M. (2014) *Social Work Perspectives on Human Behaviour* (2nd edn), Maidenhead: McGraw-Hill.

  This book provides a broader understanding of growth and development across the life course and makes this directly relevant to your practice as a social worker.

- Vourlekis, B.S. (2017) Cognitive theory for social work practice. In R. Greene (ed.) *Human Behavior for Social Work Practice.* London: Routledge.

  This chapter discusses the importance of environment and context on the production and reproduction of thinking and behaviour. Despite being US-based, the concepts and practices discussed are applicable across many countries, and it will provide you with a clear introduction.

References

Bandura, A. (1969) *Principles of Behaviour Modification.* New York: Holt, Rinehart & Winston.

Bandura, A. (1977) Self-efficacy: Toward a unifying theory of behaviour change, *Psychological Review*, 84(2): 191–215.

Bandura, A. (1986) *Social Foundations of Thought and Action.* Englewood Cliffs, NJ: Prentice-Hall.

Chen, J.-Q. and Gardner, F. (2005) Assessment based on multiple-intelligences theory. In D. Flanagan, J. Genshaft and P. Harrison (eds), *Contemporary Intellectual Assessment: Theories, Tests, and Issues* (2nd edn). New York: Guilford, pp 77–102.

Ewen, R. (2010) *An Introduction to Theories of Personality* (7th edn). London: Psychology Press/Taylor & Francis.

Fenichel, M. (2000). New concepts in practice: On therapy – a dialogue with Aaron T. Beck and Albert Ellis. American Psychological Association 108th Convention. Current Topics in Psychology. Available from: http://www.fenichel.com/Beck-Ellis.shtml (accessed 12 January 2008).

Gardner, F. (1983) *Frames of Mind: The Theory of Multiple Intelligences.* New York: Basic Books.

Joravsky, D. (1979) Scientists as servants. *New York Review of Books*, 28 June, p 260.

Kelley, H. (1971) *Attribution in Social Interaction.* Morristown, NJ: General Learning Press.

Kelly, G. (1963) *A Theory of Personality: The Psychology of Personal Constructs.* New York: Norton.

Luria, A. (2004) Vygotsky, Lev (1896–1934). In R. Gregory (ed.), *The Oxford Companion to the Mind* (2nd edn). Oxford: Oxford University Press.

Parrish, M. (2014) *Social Work Perspectives on Human Behaviour* (2nd edn). Maidenhead: McGraw-Hill.

Passer, M., Smith, R., Holt, N., Brenner, A., Sutherland, K. and Vliek, M. (2009). *Psychology: The Science of Mind and Behaviour* (3rd edn). Boston: McGraw-Hill International.

Peterson, C. and Seligman, M.E.P. (2004) *Character Strengths and Virtues.* Oxford: Oxford University Press.

Piaget, J. (1970) Piaget's Theory. In P.H. Mussed (ed.) *Carmichael's Manual of Child Psychology* (3rd edn) Volume 1. New York: Wiley, pp 7033–32.

Seligman, M.E.P. (1979) *Helplessness: On Depression, Development and Death.* San Francisco, CA: Freeman.

Vourlekis, B. (2009) Cognitive theory for social work practice. In R. Greene (ed.), *Human Behavior Theory and Social Work Practice* (3rd edn). New York: Aldine Transaction, pp 133–163.

Weiner, B. (1986) *An Attributional Theory of Motivation and Emotion.* New York: Springer.

3

Moral, spiritual and existential development

Peter Szto

Introduction

Human service professionals believe in helping people. The desire to help is so that people can live healthier, more meaningful and productive lives. The belief is that the healthier people are, the healthier is society. Any link between the individual and the well-being of society is important. The focus of this chapter is on the contribution of spirituality to how human service professionals provide care. Spirituality is defined as:

> A process of human life and development focusing on the search for a sense of meaning, purpose, morality, and wellbeing, in relationship with oneself, other people, other beings, the universe, and ultimate reality, however understood (e.g. in animistic, atheistic, nontheistic, polytheistic, theistic, or other ways). (Canda and Furman, 1999, p 3)

The definition posits spirituality as a relational process between individuals and their social environment. It is a dynamic, rather than static, relationship that involves transpersonal and transcendent discovery. A slightly different definition of spirituality is 'how you embody or make manifest in the world, that which is most important to you, which you value most' (Vanderbilt, n.d.). Here, spirituality constitutes the core of one's innermost being. Both definitions suggest that spirituality is relevant to human service professionals because helping people involves a quest for meaning, purpose, morality and existential development.

Chapter objectives

Framing this examination of spirituality for human service professionals are four objectives:

- analyse the relationship between spirituality and religion;

- look at how human service professionals have historically responded to spirituality with a focus on the profession of social work;

- explore the relationship between spirituality and personhood from an East–West historical perspective;

- examine spirituality in relation to social welfare and visualisation.

Three case studies are presented to deepen understanding of the chapter objectives.

Background and context

This chapter will examine spirituality through the lens of personhood – the status and condition of being a person. Despite the contentious debate surrounding personhood, i.e. human origins, slavery, abortion, human trafficking, sex workers, euthanasia, etc., the definition of a person is vital to this discussion on spirituality. It is assumed here, that persons the world over share a common humanity, but that across societies and locations the experience of personhood varies due to culture, language, social environment and historical circumstances. In addition, spirituality involves a person accessing their 'inner core' and being able to express whatever this is to others. Having one without the other creates an existential moral dilemma. Not being able to look inward, and not being able to externalise meaning, is a spiritual problem. A noteworthy example of overcoming this dilemma by achieving spiritual balance is India's independence leader, Mahatma Gandhi (1869–1948). In *The Story of My Experiments with Truth*, Gandhi (1957) wrote, 'What I want to achieve – What I have been striving and pining to achieve these thirty years is self-realization, to see God face-to-face, to attain Mokshat.' Mokshat is the Hindi term about release from the cycle of rebirth. It is attainment of a transcendental state after overcoming emancipation, release, and liberation from worldly ignorance and material desires. After Gandhi's long struggle to access his inner core, he eventually came to realise that spirituality offered him a wellspring of personal meaning and motivation. Accessing his inner core enabled Gandhi to engage in untold opportunities with the outer world, that is, social action. Using previously hidden ways of seeing the world, through spiritual eyes, Gandhi could now see clearly the organic unity of the person.

The unity of the person is important for human service professionals to maintain. For analytical reasons, reducing the whole person into parts is important for the study of human anatomy, probing psychological dynamics, or to understand mind-brain interactions. However, defining the person by its parts does diminish the dignity and worth of the whole person. It also, unfortunately, privileges one part of the person over another. The nursery rhyme Humpty Dumpty foretells the dangers of reducing the whole into parts.

Humpty Dumpty sat on a wall,
Humpty Dumpty had a great fall.
All the king's horses and all the king's men
Couldn't put Humpty together again.

Once separated, it becomes difficult to put Humpty Dumpty back together again. This nursery rhyme is a cautionary tale for human service professionals about reducing the whole person. The concept 'bio–psycho–socio–spiritual' is a good illustration of this. The hyphenation reduces the person into parts, in order to isolate these parts, before stringing them back together (Hutchison, 2008). The descriptor infers a whole person, but the person described is only a sum of its parts. Moreover, earlier constructs of this hyphenated descriptor did not include spiritual. Only after critics pointed this out was spirituality appended to the incomplete description (Cohen and Koenig, 2003). Ironically, the American psychiatrist, Dr. George Engel (1913–99), had coined the descriptor 'bio–psycho–social' in response to how the medical model reduced the person into organs (Engel, 1977). Engel was dissatisfied with the biomedical model's excessive narrowness, especially how it treated patients as passive objects and ignored their subjective experiences. He opposed its linear and causal framework, arguing that illnesses were much more complex and multi-faceted. He sought language that was holistic and based on a scientific framework. Although his alternative construct challenged the medical model's reductionism, he did not sufficiently eliminate it. His attempt for a holistic perspective is welcome and eventual inclusion of spirituality. This inclusion is important to re-assess and re-claim spirituality and personhood. Shonin (2013) observed:

> There is increasing scientific evidence that spirituality plays a significant role in the etiology, maintenance, and treatment of mental health problems. Types of spiritual aptitudes that have been shown to be influential in this regard include (for example) dispositional mindfulness, faith, meditative insight, loving-kindness, compassion, death-awareness, and patience. (Shonin, 2013, para 1)

In this discussion on personhood and spirituality, the role of language is significant. In English, the meaning of spirituality, and its cognate root, spirit come from the Latin *spiritus*, meaning to breathe. Ancient Latin speakers understood the intimate relationship between breathing and life itself. The two were considered one, as reflected in their language. Without the capacity to breathe, a person cannot survive and will surely die. In other words, being alive was equivalent to spirituality. All persons are, therefore, by definition, spiritual. More explicitly, spirituality is central to human existence. The interdependency of breathing and being alive speaks volumes to the intimate relationship between spirituality and personhood. This perspective is evident in ancient Hebrew. For example, the Hebrew word *ruach* (רוּחַ) denotes spirit, meaning breath or wind. Spirit signified the immaterial dimension of the person we moderns call the soul. The divine ruach meant the ultimate source of human life, as when the Old Testament prophet Moses wrote, 'the Lord God formed the man from the dust of the ground and breathed into his nostrils the breath of life, and the man became a living being' (Genesis 2:7). Ruach refers to God breathing life into the material body, giving it life, meaning and purpose. In the language of the New Testament, Biblical Greek also equates spirit with life itself. The Gospel of Luke describes giving up one's spirit as equivalent to giving up one's life. In Luke 23:46, 'Jesus called out with a loud voice, "Father, into your hands I commit my spirit." When he said this, he breathed his last.'

Spirituality is relevant for human service professionals (Dooyeweerd, 1986; Christie and Gauvreau, 1996). A spiritual perspective offers professional practitioners a unique framework to engage everyday life, social relationships, professional identity and the healing arts. Gandhi, remarkably demonstrated how becoming spiritually self-conscious yielded purpose, meaning and social action. Not everyone, though, can be a Gandhi. And, in modern Western societies, spirituality has actually diminished due to the rise of secular science. It is more likely to garner suspicion than uncritical acceptance. Human service professionals should expect misunderstanding and possibly hostility towards a spiritually sensitive practice. Social work academic, Weaver Nichols (Moser, 2008), observed, 'Spirituality has become more acceptable to talk about, use in practice, write about, and research, but it is still considered by some people to be a little bit on the fringe' (p 33). This aversion towards spirituality is curious given the profession's value for diversity, cultural difference and being non-judgmental. The recent turn towards spirituality though is promising. Holloway and Moss (2010, p 2) speak of a rediscovery of spirituality and point to the 'pros and cons' of spirituality for professional practice: '… we shall be arguing that our exploration of spirituality will take us to the very heart and spirit of social work'. A decade prior, Canda (1998) embarked on groundbreaking scholarship on the legitimate role of spirituality in professional practice. As the founding director of the Society for Spirituality in Social Work in 1990, Canda has led a community of scholars to produce evidence-based research and fresh insights on spirituality. Interest in spirituality continues to spread as indicated by the increase in number of journals, conferences and published works by organisations devoted to the study of spirituality.

Key theories and thinkers

The historical relationship between spirituality and religion is examined next. For various reasons, the relationship between the two has splintered, so that they are often confused or lumped together. In fact, the two are more complementary than opposing, and so it is important to understand why, in the modern era, they are viewed as separate. Historically, among the five major religions, that is, Judaism, Hindu, Buddhism, Christianity and Islam, spirituality was central to their beliefs and practices. For brevity, two are highlighted here. First, in Judaism, storytelling plays a key role in expressing Jewish spirituality. For example, the Maggid is a storyteller who is highly skilled in narrating stories from the Torah. The power of re-telling stories of enslavement and escape from captivity reminds Jewish people of the promises God made to them about liberation. The ritual of repeating these stories keeps alive their collective memories and provides meaning to their spirituality. Buddhist practice also uses rituals to cultivate and express spirituality. In Buddhism, one's spiritual journey involves various self-discipline practices to attain inner peace and enlightenment.

REFLECTION POINT 3.1

Think of your own beliefs, practices and the meanings you make of life. Consider where they have come from whether that is family and friends or from searching for a meaning to 'big' questions. Consider how these personal views might influence your social work practice, and what you can do to ensure they do not have a negative impact on the people you work with.

The spiritual and religion divide is also related to the sacred/secular dichotomy, that is, dividing life into two distinct worldviews. Sacred refers to personal faith, private piety, holiness and things related to a divine. Secular refers to anything public, such as the workplace or everything that has nothing to do with the divine. Some argue that this dichotomy is a false one and arbitrarily constructed to restrict spirituality from everyday life. The goal of secularism is to remove spirituality from every day public life, then reconstitute it as non-normative, and furthermore, to restrict it to private and personal beliefs only. The phrase 'spiritual, but not religious' expresses an outcome from having separated religion from spirituality. Spiritual counsellor Sven Erlandson (2000) coined the phrase as a response to the ascendency of transpersonal experiences, but without the restraints of religion. Liberal Protestant pastor and author, Lillian Daniel (2013), further popularised the idea of spirituality, but without the institutional baggage and doctrinal demands of organised religion. Post-Enlightenment writers Erlandson and Daniel came to their respective conclusions because they viewed religion in anachronistic and pragmatic terms. They saw religion as ignorant of modern science, devoid of rigorous rational analysis and, thus, unsophisticated. In their understanding, the modern person relies on reason, rational discourse and science, not on beliefs and inferences not verifiable. Without the advantage of higher-ordered reasoning, religion has become outmoded, narrow, rigid and is perhaps, naively, holding onto outdated beliefs.

The roots of modern religio-spirituality can be traced to the 18th-century German theologian, Friedrich Schleiermacher (1768–1834). Schleiermacher laid the conceptual groundwork for modern spirituality by arguing human emotions and imagination are central to epistemology over logical analysis alone. He argued for subjectivity to explain human experiences supplanting the longstanding dependence on transcendence. In this modern view, religion lost its epistemological prominence on matters spiritual. Most significantly, religion morphed into a self-serving bureaucracy with outmoded rites and rituals that no longer provided a primary source of meaning and purpose. Yet, a religion-free spirituality unintentionally created its own limitations and challenges. For example, a common definition of spirituality is elusive due to the broad variety and diversity of human experiences. All subjectivities are not the same. If everyone decides their own spirituality, then no one decides for everyone making it impossible for a common definition. Subjectivism precludes anything universal. In the modern West, spirituality has become highly individualistic and subjective. Postmodernists prefer a definition of spirituality in personal (some say self-referential) terms rather than in terms of a grand narrative. See Case Study 3.1, where the history of American social work is examined in order to understand the impact dividing religion and spirituality on human service professionals.

CASE STUDY 3.1

Faith-based organisations had been the main providers of social services up until the late 19th-century when 'scientific philanthropy' emerged. Rapid urbanisation, industrialisation, immigration and social mobility challenged church's teachings, and its spiritual-sensitive approach. The new approach alternatively found inspiration in logical positivism, rather than religious faith to help the poor. Secularisation,[1] for sure, profoundly challenged faith-inspired volunteers given the roots of social work in Judean-Christian teachings. Despite the shift from faith to science, the legacy of social work pioneers such as Charles Loring Brace (1826–90), Graham Taylor (1851–1938), Jane Addams (1860–1935) and Mary Richmond (1861–1928) were many agencies and programmes inspired by Christian teachings (see Brace, 1894).

The Settlement House movement, for example, was a social intervention rooted in a spiritual view of the social world. The Reverend Samuel Barnett, an Anglican cleric from London's East End, sought to transform its blighted communities. He argued that Christians should resist fleeing the city and instead engage its poverty through a spiritual lifestyle of radical activism. In 1884, he established Toynbee Hall as the world's first settlement house. Jane Addams emulated Barnett in establishing Hull House in Chicago. On a second trip to Europe in 1888, Addams visited Toynbee Hall, and was inspired by its vibrant faith community of like-minded progressives devoted to social change. Hull House expressed her faith in action.

Faith in action also inspired the Social Gospel movement. Liberal Protestant clergy preached that the Gospel should not be disconnected from America's social ills. Authentic spirituality meant helping others. The intellectual architect of the Social Gospel movement was Walter Rauschenbusch (1861–1918). He argued in *A Theology of the Social Gospel* (1917, p 2) that a socially engaged gospel should be 'a permanent addition to our spiritual outlook and that its arrival constitutes a state in the development of the Christian religion'. Rauschenbusch advocated for a holistic spirituality where temporal and eternal welfare co-existed. The Social Gospel movement played a key role shaping the Progressive Era and New Deal of American social welfare. The spiritual concept 'Kingdom of God' underpinned programmes to fight social injustices and advance social reforms. Many charitable organisations and social service agencies were established to address child labour, a living wage and a five-day work week. Over the course of the 20th century, though, many of these organisations would cut ties with their spiritual origins. Although Jane Addams's formative years were steeped in religious teachings and activities, she was quiet on things spiritual later in her life.

Secularisation never sought to eliminate spirituality from civic life – only to privatise it, making it personal rather than public. Spirituality, however, remains a valid dimension of social life and formal inquiry. The American organisation that accredits schools of social work – the Council on Social Work Education (CSWE) – states, 'Social workers are expected to work ethically and effectively with religion and spirituality as relevant to clients and their communities and to refrain from negative discrimination based on religious or nonreligious beliefs' (2018, para 4). This statement sets clear expectations for professional practice by recognising spirituality and sanctioning space for its existence.

Questions
1. What historical lessons can be drawn about secularisation for today?
2. How can social workers and other human service professionals be sensitive to spirituality in a secular age?
3. How might the position described concerning the US affect how you practice in your own country?

Discussion
Case Study 3.1 illustrates how American social workers and human service professionals historically handled spirituality. These may be different from culture to culture but also from person to person. Being sensitive to the many ways in which people make sense of the world for themselves can help you appreciate both your own and other people's spirituality. Another perspective on spirituality is a cross-cultural perspective. That is, the Eastern ways of knowing are qualitatively different and examined next.

East–West perspective on spirituality

In ancient Eastern civilizations, the role of the sage was to reflect on things spiritual. These reflections were often written down for future generations to benefit. To directly access these reflections requires knowledge of the original source language. Having full access to these reflections is ideal but not always possible. Fortunately, highly reliable translations are available for non-native researchers to read.

The major Eastern philosophical systems are Hinduism, Buddhism and Taoism. Each holds distinct views on personhood, albeit with different historical beginnings, geographical contexts and epistemological frameworks. Despite the diversity, they share a common bond in spirituality and belief in an afterlife. The dominant Eastern philosopher on spirituality is the Chinese sage, Confucius (551–479 BC). Confucius was an itinerant teacher, who did not personally inscribe his own ideas, but instead his disciples wrote and disseminated them. Today, we have access to Confucius's thoughts by way of his primary texts, The *Four Books* and *Five Classics* (五经, Wǔjīng). Written before 300 BC in different genres, they include poetry, dialogue, commentary, divination and historical analysis. Of particular interest is the Chinese word for Confucianism, *rujiao* (儒教). It does not refer to Confucius himself, but to a 'learned person'. *Rujiao* suggests that the pursuit of all things requires an integrated self, that is, one who is educated, moral and benevolent. The Confucian ideal of a spiritually mature person is one who reflects *rujiao*. This person was known as ren (人) and was considered the Confucian ideal of an individual living in harmony with others under the same mandate of Heaven. Fulfilling *ren* involved a life journey of spiritual cultivation to attain full integration and a mature self.

Confucianism expected individuals to cultivate spirituality through self-discipline. Confucius believed the everyday practice of social ethics was critical to produce a self-regulating and harmonious society. A highly moral society was possible but required citizens to practise self-discipline and self-cultivation to harness the darker side of human nature. In Confucian social welfare, the person was communally embedded within a web of overlapping and interlocking relationships, that is, kinship bonds and social structures. Furthermore, a complex system of rites and rituals governed relationships to produce civil society, specifically, practising gift giving, courteous behaviours and filial piety. The person was not considered an autonomous or independent moral agent, as in Western societies. Neo-Confucian scholar Tu Wei-ming (1985, p 12) describes the embedding as a 'sociality of Confucian self-hood'. The phrase defined persons as deeply rooted in familial bonds and communal obligations, an attitude opposite to Western individualism and human autonomy. The Confucian view of the person was holistic, integrated and social-oriented (Case Study 3.2). Confucian anthropology did not separate the whole person into mind and body.

CASE STUDY 3.2: SPIRITUALITY AND CHINESE SOCIAL WELFARE

This second case study highlights how the Chinese conceptualised and responded to existential issues of health, suffering and human relationships. Taoists developed Confucian concepts using highly metaphoric symbols to describe the natural world and human agency. One of the more widely recognised symbol is Yin-Yang (Figure 3.1):

Figure 3.1: Yin-Yang

The Yin-Yang symbol denotes apparent opposites that are in complementary relationship to each other. What appear to be binary or dichotomous are actually interconnected and overlapping. This perspective recognises the mutuality of opposites held together by an inner unity. For example, male and female appear opposite on such measures as genitalia, ways of knowing and masculinity/femininity. These measures, though, are merely surface differences that belie a deeper unity. Understanding Taoist metaphors requires nuanced knowledge about the host culture to grasp its spiritual roots. For example:

> [T]he word spirit has rich semiotic connections to natural, biophysical phenomena, such as breath, wind, fire, and winged creatures, all of them metaphors for the power of creation, life, and healing that pervades the world. (Tu, 1985, p 8)

A context-sensitive approach to this metaphor is important to understand Eastern ideas on spirituality. The Chinese concept Qi, or chi (氣), is one such idea. Qi refers to the material life force, or vital energy flow, that animates humans. Breath and wind also describe Qi in terms of non-material phenomena. Lee (2014) describes Qi as 'psychophysical stuff' (p 42). In ancient Chinese thought, Qi indicated a person's health, moral status and social relationships. These relationships were embedded within a dynamic flow of events and circumstances moving in multiple directions. The flow indicated constant change and disequilibrium. The function of Qi was to cultivate balance and harmony between internal and external relationships. Qi presupposed that the person was a social being versus an autonomous human being. The Confucian unit of measure for personhood was the kinship-clan system. The moral measure of a person was the degree to which they achieved balance and social harmony.

Traditional Chinese Medicine (TCM) relied on Qi to diagnose a person's health, that is, the efficient flow of Qi throughout the body. The pulse gauged strength and flow of Qi. Poor flow indicated imbalance or illness. The location of symptoms and cause were not necessarily 1:1 correspondence. A sore shoulder could be due to injury to the shoulder itself. Or, it could also be a symptom of an underlying issue elsewhere in the body, like the gall bladder. To heal the sore shoulder involved restoring the person's balance, strengthening and stimulating the person's immune system through natural or non-intrusive means. Herbal remedies, diet, food, massage and acupuncture are but a few TCM treatments proven to be highly effective over millennia.

Questions

1. How can human service professionals apply the Chinese concepts outlined in this case study to their everyday practice of helping?
2. How can Eastern approaches to spirituality be integrated with Western approaches?
3. How might the thinking contained within this case study influence your own practice?

Discussion

It is important, whatever our perspective and cultural position, that we do not privilege one way of thinking, believing or 'doing' spirituality as being the 'right way' or letting it become unconscious and assumed – what social scientists would call a normative approach. In the subsequent discussion, we look at Western and Confucian thought and compare both some of the similarities and some of the differences. Taking time to consider these approaches will help to make you more aware of the other, but also of oneself.

Ancient Western societies also developed ideas on spirituality and personhood. The ancient Greek philosophers Socrates, Plato and Aristotle laid the intellectual foundations for Western thought on personhood and spirituality. Socrates held to a holistic view of the person, '... just as one should not attempt to cure the eyes apart from the head, nor the head apart from the body, so one should not attempt to cure the body apart from the soul' (Cooper, 1997, p 643). He believed persons should be understood in their fullness and not by their parts. In the Hellenistic world, this holistic attitude influenced not only medical treatment, but all of life. The ancients held to an integrated and total view of the person. The totality included both body and soul. They were two unique but different parts, substantively distinct, yet fully integrated as a whole person. Reducing the whole person to its material dimension, that is, corporeal and carnal, was alien to ancient Greek thought. The Greeks believed personhood embodied a physical body and a non–material soul. The soul was significant for a host of human qualities: thinking, perception, emotional states, moral judgements and other psychological functions. This holistic view was the dominant attitude in the ancient Western world until the 17th century, when the French philosopher, Rene Descartes, re-conceptualised and separated the person into two distinct substances – mind and body. Cartesian dualism deconstructed the whole person into two discrete parts.

In both the Hellenistic and the Confucian worlds, the person was understood as a fully integrated whole. For the Hellenists, whole referred to an autonomous person whose identity and commitment was to the individual, rather than the social environment. Confucian wholeness was inextricably communal and akin to the social work construct 'person-in-environment'. Interaction between the person and the social environment created a gestalt where the whole was more than the sum of the individual parts. This Confucian-gestalt view of the person created a unique framework that continues to the present.

Is the Chinese Qi equivalent to the Western soul or spirit? This is a fundamental question for human service professionals in the West interested in 're-discovering' spirituality. Is it re-discovery or perceiving a reality always there? Comparative theologian, Hyo-Dong Lee (2014), suggests modern Western notions of spirituality de-emphasise and overlook psychophysical processes. The modern West continues to favour a dualistic and materialist stance towards spirituality. He argues that the demands of science for rational and evidence-based explanations squeezes out the possibility for non-material perspectives. The result has been a diminished view of spiritualty and truncated view of the person. Interactions between mind and body are minimised in favour of a reductionist view of the person, 'Western Learning, or Christianity, lacked an understanding of the vital and intimate connection between Lord Heaven and humanity, between human beings, and between human and nonhuman creatures' (Lee, 2014, p 5). Lee explains that when Western liberal Christianity de-valued and denied the Creator-creature distinction (Van Til, 1940), it ontologically untethered humans from things external or transcendent to the human experience. Even pantheism recognised 'a spiritual reality that is one with observed natural and human reality' (Poplin, 2014, p 166). The Creator-creature construct presupposes that humans are spiritual because of their ontological standing. Does the West's minimisation of mind-body interactions suppress an underlying ontic order, that is, spirituality?

REFLECTION POINT 3.2

How can human service professionals benefit from Eastern and Western views of personhood and healing practices?

In practical terms, both can be complimentary and blended to facilitate holistic service delivery. Traumatic brain injuries, rehabilitation services, palliative medicine, case management and all other human service professional functions stand to benefit from Qi, TCM and holistic thinking.

Making it real: applying knowledge to practice

Spirituality and social welfare

The current human service literature on spirituality focuses more on the individual experience than the well-being of society (Ben Asher, 2001). The search for meaning and purpose at a societal level is equally as important for human service professionals as is helping individuals (Crisp, 2008). As noted previously, secularisation did not eradicate spirituality but merely shifted the discourse on spirituality away from religion and theology towards parapsychology and the mystical. In addition, post-modern scrutiny questioned the validity of grand narratives and rejected the possibility of the supernatural on the grounds it could not be scientifically verifiable. Religion and spirituality were seen as 'biased, unscientific, lacking objectivity, or not based in measurement and replication' (Land, 2015, p 5). Post-modernism claimed to be wholly rooted in facts, observation, and thus free from subjective bias. Scientific objectivity, not faith, was the new gold standard to measure societal well-being. This secular worldview became the dominant paradigm for human service professionals. Voices of resistance, however, are emerging and challenging the status quo by questioning the validity and sufficiency of the scientific world view. In particular, the values of human service professionals regarding client self-determination, respect for human diversity, social justice, and protecting the marginalised, begs the question whether there is adequate space within the human services for religion and spirituality (see Gray, 2008)?

Social work scholar writing on spirituality, Helen Land (2015), introduces the idea of 'sacred-sensitive' practice for human service professionals to engage clients. The idea affirms the legitimate role of spirituality within human services, especially when it is clients who first raise spiritual issues. The challenge for human service professionals is how to appropriately respond when spirituality is the 'elephant in the room'. For sure, imposing beliefs is unethical and inappropriate, yet when human service professionals are neither trained nor knowledgeable about their clients' spirituality, naivete is an unfortunate disservice to clients. The increase of clients seeking spirituality is an opportunity for human service professionals to respond with relevant answers. An approach worth examining that integrates spirituality and social welfare are the ideas of Thomas Merton (1915–68). Merton was an American Catholic Trappist Monk, and scholar, who was well versed in both Western Christianity and Eastern religions. He explained how Western faith traditions abandoned their mystical heritage and sense of awe, only to replace it with empirically based rational discourse. Verbalism replaced allegory, precision replaced mystery, and words replaced visualisation. Merton observed that in Zen Buddhism enlightenment 'went beyond cultural and social structures' (Merton, 1968, p 5). Spirituality resisted the necessity to always reduce and categorise phenomena into words. How can human service professionals extend Merton's insights for future practice?

Visualising spirituality

As we have already seen, East and West expressions of spirituality are uniquely different. One expression relevant to human service professionals is the visual arts, for example, painting, illustration, social media, tattoos, graffiti, video, and photography. Visualising spirituality encompasses seeing and expressing a spiritual perspective. Photographer Christine Valters Painter explains in *Eyes of the Heart* (2013) that spirituality and photography can be a 'contemplative practice'. The process of taking photographs is empowering to 'slow down' and to 'gaze deeply'. Photography allowed space for her to decompress and for eternity to come into her day. It allowed the camera to hold the moment. Likewise, London-based amateur photographer, Philip J. Richter, in *Spirituality in Photography* (2017), advances an innovative approach to photography framed in spiritual-sensitivity. He promotes an existential minded way of visualising the world. His spirituality is a deliberate, unhurried and measured stance the photographer takes to absorb the subtle and gentler dimensions of life. He calls for patience. Patience allows the photographer to engage the subject with respect and humility. It also assumes reciprocity between image and image-maker. In that special moment of reciprocity, photography becomes a reflexive process of visual intercourse.

The benefit of photography for human service professionals is how it encodes and decodes information. Photography is an observational tool with the uncanny ability to capture reality and encode visual memory. Human service professionals are also keen observers of the social environment. Case notes and other forms of written documentation are necessary to encode what happens. The adage if it is not written then it did not happen underscores the importance of recording events. Decoding is equally important in casework. Words though can be misconstrued to manipulate the memory and meaning of events. Photography does not depend on words to communicate to offer human service professionals another means to record events as the following Case Study 3.3 indicates.

CASE STUDY 3.3

This third case study examines a concrete way to see spirituality. A brief glance at American photographer, Diane Arbus (1923–71) will conclude this section on visual spirituality. Arbus started her photography career shooting commercial work for fashion magazines *Vogue*, *Harper's Bazaar*, etc. The work left her disenchanted with the fashion industry, especially its commercial side. She quit fashion photography in 1956 to pursue her own artistic vision far removed from commercial photography. Arbus had felt a special kinship with the fringes of society such as transvestites, dwarfs, nudists and circus performers. Photography permitted her to photograph the marginalised and show them to mainstream society. Unlike portraitists, documentarians, or war photojournalists, Arbus broached formal genres to record striking observations of society's most vulnerable. It did not bother her to push social conventions of her day, or ruffle established norms to pursue what was taboo. John Szarkowski, esteemed historian of photography, said of her tenacity, 'Arbus did not avert her eyes' (*NYT*, 8 March, 2018). Her photography was all about getting others to look at human diversity. She photographed to reveal the most hidden among us. She produced visually compelling portraits about the human condition. Arbus intentionally avoided taking photographs for social justice reasons. Raw curiosity motivated her to photograph. Her images were spiritual portraits of individuals in 'search for a sense of meaning' (Canda, 1999) and 'how you embody or make manifest in the world' (Vanderbilt, n.d.).

The burden of looking at Arbus's photographs was overbearing for some. Cultural critic Susan Sontag said, 'Arbus's photographs suggest a world in which everybody is an alien—hopelessly isolated, immobilised in mechanical, crippled identities and relationships' (Sontag, 1973). Sontag found disturbing Arbus's allure to photograph the vulnerable because 'all the people are grotesques' (1973, p 2). For human service professionals this reaction raises pertinent questions. Is it professional to react with cold indifference or to show horror towards clients? Does grotesque matter? More penetrating, Sontag (1973, p 5) questions Arbus's motives to photograph, 'Arbus's work shows people who are pathetic, pitiable, as well as horrible, repulsive, but it does not arouse any compassionate feelings.' Perhaps Sontag is overly critical. Arbus defends herself by saying, 'I just used to adore them.' In fact, Arbus actually had deep empathy and rapport with her subjects. Human service professionals stand to gain from Arbus's images exactly because they are freaky and grotesque. Sontag reluctantly agreed to Arbus's spirituality: 'One needs a camera to show that "right through the dull and marvelous opacity called the United States" are spiritual patterns.'

Questions
1. How can human service professionals directly benefit from photography?
2. How might other visual arts help make spirituality more visible and practical?
3. Can you think of ways that you as a social worker might help people to visualise and vocalise their own spirituality?

Discussion
Spirituality and meaning making in life changes and develops throughout one's life. For social workers it is important to find a range of meaningful ways (some more than others to different individuals perhaps) to show, share and support people's beliefs and views, to encourage them to actively own their social, cultural and spiritual positions and to use them in fostering positivity in their lives.

Conclusion

The purpose of this chapter was to examine moral, spiritual and existential development for human service professionals. Spirituality is important because it animates everyday moral choices for clients and human service professionals. The chapter focused on what it means to be a person and how individuals express spirituality. An East–West perspective guided this examination recognising that a trans–cultural approach and historical perspective would yield insight into the human spirituality.

A look at ancient societies in the East and the West revealed both embraced a holistic view of personhood. Western societies shifted to a dualistic view which separated the whole person into two parts, body and soul. Secularisation further atomised personhood by separating spirituality from religion. The consequences of Cartesian dualism and secularisation on human service professionals has significantly influenced attitudes towards spirituality. The history of Eastern spirituality, on the other hand, has been more constant and stable. The Chinese construct Qi continues to undergird Asian thinking about personhood and spirituality. Particularly in the healing arts, Traditional Chinese medicine continues to provide healing as an alternative to Western medical science. Eastern ideas are also influencing Western practices, consider mindfulness, meditation, and other natural healing modalities.

Reflective questions

Questions remain as to the spiritual lives of clients and at least three come to mind:

1 How do specific human service professionals respond to spirituality and religious diversity? For example, how can social workers respond appropriately to the elderly with different expressions of spirituality?

2 How is spirituality experienced in different countries and cultures? Cross-cultural comparative analysis will help identify the varying expressions and belief systems people have.

3 How can dialogue on spirituality continue? Critically reflect on how arts can be used in human service work. The introduction of photography to spirituality and human services is a promising beginning.

Further reading

• Ebaugh, H.R., Chafetz, J.S. and Pipes, P. (2006) Where's the faith in faith-based organizations? Measures and correlates of religiosity in faith-based social service coalitions, *Social Forces*, 84(4): 2259–72.
This paper considers the use of faith-based charities or public social services and how the debate has developed in the context of welfare reform in late modern societies.

• Koenig, H.G. (2011) *Spirituality and Health Research*. West Conshohocken, PA: Templeton Press.
This book is very comprehensive in considering the place of spirituality in health research. It is based on over 25 years' worth of research by the author. A good place to start if you want to learn more about this area.

> • Squiers, C. (2005) *The Body at Risk: Photography of Disorder, Illness, and Healing.* New
> York: International Center of Photography.
> This book looks at photojournalism its place and impact on illness, health and healing.
> It is a good place to begin reading if you are interested in creative ways of practising
> social work.

Note

1   The concept 'secularisation' here refers to the insights of sociologist Peter L. Berger (1999), who
argued against the notion that modernity necessarily demands the removal, decline, or absence
of religion. Rather, the persistence of religion indicates a reconfiguration or realignment of the
role of religion and spirituality in society.

References

Ben Asher, M. (2001) Spirituality and religion in social work practice, *Social Work Today,* 1(7): 1–5.

Berger, P.L. (ed.) (1999) *The Desecularization of the World: Resurgent Religion and World Politics.* Grand Rapids, MI: William B. Eerdmans.

Brace, C.L. (1894) *The Life of Charles Loring Brace: Chiefly Told in his Own Letters, 1826–1890.* New York: Charles Scribner's Sons.

Canda, E.R. (ed.) (1998) *Spirituality in Social Work: New Directions.* New York: The Haworth Press.

Canda, E.R. (1999) Spiritually sensitive social work: key concepts and ideals, *Journal of Social Work Theory and Practice,* 1(1): 1–15.

Canda, E.R. and Furman, L.D. (eds) (1999) *Spiritual Diversity in Social Work Practice: The Heart of Helping.* New York: The Free Press.

Christie, N. and Gauvreau, M. (1996) *A Full-Orbed Christianity: The Protestant Churches and Social Welfare in Canada, 1900–1940.* Montreal, Quebec: McGill-Queen's University Press. Available from: http://www.jstor.org/stable/j.ctt81ddd.

Cohen, A. and Koenig, H. (2003) Religion, religiosity, and spirituality in the biopsychosocial model of health and aging, *Ageing International,* 29(3): 218–236, http://www.jstor.org/stable/j.ctt81ddd.

Cooper, J.M. (ed.) (1997) *Plato: Complete Works.* Indianapolis: Hackett Publishing Company.

Council on Social Work Education (2018). Religion and Spirituality Clearinghouse. Available from: https://www.cswe.org/Centers-Initiatives/Curriculum-Resources/Religion-and-Spirituality-Clearinghouse.aspx.

Crisp, B. (2008) Social work and spirituality in a secular society, *Journal of Social Work,* 8(4): 363–375.

Daniel, L. (2013) *When 'Spiritual but Not Religious' is Not Enough: Seeing God in Surprising Places, even the Church.* Oxford: Jericho Books.

Dooyeweerd, H. (1986) *A Christian Theory of Social Institutions.* La Jolla, CA: The Herman Dooyeweerd Foundation.

Engel, G. (1977) The need for a new medical model: A challenge for biomedicine, *Science*, 196(4286): 129–136.

Erlandson, S. (2000) *Spiritual but Not Religious: A Call to Religious Revolution in America*. Bloomington: University Press.

Gandhi, M. (1957) *An Autobiography: The Story of my Experiments with Truth*. Boston: Beacon Press.

Gray, M. (2008) Viewing spirituality in social work through the lens of contemporary social theory, *British Journal of Social Work*, 38(1): 175–96.

Hutchison, E.D. (2008) *Dimensions of Human Behavior: Person and Environment* (3rd edn). Thousand Oaks, CA: Sage Publications, Inc.

Holloway, M. and Moss, B. (2010) *Spirituality and Social Work*. New York: Palgrave/Macmillan.

Land, H. (2015) *Spirituality, Religion, and Faith in Psychotherapy: Evidence-Based Expressive Methods for Mind, Brain, and Body*. Chicago: Lyceum Books, Inc.

Lee, H. (2014) *Spirit, Qi, and the Multitude: A Comparative Theology for the Democracy of Creation*. New York: Fordham University Press.

Merton, T. (1968) *Zen and the Birds of Appetite*. New York: A New Directions Book.

Moser, E.W. (2008) Spirituality in social work – the journey from fringe to mainstream, *Social Work Today*, 8(2): 32.

Painter, C.V. (2013) *Eyes of the Heart: Photography as a Christian Contemplative Practice*. Notre Dame, IN: Sorin Books.

Poplin, M. (2014) *Is Reality Secular? Testing the Assumptions of Four Global Worldviews*. Downers Grove, IL: Intervarsity Press.

Rauschenbusch, W. (1917) *A Theology for the Social Gospel*. New York: Abingdon Press.

Richter, P.J. (2017) *Spirituality in Photography: Taking Pictures with Deeper Vision*. London: Darton, Longman & Todd.

Shonin, E. (2013) *The Biopsychosocialspiritual Model of Mental Illness*. https://edoshonin.com/2013/06/30/the-biopsychosocialspiritual-model-of-mental-illness/

Sontag, S. (1973) *The Freak Show*. New York: The New York Review of Books.

Tu, W.-M. (1985) *Confucian Thought: Selfhood as Creative Transformation*. New York: State University of New York Press.

Van Til, C. (1940) *Junior Systematics*. Philadelphia: Reformed Episcopal Seminary, Syllabus.

Vanderbilt University (n.d.) *Spirituality and Photography*. Powerpoint, available at https://www.vanderbilt.edu/olli/class-materials/Spirituality_and_Photography2.pdf.

4

Adults, families and social networks in the relational social work method

Fabio Folgheraiter, Valentina Calcaterra and Elena Cabiati

Introduction

In this chapter, the authors present a reflection inspired by the *relational social work method*. Relational social work (RSW) has developed bespoke theoretical and methodological perspectives that provide a more precise idea of what in practice it means 'to work within relationships'. RSW offers a theoretical framework to understand and utilise the dynamic relationship between those who help and those needing help, and it offers a novel interpretation of the role and function of practitioners. The key concepts here presented could support social workers in guiding and facilitating relationships in a human network aimed to cope with life difficulties.

Chapter objectives

Combining the description of RSW key concepts with suggestions for social work practice, the chapter has four main objectives:

- share the core principles of the *relational social work method*;

- show the practice applications of these principles in social casework;

- illustrate how social workers should assume *Relational Guide* functions to guide and to facilitate relationships in a coping network;

- introduce some peculiarities of working with people in intercultural settings.

Background and context

Relationship-based social work can be traced back to the person–centred practice of Rogers (1961), the social case work of Hollis (1964) and the ethical focus of Biestek (1957). The existential problems human beings experience, those which concern what it means for that person to be human, have a relational nature. That means, they develop in a context in which an individual interacts with and relates to other people. Social workers practise with people by using human–to–human relationships to encourage and develop ways of coping. This is fundamental to social work practice (O'Leary et al, 2013). According to RSW, relationships are resources that can be utilised to 'resolve' or mitigate life's difficulties (Folgheraiter, 2004, 2007). Relationship-based work has been part of children's social work research for many years (Ruch, 2005; Cooper, 2015). In many difficult family situations, however, the ways in which people interact may appear dysfunctional and contribute to the problem nexus or set of problems they are experiencing. Relationships are key for social workers. Relationships important for social workers include: the interactions between social workers and families, between members of those families, between other families, their social networks, friends and other people in local communities. A growing literature is developing around relationship-based social work (Ruch et al, 2010; Megele, 2015; McColgan and McMullin, 2017). Here, we add a perspective based on work with adults and families from an Italian social work perspective, which offers an additional way of approaching practice.

As well as relationships being essential for social work, it is also recognised that relationship difficulties can seriously hinder the quality and effectiveness of social work. In helping settings, relationships with adults and families in need can be considered in many different ways such as procedural, legal, social and clinical ones.

An image of social work that is commonly presented is that of a dual relationship with service users. All social workers engage with relationships, but their ways of doing so differ considerably; the most positive image is to see social workers as relationship builders (Insall, 2016), relationship repairers (Specht and Courtney, 1994), relationship clinicians (Arns-Caddigan and Pozzuto, 2008) or relationship guides (Folgheraiter, 2007). All social work theories and methods promote the idea that to be helpful requires working with human relationships, starting from the perspective of those needing support and care but also control and guidance. In this sense, all social work is relational, meaning that social work practices at the heart of human relationships. To manage people's human growth and development concerns, social workers need relationships and relationship skills so they can enter into the everyday lives of people who are in some way vulnerable in a respectful and reflexive manner (Howe, 1998; O'Leary et al, 2013). This helps social workers to support actions towards growth and change of these people themselves, despite their difficulties and vulnerabilities.

RSW focuses on relationships as the basis for change among all the people involved in the coping process, not only between service users and social workers (Howe, 1998). RSW encourages those involved to work together to effect change by forming a network of relationships that is active in coping with the problem. The central idea is that change emerges from reciprocal aid. The practitioner helps the relationship network to develop reflexivity and to develop skills and capabilities in enhancing welfare, and in turn, the network helps practitioners to better understand how they can facilitate the network's helping action. It is very much a two-way process, and disrupts the assumed balance of power between social workers and the people they work with. RSW, therefore, challenges social work theory and practice. It overturns the traditional idea of dispensing aid in favour of a strength-based approach to helping. RSW urges social workers to consider the people involved in a problematic situation as active protagonists in the definition of their needs, together with the social worker, and how to achieve their goals (Folgheraiter, 2004, 2007, 2012). This idea is consistent with conventional social work principles and values, such as self-determination, participation, partnership and subsidiarity (Folgheraiter and Raineri, 2012).

Although RSW informs social work practice at case, group and community level, and also social work education too, the reflections presented in this chapter relate to social work with adults and families, with a particular attention to social work in intercultural settings.

Key principles of relational social work

A first principle concerns the idea that social problems may often have solutions, but they can never be *solved*. People may change (as they constantly do) but they cannot ever *be changed* by someone (Prochaska et al, 1992). In RSW service users are engaged not as recipients, but as co-producers of interventions designed to help them (Donati, 2010). This changed dynamic is necessary and follows from the idea that the life changes emerge from the relationships and not from technical treatments.

To support people in coping with problems of living, the social worker must not manipulate people so that their lives comply with want she or he wants them to be (Seikkula and Arnkil, 2006; Folgheraiter, 2004). For instance, it would not be helpful to make someone change the way they interact with others in order to receive some practical assistance that they want. This would not be right methodologically – because intervening in this way would not work – or ethically – because in this way the principle of self-determination would be violated (Banks, 2006). A helping relationship undertaken with the core purpose of changing the other for the better, or with the intention of making the other '*conform to my idea*' of him or her (Lévinas, 1987), forces the social worker into a position of power as the *solver*. RSW on the other hand sees the relationship as balancing power and engaging together to resolve issues that matter to the person.

Social worker distress, or even burnout, often results from the impossibility and misguidedness of solving people's problems of living. How could a social worker solve a family's problems alone simply by using all his/her knowledge and expertise? The social worker could certainly provide help or resources to a family in need, but this would be a temporary, ineffective or, at best, partial solution. No social worker can unilaterally eliminate other people's problems just because she or he 'knows' what needs to be done. Nor is this possible if the practitioner associates with other colleagues in a 'multidisciplinary team' – which is like forming a powerful phalanx from a range of perspectives to deal with social problems rather than including the person themselves.

The principle of reciprocity, however, is useful in assisting social workers in developing new ways and reducing power imbalances in helping. This kind of exchange is at the core of RSW and indicates that people can receive true help only if they can engage relationally with those from whom they accept that help – a reciprocal part of the helping relationship (Freeberg, 2007; Petterson and Hem, 2011). Likewise, social workers can give help and assistance (as prescribed by their role) only if they recognise that they also receive benefits from their own relationships with service users and they know how to ask for and receive help primarily from their 'needy' partners (O'Leary et al, 2013). This is, perhaps on the surface, somewhat controversial, but, thinking literally, 'helping relationship' means that the help arises from reciprocal interaction between people. This arises from a synergy between two or more people engaged with equal commitment and dignity in achieving shared improvements (Folgheraiter, 2004).

According to RSW, well-being and solutions to the problems of living do not arise from individuals, but from coping networks acting with reflexivity (close intrapersonal questioning) and action (working alongside another). In this model, the 'subject' of social work is not 'vulnerable people' (however this contested concept is defined), but the relationships between those people involved in a particular problem situation. In order to develop an effective shared reflexivity and action oriented towards a pathway to change, those involved must be motivated to work together and need to meet in a dialogical space (a space where dialogue is shared and of equal worth). It is important to be open to embracing counterintuitive and novel ideas in order to be able to work with all the people involved in a difficult situation, including those who 'have the problem'. To generate well-being in complex ecological or living situations requires all those involved to leave the role of 'passive user' to join a helping partnership that necessarily includes social workers and those using services. People in need can help social workers in helping them by deploying their experiential knowledge about their life and their difficulties, as indicated by Borkman (1976, pp 446–447):

> Experiential knowledge is truth learned from personal experience with a phenomenon, rather than truth acquired by discursive reasoning, observation, or reflection on information provided by others. It tends to be concrete, specific, and commonsensical, since they are based on the individual's actual experience, which is unique, limited, and more or less representative of the experience of others who have the same problem. [...] Besides experiential knowledge, there is experiential expertise, which refers to competence or skill in handling or resolving a problem through the use of one's own experience.

People can explain to social workers what they have already done to cope with their problems, what works and what does not work for them, what they imagine they can do differently and how they would change their situation. In this they are 'experts by experience' and understanding this assists in breaking down the power imbalance between social workers and the people with whom they work. This way of working is vital to helping social workers who, using their professional expertise, identify and offer various ways of tackling a situation until full agreement of those involved is reached.

Adults and families in need

In working with adults and families, social workers should also consider that difficult life situations usually affect more than one person because their actions and attempts to cope relate to everyone within their ecological networks (their living environment). Despite social workers interacting with people often labelled as severely vulnerable, the basic assumption of RSW is to recognise these people as partners, alongside social workers, in the helping process. This is methodologically coherent with the idea that in RSW there is a dynamic and equalised relationship between the 'helping' and the 'helped'. Possibilities to increase well-being in difficult life situations stem from relationships between motivated people with good intentions. This concept breaks with the traditional idea of the helping intervention, filling the gap between helper and service user. In RSW, 'relational' means both actors (practitioners and service users) are in a true helping relationship, aiding each other (Folgheraiter, 2007). A relational social worker has to recognise and strengthen the motivation of service users who are moving, or intending to move, towards a desired improvement in their life situation.

Working in a relational way means adopting an approach in which social workers, service users and others are motivated to work together to identify the problems faced and how best to address them (Folgheraiter, 2004). RSW does not attempt to 'treat' dysfunctional relationships or work on people's networks; rather, they work with 'coping networks', a set of relationships between people worried about common life problems *and* who are willing to act together to address them (Folgheraiter, 2015).

Coping networks require a process of sharing and social workers act as guides to the process but share with network helpers' ideas, power, decisions and responsibility. It is a developmental approach in which indeterminacy and uncertainty represent open possibilities to act together and develop joint and unimagined actions. Coping networks can be observed in everyone's everyday life even when families have difficulties that make it necessary to ask for help. Coping networks are defined structurally by five elements (Folgheraiter, 2015):

1. *Shared aim* – the element around which the coping network forms and acts;
2. *Time* – that does not focus on the past or the causes of a given problem situation but on the 'here and now' and on the future actions and hopes of motivated people to cope with the problem;

3. *Network* – comprising people who experience the situation as problematic and desire to engage in the situation to improve it;
4. *Environment* – composed of people not directly involved in the coping network but connected with the problem, and who could be a future help;
5. *Relational guide* – the concept of 'relational guide' helps in identifying the role and the function of a relational social worker.

REFLECTION POINT 4.1

Think of a time you were facing a problem and consider the 'coping network' around you at that point. Can you identify the five elements we set out previously?

When reflecting on this, it is possible that you could see a shared aim in resolving whatever problem you were experiencing as something everyone around you agreed upon. In focusing on the problem at hand we are able to see how this affects us at that moment in time. For many of us, when we think about this we consider our family and friends as the core network, but those people may have wider connections that offer us future support in the environment. While many may not have experienced a relational guide as a social worker, it is likely that someone has been in a position of helping us to deal with difficult challenges and situations and has stuck with us to do so. This is a relational guide and shows some of the social work role.

The social worker, as a relational guide, is a member of the coping network contributing as others by expressing opinions and providing resources. However, the social worker is also a facilitator of the coping process and adopts a 'superordinate posture' (Folgheraiter, 2007). It is the guidance of the social worker that allows people who are interested in the achievement of a common goal to focus on this and to work together, forming a coping network. This recognises that the social worker, while a partner also has expertise and a clear professional role in helping as well as walking alongside others.

The dialogical nature of a network in motion requires variety and freedom across its members. The greatest degree of freedom is perhaps provided by a certain amount of 'ignorance'. Not having the precise knowledge to direct future action may be, paradoxically, 'freedom'. When the lack of knowledge is something that should be but is not known by social workers that lack is to be avoided; it is unbecoming to that profession. But when the knowledge does not exist, and cannot exist, or when it exists in the abstract but has no reference to the specific matter in hand, then admitting ignorance is not just an honourable and honest thing to do but a necessary strategy that opens the possibility of dialogue with people involved in the difficult living situation. The ethical orientation of social workers and their ability to organise concrete help allows practitioners to meet the difficult life situations of service users, to identify the problems to be addressed and to imagine what might be useful in specific situations. This position of social workers does not conflict with the importance of discussing with service users what they themselves think of their situations. Above all, it does not negate the possibility of facilitating service user participation (Beresford and Carr, 2012), both in defining the goals of the helping process and in identifying what it is necessary to do together.

It should also be remembered that people have the right to decide, understand and play active roles in the changes that affect them and their vulnerable and precarious situations experienced do not deprive them of this right (Doolan, 2007; Morris, 2012). Most people are motivated to participate in that which closely concerns them if they see its utility and if they are helped to develop trust in others (Adams, 2008; Warren, 2007).

When a social work intervention works, it does so, above all, because the people involved in the helping relationship have, metaphorically, 'taken each other by the hand' and together generated additional human energy (something that is greater than the sum of the individuals). This energy from working together gradually, and unpredictably, alters the situation and produces the shared value that it is known as a 'relational good' (Donati, 2010). According to RSW as a practice paradigm, practitioners identify and resolve problems together with others by facilitating coping networks to enhance their resilience and capacity for action at both individual and collective levels.

Guiding and facilitating relationships in a network

Social workers facilitate relationships between active and motivated people who present complex life events. They do so by recognising family strengths and promoting open dialogue (Seikkula and Arnkil, 2006). We can identify the work of social workers with relationships by considering Case Study 4.1.

CASE STUDY 4.1

Susan, a social worker, met with Peter and his parents at their home. Peter is 30 years old and was a labourer in a small factory not far away from his home. He lost his job because of the economic crisis. He is looking for a new job, but it is not so easy to find one. Peter is also worried about his parents: his mother is a housewife and his father has experience as carpenter. His father lost his job five years ago and from that moment his alcoholism became worse. The house is very small and dirty. There are plastic bags, old newspapers and trinkets everywhere. Talking with the family members, Susan understands that the mother is also unhappy with their situation and she has asked for help from the social worker to change it. This is not the same for the father, who seems disturbed by the presence of the practitioner. The social worker discusses with Peter and his mother if they agreed to meet together another time at her office to reflect on how they might improve the family situation. Peter and the mother agree with the social worker who also asks if there are any others who may be interested in participating in the meeting. The mother suggests inviting the priest who visits the family every week. The next week Susan, Peter, his mother and the priest meet together. The social worker starts the meeting, reminding everyone present of the aim of the meeting: thinking together about how to improve the family situation. Susan asks each participant to state what they think might achieve this aim. At the end of the meeting, the participants agree to a plan in which everyone has an assignment or task to complete. They decide also to meet together once a month to monitor the situation.

Questions

1. Think of the ways in which Susan, the social worker, develops relationships with members of the family and identify some of the social work values that underlie this process.
2. How does Susan develop the role of a relational guide?
3. How may you work as a social worker using relationships?

Discussion

A social worker is a professional who tries to produce as yet unknown solutions by connecting people who are motivated to develop new ways of living. Contrary to positivist or clinical traditions, relational social workers do not seek technically to repair something that has already happened and perhaps hardened into a rigid problem structure. Rather, they help a meaningful potential alternative to evolve in a social and relational context. In general, therefore, relational social workers are facilitators of human relations able to produce ethically directed thoughts towards novel coping actions. As we can see in Case Study 4.1, the social worker seeks to bring out positive coping elements, however scarce they may be, from within the difficult family situation. The social worker recognises the willingness of Peter and his mother to do something to change the situation even if they do not, as yet, know what to do. Susan makes a link with Peter and his mother and orients the process in a relational way, not specifying a solution, but rather asking people to reflect together to identify a suitable strategy for that specific situation. Networking takes shape as a professional social work method when a social worker does not directly provide help, but supports that helping as it comes into existence (Folgheraiter, 2004).

The social worker joins the social relations together in the direction of a better outcome for all. In Case Study 4.1, we can read that the father is not worried about the situation, thus he is not involved in the reflective process. However, we have to consider that if other members of his family reflect to change their situation, it will necessarily involve him; the situation should also improve for the father. Furthermore, the social worker, Susan, asked the family members to indicate other people (such as the priest) who may be interested in taking part in the helping or coping network. This is really important because it allowed the network to include other strengths and resources that the social worker would not have reached without the active collaboration of the family members.

As we can see, the network mostly comprised family members rather than practitioners. This is a point of strength because if strategies were defined with the family's participation, it would be more likely that the agreed plan of help fits with what people desire and feel able to do. It is more likely that the family will be active in implementing the plan and indeed it may facilitate better coping or problem resolution in the future by learning how to work together through life's difficulties.

REFLECTION POINT 4.2

Social work in the West is likely to focus more on the individual than the family or living eco-system in which the individual seeking support lives. This may make the inclusion of a problem-solving or relational nexus difficult. What do you think some of the difficulties might be of including others and how might you get around them? Reading through this chapter you may see that relational social work practice shifts the focus somewhat and the dialogues and relationships created may open new opportunities for action.

As a relational guide, the social worker's actions are secondhand: they do not act directly, instead they seek to facilitate the actions of others. Relational social workers act responsively to what the network has shown that it wants to do. But this does not imply that their presence is not also proactive. Social workers respect people's decisions, while they remain within the broad direction of the general aim and are not destructive or harmful to the social interactions within the network. Their role as facilitator entails that they must foster any creativity that leads forward, and block or ignore everything that leads backwards or causes the process to stall. So they are active participants in the change process. What relational social workers do not do is to provide answers or give direct advice. Acting relationally, social workers provide reflexive feedback by referring everything back to the network that they see is happening to it but that the network itself does not perceive.

We can see another example of social workers guiding a network in Case Study 4.2:

CASE STUDY 4.2

A social worker looks after an older woman. She notes that the woman seems depressed and she talks about her concern in a meeting with her social worker coordinator. The coordinator invites the care social worker to monitor the situation. She notes that the elder woman stays often in the attic. One day she follows the woman and notes that she is bustling with a rope. The care social worker discusses this with some colleagues and with the social worker coordinator. Together they decide to contact the psychiatrist, who thinks that it is better to check the situation. In a home visit, they have confirmed a certain risk of suicide. The social worker coordinator, the care social worker, the psychiatrist and a volunteer meet together and define a strategy to control the situation. Then they decide to contact a relative of the older woman and with her they think about how to support the woman.

Questions

1. How is the social worker active and facilitative in this situation?
2. How do the social worker's actions fit with the model of relational social work?
3. What might you learn for your own practice as a relational social worker?

Discussion

In Case Study 4.2, we can find involved in the coping network the two practitioners, a volunteer and the psychiatrist; they think together about how to protect the older woman. Also, the psychiatrist works in a relational way because, after the diagnosis of the suicide risk, he could keep in charge of the situation without the involvement of other practitioners. However, he discusses the problem with the coping network, allowing the reflective process of aid to continue. At this time, a new aim arises, which is to maintain the woman's increased safety. To reach this aim, the network needs help, thus they invite the older woman's relative. Her involvement is not only to find an executor of what practitioners define; rather, she is involved in the reflective process to understand how to reach the aim and she can contribute with her experiential knowledge of the situation. This because the network is coping with an open problem, without a defined path of aid to follow.

The relational guidance of the social worker helps people who come together to recognise each other's needs to work together towards a common goal and to recognise the specific skills of each participant. What the relative thinks and says has the same value as what the psychiatrist thinks and says; they have different competences and roles to play but each is necessary. The social worker's role is to support this helping network through reciprocal relationship building.

In social work, the relational guidance is the reciprocal influence between a network–in–motion and an expert who seeks to intercept and deflect that motion. To some extent, s/he too is caught up in the movement and is thus part of the network's inertial system. But s/he also remains partly external to it with his/her feet firmly planted on the ground. S/he is able from this steadier position to influence the network's inner relational dynamics and its axial shifts as it moves towards solution of the problem (Folgheraiter, 2004, p 175). The relational guide function does not exclude the possibility of social workers participating in networks as members who actively reflect on the situation with others. Social workers introduce technical expertise and knowledge into the network (those centrally involved in the problem situation). However, it is important that the relational guidance be ongoing and sufficient, and that social workers contribute to the network's dialogue and agreement about what to do but without exercising their decision-making power and ideas for change. The role is rather to facilitate joint reasoning among all of the members of the network. In doing this social workers' relational position within the coping network needs to be secure, consistent, responsive and positively regarding (Howe, 1998).

The realisation of the strategies must also proceed in a shared manner. It is the responsibility of the relational guide to walk alongside the network and to mark out sufficient time for discussion of any issues that arise from the implementation of the tasks and roles decided by the network. Monitoring the way things are going by organising regular network meetings might seem more expensive in terms of time and effort for the social worker; however, the network meetings respond to the operating principle that every problem, as large or small as it might be, does not relate only to the individuals who are directly involved but concerns everyone who has contributed to it. Therefore, the solutions to the problems of implementation of the approved strategies can only be identified if each member of the network brings his/her contribution according to his/her point of view and expertise. In the end, spending enough time to monitor progress and to work with issues arising is likely to save time and to ensure the achievement of agreed goals.

Some peculiarities of working with families in intercultural settings

Social work is a profession that is committed to celebrating diversity and difference (Jenkins, 2008), regardless of whether people are born in a country other than that of the social worker. Social workers meet 'differences' in everyday practice because their work is based on encountering diverse families and their unique life stories. Although differences are not only cultural, ethnic or national, social workers have stressed the importance of respect for clients from diverse backgrounds from the beginning of the profession onwards (Addams, 1911), showing specific interest in vulnerable and oppressed populations (Williams and Graham, 2016).

The ethical duty to work positively with difference and 'Otherness' is presented and promoted by international associations, official statements and codes of ethics (IFSW, 2014). It has been emphasised since the 1970s that practitioners need to act positively across different cultures when working with adults and families (Cheetham, 1972). Several approaches have been developed to guide social workers to act in interculturally competent ways (Bennett, 1993; Park, 2016; Dominelli, 2002, 2008, 2012; Fong, 2009; Cross et al, 1989) and social work education has also paid increasing attention in preparing students for this challenge (Funge, 2011; Puntervold, 2015).

The responsibility to promote anti-racist social work practices is commonly shared, but in daily practice, the intercultural dimension can amplify dilemmas, increasing the difficulties in the helping relationship between practitioners and families experiencing troubles. Several international social work studies have alerted us to the pervasive and destructive nature of racism in practice, but less has been written about the best ways to combat it (Pedersen et al, 2005). Despite the urgency from the literature expressing the need for more culturally competent practices and services, there is still a gap in providing culturally relevant interventions (Fong, 2009). On the other hand, it has become more and more evident that health and social care services need to respond to the rapidly changing demographics in those using the services (Harrison and Burke, 2014).

Inspired by RSW, it is possible to reflect on intercultural social work with families, drawing clear attention to ethical and relational dimensions. One of the main intercultural challenges for social work is to overcome the risk of misunderstanding between practitioners and families that come from different countries or cultures. Considering that the risk of misunderstanding between social workers and families may occur at all levels of intervention, in intercultural settings it is important to manage some specific issues that could negatively influence the helping relationship. These may be due to specific challenges arising from communication problems, cultural shocks, different codes of behaviour, gender roles and child-rearing practices. These issues need to be managed with prudence and care in order to avoid the differences affecting and upsetting the helping relationship. Working towards reciprocal understanding between families and social workers is important.

A primary critique of cultural competence concerns the simplistic idea that one can truly know another's culture or be an expert in cultures and subcultures. Social workers must avoid assuming this naïve and unrealistic view driven, as it is, by the need to understand how to assess specific needs or behaviours of families from different cultural backgrounds (Parker et al, 2017). It is clear in the example of child protection services where 'white practitioners' have shown their inability to address problems that affect 'black families' (Chand, 2000; Dominelli, 2008). Perceiving competence to successfully work with families of different cultural backgrounds, practitioners could fall into the trap of assumed knowledge, in which they become 'cultural assimilators' (Brislin, 1986; Triandis, 1995) of other cultures. Practitioners may react to difference and diversity by risking 'an arrogance of knowing' (Dorsett and Fronek, 2009, p 256), seeking help from knowledge and looking for a rational explanation towards the understanding of that family's needs. In this manner, 'culture' risks becoming a monolithic object to be learned and applied to all (Gilroy, 1990; Kim, 1988; Bennett, 2013); people are reduced to a common denominator, without regard to the social and relational position they occupy specifically.

Furthermore, RSW encourages us to avoid homogenising groups and peoples (Kroebar and Kluckhohn, 1985; Williams, 2006) and their *experiential knowledge*. According to Ben-Ari and Strier (2010), the approach to working with cultural diversity implies, first and foremost, an ethical and relational position towards difference. To maintain a relational position towards families of different cultural backgrounds, a key concept of RSW, is central. As mentioned before, the principle of *reciprocity* states that people can receive true help only if they themselves can give help to those from whom they accept it (Folgheraiter, 2007). In intercultural social work settings, the help given from the family to the social worker could help in better understanding the intercultural dimensions in which attitudes and behaviours occur. A practitioner's position of humility and not knowing is a powerful antidote to elude not only discriminatory and racist practices, but also to avoid the common risks of ethnocentrism (Bhawuk and Brislin, 1992), essentialism (Hollinsworth, 2012; Dominelli, 2010; Dominelli et al, 2001) and relativism (Bennett, 2013). To ensure that one listens to the specific life expertise of each family and family member, social workers have to show capabilities to use the given information to change and, consequently, to better orient their assessment and intervention.

Conclusion

At the outset of the work of a relational social worker it is important is to expand his or her view of the problem to include the wants, wishes and motivations of people to recover from the situations they are experiencing and wish to change. The social work encourages and guides the attempts to make changes in the direction of well-being. RSW suggests that each change in the helping relationship with a family or a service user requires also that the social worker is able to change in order to facilitate the service user's change (Cabiati and Folgheraiter, 2017).

Believing in the principle of reciprocity necessitates creating space for the reciprocal influence in the helping relationship: not only do social workers and institutional cultures influence family cultures, but a family's culture also influences a practitioner's view. Because all relationships are in some manner two-way, and considering that we are all 'bearers of culture' (Qureshi, 2009, p 207), practitioners have to focus primarily on the relationship. The focus is not only on the social worker's culture (as something to adopt) or even on the family's culture (as something to critically examine). The focus and the understanding efforts are towards the relationship, with awareness of the 'Other'. The relationship between 'Self' and 'Other' is inevitably distant and respectful (Lévinas, 1987) and infinitely beyond comprehension, control and consumption (Kunz, 1998).

Without the presumption of being able to assimilate the others' culture, a prudential position of openness is required for social workers: the same openness that families beforehand have been expected to show towards a welfare system that is often unprepared in addressing their specific needs (Puntervold, 2015) and is based on Western social work models. RSW emphasises the primacy of relation to knowledge, avoiding the ethical problems of over-emphasising competence and technicality (Rossiter, 2011). In intercultural settings this assumes more importance. The social worker's ability to be able to change perspective, to open his or her worldview, to adapt 'Western' tools and patterns to make explicit their beliefs that could not meet those of families take on a fundamental importance.

Reflective questions

1 What is the central idea of the relational social work method?

2 What does it mean that help arises from relationships?

3 Who can be a member of a coping network?

4 How could the principle of reciprocity help practitioners in overcoming the intercultural challenges existing between them and families?

Further reading

- Cabiati E. (2015) The need of participate interventions in child protection: Fieldwork voices in Nuevo León State, *Social Sciences*, 4: 393–420.
  By using a case study of child protection in Mexico, Cabiati explains how the relational method works towards developing agreed solutions to family problems.

- Folgheraiter, F. (2019) The relational gaze in social work: four vertical levels of professional observation, *Relational Social Work*, 3(1): 2–14.
  This article presents levels of professional observation in relational social work.

- Folgheraiter, F. (2007) Relational social work: Principles and practices, *Social Policy and Society*, 6(2): 265–274.
  This article sets out some of the core principles that we have discussed within the chapter.

- Raineri, M.L. and Calcaterra, V. (2015) Social work strategies against crisis in everyday practice: An anti-oppressive case study, *International Social Work*, doi: 10.1177/0020872815606793.
  This paper shows how relational social work methods can be employed to foster an anti-oppressive and inclusive approach to social work practice.

References

Adams, R. (2008) *Empowerment, Participation and Social Work*. Basingstoke: Palgrave Macmillan.

Addams, J. (1911) *Twenty Years at Hull House, with Autobiographical Notes*. New York: Macmillan.

Arns-Caddigan, M. and Pozzuto, R. (2008) Use of self in relational clinical social work, *Clinical Social Work Journal*, 36(3): 235–243.

Banks, S. (2006) *Ethics and Values in Social Work*. Basingstoke: Palgrave Macmillan.

Ben-Ari, A. and Strier, R. (2010) Rethinking cultural competence: What can we learn from Levinas?, *British Journal of Social Work*, 40(7): 2155–2167.

Bennett, M.J. (1993) Towards ethnorelativism: A developmental model of intercultural sensitivity. In R.M. Paige (ed.), *Education for the Intercultural Experience*. Yarmouth, ME: Intercultural Press.

Bennett, M. (2013) Ethnocentrism/xenophobia. In C. Cortes (ed.), *Multicultural America: A Multimedia Encyclopedia*. New York: Sage.

Beresford, P. and Carr, S. (eds) (2012) *Social Care, Service Users and User Involvement*. London: Jessica Kingsley.

Bhawuk, D.P.S. and Brislin, R. (1992) The measurement of intercultural sensitivity using the concepts of individualism and collectivism, *International Journal of Intercultural Relations*, 16(4): 413–436.

Biestek, F. (1957) *The Casework Relationship*. Chicago: Loyola University Press.

Borkman, T. (1976) Experiential knowledge: A new concept for the analysis of self-help groups, *The Social Service Review*, 50(3): 445–456.

Brislin, R.W. (1986) A culture general assimilator: Preparation for various types of sojourns, *International Journal of Intercultural Relations*, 10(2): 215–234.

Cabiati, E. and Folgheraiter, F. (2017) *Let's Try to Change (at First Ourselves)*. Paris: UNAFORIS, European Conference.

Chand, A. (2000) The over-representation of black children in the child protection system: Possible causes, consequences and solutions, *Child and Family Social Work*, 5(1): 6–77.

Cheetham, J. (1972) *Social Work with Immigrants*. London: Routledge.

Cooper, A. (2015) Emotional and relational capacities for doing child protection work. In: L. Waterhouse and J. McGhee (eds), *Challenging Child Protection: New Directions in Safeguarding Children*. Research Highlights in Social Work 57. London: Jessica Kingsley, pp 141–153.

Cross, T., Bazron, B., Dennis, K. et al (1989) *The Cultural Competence Continuum. Toward a Culturally Competent System of Care: A Monograph on Effective Services for Minority Children Who are Severely Emotionally Disturbed*. Washington, DC: Georgetown University Child Development Center.

Dominelli, L. (2002) *Anti-Oppressive Social Work: Theory and Practice*. London: Palgrave Macmillan.

Dominelli, L. (2008) *Anti-Racist Social Work*. London: Macmillan.

Dominelli, L. (2010) Globalization, contemporary challenges and social work practice, *International Social Work*, 53(5): 599–612.

Dominelli, L. (2012) *Green Social Work. From Environmental Crises to Environmental Justice*. Cambridge: Polity Press.

Dominelli, L., Lorenz, W.E. and Soydan, H. (2001) *Beyond Racial Divides*. Aldershot: Ashgate.

Donati, P. (2010) *Relational Sociology: A New Paradigm for the Social Sciences*. London: Routledge.

Dorsett, P. and Fronek, P. (2009) Case management: Practitioner standards and skill development. In E. Moore (ed.), *Case Management for Community Practice*. South Melbourne, Australia: Oxford University Press.

Doolan, M. (2007) Duty calls: The response of law, policy and practice to participation right in child welfare systems, *Protecting Children*, 21(1): 10–18.

Folgheraiter, F. (2004) *Relational Social Work: Toward Networking and Societal Practices*. London: Jessica Kingsley.

Folgheraiter, F. (2007) Relational social work: Principles and practices, *Social Policy and Society*, 6(2): 265–274.

Folgheraiter, F. (2012) *The Mystery of Social Work*. Trento: Erickson.

Folgheraiter, F. (2015) Relational social work. In J.D. Wright (ed.), *International Encyclopedia of the Social and Behavioral Sciences* (pp 221–226). Oxford: Elsevier.

Folgheraiter, F. and Raineri, M.L. (2012) A critical analysis of the social work definition according to the relational paradigm, *International Social Work*, 55(4): 473–487.

Fong, R. (2009) Culturally competent practice in social work. In D.K. Deardoff (ed.), *Intercultural Competence*. New York: Sage.

Freeberg, S. (2007) Re-examining empathy: A relational-feminist point of view, *Social Work*, 52(3): 251–259.

Funge, S. (2011) Promoting the social justice orientation of students: The role of the educator, *Journal of Social Work Education*, 47(1): 73–90.

Gilroy, P. (1990) The end of anti-racism, *New Community*, 17(1): 71–83.

Harrison, P. and Burke, B. (2014) Same, same, but different. In M. Lavalette and L. Penketh (eds), *Race, Racism and Social Work*. Bristol: Policy Press.

Hollinsworth, D. (2012) Forget cultural competence; ask for an autobiography, *Social Work Education*, 32(8): 1048–1060.

Hollis, F. (1964) *Casework: A Psychosocial Therapy*. New York: Random House.

Howe, D. (1998) Relationship-based thinking and practice in social work, *Journal of social work practice*, 12(1): 45–56.

Insall, L. (2016) Social worker as relationship builder. In *Named Social Worker, Social Care Institute for Excellence*. Available from: https://www.scie.org.uk/news/opinions/named-social-worker

International Federation of Social Work (2014). *Global definition of social work*. Available from: http://ifsw.org/get-involved/global-definition-of-social-work (accessed on 7 July 2017).

Jenkins, R. (2008) *Social Identity*. London: Routledge.

Kim, Y.Y. (1988) *Communication and Cross-Cultural Adaptation*. Clevedon: Multilingual Matters.

Kroebar, A. and Kluckhohn, C. (1985) *Culture: A Critical Review of Concepts and Definitions*. New York: Random House.

Kunz, G. (1998) *The Paradox of Power and Weakness: Levinas and an Alternative Paradigm for Psychology*. Albany, NY: University of New York Press.

Lévinas, E. (1987) *Time and the Other*. Pittsburgh: Duquesne University Press.

McColgan, M. and McMullin, C. (2017) *Doing Relationship-Based Social Work*. London: Jessica Kingsley.

Megele, C. (2015) *Psychosocial and Relationship Based Practice*. Northwich: Critical Publishing.

Morris, K. (2012) Thinking family? The complexities for family engagement in care and protection, *British Journal of Social Work*, 42(5): 906–920.

O'Leary, P., Tsui, M.S. and Ruch, G. (2013) The boundaries of the social work relationship revisited: Towards a connected, inclusive and dynamic conceptualization, *British Journal of Social Work*, 43(1): 135–153.

Park, H.J. (2016) Ageing in anomie: Later life migration and its implications for anti-anomic social work practice, *International Social Work*, 59(6): 915–921.

Parker, J., Ashencaen Crabtree, S., Azman, A., Nikku, B.R. and Nguyen, U.T.T. (2017) A comparative study of social work assessment in Malaysia, Nepal, Vietnam and the United Kingdom: Towards an understanding of meaning, *Social Work and Society Online International Journal*, 15(2): 1–17. Available from: https://www.socwork.net/sws/article/view/530/1031

Pedersen, A., Walker, I. and Wise, M. (2005) 'Talk Does Not Cook Rice': Beyond anti-racism rhetoric to strategies for social action, *Australian Psychologist*, 40(1): 20–31.

Petterson, T. and Hem, M.H. (2011) Mature care and reciprocity: Two cases from acute psychiatry, *Nursing Ethics*, 18(2): 217–231.

Prochaska, J.O., Di Clemente, C.C. and Norcross, J. (1992) In search of how people change: Applications to addictive behaviors, *American Psychologist*, 47(9): 1102–1114.

Puntervold, B. (2015) Social work in a multicultural society: New challenges and needs for competence, *International Social Work*, 58(4): 562–574.

Qureshi, N. (2009). Kultursensitivitet i profesjonell yrkesutøvelse. In K. Eide, N. Qureshi, M. Rugkåsa and H. Vike (eds), *Over profesjonelle barrierer. Et minoritetsperspektiv i psykososialt arbeid med barn ogunge*. Oslo: Gyldendal Akademisk.

Rogers, C. (1961) *On Becoming a Person: A Therapist's View of Psychotherapy*. London: Constable.

Rossiter, A. (2011) Unsettled social work: The challenge of Levinas' ethics, *British Journal of Social Work*, 41(5): 980–995.

Ruch, G. (2005) Relationship-based practice and reflective practice: Holistic approaches to contemporary child care social work, *Child and Family Social Work*, 10(1): 111–123.

Ruch, G., Turney, D. and Ward, A. (2010) *Relationship Based Social Work: Getting to the Heart of Practice*. London: Jessica Kingsley Publishers.

Seikkula, J. and Arnkil, T.E. (2006) *Dialogical Meetings in Social Network*. London: Karnac Books.

Specht, H. and Courtney, M.E. (1994) *Unfaithful Angels: How Social Work Has Abandoned its Mission*. New York: The Free Press.

Triandis, H.C. (1995) Culture specific assimilators. In S.M. Fowler (ed.), *Intercultural Sourcebook: Cross-Cultural Training Methods*. Yarmouth, Maine: Intercultural Press.

Warren, J. (2007) *Service User and Career Participation in Social Work*. London: Sage.

Williams, C.C. (2006) The epistemology of cultural competence, *Families in Society*, 87: 209–220.

Williams, C. and Graham, M.J. (2016) *Social Work in a Diverse Society: Transformative Practice with Black and Minority Ethnic Individuals and Communities*. Bristol: Policy Press.

5

Critical perspectives on human growth and development in adults

Jonathan Parker and Sara Ashencaen Crabtree

Introduction

In this chapter, we will examine theoretical and conceptual models that are relevant to the topic of adult human development and growth. That said, we recognise that while such theories and models aim to provide useful and practical explanations and understandings of the social world they can often appear divorced from it, leaving readers perplexed and unsure how to apply these ideas. Consequently, feelings of alienation from using theories and models may skew the value of theories and theorising in the minds of some away from understanding, explaining and developing acceptance of diversity, fluidity and uncertainty as central conditions for the helping professions. In reaction to this we may, at times, simply accept, without question, the axioms elucidated within certain theories or, at the other end of the spectrum, to reject in total the utility of traditional development theories in the human services. Elsewhere, we have written of an anti–theoretical and anti–intellectual perspective and argued strongly for an appreciation of theories and models for practice that adds to our understanding and helps us question received ideas (Parker, 2012, 2017). This is central to critical social work practice.

Previous chapters in this section of the book have outlined some of the traditional approaches to human growth and development, although these are usually discussed in respect of children and young people, rather than adults. We have also discussed a growing appreciation of existential or spiritual aspects of what it means to be human. In this chapter we will take a critical approach, emphasising the centrality of observing and questioning at all times. This is an approach we took in the companion volume, considering specially some sociological critiques of human growth and development. Whilst they relate to children and young people, you may wish to read that chapter and apply the thinking to adults. In this chapter we focus on some of the major changes in life, such as the menopause in women, and explore these as they affect the lives of adults at different points in the life course.

Chapter objectives

- critically review some of the accepted paradigms in human growth and development in adults;

- examine approaches that emphasise the social, structural and agentic as important in human growth and development;

- consider concepts and theories relating to gerontology;

- provide alternative perspectives to help social workers and other human service professionals negotiate the thorny paths of theoretically informed practice.

Background and context

This chapter brings together the preceding theoretical background chapters setting the scene for an exploration of themes pertinent to contemporary social work practice with adults. We will explore sociological theories in a questioning and analytic manner reflecting the approach social workers need when entering the social world of others. There are many diverse ways in which the world in which we live is experienced, and taking a critical perspective means that we take issue with the idea there is one single, objective reality to be known. Indeed, because social works practise in fluid environments where diversity, difference, uncertainty and ambiguity operate we must beware of normative interpretations that privilege one group over another. Whether one is male or female, whatever one's sexual orientation, ethnicity, age and socio-economic status amongst other different social positions we experience the world differently. We also influence, by interacting with the world around in different ways. This social and environmental understanding of difference and diversity provides social workers with the theoretical knowledge to understand that people experience life in various ways and helps to organise responses alongside people that meet their needs rather than fit neatly into a particular theoretical model that bolsters the power of certain groups in society.

These influences will be examined and questioned in this chapter using particular and non-exhaustive examples from a range of adult perspectives. This builds on the understandings we set out in the companion volume, which we applied to children and young people, and extends our journey across the life course. However, it is important to remain tentative in whatever we discuss. This is because no single perspective can be held to be more important than others, as this may diminish the experience of those who do not fit that particular paradigm. Of course, such a postmodern position is open to criticism that suggests values and ethics become unimportant and relative to the time, setting and cultures where they are enacted. In social work we are clear that human rights and social justice are paramount and therefore must critique different perspectives against those core characteristics.

To gain the most from an immersion into theories and models a certain agile and sceptical intellectual position needs to be taken up and this is what we mean by adopting a 'critical perspective'. In the companion volume we explored the term 'critical' which certainly needs some explanation before considering a 'critical' approach to social work practice. To recap, we noted that often it is used in a negative sense to suggest that one is looking at what is wring or even judging something to be less than one's preferred perspective. For instance, as a teacher one may be described as critical of one's pupils behaviour, dress sense and attitudes or one might be said to be critical of the work that has been presented, meaning that it does not reach the standards that are expected for study of that subject. However, these are popular ways of understanding the term and not how we are using them in this chapter. As in the companion volume, we are using the term to convey a continually questioning approach to the situations and explanations for them that we, as social workers, find ourselves in. We seek to instil a questioning approach to ways of understanding and theorising so that no one position is taken to be the correct one; we are challenging normative approaches. Continual questioning is highly important in all professions working with people, and especially within social work, as it is the person-in-context who forms the focus of concern (Germain, 1973).

This questioning approach also recognises that what we do as social workers is increasingly state mandated as a means of regulating the private and social lives of adults. It helps social workers to understand the tense position they hold between state and marginalised people (Ferguson, 2008). Of course, social work is practised in many other environments as well – charities, voluntary organisations, community development schemes – but the UK trend has been towards social work as a local government operated social regulator (Parker, 2019). So, adopting a critical approach allows social workers to see this position and to consider how best to act when there are competing demands and views. The critical practitioner's role is to be creative and inspirational rather than instrumental and bureaucratic, a highly skilled yet principled role to take.

A critical approach does not privilege one approach to society or another. It questions. Thus, as suggested by Fook (2016), aspects of agency (the person or individual and his or her capabilities) interact with structure (the macro elements written into society and reflected in the assumptions we make about that society, or direct the ways in which we begin to regulate our behaviours). In social work, this recognition of agency and structure is important (see Thompson, 2016).

Another important way in which the terms critical, criticism and criticality are used will be seen in your academic studies. It is important to mention this here because it relates, again, to the central message to question everything and to search out what seems to be going on underneath the overt, observable situation you are faced with. Rutter and Brown (2019) present a very useful introduction to critical thinking that you can apply to your practice a much as your academic work. Criticality forms one of the cornerstones of anti-oppressive social work practice (Thompson, 2016). Taking one example, as part of the reach of post-colonial thought, we have begun to recognise colonising perspectives start from an assumed, normative position, whereas continued questioning and subjecting everything to scrutiny, including our own approaches, thoughts and behaviours as social workers helps to guard against such.

In this chapter, therefore, as throughout this textbook, we are not using a critical position to be negative and to reject those beliefs or practices we do not like or approve. Rather we are using it to stress the importance of being mindful of the context in which we practice and to question, challenge, reflect and act creatively to achieve the goals of our service users. Social work and, indeed all, human service professions demand criticality and even more so in times of continued service reduction and austerity (Parker and Ashencaen Crabtree, 2018). It is a moral necessity and reintroduces such at a time that social work and many human services have become purely instrumental and regulated as an impersonal function rather than a human interaction. To consider some of these issues we will provide an overview of gerontological thinking, feminisms, ill-health and the menopause. These represent aspects of adult life that can be approached critically and act as examples from which you can transfer your understanding and thinking.

Exploring the theoretical context

Gerontology concerns the study of ageing across the lifespan although it is most often associated with older age which, in itself, suggests older age is associated with specific discourses that require the attention of helping professions, policymakers and so on. As social workers recognising this as an arbitrary social division will keep a clearer focus on the needs of the adults one is working with rather than applying assumed knowledge. Gerontological theory adopts a range of perspectives – biological, psychological and sociological (Phillips et al, 2006).

Within the literature, social gerontological theories are introduced in a linear, chronological way or through shifts in thought (Bengtson et al, 1997; Putney et al, 2005). However, looking at theories from macro, meso and micro, or structural, professional and interpersonal approaches allows us to avoid the pitfalls of privileging the idea of a progressive discourse that not only suggests theories are improving in their explanatory power but also dismisses the value of previous theorising (Lymbery, 2005; Penhale and Parker, 2008). Powell and Hendricks (2009) highlight four core themes, which cut across the macro, meso and micro explanatory levels, as central to critical social gerontology.

Economic and political theories influence the global world and policy assumptions and developments. They also demonstrate the impact of power imbalances and how different age groups in societies are theorised according to reproductive capacities, youthfulness and currently privileged aspects of economic productivity. This leads to inequalities at all levels which have a profound effect on people's developmental capabilities. Critical social gerontology also highlights how individual approaches to ageing have become fragmented and subject to popular discourses that promote cosmetic surgery, bio-technologies and lifestyle choices as reactions to ageing. Individuals are also exposed to increased surveillance through the promotion and use of assistive technologies which alter ways in which social care is experienced (Foucault, 1979; Parker, 2005). The capacity of people to make choices, to be private changes the daily performance of living and the potential for development, as well as potentially enhancing lifestyles.

Traditional sociological approaches to ageing, and originally this was taken to refer to ageing in older age, derived from functionalist schools in which society was assumed to be ordered and regulated to provide the best possible fit for all its members (Parsons, 1951). The roles that people took on at each age throughout their lives were assumed to be taken on so that society functioned and ran smoothly and that children, once educated, would become the new workers and family builders before happily moving into retirement and out of mainstream society as they grew older.

In studies of ageing this became known as disengagement theory, moving from active involvement in functionalist tasks in political, economic and social life as a way of preparing for a new generation to take over these functions (Cumming and Henry, 1961). Ageing was simply viewed as inevitable decline. There were obvious flaws with this way of theorising. For instance, it ignored political economy, culture, and power relations and was based on monocultural studies that privileged the West, and the power relations that predominated there. However, disengagement theory does have some explanatory power of socio-political relations.

Havighurst and Albrecht (1953) and Lemon et al (1972) offered a similar perspective, that of role and activity theory. These focused on changing roles and activities throughout the different stages of the life course stages. These reflect age related assumptions and shifts in the balance of power (see Erikson's psychological stages of development, widely available on the Internet and in relevant literature).

Decline, burden and pathologisation represent the key discourses underlying functionalist approaches. Whilst at a surface level these criticisms might appear to be addressed in contemporary moves towards a focus on active ageing. Taking a critical stance we can see that it also reflects a macro economic theory concerned with reducing the financial burden of health and social care for older people and retaining an active, informal workforce and child carers (Parker, 2012; Parker and Ashencaen Crabtree, 2014). People living into active old age are also greater consumers and so add to economic growth. Of course, active ageing and healthier ageing are good things for the individuals involved and this must not be forgotten. However, we need, as social workers and other helping professionals to take an informed approach to them and not to accept programmes and services developed to promote active ageing without questioning them closely.

Political economy, feminism and critical gerontology

Discourses of ageing have been constructed and developed for political ends. Indeed, the ways political and economic forces act to determine the allocation of resources where older people are considered to be a drain not to contribute to society leads to discrimination and a reduction in opportunities for living. Moreover, economic prosperity is often described as being gendered in terms of the so-called feminisation of poverty, which begins from the big disparities in pocket money given to boys and girls according to a Halifax Building Society survey (BBC, 2016). This in turn is aggravated by lower wages that traditional female work in service and care industries command together with gendered pay gaps prevalent in employment, including social work, health care work and teaching, and part-time work often associated with working mothers (Office for National Statistics, 2018). Gendered disparities accumulate over life resulting in women's poorer retirement pension entitlements compared to that of male counterparts in old age (Jones, 2018).

Since austerity this has become more entrenched as Grenier et al (2017) have shown in respect of dementia. They talk of precarious ageing as a counterfoil to active ageing suggesting this has four indicators:

- casualisation of older workers and alienation from the workforce;
- environmental challenges such as climate change and spatial injustices which reduce housing and living options for older people;
- resource uncertainty from deregulated pensions, provision of or entitlement to health and social care and so on;
- precarious deep old age where the existential meets the biomedical – such as dementia.

Social workers have a clear role in identifying these restrictions in life style and choice, challenging these and, along with Grenier et al, call for changing cultures of life-course and ageing.

Feminist theories and their developments

Feminist theories are widely divergent, although all are premised on achieving gender equality and challenging patriarchal structures, institutional sexism and modes of thinking that deny full humanity to women and are supportive of gendered male prerogatives (Wharton, 2012). The issue of how language both articulates patriarchy and the pre-eminence of men over women has been challenged using postmodernist deconstruction. For instance, many people nowadays would raise an eyebrow at the use of 'men' or 'mankind' to refer to all people and many institutions have adapted the term 'chairman' to the shorter, gender neutral term 'chair'. Yet as has been shown by the gender pay gap as reported by companies and higher education institutions, there is a long way to go before gender equality is really achieved.

Nonetheless, the ways in which gender relations have influenced the lives of women, and men, over their life courses represent interesting examples of just how fluid and malleable human life can be. Let's consider the example of a woman born in the early 1950s, her experiences and family in Case Study 5.1.

CASE STUDY 5.1

Gail married Tom when she was 19 and he was 21 years old. She worked as a secretary after leaving school having completed two A levels in English and History. As a teenager, she had wanted to become a doctor, but was dissuaded by the school and her mother. The school suggested she would be better suited to less scientific subjects and her mother had said she'd frighten men away if she went to university and became a doctor – 'men don't like clever women'.

She was happy in her marriage with Tom, an engineer who worked with a local firm. They had two children, Annette, born in 1971, and James, born two years later. When the children were born, she stopped working to look after them and did not return to work until they were both settled in senior school in 1985. She had little experience to draw on and went to work in the local school as a welfare assistant, serving meals and supervising the children at meal times and breaks.

As Annette grew up it was expected that she would go to university, as it was with James. Annette did not pursue her mother's earlier dream of studying medicine but choose to read geography, as she wanted to work in social planning. She gained her degree and began work for a local authority planning department. James studied history, as he was interested in teaching. He found teaching in a primary school a satisfying choice of career. They were both supported in career choices by their parents. When Annette had her first child, Kyle, she went back to work fully supported by her mother who was able to offer some child care support. Gail and Tom were not quite so supportive when James gave up work to look after his child.

James argued this was sexist, but Gail said it was protective and important for a woman or a man to earn their own living and not to be dependent. She had experienced dependency herself in a kind and loving relationship but had seen friends who had nothing to fall back on or to make ex-husbands and partners pay for their living expenses as well as those of children and she found this to be against all the gains women had made and for which they had been arguing.

Questions

1. How far do you think that social conventions regarding gender norms have shaped Gail's life?
2. How would you compare the differences and similarities in the lives and behaviour of mother (Gail) and daughter (Annette), father (Tom) and son

(James)? Do these resonate or contrast with your family history and those of people you know?

3. What do you think of Gail's argument about the dangers of financial dependency in adult relationships? Do you agree with her?

Discussion

In this case study there had been many changes in expectations and daily practices that demonstrate the plasticity (or changing nature) of society and the world. It is important that we are aware of how the structures of society exert great pressure on the ways in which we think and behave. It is also important that we see that fulfilment and actualisation and freedom from exploitation are central to our role as social workers when working with people.

The example of the #MeToo movement is also useful here. The movement started in 2006 when activist and founder Tarana Burke supported the development of a culturally-informed system of support for Black women who had experienced sexual abuse (Me Too, 2018). In 2017, however, the movement grew in popularity via the use of social media no doubt assisted significantly by widespread anger at the sexually dismissive and violent pronouncements made by President Trump in the US and a number of high profile cases of powerful people in the film and media industry taking advantage of their positions to sexually abuse others.

The movement has brought the often-taboo subject of sexual harassment and abuse at a range of levels, including the everyday, to the attention of wide audiences, as a result of social media. The importance of this is that it signals the importance of questioning and challenging received wisdoms and the assumed acceptability of the unacceptable. It represents a developmental shift, especially in the West but more globally as well, as it demonstrates how social and political change influences how we live and organise socially whatever age we are. If we look at the way Laura Bates's *Everyday Sexism Project* started in 2018 (https://everydaysexism.com) and has also brought to people's attention some of the taken-for-granted discourses that have regulated gender relations and allowed the growth of challenges to them, we again see the potential for growth and development.

We can theorise how this happens by considering the concept of daily practices as a means of critically questioning how things are and offer alternatives to the accepted, normative ways of looking at adults. The idea of everyday practices is important in formulating notions concerning social actions and relations, how they are both representative of the world and constitutive of it (Parker and Ashencaen Crabtree, 2018). The original concept of practices has taken root within social theory but stems from debates that began in family studies. The ways people act in social life and organisations such as families are seen to be constitutive of them as well as representing what those actors think of them. These ideas can be applied more widely to the ways in which everyday practices construct and adapt all social entities and can help us consider aspects of growth and development as adults in social and ecological contexts (Schatzki, 1996). The thinking behind practices, or what we do in our mundane interactions with the world around us, owes much to Berger and Luckmann's (1966) work on social constructionism. In analysing the ways in which knowledge of the world, its institutions, those around us and ourselves Berger and Luckmann discussed the ways in which the external world is internalised and interpreted by our experiences and expectations of it. It is then projected back on to that tacitly assumed external world (re)producing and (re)creating it.

So, if we consider the ways in which a homosexual man may have been perceived in the UK in the 1960s the external presentation may have been considered effete, there may have been an expectation of 'camp' gestures and language, an unconscious association with over-the-top characters from film, television or theatre. This 'external' presentation may be internalised by someone observing this man and they may use these perceptions to constitute gay men in the world. When taken alongside other social constructions of approved masculinity the perception of the gay man would seem 'deviant' and therefore may attract less favourable or, indeed, hostile treatment. The construction of being gay in the 2000s is likely to have changed significantly from this rather negative portrait from 50 years ago as indicated in Case Study 5.2. However, the ways the constructions are internalised and experienced in each time is likely to have had considerable impact on the emotional and mental health of each. It is also likely to affect how they interact socially and the situations they would enter or feel comfortable in. In this way social constructions represent time specific influences on growth and development.

The theory of everyday practices began with Pierre Bourdieu's (1977) work. Like Berger and Luckmann (1966), he attempts to explain how the external world is internalised by individuals and how this is then reflected back onto the world. This process leads to the development of cognitive structures that are constitutive of a particular type of environment or part of the social world. Bourdieu termed these *habitus*. Habitus are:

> ... [S]ystems of durable, transposable dispositions which orchestrate the generation and structure of practices, or what we do, at an everyday level. Whilst the individual agent is the producer and reproducer of objective meaning, actions and words are often the product of an unconscious assumption and internalization of external social relations. One of the effects of the habitus is the production, therefore, of a commonsense world endowed with objectivity, which is secured by a consensus view of the meaning of certain practices. (Parker, 2005, p 262)

This shared or taken-for-granted view of the apparent meaning of certain everyday practices is interpreted by Bourdieu using Husserl's concept of *doxa* which concerns a misrecognition of how constructions are structured in the world

(Myles, 2004). Bourdieu (1977, 1996) can be quite complex in his theorisation of practice. However, if we explore this through examples it should become clear how understanding daily practices helps in developing critical practice as a social worker (Parker and Ashencaen Crabtree, 2018).

Habitus can be considered as either an objective or subjective social category, something that is seen as external to the observer or something internal to them. The first objective social category is a *structuring structure* – one that helps to create what it is and how it is understood – whilst a subjective social category is a *structured structure* – one created by the objective social category. The different ways two people think of their relationship will be structured by their underlying dispositions of what a relationship should be like, what roles should be played, what is expected and what is considered wrong (see Case Study 5.2 for an example of what this might mean). In this sense, the objective social category helps to order or police one's actions and the ways in which perceptions are constructed.

CASE STUDY 5.2

Julie and Stefan had been married for ten years. Their daughter, Jeanne, was eight years old. Both Julie and Stefan realised that their relationship was breaking down. When Julie met Karin, she realised how attracted she was to her. Julie and Stefan separated, and Julie moved in to live with Karin. Although the separation was fairly amicable it raised thoughts and perceptions that had not been recognised explicitly previously.

Julie took time to come to terms with a change from thinking she was heterosexual to understanding her sexuality was not quite as fixed as she thought. She struggled with this because of her experiences of heteronormative families throughout her life, and from the dispositions strengthened by her parents who believed same-sex relationships were 'just not normal'.

Stefan, on the other hand, was surprised when he found himself criticising Julie's choice and thinking that she was failing as a mother by moving in to live with another woman. He had consciously thought of himself as accepting and non-judgemental in his views. He had to question himself deeply whether this was a reaction against the breakdown of his relationship or deeper taken-for-granted views that had surfaced and had perhaps structured his performance of family beforehand.

Questions

1. Consider what emotional issues may arise for the individuals portrayed here in adjusting to the new relationship structure. Think about this from the hypothetical point of view of Julie, Stefan, Karin and their shared children.
2. How far do you think social norms regarding sexual conventions and that of being a 'good mother' may influence how lesbian parenting relationships are viewed?

Discussion

Working through these changes in thought, behaviour and family structure demonstrates some of the ways that change, and adaptation takes place throughout adulthood. It also indicates that social workers and other human service professionals can seek to illuminate hidden dispositions underlying many of the daily practices that we and those people we work with perform without conscious thought.

These dispositions, according to Bourdieu, are durable and transferable. Perhaps both Julie and Stefan in Case Study 5.2 had reflected their assumptive world outwards and maybe reproduced the objective social category. If so, this could have communicated to Jeanne that her mother was doing something wrong and so replicating discourses that discriminate and oppress.

The family theorist David Morgan (1999) suggests that whilst Bourdieu's theory of practice accounts for the reproduction of social entities, a major criticism levelled against it is that it does not seem to account for the possibilities of change and challenge to existing orders. It is also important to recognise the influence and impact of our involvement as social workers. By virtue of our involvement, a statement is being made and discourses formed of the situations we are involved in, and this is recreated through our practices.

Morgan (1996, 1999) provides the clearest articulation of practices. He introduces concepts of difference and diversity as core to understanding them and challenges the uncritical usage of the term 'family' as potentially rigidifying and normalising. Seeing this as a verb rather than a noun helps us to understand how we might respond to it in society because we understand something if its generation. Practices draw upon common sense, everyday understandings and how these are used reflexively to structure that world. Bernades (1997) adds that they also demarcate from practices not assumed or considered to be part of that site of practice. In general, practices are defined by all the social actors involved, by service users, practitioners and observers in the general public. Social work accounts, and those of cognate professions, are influential, and there is a need for reflexive monitoring of one's own routine practices which may reproduce unspoken normative understandings.

Criticality can also stem from Marxist perspectives, which, although they emanate from a structural focus, can still offer explanations that relate to the individual in context and his or her growth and development throughout life. Marx was particularly interested in the concept of alienation that he considered to be rooted in the dynamics between different social groups. Whilst Marx was concerned primarily with economic and class relations his thinking could equally be applied to ageing.

A Marxist analysis would suggest that alienation takes place when a person is separated from the creative and meaningful aspects of living seen in the exploitation of one group by another. So intergenerational conflict and resulting political economic arguments of decline, retirement and economic non-productivity creates conflict. However, this conflict is necessary to changing things (see Parker and Ashencaen Crabtree, 2018). Marxist thought indicates that conflict can produce positive change – a new way of engaging in social, and economic production. This dialectic can be harnessed by older people marginalised people in society acting alongside social workers (see Case Study 5.3).

REFLECTION POINT 5.1

How might you as a social worker incorporate critical thinking into your practice? How might this be affected by your own approach to politics (with a small or a big 'P')? Think how your own behaviours, ways of communicating and thinking present a picture of yourself to others and send a message about what you think of them. How might you use this in your social work practice?

CASE STUDY 5.3

Seamus has been diagnosed with a life-limiting condition after 30 years in teaching, eventually becoming deputy head for pastoral concerns at a large school in Oldtown. Seamus had been a respected member of his independent school and local community. He was influential in driving community change and organising social events in the neighbourhood but found himself increasing side-lined as his mobility and speech deteriorated. It has been suggested by the school governors that he should devote most of his professional time to the administrative side of teaching rather than in the classroom owing to his disability and possibly evoking discomfort or misunderstanding in the children. Using his skills and knowledge from teaching and community work, Seamus wrote to the local newspapers, community groups, social workers and health care professionals articulating his position. This caused some consternation among colleagues, parents and neighbours.

Questions

1. What issues and implications are raised by the suggestion that Seamus spends less time in face-to-face interactions with the pupils raise?
2. Could there be any benefits to himself or others in continuing his direct teaching practice? What might these be?
3. What more do you think can be done to help Seamus (and others) to find ways to promote his involvement in the community?

Discussion

The position which Seamus's colleagues have put him in indicates that often well-meaning attempts to prevent upset or misunderstanding leave the person out of decision making and impose a normative sense of order on a situation. The social model of disability (see Chapter 12) adds an important corrective to a model that only sees the disability or what is assumed to be wrong.

Let us now turn our attention to the controversial ways in which the menopause has been considered in contemporary society.

The menopause: women and ageing

The menopause, such a socially hidden and taboo topic, has recently come out of the closet and forms the basis of a case study in Chapter 1. The menopause has until now been largely a hidden topic but provided women do not die prematurely then they will all undergo the menopause. We might question why it is only now that we hear about it on the radio and television, and read about it in the media. Institutions are also now beginning to take notice of this natural life event among their employees, with the University of Leicester establishing a formal menopause policy to support staff, where one of their academics suggests that men should say 'menopause' three times a day, as a kind of cure for the complete male disinterest traditionally shown to 'women's problems' (George, 2018). However, a short scan of academic library contents will reveal that the greatest number of references to the menopause direct the reader to a medicalised perspective on the condition, rather than viewing the menopause as both a physical but also culturally-constructed social phenomenon. A pertinent question may be why should social workers be interested in female ageing processes and the menopause?

REFLECTION POINT 5.2

If you are asking yourself this exact question, reflect now on why that might be. Think why it might be important to focus on women and ageing. If you are a man, reflect on why this may be an important matter for you to consider. The following discussion will help you to refine and develop your thinking.

Medicalised discourses (see Chapter 13) tend, by their very nature, to offer a pathological interpretation of body and mental states. While this obviously has its great merits in alleviating human suffering, how such states are viewed within the context of cultures and social values is a domain of human experience that is not taken into account. However, this can be all-important. Dickson (1990) argues that medical discourses referring to the menopause act as a form of social control of menopausal women and the reinterpretation, and often denial, of how the menopause is individually experienced. Ferguson and Parry (1998), in turn, consider how the combined, politically-gendered facets of the menopause relating directly to femininity, sexuality ageing in conjunction with a medicalised discourse do not help to facilitate women's acceptance of and adjustment to this stage of human development.

To return to why social workers might need to consider the psychosocial, biophysical impact of the menopause let us consider the following. The menopause and menopausal women have long been the butt of many jokes of the 'take my ...' mother-in-law variety. In patriarchal societies, women's biological role has been emphasised where primarily they have been valued as sexual and reproductive beings. Beauty and sexuality in women has long been viewed as the possessions of male guardians and not as assets that belong to the women themselves. The traditional role of the father-of-the-bride who ceremoniously walks his daughter down the aisle to pass her to the groom is a ritualised but stark enactment of patriarchy in action in relation to the ownership of women among men – however sentimentally it may be viewed witnessed from the pews.

Accordingly, once the biology of women moves her past the physical stages that are valued by patriarchal society to a new physical state that may not be socially legitimised, this in turn undermines woman as a patriarchal commodity of value. Yet, it is also true to say that not all cultures, including patriarchal ones, view women's human development in the same light. In some cultures, such as those of the Muslim Middle East, a woman may look forward to the post-menopausal years as bringing her more freedom of movement than she was permitted in her younger, fertile years (Ashencaen Crabtree et al, 2016). In other societies, such as Japan, this time of life can release women from child-bearing and rearing duties, enabling women to be recognised as taking up a new socially valued role, that perhaps of the wise elder to whom the younger generation defer (Karasawa et al, 2011). In others, the active, hands-on grandmother role will bring both its new demands as well as enabling women to make important new contributions to the family. In African societies, this grandmother (rather than grandparenting per se) role is connected to the improved nutrition and therefore survival of grandchildren (Sear et al, 2000).

However, in Anglo-Saxon society, menopausal women are surrounded by negative stereotypes of the ageing woman, diminished in the commodification of her fertility, her sexuality questioned, anxieties about fading looks exploited by beauty companies – and additionally uncompensated for by recognition of her accumulated wisdom. Like most male counterparts many women reaching the menopause will be in paid employment. However, as we have already discussed, gendered 'glass ceiling' barriers to progression will have taken their toll on women's rates of progression in comparison with male counterparts, thus depriving women of gaining as much kudos and associated privileges in the workplace during otherwise generally productive and responsible working lives. Older women are said to complain of being invisible in contemporary society, in contrast to older men who may have secured positions of recognised power and authority. For example, the second author of this chapter heard about a visiting eminent female professor who was referred to by male colleagues as 'that old bat' purely on the grounds of her age and gender. The common terms used about older women are rarely complementary but often are either derogatory or patronising. No wonder menopause is regarded as a stigmatised condition.

Moreover, the impact of declining hormones upon the bio-physiology of women can be severe and yet by huge irony, while menopause is viewed as a medicalised condition, the seriousness of many women's suffering during the menopausal years is often trivialised and even dismissed by sceptical physicians. The symptoms of the menopause at their worst can include not only 'hot flushes' but vaginal dryness and shrinking leading to painful sexual intercourse, and this loss of elasticity can affect the urethra resulting in miserable, recurring urinary tract infections. Insomnia, anxiety and depression, frightening heart palpitations and utter exhaustion are all common symptoms that women complain of, while the onset of 'middle-aged spread' is a comparatively minor but nonetheless sad reminder of what is being lost. Women have been both encouraged to think of hormone replacement therapy by physicians at times, while at others this has been withheld from them regardless of their need. Medically unsupported menopausal symptoms are very likely to drive women to seek private health care if faced with an unsympathetic and/or ignorant GP. Social work with middle-aged and older women needs to take into account the possibilities of a burden of biophysical and psychosocial implications relating to the menopause in view of the length of the duration from start to finish of the menopause, which can be a good decade or more. This awareness needs to be extended obviously to service users but without forgetting that the menopause can equally affect all women colleagues and indeed in due course oneself. Feminist social work practice requires that the 'invisibilising' of women's experiences, to daringly coin a new verb, needs to be challenged and thought through.

Happily, some women, as they say, 'sail through' the menopausal years without any problems, and this is most encouraging – but it would be unrealistic and unfair to assume that this is the case for the majority. Recently BBC Radio 4's *Woman's Hour* programme focused on the menopause and duly received a deluge of calls and emails from women describing their menopausal experiences. The dam had burst on women's complicit silence on the menopause where, because they were given licence and encouragement to speak, expressed their thoughts and feelings vividly. Unlike the relative sympathy afforded to the wild hormonal and physio-psychological roller-coaster of adolescence, menopausal women whose bodies, and often minds, are equally undergoing dramatic changes that they must adjust to are not normally viewed with the same level of awareness and concern. The invisibility of women's gendered experiences are characteristic of their decentred position in patriarchal society, which despite some advances remains entrenched. Alarmingly, however, this is also manifested in medical care beyond that of the menopause in terms of the coined 'gender pain gap' where across a range of conditions the pain and suffering experienced by women and girls is trivialised by the medical profession in comparison with the attention given to pain reported by men (Hoffman and Tarzian, 2001). The recent scandals involving botched vaginal mesh operations and overlooked cervical smear reminders are indicative of an institutionalised casualness towards the welfare of women throughout their life course and where many of those most profound subjective experiences are viewed as invalid (Foster, 2018).

Being critical in professional practice

If we return to Ferguson's (2008) earlier work on critical best practice, there seems to be both an acknowledgement of the realities of social work practice within a state-regulated or controlled bureaucracy, alongside a demand that we question why things are done in certain ways, what assumptions these are based on and what alternative ways of thinking and acting there might be. Such an approach recognises that acting critically may be difficult, make us unpopular and lead us into conflict with those who employ us. However, the moral principles on which social work is practised allows and necessitates practice that works with people for the best possible outcomes which, in turn, may require calling out discrepancies and using the evidence of people's experiences to analyse and critique how relations at the macro or structural, meso or organisation as well as individual levels have a profound influence on how adults live and perform in their daily lives.

An ecological systems approach can help us here. We have discussed elsewhere (see 'Further reading' – Parker and Ashencaen Crabtree (2018) – how this theory shares links with social constructionist and critical theory (Parker, 2019)). Seeing the person in their environmental context allows us to identify the various influences on their lives in a way that understands the structural, organisation pressures on people as well as personal and internal changes that come with adulthood and subsequent ageing.

Conclusion

This chapter took a critical approach to traditionally accepted theories, not dismissing or necessarily debunking them but emphasising the centrality of observing and questioning at all times. This adds a transformatory perspective to our practices and should be borne in mind when using more traditional theories and models to inform practice.

Reflective questions

1 How might you challenge some of the accepted paradigms in human growth and development in adults?

2 Describe some approaches that emphasise the social, structural and agentic as important in human growth and development; and identify what possible implications these may have for those working with adults.

3 Provide alternative perspectives to help social workers negotiate the thorny paths of theoretically informed practice and highlight the importance of reflexivity and reflection in your own practice.

Further reading

- Dominelli, L. (2002) *Feminist Social Work Theory & Practice* (2nd edn). Houndmills, Basingstoke: Palgrave.
  This classic text from Lena Dominelli explores the importance of feminism and feminist practice for social work. It is central to your learning whether you are a man or woman because it deals with overt and hidden discrimination in society in which we are all, along with our service users, implicated.

- Parker, J. and Ashencaen Crabtree, S. (2018) *Social Work with Disadvantaged and Marginalised People*. London: Sage.
  We present a critical approach to social work practice in this book exploring in more depth some of the concepts we have presented in this chapter.

- Swain, J. and French, S. (2004) (eds), *Disabling Barriers, Enabling Environments* (2nd edn). London: Sage.
  Swain and French's book raises our understanding of the social and structural impacts on disability and disabling environments.

References

Ashencaen Crabtree, S., Husain, F. and Spalek, B. (2016) *Islam and Social Work: Culturally Sensitive Practice in a Diverse World* (2nd edn). Bristol: Policy Press.

BBC (2016) Pocket money: boys get 13% more than girls survey finds. 3 June. Available from: https://www.bbc.co.uk/news/business-36440161 (accessed 4 April 2019).

Bengtson, V.L., Burgess, E. and Parrott, T. (1997) Theory, explanation and a third generation of theoretical development on social gerontology, *Journal of Gerontology, Series B, Psychological and Social Sciences*, 52(2): 572–588.

Berger, P.L. and Luckmann, T. (1966) *The Social Construction of Reality: A Treatise in the Sociology of Knowledge*. New York: Doubleday & Company.

Bernades, J. (1997) *Family Studies: An introduction*. Abingdon: Routledge.

Bourdieu, P. (1977) *Outline of a Theory of Practice*. Cambridge: Cambridge University Press.

Bourdieu, P. (1996) Understanding Theory, *Culture and Society*, 13(1): 17–38.

Cumming, E. and Henry, W. (1961) *Growing Old: The Process of Disengagement*. New York: Basic Books.

Dickson, G.L. (1990) A feminist poststructuralist analysis of the knowledge of menopause, *Advances in Nursing Science*, 12(3): 15–31.

Ferguson, H. (2008) The theory and practice of critical best practice in social work. In K. Jones, B. Cooper and H. Ferguson (eds), *Best Practice in Social Work: Critical Perspectives*. Basingstoke: Palgrave, pp 15–37.

Ferguson, S.J. and Parry, C. (1998) Rewriting menopause: Challenging the medical paradigm to reflect menopausal women's experiences, *Frontiers: A Journal of Women's Studies*, 19(1): 20–41.

Fook, J. (2016) *Social Work: A Critical Approach to Practice* (3rd edn). London: Sage.

Foster, D. (2018) The gender pain gap is real. Doctors, stop dismissing women's conditions, *The Guardian* 26 November. Available from: https://www.theguardian.com/commentisfree/2018/nov/26/gender-pain-gap-doctors-women-healthcare

Foucault, M. (1979) *Discipline and Punish: The Birth of the Prison*. London: Penguin.

George, R. (2018) Should men say 'menopause' three times a day to help working women? *The Guardian*, 22 August. Available from: https://www.theguardian.com/society/shortcuts/2018/aug/22/things-help-menopausal-working-women (accessed 23 April 2018).

Germain, C. (1973) An ecological perspective in casework, *Social Casework*, 54(6): 323–330.

Grenier, A., Lloyd, L. and Phillipson, C. (2017) Precarity in late life: Rethinking dementia as 'frailed' old age, *Sociology of Health and Illness*, 39(2): 318–330.

Havighurst, R. and Albrecht, R. (1953) *Older People*. London: Longman.

Hoffman, D.E. and Tarzian, A.J. (2001) The girl who cried pain: A bias against women in the treatment of pain, *Journal of Law, Medicine & Ethics*, 29(1): 13–27.

Jones, R. (2018) UK pensions gender gap widens in past decades, figures show. Available from: https://www.theguardian.com/business/2018/mar/26/uk-pensions-gender-gap-widens-past-decade-figures (accessed 16 September 2019).

Karasawa, M., Curhan, K.B., Markus, H.R., Kitayama, S.S., Love, G.D., Radler, B.T. and Ryff, C.D. (2011) Cultural perspectives on aging and well-being: A Comparison of Japan and the US, *International Journal Aging Human Development*, 73(1): 73–98.

Lemon, B.W., Bengtson, V.L. and Peterson, J.A. (1972) An exploration of the activity theory of ageing, *Journal of Gerontology*, 27(4): 511–523.

Lymbery, M. (2005) *Social Work with Older People: Context, Policy and Practice*. London: Sage.

Me Too (2018) Website. Available from: https://metoomvmt.org.

Morgan, D. (1996) *Family Connections: An Introduction to Family Studies*. Cambridge: Polity.

Morgan, D.H.J. (1999) Risk and family practices: Accounting for change and fluidity in family life. In E. Silva and C. Smart (eds), *The New Family?* London: Sage.

Myles, J.F. (2004) From doxa to experience: Issues in Bourdieu's adoption of Husserlian phenomenology, *Theory, Culture and Society*, 21(2): 91–107.

Office for National Statistics (2018) *Understanding the gender pay gap in the UK*. Available from: https://www.ons.gov.uk/employmentandlabourmarket/peopleinwork/earningsandworkinghours/articles/understandingthegenderpaygapintheuk/2018-01-17 (accessed 16 September 2019).

Parker, J. (2005) Constructing dementia and dementia care: Daily practices in a day care setting, *Journal of Social Work*, 5(3): 261–278.

Parker, J. (2012) Landscapes and portraits: Using multiple lenses to inform social work theories of old age. In M. Davies (ed.), *Social Work with Adults: From Policy to Practice*. Basingstoke: Palgrave Macmillan, pp 285–299.

Parker, J. (2017) *Social Work Practice* (5th edn). London: Sage.

Parker, J. (2019) Descent or dissent? A future of social work education in the UK post-Brexit, *European Journal of Social Work*, first published 12 February 2019. Available from: https://doi.org/10.1080/13691457.2019.1578733

Parker, J. and Ashencaen Crabtree, S. (2014) Problematising active ageing: a theoretical excursus into the sociology of ageing for social work practice. In M.-L. Gómez-Jiménez and J. Parker (eds) *Active Ageing? Perspectives from Europe on a Vaunted Topic*. London: Whiting and Birch, pp 12–29.

Parker, J. and Ashencaen Crabtree, S. (2018) *Social Work with Disadvantaged and Marginalised People*. London: Sage.

Parsons, T. (1951) *The Social System*. Glencoe, IL: Free Press.

Penhale, B. and Parker, J. (2008) *Working with Vulnerable Adults*. London: Routledge.

Phillips, J., Ray, M. and Marshall, M. (2006) *Social Work with Older People* (4th edn). Basingstoke: Palgrave Macmillan.

Powell, J.L. and Hendricks, J. (2009) The social construction of ageing: Lessons for theorizing, *International Journal of Sociology and Social Policy*, 29(1/2): 84–94.

Putney, N.M., Alley, D.E. and Bengtson, V.L. (2005) Social gerontology as public sociology in action, *The American Sociologist*, 36(4): 88–104.

Rutter, L. and Brown, K. (2019) *Critical Thinking and Professional Judgement for Social Work* (5th edn). London: Sage.

Schatzki, T. (1996) *Social Practices: A Wittgensteinian Approach to Human Activity and the Social*. Cambridge: Cambridge University Press.

Sear, R., Mace, R. and McGregor, I.A. (2000) Maternal grandmothers improve nutritional status and survival of children in rural Gambia, *Proceedings of the Royal Society, Series B, Biological Sciences*, 267(1453): 1641–1647.

The Everyday Sexism Project (2018) *The Everyday Sexism Project*. Available from: http://everydaysexism.com

Thompson, N. (2016) *Anti-Discriminatory Practice* (6th edn). London: Palgrave.

Wharton, A. (2012) *The Sociology of Gender: An Introduction to Theory and Research* (2nd edn). Chichester: Wiley-Blackwell.

PART II

Specific developmental issues

The second part of this book concerns specific issues and particular aspects of human growth and development across the life course and in environmental contexts. These follow closely on those discussed in the companion volume but are here related to adults continuing through the life course.

Part II introduces specific issues that are commonly considered in traditional discussions of human growth and development and its relation to social work, including attachment and bonding in adulthood (Chapter 7) which leads us into a consideration of relationships and friendships, which is explored in subsequent chapters. Education, covered in Chapter 8, is considered as a lifelong stage in which we, as human beings, seek to extend knowledge, skills and understanding and that this is important in terms of our pro-social development, feeling valuable and part of the world. We use examples from your own social work education to make this more real to you and to develop your understanding. In Chapter 9, we explore how the life course can have a significant influence on adult involvement in and turn from crime. The links between children and young people and adults are made in this chapter. Next, in Chapter 10, we turn to a consideration of health and disability, exploring the context and debating the specific issues that might arise as a stepping stone to considering practice issues in the final part of the volume. These issues are tackled from a nursing perspective which adds to our multidisciplinary focus in contemporary social work. The final chapter in this part explores death as a neglected but powerful concept in late modern society. Addressed from a nursing sociologist's viewpoint, Chapter 11 provides an important theoretical insight into the ways in which death has changed throughout history.

Part II objectives

- introduce common specific issues in adult development;

- begin to question the application of models and understandings given while inculcating a critical edge;

- prepare readers for applying their knowledge to practice in Part III.

6

Critical aspects of attachment theory: empirical research findings and current applications

Gabriele Schäfer

Introduction

Attachment is one of the most studied developmental processes of psychology. Attachment theory is a psychological model that describes the interpersonal dynamics of long-term and short-term relationships between human beings. Our attachment style affects everything in our life from the way we select our partner to how well our relationships progress. Recognising our attachment patterns can be very helpful in understanding our fears, vulnerabilities and strengths in relationships. The most important tenet of attachment theory is that an infant needs to develop a close relationship with at least one primary caregiver. This complex process is essential for the child's healthy social and emotional development (for a more detailed discussion on child attachment theory in childhood (see Chapter 7 in the companion volume; Gerrig et al, 2018; Schneider and Lindenberger, 2018). The focus on studying attachment processes in children has now been extended to the research about adult attachment, which we will focus on in this chapter. Attachment theory has a number of applications for adults with respect to their parenting styles. Attachment disruptions within a primary caregiver's life can lead to serious threats to a caregiver's sensitivity and also general availability towards their children. Potentially they can activate defensive processes and expressions of attachment-related emotions such as sadness, fear and anger (see Kobak et al, 2016; Weinfield et al, 1999). Bowlby's focus for creating positive change involved working with parents' internal schemata, parenting behaviours and their relationship with their therapist (Berlin et al, 2008; Gloger-Tippelt, 2002). Another important application of attachment theory concerns the complex attachment patterns in intimate couple relationships. Hazan and Shaver (1987) extended attachment theory to adult romantic relationships. According to these authors, the affectional bonds that develop between adults in romantic relationships are conceptually similar to the same attachment behavioural system that gives rise to the affectional bonds between infants and their caregivers. This has a number of implications that will be discussed throughout the chapter.

Chapter objectives

In this chapter, research on a number of important aspects of attachment theory will be discussed:

- attachment theory in adult romantic relationships;

- the roles of gender in attachment processes;

- family violence and neglect in attachment processes;

- cross-cultural studies on the development of attachment;

- a critical analysis of the limitations of the Bowlby–Ainsworth attachment theory.

Attachment theory in adult romantic relationships

As mentioned previously, attachment theory has applications for adult relationships. However, according to Hassebrauck and Schwarz (2016), the contribution of attachment theory to the research area of interpersonal attraction is still limited. Scroufe and Fleeson (1986) point out that early attachment patterns have a strong influence on the development of personality. In this respect, the relationship between an infant and the primary caregiver becomes an internal working model for interpersonal relationships in general and romantic couple relationships as well (see Shaver et al, 1988). Hazan and Shaver (1987) extended attachment theory to adult romantic relationships. According to these authors, the affectional bonds that develop between adults in romantic relationships are conceptually similar to the same attachment behavioural system that gives rise to the affectional bonds between infants and their caregivers. Hazan and Shaver (1994) pointed out that in studies of adult attachment, anxious/ambivalent attachment is associated with a strong preoccupation with a partner's level of responsiveness. Adults with this attachment style tend to fall in love easily and experience jealousy, fear, anxiety and loneliness (even when involved in a couple relationship) and have low self-esteem (Collins and Read, 1990). They also experience a higher rate of relationship dissolution (Hazan and Shaver, 1987, for a detailed description of the research; see Hazan and Shaver, 1994). Avoidant attachment results from a consistent lack of responsiveness, so individuals avoid intimate social contact because of their fear of intimacy. They also show pessimistic views of intimate relationships and experience a relatively high rate of relationship dissolution (Hazan and Shaver, 1987). The lack of self-disclosure and discomfort with relationship partners who do self-disclosure is also a process that people with this attachment style often experience (Mikulincer and Nachshon, 1991). Hazan and Shaver (1994, p 16) postulate that 'insecure attachment might be at the root of many dysfunctional behaviors contributing to relationship dissatisfaction.'

Consistent with research on childhood attachment, secure attachment is the most stable pattern. Hazan and Shaver (1987) reported that, in their study, secure individuals experienced love relationships as very happy, friendly and trusting. Participants in their studies described that they accepted and supported their partners despite their faults. Their relationships also tended to endure longer. The attachment style has been proven to be a precise indicator for relationship quality (Mikulincer et al, 2002; Nosko et al, 2011). Hazan and Shaver (1987) found, in their studies, that about 56 per cent of people have a secure attachment, 24 per cent have an avoidant attachment and 20 per cent experience an anxious/ambivalent attachment. The results indicate 'that people with different attachment orientations entertain different beliefs about the course of romantic love, the availability and trustworthiness of love partners, and their own love-worthiness' (Hazan and Shaver, 1987, p 521). The results of these studies are supported by a study from Mikulincer and Erev (1991).

Other researchers identify four attachment styles in adults: secure, anxious-preoccupied, dismissive–avoidant and fearful-avoidant. These four styles approximately correspond to infant classifications: secure, insecure-ambivalent, insecure-avoidant and disorganised/disoriented (see Bartholomew, 1990; Bartholomew and Horowitz, 1991, for a more detailed description of the four adult attachment styles; Asendorpf, 2016). According to Bartholomew and Horowitz (1991), the secure attachment style in adults corresponds closely to the secure attachment style in children, whereas the anxious-preoccupied attachment style in adults is similar to the anxious-ambivalent attachment style in children. Both the dismissive-avoidant attachment style and the fearful-avoidant attachment patterns in adults correspond to the avoidant attachment style in children (see Van Buren and Cooley, 2002). Bartholomew (1990) explains that the differentiation in both a fearful-avoidant and dismissive-avoidant attachment style is a coping mechanism to deal with emotional conflicts with the primary caregiver (e.g. the mother). Unsympathetic or distant behaviour from the mother leads to the development of a negative outside image. An individual with a working model of dismissive-avoidant attachment wants to maintain distance to others, because their model is that the mechanism to satisfy his or her needs is to pretend like you don't have any. In this way they can avoid the painful experience of being rejected. This can lead to a situation where they select someone who is overly demanding of attention or more possessive. An example of a person with a working model of anxious–preoccupied attachment is that he/she senses that, in order to develop closeness to someone and get your needs met, you need to be with that partner all the time and get constant attention and reassurance. This can lead to a situation where they choose a partner who is isolated and difficult to connect with. These four categories resemble, to a degree, the attachment styles in adults that Hazan and Shaver (1987) identified in their studies.

Shaver and Hazan (1988) postulate that different love relationships involve different variations of behavioural systems. The typical couple relationship involves a combination of attachment, caring and sexuality. They claim that romantic love is an attachment process that includes sexuality and caring for each other.

> Romantic love, viewed from an attachment perspective, involves the integration of three behavioural systems: attachment, caregiving, and sexual mating. (Shaver and Hazan, 1988, p 482)

Attachment and caring behaviour are central components of romantic love (Carnelley et al, 1996, pp 272–275). In the first phase of a romantic relationship couples frequently experience a complex combination of sometimes contradictory emotions. People who are in love experience a mixture of sexual excitement and feelings of intense loneliness because of the uncertainty of a common future (Shaver and Hazan, 1987). After a while, the sexual attraction usually decreases, and the attachment fears either become stronger or weaker. This can create either a deepening of the relationship or more boredom that can potentially lead to the dissolution of the relationship (Shaver and Hazan, 1985).

Although there is, without question, a correlation between attachment styles in childhood and the experience of attachment in adult intimate couple relationships (see Case Study 6.1), attachment theory alone is not enough to explain romantic love in all its facets. People are potentially able to change enduring attachment patterns if they really work on it. 'The average person participates in several important friendships and love relationships, each of which provides an opportunity to revise mental models of self and others' (Hazan and Shaver, 1987, p 522). Main et al (1985) report that some parents in their study had freed themselves from the burden of cross-generational continuity, with respect to their attachment patterns and were able to work through their unpleasant experiences with their parents. These participants of their study now had developed mental models of relationships that were more typical of secure attachment. Shaver and Hazan (1987) explain that every person has an ability to reorganise their internal representations of attachment patterns although this is not an easy process. For this to occur an individual has to be self-aware and able to integrate their painful past experiences into new positive internal working models.

REFLECTION POINT 6.1

Consider the intimate adult relationships you have experienced or witnessed in your life. Do any of the previous attachment types fit those relationships in your opinion?

Gender and the development of attachment

Maccoby (1990) states that the hypothesis, that there are consistent context-independent personality differences between men and women, has not been supported by empirical research. Kindler (2009) reviewed findings from research on attachment history and gender and found that there are both differences and similarities between the genders with respect to their attachment development. On the phylogenetic level, research has not identified relevant differences in attachment development (Kindler, 2009). This means that based on natural evolutionary relationships there are no differences between men and women with respect to their attachment development. However, there are considerable differences in different cultures, which is an important factor in understanding and assessing attachment patterns in infants, children and adults. In Western cultures – that are often more individualistic and less patriarchal than collectivist cultures – it seems that mothers display similar attachment sensitivity towards their sons and daughters in their first year of life. They tend to react in a nurturing and sensitive way towards all of their children, regardless of their gender.

In German longitudinal studies in Regensburg and Bielefeld (applying the Strange Situation) of children aged between 12 and 18 months, gender differences between the different attachment classification groups could not be identified (Grossmann, 1989; Spangler and Grossmann, 1993). In nine other studies from different countries such as the US, Japan, Israel and Germany, gender differences in attachment patterns could not be identified (Ainsworth et al, 1978; Waters, 1978; Easterbrooks and Lamb, 1979; Egeland and Faber, 1984; Sagi et al, 1985; Goosens, 1986; Takahashi, 1986). In cultures where women are severely devalued, reflected in lower survival rates for girls compared to boys, this might be different. Female infanticide in India, for example, has reached a level that severely impacts on the foundations of the state. It occurs because of poverty and the dowry system. In the *Süddeutsche Zeitung* online it was reported in 2010 that the murder of girls has a long and cruel tradition in India. The article quotes results of a UNICEF report from 2009. Every day approximately 7,000 female foetuses are aborted in India. It would be interesting to find out how exactly these differences in attachment processes influence girls in their socialisation and what that means to them as adults.

In cultures where women are devalued, the perception of women in society seems to have a significant negative impact on a mother's sensitivity towards her daughters (see Miller, 1981; Mosher, 1983). Does that mean that more women in these cultures develop insecure, ambivalent or even disorganised attachment patterns in adulthood? How does that in turn influence their couple relationship and their parenting style? More research is needed to generate knowledge of whether girls and boys are treated with different levels of sensitivity and caring by their mothers and fathers in infancy as well as middle childhood and adolescence, both in cultures where women are devalued and in those where they are not devalued.

This has implications for social workers, especially when they are working with female migrants and refugees from cultures where women are sometimes encouraged to abort their daughters by either their husbands or his family or face guilt and discrimination. These social workers might encounter women who consequently have less attachment to their daughters and who find it difficult to stand up to their male partners when it comes to child welfare and the education of their daughters. They also might experience low self-esteem since they are not valued like the men in their culture.

CASE STUDY 6.1

A married couple, Thomas (aged 47) and Nicole (aged 43), with two children (a five-year-old boy named Peter and a 14-year-old girl named Phoebe) have recently split up. Throughout the relationship Thomas was always quite distant to his wife and children. He and his parents were never emotionally close and as an adult he avoided contact with them as much as possible. Nicole has a mother who was not sensitive to her needs as a child and who was also rather unpredictable in her availability. On top of that, her mother discouraged Nicole's autonomy as a child. As a result, Nicole became quite clingy and immature as a child and later as an adult felt very insecure. Her greatest fear was abandonment, and she was also very jealous of the other women that Thomas worked with.

In the couple relationship, Nicole felt abandoned because the more she tried to get close to Thomas the more he tried to avoid her. He felt that she suffocated him with her constant emotional demands, jealousy and anger. Both experienced helplessness because they did not know how to resolve their conflicts. As a result Nicole, who wanted a lot of attention and reassurance, became increasingly frustrated and angry. After many years of Thomas feeling panic because of Nicole's constant emotional demands, he withdrew even further from her and began avoiding contact with her. They constantly argued with each other and eventually their relationship broke down. Their children also suffered greatly because of their parents' problems. After a year of separation Thomas and Nicole decided that they want to reconcile and attend couple counselling.

Questions

1. What attachment issues do you think Nicole and Thomas are facing in this family?
2. Which interventions do you think would be useful to assist Thomas and Nicole in this family?
3. Which interventions do you think would be useful to assist the children in this family?
4. How can Nicole and Thomas overcome their painful past experiences with their parents and develop new positive working models?

Discussion

Your understanding of child and attachment styles and the potential consequences will come into play here. Insecure attachment can result in anxious behaviours and demands and can affect the emotional warmth of subsequent relationships. Avoidant behaviours are also likely to cause emotional problems that require you as a social worker to undertake a full, open and honest assessment of the situation. This would be best helped by a relational approach as discussed in Chapter 4, in which the family and those around can work on agreed areas to frankly confront their fears and concerns and to recognise what they might result in for others.

The consequences of violence and neglect in the family

Gasteiger-Klicpera (2009) reviewed the research on the psychological consequences of violence and neglect in the family. She concluded that, from the perspective of attachment theory, neglect, physical and sexual abuse within the family system result in deep relationship trauma. This relationship trauma changes the internal relationship representations of the affected children as well as those of adults who are abused by their partners. Manly et al (2001) found in their study that the chronicity of the abuse from early infancy to preschool age resulted in particular negative consequences for the psychosocial adjustment of children. Many studies have shown that experiencing child abuse can lead to a range of both internalising and externalising behaviour problems. As a result of child abuse children can experience a variety of psychological problems, including depression and anxiety which may persist into adolescence (McLeer et al, 1994, 1998; Widom, 2000; Wolfe et al, 2001; McCabe et al, 2005). As adults, these affected individuals possibly find it harder to form healthy attachment patterns that can lead to relationship breakdowns, violence and divorce. Even parental divorce during childhood is associated with chronic loneliness in adulthood (Shaver and Rubenstein, 1980).

However, not only children experience violence and abuse. Violence that is committed by a spouse or partner in an intimate relationship against the other spouse or partner can also disrupt family life and create attachment patterns that are insecure and anxious/ambivalent. The victims of domestic violence are overwhelmingly women, and women tend to experience more severe forms of violence (McQuigg, 2011; García-Moreno and Stöckl, 2013). In some countries and cultures, domestic violence is often perceived as justified. Especially in cases where there is a suspected or actual act of infidelity on the part of the woman, domestic violence is a common way of men to respond. According to research there is a significant correlation between a country's level of gender equality and rates of domestic violence. Countries with less gender equality experience higher rates of domestic violence (Esquivel-Santoveña et al, 2013).

Social workers who work with parents who neglected and abused their children and each other might explore their client's attachment histories and refer them to therapists if necessary. For social workers, therapists and educators it should be clear that seriously disrupted care-giving may place children at risk and consequently decrease the child's capacity for resilience into the future and into adulthood. It is also necessary to look at adult's attachment patterns and ask questions about how conflicts are resolved in the family. Policies and programmes should be developed and implemented to help men and women, who abuse each other and their children, learn to deal with conflicts in a more constructive way.

Cross-cultural studies on attachment

Attachment theorists were interested to find whether the Strange Situation classifications are culturally universal. Lohaus and Vierhaus (2015) describe the general frequency of attachment patters as: secure attachment 60–70 per cent, insecurely avoidant attachment 15–20 per cent, insecure ambivalent attachment 10–15 per cent and disorganised 5–10 per cent. Nonetheless, there are cultural variations. In empirical studies researchers found that ambivalent classifications were more frequent than expected in Japan (Miyake et al, 1985) and Israeli kibbutzim (Sagi et al, 1985). In northern Germany, a study showed that avoidant classifications were overrepresented (Grossmann et al, 1985). The outcomes of these studies were initially interpreted in cultural terms. Hence, the high frequency of ambivalent classifications observed in Japan and the Israeli kibbutzim was associated with underexposure to strangers (Miyake et al, 1985; Sagi et al, 1985). The high number of infants with an avoidant attachment pattern in Germany was attributed to a greater parental encouragement towards babies' autonomy and not to parental rejection (Grossmann et al, 1985).

In contrast to the northern German study, Lohaus and Vierhaus (2015) explain that in Western industrial nations, where individuality and independence are valued, there are a high number of children with a secure attachment pattern, whereas in cultures where family connections and community closeness is valued there is a comparatively high degree of children with an insecure ambivalent attachment style. Ambivalence can strengthen the emotional orientation towards the primary caregiver, which is wanted in close-knit societies such as Japan (Tesch-Römer and Albert, 2012). After looking at studies on child attachment in different cultures, Bretherton (1992) came to the conclusion that these interpretations were not based on systematic assessments of culturally guided parenting practices and parental beliefs. Van Ijzendoorn and Kroonenberg (1988) investigated the frequency distributions of the Strange Situation classification using over 1,000 cross-national and US studies. After analysing the data they concluded that valid conclusions about cross-national differences should not be drawn from single samples. This, according to Bretherton (1992), challenges the assumption that attachment patterns should be purely interpreted on a cultural level. There needs to be more research on the differences between attachment patterns between different cultures as well as between different groups within societies. Of course, these studies consider attachment as it has developed in studies of children and young people and we need to consider what impacts there might be on adults.

In this respect, a study of parent-infant attachment patterns among the Efe, a semi-nomadic people who live in the African rain forest, provides interesting information. The Efe, who live through foraging, horticulture and hunting, have different attachment practices compared to Western cultures (Tronick et al, 1985). Efe babies receive more care and nursing from other women than from their own mothers during the days, although during the nights, mothers are the principal caregivers. This suggests that attachment can be 'practised' differently depending on culture. In this case adult women who were not biologically related to the child developed and promoted attachment relationships. When they reach six months of age, infants begin to seek a closer relationship with their biological mothers, although other women still play a significant nurturing role. Tronick et al (1985) attribute Efe child-rearing practices to their living arrangements. The Efe live in dwellings that are closely spaced and offer little privacy. Under these circumstances, cooperation becomes a highly valued behaviour. Attachment behaviour seems to be heavily overlaid with cultural values.

REFLECTION POINT 6.2

Think about your own culture and how attachment affects you as an adult within that environment. Do you show overt affection to family members, partners? Are you expected to or assumed to be present for a significant other? What do you think might be driving these ways of behaving and how do you think it fits with adult attachment theories?

According to Posada et al (1995), despite the global cultural variations, parents want their children to feel secure in their relationships with them and adults want their children to attach securely to them. Fortunately, on a world-wide scale, more infants, and therefore dyadic parent–child relationships, fall into the secure attachment pattern than into any of the insecure classifications (Van Ijzendoorn and Kroonenberg, 1988). This, as we have shown in this chapter, also has implications for adult romantic relationships. As already explained, according to Hazan and Shaver (1987), the affectional bonds that develop between adults in close romantic relationships are conceptually similar to the attachment patterns between infants and their caregivers. Parents who experienced secure attachment as children are more likely to have healthy attachment patterns to their partners, which can increase the quality of couple relationships and marriages. In turn ambivalent or insecure attachment patterns are more likely to create problems in adult romantic relationships. Although culture, especially cultures with strong patriarchal traditions, play an important role in how men and women develop attachment patterns it seems that caring parents across different cultures bring up children with more secure attachment styles.

Social workers should be aware of intergenerational transmission of attachment patterns in different cultures and how these can impact on adult intimate relationships and also relationships between parents and their children (see Case Study 6.2).

CASE STUDY 6.2

A married couple, Nick (Caucasian, aged 46) and Jasmin (born in Pakistan, aged 45), with two children (a 14-year-old boy named Robert and a 16-year-old girl named Sina), live together as a family in a poor suburb of London. Jasmin's family emigrated from Pakistan when she was a little girl and they try to keep the traditions of their homeland alive. Jasmin has a very close relationship with her parents, but is nevertheless afraid of her father's strict authority. He has all the power in her family and made all the important decisions in the household. Her mother is a housekeeper who would have preferred to live in Pakistan but accepted immigrating to England because it meant that her children could get a better education. Jasmin has two older brothers, who always tried to control her during her childhood and adolescence. Her family was very disappointed when she married Nick and tried everything to stop her. They even cut the contact with Jasmin until Sina was born. They would have preferred her to marry a Pakistani man. Her parents live in the same suburb of London that she lives in. Nick's parents also come from London and he has a conflictual relationship with both of them. His father was violent and angry and regularly hit his mother and him and his siblings. His mother endured her painful marriage and Nick despised her inability to leave her father. He also felt that he had to protect his mother from his father.

Nick and Jasmin also experience many conflicts in their relationship. Both of them are unemployed and Nick has developed a drinking problem. When he is drunk he can get very unstable and angry. Sometimes he becomes violent towards Jasmin and the children. Jasmin is desperate but does not want to leave him because she hopes that if at least she keeps the family together he will change. In her culture a woman brings dishonour to the whole family if she leaves her husband. She does not tell her parents that Nick is violent because she fears that they would blame her for not being a good wife and mother. She is also worried about what her brothers might do to him. Instead she tries to keep the image of a happy family intact by compensating for Nick on a practical as well as an emotional level.

The children are very negatively affected by their parent's relationship and especially Robert is angry with his father. He also experiences problems in school and was suspended because of violent outbursts towards other boys in his class. Sina has become withdrawn and sometimes cuts herself. She has developed fears of going to school and prefers to be in her room most of the time.

Questions

1. What attachment issues do you think Jasmine and Nick are facing in this couple relationship?
2. Which interventions do you think would be useful to assist Jasmin and Nick?
3. Which interventions do you think would be useful to assist Sina and Robert in this family?

4. How does gender and culture influence the dynamics in this couple relationship and the parenting relationship with the children?
5. How can Jasmin and Nick overcome their past experiences with their parents and develop new positive working models?
6. How can social services assist their children? What steps have to be taken next?

Discussion

You will see in this case study that many social and cultural factors interact. It is important to note this because it can help you not to be rigid and single-minded in your intervention but to explore alongside those involved what are their preferred ways of dealing with identified problems. Bringing in your knowledge of attachment styles, the impact of different forms of attachment and taking a whole family approach will help you to work with the family to develop the best ways forward.

Limitations of the Bowlby–Ainsworth attachment theory

In this section, attachment theory will be analysed and some limitations will be identified. Some of the limitations refer to the theoretical aspects of attachment theory and others to the research design of some of the studies. These aspects have been discussed in detail in Chapter 7 in the companion volume. Bowlby and Ainsworth's attachment models are common references in Attachment theory research. However, there is also considerable criticism of their theory and experimental design. The most fundamental limitation is the stress infants are exposed to through experiments such as the Strange Situation; it risks the exposure of children to negative emotions and traumatic experiences. Since infants cannot decide whether or not they want to participate in laboratory tests the Strange Situation procedure is an ethically problematic experiment.

Field (1996) claims that how mothers and children interact together when they are not stressed demonstrates more of how the attachment model works than how the child behaves when the mother leaves and then comes back. Attachment behaviours that are directed towards the caregiver during departing and reunion times cannot be the all determining factor used when attachment is defined. The primary attachment figure is usually assumed to be the mother. However, the mother is not always the primary attachment figure and for this reason it cannot be assumed (Field, 1996). Mesman et al (2016) state that in Western and non-Western cultures children communicate with a number of attachment figures. Howes and Spieker (2016) investigated attachment relationships in the context of multiple caregivers and found that childcare providers are not long-term participants in the social networks of most children.

Limiting the examination of attachment patterns to only those between the primary caretaker and infants may decrease predictive power in a substantial way. Thus more conceptual work and empirical research has to be conducted in order to find out how experiences with different attachment figures, such as childcare providers, foster parents and adoptive parents and form coherent internal working models. In addition, Parkes (2006) points out that the categories that Ainsworth identified appear clear cut. Nonetheless, they fail to measure the strengths of the attachment patterns they describe.

Although stressed parents often seem to have insecure children, there is also the possibility that stress can provide a learning experience for the children. For example, Simpson and Rholes (1994) refer to several studies that support the notion that mild to moderate stress can even foster attachment security rather than undermine it. It has also been claimed that Ainsworth's work was biased because the research was conducted with only middle-class American families. This is only true to a degree because of her long research project in Uganda. However, it is still a valid criticism that what is generally considered an appropriate response to separation might not be the same in different cultures. Critics also believe the laboratory experiment of the Strange Situation was artificial and lacked ecological validity.

Some critics of attachment theory claim that the behavioural strategies of insecure avoidant children (under certain cultural conditions) could be as or even more adequate than strategies of securely attached children (Hinde and Stevenson-Hinde, 1990). Parkes (2006) also states that children, who, as a consequence of insecure attachment are prone to distress, should not be assumed to be poorly adapted to their social environment. Given their family circumstances, the experiences of distress might be quite appropriate. Lamb et al (1984) postulate that different attachment patterns can be understood as equivalent adjustments to different parenting styles and constitute alternative developmental paths. Fear might be an appropriate and even life-saving adaptation to situations of danger. In this respect, an infant who cries out when alarmed is probably more likely to survive than one who is silent (Parkes, 2006).

Attachment theorists have reacted to these criticisms and developed other methods to complement the Strange Situation procedure. The Attachment Q-Set can be used with infants and toddlers while there is also the possibility for primary caregivers to participate and offer their view on the quality of attachment between them and the child (Lohaus and Vierhaus, 2015). There are also a number of different measures of adult attachment as well. The most well-known measure consists of self-report questionnaires and coded interviews and is based on the *Adult Attachment Interview* (Crowell et al, 2008).

A criticism comes from Buchanan (2013), who wrote about critical social work and the problems in applying attachment theory in contexts of domestic abuse. She stresses that, by framing the mother/infant relationship without regard for micro and macro contexts, the social world outside the mother and infant is excluded. According to her, it is problematic and disempowering to have one's life deemed as deficient if one has for example grown up with domestic violence.

> Given the high prevalence of gendered abuse, these social workers
> will provide services to women and their children who are enduring

domestic violence. There is, therefore, a need for social workers to utilise knowledge of gender analysis and feminist understandings of domestic violence to critically analyse the attachment approaches they are encouraged to utilise. (p 27)

She emphasises that, if these principles are not fully understood, women living with violent partners may possibly be even further disempowered and victimised. These women could perceive themselves as being deficient in their role of being a caring mother. Additionally, others, particular men who are the perpetrators of domestic violence, are possibly absolved of their responsibility for their child's well-being. In this way society and its institutions could be excluded from accountability. Harris (1998) argues that parents should not be held totally responsible for the way their children develop. The early infant–caregiver relationships are essential but in later years children tend to rely more on their peer relationships. Since Bowlby developed his theory, research has been conducted about attachment theory in later life. During the last 30 years, attachment theory has become one of the frameworks for the study of adult attachment and romantic relationships (Fraley and Shaver, 2000). Nevertheless, attachment theory has been limited when it comes to the issue of interpersonal attraction (Hassebrauck and Schwarz, 2016). More research should be conducted in order to explore how attachment processes across different cultures impact on adult relationships. Research is also necessary in the area of helpful therapeutic interventions. By applying effective interventions negative working models of attachment could be transformed which would empower people to develop healthy bonds in adult relationships.

Conclusion

Attachment is one of the most studied developmental processes of psychology. Attachment theory has implications and practical applications in a number of different social settings, such as social policy, therapy, decisions about the care and welfare of children and mental health. In 2008, Berlin and colleagues stated that supporting early child–parent relationships is an increasingly important goal of mental health practitioners, community-based service providers and policymakers (Berlin et al, 2008). It is safe to conclude that our style of attachment affects many processes in our life, from the way we select our romantic partners to the interpersonal behaviours with our children. The majority of children grow up and develop within a complex network of attachment figures. Some of these attachment figures are enduring, while others change over the life course (Howes and Spieker, 2016). Attachment theory explains babies' behaviour towards their primary caregiver (usually the mother) during separation and reunion times (see Schäfer, 2019). It is theorised that attachment behaviours formed in infancy will have a profound impact on adult attachment relationships. Studies from a number of researchers support this hypothesis (see Shaver and Hazan, 1985, 1987; Bartholomew, 1990; Bartholomew and Horowitz, 1991; Fraley and

Shaver, 2000). However, more studies should be conducted in order to explore attachment processes in adults and how they impact on intimate relationships, as well as relationships to friends and colleagues.

In this chapter, critical aspects of attachment theory have been reviewed and empirical studies have been presented. These give an impression about the new insights that were generated in areas such as gender differences, the impact of violence and neglect in families and the differences and similarities between attachment patterns in different societies. Different cultures and societies have different values about attachment relations. In some cultures autonomy is fostered and in others more dependent relationships within families are treasured. This has implications for the behaviour in adult romantic relationships and also for the quality of parenting. Societies provide different conditions for families. In cultures with strongly developed patriarchal traditions there is no gender equality in most families and women are often discriminated against during their upbringing and later as adults. This has an impact on the relationship to their partners and on their parental coping and nurturing capacities. Bowlby's statement that '[i]f a community values its children it must cherish their parents' (1951, p 84) certainly has the same or even more relevance today than when it was made. Increasingly powerful groups in society promote their own control over the resources of society by subordinating and marginalising others (see Marris, 1991). Marris's analysis is thought-provoking, given the rise of neoliberalist policies and the decrease in size of the social welfare state across Europe, Australia, New Zealand, Canada and the US. It is important to create the societal circumstances that allow family coping and family security because these conditions, at least to a degree, support parents in building close and intimate relationships with their children.

McDonald (2005) argues that situating domestic violence as a problem that is located in dysfunctional families and/or caused by insecure early attachment patterns alone, fits well with a neoliberal perspective that denies the need for structural changes to address social issues. Valuing of attachment relations thus has moral implications and should influence public policy, public health programmes, child mental health services, childcare services, child protection agencies, family law courts, family home visiting, early intervention services and innovative interventions in therapy. Yet, although it is important that policies orientate services to prevention, early intervention, and family support, there is also a need to address the ways in which societies maintain or even increase inequalities.

Reflective questions

1 What do you consider to be the most important aspects of attachment theory for adults?

2 How does attachment influence adult couple relationships?

3 How do you think gender and culture impact on attachment processes in adult intimate relationships?

4 What can individuals do in order to change negative attachment patterns in their life?

5 What in your opinion are the most problematic aspects of attachment theory?

Further reading

- Bartholomew, K. and Horowitz L.M. (1991) Attachment styles among young adults: A test of a four-category model, *Journal of Social and Personal Relationships*, 61(2): 226–44. This research article develops a model of attachment styles based on self-image and perceptions of the image of others. It is useful to read the research that underpins the model as this shows the fluidity of the model when considering adults.

- Crowell, J.A., Fraley, R.C. and Shaver, P.R. (2008) Measurement of individual differences in adolescent and adult attachment. In J. Cassidy, and P.R. Shaver (eds), *Handbook of Attachment: Theory, Research and Clinical Applications*. New York and London: Guilford Press, pp 599–634. Attachment styles, and meanings change over time. This interesting chapter charts some of the developments that can take place from adolescence through adulthood. This is important when considering the application of attachment theory in social work practice.

- Fraley, R.C. and Shaver, P.R. (2000) Adult romantic attachment: Theoretical developments, emerging controversies, and unanswered questions, *Review of General Psychology*, 4(2): 132–154. This research focuses on romantic attachment and therefore has implications for social workers when working with families and couples.

- Gilliath, O., Karantzas, G.C. and Fraley, R.C. (2016) *Adult Attachment: A Concise Introduction to Theory and Research*. London: Academic Press. This book provides a contemporary overview of attachment theory in adults and explains the concepts and implications in some detail. It is a good text for the interested reader to take forward their knowledge.

- Mesman, J., Van Ijzendoorn, M.H. and Sagi-Schwarz, A. (2016) Cross-cultural patterns of attachment: Universal and contextual dimensions. In J. Cassidy, and P.R. Shaver (eds), *Handbook of Attachment: Theory, Research, and Clinical Applications*. New York: The Guilford Press, pp 852–878. It is important for social workers to remember that context, culture and difference are important. This chapter helps to illustrate some of the problems that can arise should attachment theory be applied too rigidly to any situation or setting.

References

Ainsworth, M., Blehar, M., Waters, E. and Wall, S. (1978) *Patterns of Attachment*. Hillsdale, NJ: Erlbaum.

Asendorpf, J.B. (2016) Bindung im Erwachsenenalter. In H. Bierhoff and D. Frey (eds), *Soziale Motive und soziale Einstellungen*. Göttingen: Hogrefe, pp 323–352.

Bartholomew, K. (1990) Avoidance of intimacy: An attachment perspective, *Journal of Social and Personal Relationships*, 7(2): 147–178.

Bartholomew, K. and Horowitz, L.M. (1991) Attachment styles among young adults: A test of a four-category model, *Journal of Social and Personal Relationships*, 61(2): 226–244.

Berlin, J., Cassidy, J. and Appleyard, K. (2008) The influence of early attachments on other relationships. In J. Cassidy and P. Shaver (eds), *Handbook of Attachment: Theory, Research and Clinical Applications* (2nd edn). New York: The Guilford Press, pp 637–665.

Bretherton, I. (1992) The origins of attachment theory: John Bowlby and Mary Ainsworth, *Developmental Psychology*, 28(5): 759–775.

Buchanan, F. (2013) A critical analysis of the use of attachment theory in cases of domestic violence, *Critical Social Work*, 14(2): 19–31.

Carnelley, K.B., Pietromonaco, P.R. and Jaffe, K. (1996). Attachment, caregiving, and relationship functioning in couples: Effects of self and partner, *Personal Relationships*, 3(3): 257–278.

Collins, N.L. and Read, S.J. (1990). Adult attachment, working models, and relationship quality in dating couples, *Journal of Personality and Social Psychology*, 58(4): 644–663.

Crowell, J.A., Fraley, R.C. and Shaver, P.R. (2008) Measurement of individual differences in adolescent and adult attachment. In J. Cassidy, and P.R. Shaver (eds), *Handbook of Attachment: Theory, Research and Clinical Applications*. New York and London: Guilford Press, pp 599–634.

Easterbrooks, M.A. and Lamb, M.E. (1979) The relationship between quality of infant-mother attachment and infant competence in initial encounters with peers, *Child Development*, 50(2): 380–387.

Egeland, B. and Faber, E.A. (1984) Infant-mother attachment: Factors related to its development and changes over time, *Child Development*, 55(3): 753–771.

Esquivel-Santoveña, E.E., Lambert, T.L. and Hamel, J. (2013) Partner abuse worldwide, *Partner Abuse*, 4(1): 6–75.

Field, T. (1996) Attachment and separation in young children, *Annual Review of Psychology*, 47(1): 541–562.

Fraley, R. and Shaver, P.R. (2000) Adult romantic attachment: Theoretical developments, emerging controversies, and unanswered questions, *Review of General Psychology*, 4(2): 132–154.

García-Moreno, C. and Stöckl, H. (2013). Protection of sexual and reproductive health rights: Addressing violence against women. In M.A. Grodin, D. Tarantola, G.J. Annas and S. Gruskin (eds), *Health and Human Rights in a Changing World*. New York: Routledge, pp 780–781.

Gasteiger-Klicpera, B. (2009) Psychische folgen familiärer Gewalt und Vernachlässigung. In H. Julius, B. Gasteiger-Klicpera and R. Kissgen (eds), *Bindung im Kindesalter: Diagnostik und Intervention*. Göttingen: Hogrefe, pp 27–35.

Gerrig, R.J., Dörfler, T. and Ross, J. (2018) *Psychologie* (21st edn). Hallbergmoos: Pearson.

Gloger-Tippelt, G. (2002) Der Beitrag zur Bindungsforschung zur klinischen Entwicklungspsychologie der Familie. In B. Rollett, and H. Werneck (eds), *Klinische Entwicklungspsychologie der Familie*. Göttingen: Hofrebe, pp 118–141.

Goosens, F.A. (1986) The quality of attachment relationships of two-year-old children of working and nonworking mothers and some associated factors. Dissertation, University Leiden, Netherlands.

Grossmann, K.F. (1989) Differential effects of attachment quality to mother and father on boys and girls. Paper presented on the 10th Biennial Meeting of the International Society for the Study of Behavioral Development.

Grossmann, K., Grossmann, K.E., Spangler, G., Suess, G. and Unzner, L. (1985) Maternal sensitivity and newborns' orientation responses as related to quality of attachment in Northern Germany. In I. Bretherton and E. Waters (eds), Growing points of attachment theory and research, *Monographs of the Society for Research in Child Development*, 50(1–2), 209: 233–256.

Harris, J.R. (1998) *The Nurture Assumption: Why Children Turn Out the Way they Do*. New York: Free Press.

Hassebrauck, M. and Schwarz, S. (2016) Interpersonale attraktion. In H. Bierhoff, and D. Frey (eds), *Soziale Motive und soziale Einstellungen*. Göttingen: Hogrefe, pp 353–377.

Hazan, C. and Shaver, P. (1987) Romantic love conceptualized as an attachment process, *Journal of Personality and Social Psychology*, 52(3): 511–524.

Hazan, C. and Shaver, P.R. (1994) Attachment as an organizational framework for research on close relationships, *Psychological Inquiry*, 5(1): 1–22.

Hinde, R.A. and Stevenson-Hinde, J. (1990) Attachment: Biological, cultural, and individual desiderata, *Human Development*, 33(1): 62–72.

Howes, C. and Spieker, S. (2016) Attachment relationships in the context of multiple caregivers. In J. Cassidy, and P.R. Shaver (eds), *Handbook of Attachment: Theory, Research, and Clinical Applications*. New York: The Guilford Press, pp 314–329.

Kindler, H. (2009) Geschlechtsbezogene Aspekte der Bindungsentwicklung. In G. Spangler and P. Zimmermann (eds), *Die Bindungstheorie. Grundlagen, Forschung und Anwendung*. Stuttgart: Clett Kotta, pp 281–297.

Kobak, R., Zjac, K. and Madsen, S.D. (2016) Attachment disruptions, reparative processes, and psychopathology. In J. Cassidy and P.R. Shaver (eds), *Handbook of Attachment: Theory, Research, and Clinical Applications*. New York: The Guilford Press, pp 25–39.

Lamb, M.E., Thomson, R.A., Gardner, W.P., Charnov, E.L. and Estes, D. (1984) Security of infantile attachment as assessed in the 'strange situation', *The Behavioural and Brain Sciences*, 7(1): 121–171.

Lohaus, A. and Vierhaus, M. (2015) *Entwicklungspsychologie des Kinder und Jugendalters für Bachelor* (3rd edn). Berlin: Springer Verlag.

Maccoby, E.E. (1990) Gender and relationships: A developmental account, *American Psychologist*, 45(4): 513–520.

Main, M., Kaplan, N. and Cassidy, J. (1985) Security in infancy, childhood and adulthood: A move to the level of representation, *Monographs of the Society for Research in Child Development*, 50(1–2): 66–104.

Manly, J.T., Kim, J.E., Rogosch, F.A. and Cicchetti, D. (2001) Dimensions of child maltreatment and children's adjustment: Contributions of developmental timing and subtype, *Development and Psychopathology*, 13(4): 759–782.

Marris, P. (1991) The social construction of uncertainty. In C.M. Parkes, J. Stevenson-Hinde and P. Morris (eds), *Attachment Across the Life Cycle*. London: Routledge, pp 77–90.

McCabe, K.M., Lucchini, S.E., Hough, R.L., Yeh, M. and Hazen, A. (2005) The relation between violence exposure and conduct problems among adolescents: A prospective study, *American Journal of Orthopsychiatry*, 75(4): 575–584.

McDonald, J. (2005) Neo-liberalism and pathologizing of public issues: The displacement of feminist service models in domestic violence support services, *Australian Social Work*, 58(3): 275–284.

McLeer, S.V., Callaghan, M., Henry, D. and Wallen, J. (1994) Psychiatric disorders in sexually abused children, *Journal of the American Academy of Child & Adolescent Psychiatry*, 35(3): 313–319.

McLeer, S.V., Dixon, J.F., Henry, D., Ruggiero, K., Escovitz, K., Niedda, T. and Scholle, R. (1998) Psychopathology in non-clinical referred sexually abused children, *Journal of the American Academy of Child and Adolescent Psychiatry*, 37(12): 1326–1333.

McQuigg, R.J.A. (2011) Potential problems for the effectiveness of international human rights law as regards domestic violence. In R.J.A. McQuigg (ed.), *International Human Rights Law and Domestic Violence: The Effectiveness of International Human Rights Law*. Oxford and New York: Taylor & Francis.

Mesman, J., Van Ijzendoorn, M.H. and Sagi-Schwarz, A. (2016) Cross-cultural patterns of attachment: Universal and contextual dimensions. In J. Cassidy and P.R. Shaver (eds), *Handbook of Attachment: Theory, Research, and Clinical Applications*. New York: Guilford Press, pp 852–878.

Miller, B.D. (1981) *The Endangered Sex: Neglect of Female Children in Rural North India*. Ithaca, NY: Cornell University Press.

Mikulincer, M. and Erev, I. (1991) Attachment style and the structure of romantic love, *British Journal of Social Psychology*, 30(4): 273–291.

Mikulincer, M. and Nachshon, O. (1991) Attachment styles and patterns of self-disclosure, *Journal of Personality and Social Psychology*, 61(2): 321–331.

Mikulincer, M., Florian, W., Cowan, P.A. and Cowan, C.P. (2002) Attachment security in adult relationships: A systematic model and its implications for family dynamics, *Family Process*, 41(3): 405–434.

Miyake, K., Chen, S. and Campos, J.J. (1985) Infants' temperament, mothers' mode of interaction and attachment in Japan: An interim report. In I. Bretherton and F. Waters (eds), Growing points of attachment theory and research, *Monographs of the Society for Research in Child Development*, 50(1–2): 276–297.

Mosher, S.W. (1983) *Broken Earth: The Rural Chinese*. New York: Free Press.

Nosko, A.T., Lawford, H. and Pratt, M.W. (2011) How do I love thee? Let me count the ways: Parenting during adolescence, attachment styles, and romantic relationships in emerging adulthood, *Developmental Psychology*, 47(3): 645–657.

Parkes, C.M. (2006) *Love and Loss: The Roots of Grief and its Complications*. London: Routledge.

Posada, G., Waters, E., Crowell, J. and Lay, K.L. (1995) Is it easier to use a secure mother as a secure base? Attachment q-set correlates of the adult attachment interview. In E. Waters, B. Vaughn, G. Posada and K. Kondo-Ikemura (eds), Caregiving, cultural and cognitive perspectives on secure-base behaviour and working models: New growing points of attachment theory and research, *Monographs of the Society for Research in Child Development*, 60(244): 133–545.

Sagi, A., Lamb, M.E., Lewkowics, K.S., Shoham, R., Dvir, R. and Estes, D. (1985) Security of infant-mother, -father, and metaplet attachment among kibbutz-reared children in Israeli children. In I. Bretherton and E. Waters (eds), Growing points in attachment theory and research, *Monographs of the Society of Research in Child Development*, 50: 257–725.

Schäfer, G. (2019) The making of affectional bonds: An introduction to the principles of attachment theory. In J. Parker and S. Ashencaen Crabtree (eds), *Human Growth & Development* (Vol. I). Bristol: Policy Press.

Schneider, W. and Lindenberger, W. (2018) *Entwicklungspsychologie* (8th edn). Basel: Beltz Verlag.

Scroufe, L.A. and Fleeson, J. (1986) Attachment and the construction of relationships. In W.W. Hartup, and Z. Rubin (eds), *Relationships and Development*. Hillsdale, NJ: Lawrence Erlbaum, pp 51–71.

Shaver, P. and Rubenstein, C. (1980) Childhood attachment experience and adult loneliness. In L. Wheeler (ed.), *Review of Personality and Social Psychology* (Vol. 1). New Haven: Yale University Press, pp 42–73.

Shaver, P. and Hazan, C. (1985) Incompatibility, loneliness, and 'limerence'. In Ickes, W. (Eds.), *Compatibility and Incompatibility in Relationships*. New York: Springer Verlag, pp 163–184.

Shaver, P. and Hazan, C. (1987) Being lonely, falling in love, *Journal of Social Behavior and Personality*, 2(2): 105–124.

Shaver, P. and Hazan, C. (1988) A biased overview of the study of love, *Journal of Social and Personal Relationships*, 5: 473–501.

Shaver, P., Hazan, C. and Bradshaw, D. (1988) Love as an attachment: The Integration of the three behavioral systems. In R.J. Sternberg, and M. Barnes (eds), *The Psychology of Love*. New Haven, CT: Yale University Press.

Simpson, J.A. and Rholes, W.S. (1994) Stress and secure base relationships in adulthood. In K. Bartholomew and D. Perlman (eds), *Advances in Personal Relationships*, Vol. 5: *Attachment Processes in Adulthood*. London: Jessica Kingsley Publishers, pp 181–204.

Spangler, G. and Grossmann, K.E. (1993) Behavioural organization in securely and insecurely attached infant, *Child Development*, 64(5): 1439–1450.

Süddeutsche Zeitung (2010) *Massenabtreibung weiblicher Föten*. Available from: http://www.sueddeutsche.de/panorama/unerwuenschte-toechter-in-indien massenabtreibungen-weiblicher-foeten-1.667180

Takahashi, K. (1986) Examining the strange situation procedure with Japanese mothers and 12-month-old infants, *Developmental Psychology*, 22(2): 265–270.

Tesch-Römer, C. and Albert, I. (2012) Kultur und sozialisation. In W. Schneider and W. Lindenberger (eds), *Entwicklungspsychologie* (7th edn). Basel: Beltz Verlag, pp 137–159.

Tronick, E.Z., Winn, S. and Morelli, G.A. (1985) Multiple caretaking in the context of human evolution: Why don't the Efe know the Western prescription to child care? In M. Reite and T. Field (eds), *The Psychobiology of Attachment and Separation*. San Diego, CA: Academic Press, pp 293–321.

Van Buren, A. and Cooley, E.L. (2002) Attachment styles, view of self and negative affect, *North American Journal of Psychology*, 4(3): 417–430.

Van Ijzendoorn, M.H. and Kroonenberg, P.M. (1988) Cross-cultural patterns of attachment: a meta-analysis of the strange situation, *Child Development*, 59(1): 147–156.

Waters, E. (1978) The reliability and stability of individual differences in infant-mother attachment, *Child Development*, 49(2): 483–494.

Weinfield, N.S., Sroufe, L.A., Egeland, B. and Carlson, E.A. (1999) The nature of individual differences in infant-caregiver attachment. In J. Cassidy and P.R. Shaver (eds), *Handbook of Attachment*. New York: Guilford Press.

Widom, C.S. (2000) Childhood victimization: Early adversity, later psychopathology, *National Institute of Justice Journal*, 242(1): 2–9.

Wolfe, D.A., Scott, K., Wekerle, C. and Pittman, A.L. (2001) Child maltreatment: Risk of adjustment problems and dating violence in adolescence, *Journal of the American Academy of Child & Adolescent Psychiatry*, 40(3): 282–289.

7

Families and friends: relationship development in Muslim cultures

Sara Ashencaen Crabtree

Introduction

After some considerable time in the wilderness, social work is now turning away from a secular and somewhat insular focus, to embrace the idea that social work awareness relating to anti-oppressive attitudes towards ethnic and cultural diversity must include socio-religio perspectives, where the faith is a very important dimension of the human experience (Parker et al, 2018).

The institution of marriage and the pre-eminent position of the family in its influence over the individual continues to hold an unshakeable position as the primary social institution in Islam. Gender politics, in terms of the right to pursue fluid and reshaped identities, along with a questioning of the institution of marriage, may be shaping the landscape in many societies, including the UK. However, whatever the personal politics of the individual are, this appears to have had little impact on how family is perceived among Muslim minority ethnic (ME groups). This is not to say that contentions regarding gender, sexuality, feminism, masculinities, family relations and the family per se are being debated (and hotly so at times) (Afshar et al, 2005); but such debates have yet to undermine the fundamental position of a heterosexual, cohabiting, reproductive family life as the central unit of social organisation among Muslims in the way that has occurred among some other groups in British society, for example.

Chapter objectives

- explore aspects of the family within the context of the Muslim faith;
- examine current and relevant demographical information regarding the diverse community of British Muslims;
- consider backdrop stressors, such as Islamophobia, inequality and disadvantage;

> • reflect on personal and professional qualities useful to social workers working with unfamiliar faith-based or ethnic minority groups.

Background and context

In this chapter, aspects of the family are explored as outlined in the chapter objectives, where analytical insights about the family will be developed from contemporary research literature with case examples used to illuminate the discussion throughout. In considering the family within the Muslim faith, we will examine relationships in adult life in terms of acquiring adult status and associated responsibilities, undertaking marriage and starting families. Gender normativity will be discussed as prescribing marital and parental duties; while expectations governing extended family members will be considered. The issue of family here will be reframed as a verb – 'doing family' – and thus what that may mean within the context of Muslim faith and culture in the UK (Finch, 2007). Family morphologies therefore will be considered, in terms of what marriage may look like, as informed by Islamic family law, better known as *Sharia*.

The second section (Relationships in adult life) considers adult relations in the family, while the third section (Sexuality and gender) explores conflict within the family. This topic covers the wide area of gender, sexuality, culture and religion, where we revisit gender normativity within the context of modesty and propriety, as well as conventions regarding marriage, childrearing and transitions within childhood.

The final section (Expanding knowledge and applying it) explores the implications of issues raised for social work, reflecting upon the social work role in working with particular faith communities. In addition, we will consider how social workers may transfer that knowledge as gained through study and practice experience to other diverse groups. Such considerations will be developed via an understanding of the processes of self-reflectivity and reflexivity.

The Muslim population of the UK, despite Islamophobic propaganda of a massed army of unwanted migrants (see Grosfoguel and Mielants, 2006), is numerically very small, being under three million people (MCB, 2015). Muslim ME groups are also composed of a highly diverse ethnic population relating partially to waves of immigration that have taken place over the decades, as well as through conversion within the UK. Some of the first UK Muslim migrants were part of the South Asian diaspora to Britain back in the late sixties. The expulsion of East African Asians from primarily Uganda led to another wave of migrants in the seventies. Bangladeshi communities set up home in the UK in the 1980s, and since then others have arrived from the Middle East, Europe and Africa, some arriving for employment opportunities (the main driver for previous Middle Eastern (ME) migrants) and others being forced to migrate due to violence and oppression in their own countries (Ashencaen Crabtree et al, 2016).

Denominational difference is a feature of Islam (just as it is of Christianity and Judaism) where each carries its own distinctive tradition and philosophy as well as geo-political spheres of power and influence. A key example is *wahabism*, a very conservative form of Sunnism, which is supported by the political structures and vast wealth of countries such as Saudi Arabia. Similarly to Christianity, sectarian oppression is also found in Islam in relation to the Shi'a community and the Sunni. Many Shi'a are regarded as non-Muslims by some more extreme elements and are duly oppressed.

Despite great ethnic and cultural diversity, deprivation and underprivilege in the UK has affected Muslim ME groups overall set beside comparator faith groups in terms of employment, education, housing and income; additionally there are correlations with ill health and disability (Ashencaen Crabtree et al, 2016; MCB, 2015). Islamophobic prejudices play their part in these circumstances, as has the heightened anxieties within the community, raised by the association of terrorism with Muslims and the rise of Alt-right racism and intolerance towards migrants in general.

Relationships in adult life

In Chapter 11 of the companion volume of this series, Muslim childhood was explored as a transitional stage in human development. Transitions of any sort suggest a move, whether fluid or obstacle-ridden, from one state to another (Becket and Taylor, 2016). The transition from childhood to adulthood will, in most societies, involve a marked change of status and the undertaking of new roles and responsibilities. These human development stages will differ across cultures, groups and individuals, including when such transitions are expected to take place in the life stage. To give an example, the average age of marriage for most Britons today takes place later in an individual's life now than was the case 50 years ago. Yet, the period between an individual's adolescence and undertaking marriage may be much shorter in some cultures and thus the transition period lessened between childhood and adulthood. It is a general truism that reduced transitional periods can characterise a Muslim experience of attaining adulthood, especially for daughters (Ashencaen Crabtree et al, 2016).

The transition from childhood to adolescence and from that to adulthood is marked by the family's awareness of future intimate relationships as part of adult life. Marriage among a number of ME communities may be viewed more along the lines of contracts between families first and foremost — and not simply intimate alliances between individuals primarily. Such extended marriages will be viewed as strengthening both families and potentially making an important contribution to the local community. This outlook carries both strengths and weaknesses, as will be discussed further.

Heteronormativity in intimate relationships is most likely to be implicitly assumed given the difficulties of adopting a gay/lesbian identity for many Muslims (an issue we will discuss later in the chapter). The shorter transition between adolescence and adulthood occurs usually through early marriages, which are often encouraged among many Muslim communities globally for a number of reasons. Firstly, marriage confers adult status and particularly so for girls, where waged work and careers may not be viewed as this pivotal step towards adult independence. This attitude may be transferred to majority non-Muslim societies, where among British Muslims 18 per cent of women aged 16–74 occupy the 'Looking after home or family' category compared to 6 per cent of women in the general population (MCB, 2015). That said, the comparable numbers of young Muslims of both sexes entering higher education nationally offers others facets to consider apart from the domestic picture (MCB, 2015). Islamic principles emphasise, regardless of culture interpretations, that seeking knowledge and education is a duty of both sexes (Haw et al, 1998).

REFLECTION POINT 7.1

From what you have learned so far, how closely does this fit the general media portrayal of Muslims in the UK? Explain your response.

Marriage is thought to ensure a legitimised channel for sexuality in cultures where virginity and chastity are highly prized. In Islam, sexuality is regarded as a pleasurable outlet for normal human appetites between both sexes; and where sexual frustration is viewed as a cause mischief and social discord (Ashencaen Crabtree et al, 2016). These attitudes have differed markedly from traditional British views of driving male sexual appetite and the 'nice girls' disinterest, as well as the even older Christian Augustinian view of the superiority of a chaste, single life over that of marital indulgence. Better to marry than to burn (with desire), to paraphrase Chaucer's Wife of Bath, has long been thought of as the best course of action applicable to all Muslims reaching the transitions to adulthood. Equally, however, it is not acceptable for children to be born out of wedlock and such situations will bring disgrace to a single mother and her family.

Marriage will therefore entail children, or at least the expectation of having them, as a normal life course for most Muslims, where childbirth stamps the seal of achieving womanly status for instance. Children are not only expected, but usually deeply wanted. Larger family sizes tend to characterise Muslim families in the UK, along with a prevalence of younger Muslims, compared to over-60s (MCB, 2015). Once born, the Muslim *ummah* (the global community of the faithful) shows great variation in terms of attitudes towards the infant's gender, but while in some cultures sons are undoubtedly valued over daughters, in others daughters are deeply prized. In general, for many Muslim families, a new baby may well be viewed as a treasure, regardless of sex. Yet notably, and in contrast to some stereotypes of patriarchal dominance, in Muslim communities, such as those found in Southeast Asia (Malaysia and Indonesia primarily), the lineage is traced through the mother, where both matrilineal and matrilocal Muslim cultures exist. Matrilocality indicates that the groom is expected to move in with the bride and her family to contribute his labour, rather than families seeing the departure of daughters to her husband's family. Such kinship models tend to affirm the value of new-born girls as an overall asset to her family and community, as opposed to patrilineal and patrilocal kinship types, which emphasise the lineage and prerogative of the male (Ashencaen Crabtree et al, 2016).

Muslim marriages tend towards clear gendered divides in terms of roles and duties in keeping with Islamic principles, where men are responsible for earning the family income and women responsible for the running of the home and care of the family (Stang Dahl, 1997). Women may seek waged work, provided that this does not interfere with their primary domestic duties, and under these circumstances they are not obliged to contribute their earnings to the family purse but may keep them for their own use. Owing to these differences, Muslim women may inherit but only a proportion in comparison with their brothers, owing to men's perceived greater financial responsibility, which can be extended to supporting a widowed mother or unmarried sisters, for instance (Siraj, 2010). These gendered polarities do not, in principle, suggest a superior-inferior division of labour, merely gendered differences, although women are viewed as subject to the guardianship of male relatives owing to their perceived greater vulnerability. How far such guardianship will be used to control women's autonomy will largely depend on a variety of factors, including culture and education. In more conservative families and communities a woman may be expected to observe *purdah*, in which she will avoid all contact with men beyond a small circle of close male relatives to whom she is legally unable to marry because of consanguinity or marital status (Rehman, 2003). In other words, this would include male relatives such as her father, her brother and a grandfather, although an unmarried cousin would be viewed as a potential marriageable option; and thus some women will be expected to guard their virtue in social interactions with these relatives. The veil, which has been viewed as such a contested symbol in the West as well as many Muslim societies, indicates piety and a form of purdah, while acting as a physical barrier against improper interactions that threaten impropriety (Moghissi, 1999). Accordingly, some Muslim women will don a veil in public or if socialising at home with male visitors not counted as part of her *mahram*. The Moroccan feminist Fatima Mernissi (1975) comments that the veil acts as a patriarchal device in symbolising that a woman is present but nonetheless invisible in the male sphere. That said, wearing the veil has permitted many professional women in countries such as Malaysia to feel they can participate in waged labour with religious integrity intact (Ong, 1995).

The morphology of the family varies widely throughout the Islamic world, where in addition to matrilineal and matrilocality, extended families have been commonplace with several generations living inter-dependently under one roof. However, with the rise of industrialisation and the demise of agrarian, subsistence communities, together with migration, this has led to the development of smaller, nuclear families (Ashencaen Crabtree et al, 2016). Polygamous marriages of up to four wives are accepted in Islam under certain conditions; although where Islamic *Sharia* family law is not legally binding, such as the UK, such marriages are not recognised (Charlsey and Liversage, 2013). The issue of polygamy and some of the dilemmas it raises are considered in Case Study 7.1 and has been associated with marital discord and compromised mental health status in Muslim women (Al-Krenawi et al, 2002; Al-Shamsi and Fulcher, 2005). Yet, de facto polygamy can still occur by undertaking a state-recognised civil marriage to one woman and an Islamic marriage, the *nikah*, to another. The *nikah* is not an anomalous, minority ceremony of small importance in Britain, but a growing trend, including among younger women, where according to a recent survey by *Channel 4*, nearly all Muslim married women participants had gone through this ceremony. Yet almost 61 per cent had not followed this by a recognised civil wedding in the UK. Until recently, this left such women unprotected by legal rights in the event of a relationship breakdown (Sherwood, 2017). However, a recent court hearing has decided that the *nikah* does come within English matrimonial law in reference to divorce (Sherwood, 2018). The implications of this decision are great, not merely in reference to the sharing of matrimonial assets, but in respect of some recognition in British law of faith-based marriage ceremonies. How far this may accommodate other interpretations of traditional *Sharia* family law, previously considered invalid in the UK, has yet to be tested in the light of this ruling. However, the implications are indicative towards noting religious plurality governing the lives of ME individuals; and, secondly, that multicultural societies need to address, if not always accommodate, other religio-cultural frameworks of justice and equity. Yet this is not an uncontroversial position, as we will further explore.

CASE STUDY 7.1

Abdul Zahed has been married under British marriage law for seven years to Lisa, a white British woman who converted to Islam upon marriage. The couple have one daughter. The Zaheds have been trying to have another baby for some time without success. Both have been medically investigated but nothing serious has been detected, although it is true that Lisa has a somewhat irregular menstrual cycle and Abdul a fairly low but not abnormal sperm count. Lisa has now sought advice from her local mosque regarding Abdul's new idea, which is that he takes a second wife, having someone already in mind as a suitable spouse and whom he believes would fit in with their family well. He has earnestly assured Lisa that she will not be replaced in his affections and that in keeping with Islamic principles he will be fair in all his dealings with both wives, but that this is the obvious solution to their fertility problems. The mosque informs Lisa that unless there was a provision to the contrary made in any Islamic marriage contract they drew up, Abdul is completely within his rights according to *Sharia* law, especially as he has promised to treat both wives equally. Her confidante at the mosque advises her to try and accept the situation by making friends with the second wife and look at the matter positively. Lisa has tried to do so but finds herself deeply in conflict in terms of her commitment to Islam and her great dismay at the thought of being in a polygamous union.

Questions

1. How would you describe the different viewpoints being brought to bear in this situation?
2. What concerns might you have as a social worker speaking with a second wife in a polygamous union who seems distressed by her situation?
3. In dealing with service users seeking advice about issues arising from a polygamous union what kind of multidisciplinary assistance within health and social services and the community might you wish to draw on?

Discussion

Polygamous marriages are recognised under *Sharia* (Islamic) family law although they are not specifically recognised under UK law in that a man cannot legally marry two women at the same time. However, the *nikah* ceremony is a common compromise among British Muslims and this is presumably what Abdul means when he talks about taking an additional wife. It would be an error to think that all Muslim women are complacent towards polygamy, many are not and would not agree to this idea, and many Muslim men would not consider it either. Lisa, as a convert to Islam, will not have grown up with such expectations, even though theoretically this scenario could have occurred, as is now proposed. Abdul's reassurances are in line with Islamic expectations of equal treatment of all wives by husbands; however, this does not take into account the emotional and psychological aspects polygamy can bring, nor here the reasoning offered for the suggestion, which again is not an uncommon excuse. Issues surrounding religious orthodoxies, tacit negotiation of marriage by couples and changing marital expectations over time are all to be considered here, along with assumed gender norms and differing cultural values and beliefs. Not forgetting the emotional fallout hinted at in Case Study 7.2 relating to possible feelings of frustration, rejection, abandonment, potential humiliation and social stigma that will require very sensitive help.

In relation to socio-cultural and religious norms prescribing social relations, duties of care and welfare, as well as those dictating gender conventions, may carry a high profile in some ME communities. However, these are values and associated conduct that do not stand apart in a social vacuum. Instead these need to be read against the larger text of dominant society projecting prevailing social values, which may complement or contradict minority group perspectives. Such is the position of ME Muslim communities living in the UK. Negotiating different value systems in daily life, which is the experience of many ME people, can be meaningful, exciting, liberating, disorientating, disempowering or threatening at times. Clearly it can also create tension and conflict; although for wider society socio-religo-cultural diversity adds immensely to the richness of social experiences, as well as to the development of more tolerant and nuanced civic and political democratic spaces.

Encountering new philosophies, people and ways of being attracts curiosity (as well as hostility), with the natural result that some people will convert to other faiths. The rates of conversion to Islam in Britain are debatable, but it is known that thousands of people convert every year. Indeed, Al-Krenawi (2012) notes that Islam is the second largest religion in Europe and one of the fastest growing globally. One estimate, using the Scottish Census 2001, gives the approximate figure of 60,669 converts overall, where white Britons make up a slender majority (Brice, 2010). It has also been noted that many offenders convert to Islam in prison, which is a time of crisis that is personally and existentially testing (Ashencaen Crabtree et al, 2016). The sense of brotherhood (this appears to be a predominantly male phenomenon), along with the routines and conditions the faithful observe daily, may provide structure and meaning to otherwise chaotic, constrained and wretched life circumstances.

While Muslim men are free to marry beyond the faith to women of 'the Book' – referring to the sacred texts of Judaism and Christianity (and thus such women who are not obliged to convert, unlike other faiths), Muslim women are generally expected to marry within the faith, commensurate with the patriarchal view of women as important transmitters of cultural norms and beliefs (Ashencaen Crabtree and Husain, 2012). Raising children to practise the faith is considered a duty of Muslim motherhood (Ashencaen Crabtree et al, 2016), while less benignly the cultural weight of embodying values and belief systems falls unfairly on the shoulders of women – not dissimilar in fact to the dichotomy of shame and honour implicating women rather than men in patriarchal Catholic Latin cultures (Scheper Hughes, 1992). It would appear that this assumption that women are responsible for religious purity for the community continues, where evidence from the multicultural and migratory haven of Canada is that Muslim women are the least likely to marry outside of their faith compared to all other religious groups (Cila and Lalonde, 2014). This can carry drawbacks, however, in terms of social integration issues and the pressure to conform to norms and values that may not always be shared in wider society, such as in the case of Lisa Zahed (Case Study 7.1), leading to family conflict and individual distress.

Sexuality and gender

An assumed trajectory of human life, as viewed in the West, is that transitions in childhood to youth will lead to an exploration of sexuality and gender (Kumar Kar et al, 2015). Arguably, this is an increasingly prevalent area of preoccupation for many, mostly young, adults, where the traditional categories of gender have been challenged and subject to many variations, reclassifications, subdivisions and fluid morphologies. This is in keeping with contemporary, tribal identity politics – the unique characteristic of the 21st century (Fukuyama, 2018).

The general Muslim community in the UK has so far kept largely aloof from such debates, although it should be said that opprobrium is attached to sexuality that deviates from a heteronormative position as against Islamic principles. Indeed the recent BBC (2018) report on the public caning of two women in Malaysia caught in lesbian acts (and the persecution and even execution of gay men in the Muslim world) indicates high levels of intolerance. Many otherwise gay/lesbian Muslims across the world will be expected to make their peace with the social pressures to conform to a heterosexual destiny, as was typically the case in Western society until comparatively recently. In the UK, such extreme retribution is obviously illegal, yet adopting a gay identity as a Muslim is nonetheless fraught and hazardous. Defying family and community expectations in this way may bring down serious consequences on the head of individuals with possibly lifelong repercussions, including social rejection and potentially violence. Such scenarios directly concern social workers who may find themselves having to deal with domestic violence incidents, while attempting to negotiate across unfamiliar cultural terrain in addition to safeguarding those in danger.

REFLECTION POINT 7.2

What kinds of issues or hazards may social workers need to think about when working with domestic violence and unfamiliar minority ethnic communities?

We have mentioned marital alliances between families, which serve to create strong bonds of intermeshed relations that in optimum circumstances are highly supportive and protective of group members, including the newly married couple. For this reason, as well as the advantage of retaining wealth within the family, first cousin marriages have been very popular among many Middle Eastern and Asian Muslim families in serving to bind the extended family still closer (Ashencaen Crabtree et al, 2016). However, such alliances, if linked to a public façade of family standing and honour, and especially when not initiated and brokered by the couple themselves, have the potential to create highly coercive and abusive situations, as exemplified by the case study of Fawzia (Case Study 7.2). Marital arrangements may otherwise be brokered as 'assisted' alliances, where young people are brought together socially by their families or an interested other party, with a view to assessing their compatibility for marriage. Other couples may be expected to entrust the entire matter to senior family members to organise and may find themselves only meeting for the first time on their wedding day. Notoriously, some young British girls/women have been forced or tricked by their families into going abroad for apparently innocent reasons, only to find themselves marooned in a foreign country forced by coercion to marry a man that unbeknowingly they were promised to (Summers, 2018).

CASE STUDY 7.2: THE ENFORCED MARRIAGE

Fawzia, a 20-year-old university student, has returned home for the vacations. Her sibling has warned her parents that Fawzia was seen writing an intimate text to her girlfriend. Fawzia's parents confront her angrily with this information where she feels obliged to tell them she is a lesbian and is in love with another female student. This revelation results in a tremendous row where her siblings side with her parents in their disgust and condemnation. Fawzia is hit and then confined to the parental home while her phone, passport, cash and bank cards are confiscated. A few days later her parents inform her that they have arranged a rapid marriage for her with a male cousin back in their home country and that if she does not agree to this then her family will have no choice but to promptly disown her owing to the disgrace she is bringing upon them. Fawzia is very distressed by the situation, but knowing that all her close female relatives have undergone arranged marriages feels helpless to resist effectively against such united and powerful family pressure.

Questions
1. What are the immediate priorities for Fawzia in this situation?
2. What advice could be offered to Fawzia about her rights?
3. What do you think the implications would be if she decides to go against the arranged marriage?
4. What help might be available to Fawzia?

Discussion

Islam is often viewed as a faith that is not tolerant towards sexual diversity, although naturally this view is open to contestation and challenge, as well as family diversity of what is accepted or otherwise. Nonetheless, the evidence shows that not only are enforced marriages a concern in the UK but that gay and lesbian lifestyles can be viewed as deviant requiring family and social control of individuals (Ashencaen Crabtree et al, 2016). Girls and women as family assets to be disposed of without much concern for their views is not endorsed by Islam, but can be enacted as a cultural norm underpinning collective family honour, in which alliances with other families through marriage are highly prized over the individual's wishes. Here, Fawzia's apparent 'deviancy' legitimates in the eyes of her family their right to impose a fate upon her that would redeem her within the family and her community. In so doing, however, they reject her right to autonomy as it is viewed within UK law and socio-cultural conventions.

The question of family honour and the jeopardy of potentially losing 'face' to the surrounding community (as seen in Case Study 7.2) should not be underestimated. To contextualise this matter we need to adopt an historical, less ethnocentric perspective; the post-war culture has shifted away from collective responsibility and the value of conventionality towards increasing individualism, such as typically found in the US and the UK. This change, strongly supported by neo–liberal politics in the UK, has been viewed as emancipatory in many positive ways for individuals who felt otherwise on the margins of society. However, taken too far, individualism can also be destructive to community cohesion, which in turn beneficially influences individual well–being and a sense of shared purpose (Putnam, 2001). It is perhaps no coincidence that while the politics of individualism is at its zenith in the UK, so too is depression and anxiety among those most likely to be exposed to it – young people (Centre for Longitudinal Studies, 2017). Jordan Peterson (2018), like Robert Putnam, another North American public intellectual, speaks of meaningfulness as connected to taking responsibility for one's life, which is argued to be the central tenet of human life, rather than the pursuit of happiness (or its antithesis, the attraction of nihilism). This is not a new idea: logocentricism (logos = meaning) has been around for quite a while. Peterson (2018) argues that pursuing the meaningful good rather than egocentric hedonism helps the individual as a vital entity that contributes to the social weald (societal good). Such arguments can be secular, but certainly this also comfortably resonates with many religious positions: social good has often been tied to religion; and faith-based organisations have historically often been immersed in social welfare initiatives (Prochaska, 2006).

By contrast, many ME communities retain a strong sense of shared and communal values, along with clear demarcations of the boundaries of human conduct contained within the ecology of family and community. Dominant norms and values are bolstered by community engagement in rituals (the Friday mosque, Sunday Church, synagogue on the Shabbat, come to mind), along with guidelines on appearance, behaviour and ritualised food consumption: religious food taboos (such as avoiding pork etc.) or fish on Friday for observant Christians, for example.

Ritual and sacred purity, and the division between that and the unclean, has been viewed as a very important consideration for many communities (one may consider halal and kosher food for Muslims and Jews respectively), while purity of thought may also be highly valued. These aspects serve to shape community expectations and behaviour, although purity distinctions can also be found in individualism such as the rise of veganism for instance. Individualism has been formed through the fracturing of a belief in collective norms, and in its more extreme manifestations is viewed as forms of tribalism (Fukuyama, 2018) as typified in atomised identity politics. Consider the current notion of 'safe spaces' in universities with proponents arguing against open debating forums, once a common feature of university life, where one might well be exposed to views sometimes earnestly disagreed with. The notion of a right to a 'safe space' in this sense relates directly to the concern for bounded purity dictated by what the 'tribe' in question considers acceptable (good, right, permitted/included) – or otherwise unacceptable (wrong, bad, rejected/excluded). Whether such rigid boundaries serve students and wider society well is highly debatable (see the interesting BBC Radio 4 podcast 'Morality in the 21st century' for a fuller investigation of these ideas).

Evidently then, levels of inclusivity as well as insularity can be found in both communal and individualistic groups. The danger for the individual comes from coercion and abuse, which again is found across both groups by forcing individuals to conform or to be ritualistically rejected or expunged. Two terms of great significance to Muslims help us to draw out some of the implications of protection versus coercion. *Ishan* refers to enacting one's inner religious conviction through actions of social responsibility and care towards other – applicable concepts to the family, the tribe or wider community, which governs interpersonal relations. *Izzat* refers to respect again, but also to honour. Both terms are applicable at the smaller or larger ecological levels, but are usually applied in relation to the family. That which threatens a family's *izzat* exposes them to family dishonour and public vulnerability. Retribution by the family may be visited upon the individual who has shamed it. This family reaction of rejection is often thought to wipe the publicly exposed stain out. Honour-based violence (HBV) is predicated upon such thinking (as in the case of Fawzia in Case Study 7.2), where there have been a number of notorious court cases brought to justice in relation to this crime, such as the torture and murder of Banaz Mahmod, a young British Kurdish woman, by male relatives (for more information see the documentary 'Banaz, a love story' at http://watchdocumentaries.com/banaz-a-love-story/). While the police involved at that time pursued this case across international borders with great tenacity, the UK police force in general have been accused of failing to refer more than 5 per cent of HBV crimes to the Crown Prosecution Service (Summers, 2017). HBV is also implicated in hostile responses to perceived illicit sexuality connected to LGBT issues and indeed to other behaviours associated with improper interactions, otherwise known as *zina*, between males and females, beyond the guardianship of the *mahram* (Ashencaen Crabtree et al, 2016).

Expanding knowledge and applying it

Topics surrounding difference and diversity have dominated social work for many years, yet these have often focused on specific areas, such as 'race'/ethnicity, gender and sexuality – all very important topics, but where the issue of faith was largely excluded with a few exceptions. This was an interesting omission in the social work literature given that religion was the foundation and cornerstone of early social work (Prochaska, 2006). Increasing secularisation of the new profession encouraged a split from social work's faith-based roots, along with an increasing disdain for religion as social work professionalised in a sociological sense. An untested assumption framed religion in the West as equated to Christianity, which was in turn viewed as responsible for the oppression of others (Parker et al, 2018). Such bigotry in its antagonism towards Christianity tended to marginalise many social workers, among whom could be found practitioners from non–white ethnic groups. Yet, while Christianity was being cold-shouldered in social work, this was not overly compensated for by genuine interest in other religions. Thus a paradox was created whereby social work appeared interested in ethnic diversity and marginalised ME groups but not specifically in the religo-cultural beliefs that shaped and nurtured such groups (Ashencaen Crabtree et al, 2008).

Fortunately, however, there has been a renewed interest in religion and social work after years of secular marginalisation in the profession concerning this very important human domain (Parker et al, 2018; Crisp, 2017; Furness and Gilligan, 2010). Yet, it would be true to say that it has only been in the recent past that the research canon has embraced Islamic perspectives on social work. Writing from the US, Hodge (2005) began to offer the first tentative papers on this area, following from one of the earliest papers on the topic by Ashencaen Crabtree and Baba (2001) examining social work education in Malaysia; although prior to this there had of course been research work on aspects of psychosocial, health issues and community issues in relation to Muslims globally. In 2008, Ashencaen Crabtree et al produced the first comprehensive social work text on Islamic perspectives, with a second edition following in 2016. Since these earlier years it has been gratifying to see that there have been additional valuable contributions covering a wide area of practice, including social work, Islam and human rights (Al-Krenawi, 2012), the UK Muslim service user experience (Warden et al, 2016), social work implications for counter-terrorism and Muslim families (Guru, 2012), Islamophobia and social work considerations (Beck et al, 2017), feminism in Islam (Yamani, 1996), ageing and Islam (Ashencaen Crabtree, 2014) and Islamophobia (Ashencaen Crabtree, 2014) – along with a host of other interesting papers referring to intercultural marriage and social work (Al-Krenawi and Jackson, 2014), mental health services and Muslim women (Pilkington et al, 2015), and disability and gender in the Middle East (Abu-Habib, 2007). The best place for the interested reader to begin sourcing research material on social work and Islam/Muslims is to search online journal databases and to study the reference list of specific books on such subjects.

How best then should one apply the knowledge gained? Clearly, while reading widely around a topic, such as faith, this will greatly increase your understanding and appreciation of it, but this will not necessarily make you into a culturally competent expert of social work practice with Muslim service uses. Yet, having a good understanding of the rich diversity of the Muslim world, as found not only globally but within your own community or nation, shows interest and respect (Ashencaen Crabtree and Parker, 2014; Ashencaen Crabtree, 2017a, 2017b).

Thankfully such defamatory political antics will of course not tarnish the reputation of any but the very rarest social work practitioner, yet the point is made. Ensuring that you know as much as you can about the lives and socio-religio-ecological context behind the casework file will pay dividends, as will noting the usual social work caveat of avoiding assumptions, and finally showing interest and humility in your dealings with service users and their families. In my experience, as a former social worker practitioner working with Muslim client groups, most Muslim service users will be more than happy to help to educate you about what is meaningful to them – and usually with generosity and graciousness. There will be, as in my case, many a faux pas made along the way while a steep learning curve will rise ahead when working with family conflicts, different norms and assumptions regarding gender, childrearing, disability, sickness and ageing, but courtesy and a genuine interest to hear what others have to teach us can usually pave the way. Social workers have an ethical duty to adhere to and legal obligations to observe, so that a relativistic position of different cultures, different mores can only take us so far. Practices deemed harmful by law, remain unacceptable and can be lawfully punished, but meeting unfamiliar situations with an open mind, heart and hand leads to trust and better working relationships.

What else can be gained from acquiring and using such knowledge? Knowing better how a faith influences and shapes the social and spiritual existence of people not only will also deepen your awareness of communities and particular religious principles, but also help you appreciate the vital relevance religion holds for the majority of people in the world. The assumption that in the West we live in an increasingly secular age is not necessarily so; forms of faith change over time and adapt to new ways of seeing the world and new ideas although admittedly many devotees might state that the Holy Qur'an, the Bible and the Torah are guides for life that stand for all time, being immutable – although this again is a view decidedly not shared by all.

Furthermore, while there are those who do not express an allegiance to a specific religion this does not imply that the spiritual domain of human existence has no relevance to these individuals, for the most profound existential difficulties that all conscious humans must confront in their lives are fundamentally embedded in religious thinking (Peterson, 2018). What is the meaning of life? Is death the end of existence? What is human life worth? How should one behave to other people, probably other living creatures, maybe also the earth? Are there really such forces in the universe as good and evil? These questions are fundamental areas of religious and spiritual inquiry that people have grappled with since the beginning of human consciousness. Those questions remain as relevant to people living today as they did 20,000 years ago and possibly well before that.

Conclusion

In conclusion, faith and religion intrinsically focus on the value of human life, even though suffering is rife, problems abound, illness is a universal experience and death awaits us all – these aspects do not diminish human life as faith and spirituality affirm. Islam provides one of the great pathways to a meaningful life and ultimately human transcendence – as do all the other recognised faiths that readers will have heard of. Faith itself is not usually the problem in the lives of people we encounter but (mis)interpretations of it can be, as for instance, Islamist extremism demonstrates. It is those attitudes, whether culturally grounded or not, that regards other people as objects and possessions to be manipulated or commodified, such as underpins HBV, for example (or even totalitarian politics), that are decidedly harmful.

How to work with skill and compassion across diverse groups of people will challenge the abilities of any practitioner (although therein lies the professional excitement that will keeps one keen and alert). A thirst for knowledge, its application used with care and humility and a sincere willingness to keep on learning, is the greatest gift any practitioner can offer another person and the profession.

Reflective questions

1 How might your own beliefs have an impact on working with diverse communities?

2 What kinds of personal and professional qualities do you feel are important to beginning social work practice with unfamiliar minority ethnic or faith communities?

3 How far do you think any political discourses you can identify taking place in today's society affect the perception of minority ethnic communities?

Further reading

• Ashencaen Crabtree, S., Husain, F. and Spalek, B. (2016) *Islam and Social Work: Islam and Social Work: Culturally Sensitive Practice in a Diverse World* (2nd edn). Bristol: Policy Press. This unique book offers readers a thorough introduction to Islamic philosophies, beliefs and worldviews in relation to a discussion of related social work issues.

• Furness, S. and Gilligan, P. (2010) *Religion, Belief and Social Work: Making a Difference.* Bristol: Policy Press. A valuable book that considers the interface of social work with religion, exploring this in connection with commonly known faith communities.

• Laird, S. (2008) *Anti-Oppressive Social Work: A Guide for Developing Cultural Competence.* London: Sage. An important text that assists social worker to understand what is cultural competence and how this relates to core social work values.

References

Abu-Habib, L. (ed.) (2007) *Gender and Disability: Women's experiences in the Middle East.* Oxford: Oxfam Publication.

Afshar, H., Aitken, R. and Franks, M. (2005) Feminisms, Islamophobia and identities, *Political Studies*, 53(2): 262–283.

Al-Krenawi, A. and Jackson, S.O. (2014) Arab American marriage: Culture, tradition, religion and the social worker, *Journal of Human Behavior in the Social Environment*, 24(2): 115–137.

Al-Krenawi, A. (2012) Islam, human rights and social work in a changing world. In: S. Ashencaen Crabtree, J. Parker and A. Azman (eds), *The Cup, The Gun and the Crescent: Social Welfare and Civil Unrest in Muslim Societies*. London: Whiting & Birch, pp 19–33.

Al-Krenawi, A., Graham, J.R. and Slonim-Nevo, V. (2002) Mental health aspects of Arab-Israeli adolescents from polygamous versus monogamous families, *Journal of Social Psychology*, 142(4): 446–460.

Al-Shamsi, M.S.A. and Fulcher, L.C. (2005) The impact of polygamy on United Arab Emirates' first wives and their children, *International Journal of Child and Family Welfare*, 8(1): 46–55.

Ashencaen Crabtree, S. (2014) Islamophobia and the Manichean constructions of the 'Other': A contemporary European problem. In S. Ashencaen Crabtree, (ed.), *Diversity and the Processes of Marginalisation and Otherness: Giving Voices to Hidden Themes. A European Perspective*. London: Whiting & Birch.

Ashencaen Crabtree, S. (2017a) Problematizing the context and construction of vulnerability and risk in relation to British Muslim ME groups, *Journal of Religion and Spirituality in Social Work*. Available from: doi/abs/10.1080/1542 6432.2017.1300080

Ashencaen Crabtree, S. (2017b) Social work with Muslim communities: treading a critical path over the crescent moon. In Beth Crisp (ed) *Routledge Handbook of Religion, Spirituality and Social Work*. Routledge, pp 118–127.

Ashencaen Crabtree, S. and Baba, I. (2001) The Islamic perspective in social work education. *Social Work Education*, 20(4): 469–481.

Ashencaen Crabtree, S. and Husain, F. (2012) Within, without: Dialogical perspectives on feminism and Islam, *Religion and Gender*, 2(1): 128–149.

Ashencaen Crabtree, S. and Parker, J. (2014) Religion, Islam and active ageing. In M.L. Gómez Jiménez and J. Parker (eds), *Active Ageing? Perspectives from Europe on a Much Vaunted Topic*. London: Whiting & Birch.

Ashencaen Crabtree, S., Husain, F. and Spalek, B. (2008) *Islam and Social Work: Debating Values and Transforming Practice*. Bristol: Policy Press.

Ashencaen Crabtree, S., Husain, F. and Spalek, B. (2016) *Islam and Social Work: Culturally Sensitive Practice in a Diverse World* (2nd edn). Bristol: Policy Press.

BBC (2018) LGBT Rights: Malaysia women caned for attempting to have lesbian sex. Available from: https://www.bbc.co.uk/news/world–asia–45395086

Beck, E., Moon, I.-A., Ferdoos, A.B. and Wahab, S. (2017) Undoing Islamophobia: Awareness of Orientalism in social work, *Journal of Progressive Human Services*, 38(2): 58–72.

Becket, C. and Taylor, H. (2016) *Human Growth and Development*. London: Sage.

Brice, M.A.K. (2010) *A Minority Within A Minority: A Report on Converts to Islam in the United Kingdom*. Report on Behalf of Faith Matters. Swansea University.

Centre for Longitudinal Studies (2017) *One in Four Girls is Depressed by Age Fourteen*. University College London. Available from: http://www.cls.ioe.ac.uk/news.aspx?itemid=4646anditemTitle=One+in+four+girls+is+depressed+at+age+14%2c+new+study+revealsandsitesectionid=27andsitesectiontitle=News andreturnlink=news.aspx%3fsitesectionid%3d27%26sitesectiontitle%3dNews

Charlsey, K. and Liversage, A. (2013) Transforming polygamy, migration, transcultural multiple marriages in Muslim minorities, *Global Networks*, 13(1): 60–78.

Cila, J. and Lalonde, R.N. (2014) Personal openness towards interfaith dating and marriage among Muslim young adults: the role of religiosity, cultural identity, and family connectedness, *Group Processes and Intergroup Relations*, 17(3): 357–370.

Crisp, B. (2017) Religion and spirituality in social work: creating an international dialogue. In B. Crisp (ed) *The Routledge Handbook of Religion, Spirituality and Social Work*. Oxon: Routledge, pp 1–3.

Finch, J. (2007) Displaying families, *Sociology*, 4(1): 65–81.

Fukuyama, F. (2018) Against identity politics: The new tribalism and the crisis of democracy, *Foreign Affairs*, 1 September: 90–114.

Furness, S. and Gilligan, P. (2010) *Religion, Belief and Social Work*. Bristol: Policy Press.

Grosfoguel, R. and Mielants, E. (2006) The long-durée entanglement between Islamophobia and racism in the modern/colonial capitalist/patriarchal world-system: an introduction, *Human Architecture: Journal of the Sociology of Self-Knowledge*, 5(1): 1–12.

Guru, S. (2012) Under siege: Families of counter-terrorism, *British Journal of Social Work*, 42(6): 1152–1173.

Haw, K.F., Shah, S. and Hanifa, M. (1998) *Educating Muslim Girls: Shifting Discourses*. Buckingham: Open University Press.

Hodge, D.R. (2005) Social work and the house of Islam: orientating practitioners to the beliefs and values of Muslims in the United States, *Social Work*, 50(2): 162–173.

Kumar Kar, S., Choudhury, A. and Pratap Singh, A. (2015) Understanding normal development of adolescent sexuality: A bumpy ride, *Journal of Human Reprodcutive Science*, 8(2): 70–74.

MCB (Muslim Council of Britain) (2015) *British Muslims in Numbers: A Demographic, Socio-Economic and Health Profile of Muslims in Britain Drawing on the 2011 Census*. London: Muslim Council of Britain. Available from: https://www.mcb.org.uk/wp-content/uploads/2015/02/MCBCensusReport_2015.pdf

Ong, A. (1995) State versus Islam: Malay families, women's bodies and the body politic in Malaysia. In A. Ong and M.G. Peletz (eds) *Bewitching Women, Pious Men: Gender and Body Politics in Southeast Asia*, Berkeley, CA: University of California, pp 159–194.

Parker, J., Ashencaen Crabtree, S., Reeks, E., Marsh, D. and Vasif, C. (2018) River! that in silence windest: The place of religion and spirituality in social work assessment: sociological reflections and practical implications. In C. Spatscheck, S. Ashencaen Crabtree and J. Parker (eds), *Methods and Methodologies of Social Work: Reflecting Professional Intervention*. Erasmus SocNet (Vol. III). London: Whiting & Birch.

Peterson, J. (2018) *12 Rules for Life: An Antidote to Chaos*. UK/USA: Allen Lane/ Penguin.

Pilkington, A., Msetfi, R.M. and Watson, R. (2015) Factors affecting intention to access psychological services amongst British Muslims of South Asian origin, *Mental Health, Religion and Culture*, 15(1): 1–22.

Prochaska, F. (2006) *Christianity and Social Services in Modern Britain*. Oxford: Oxford University Press.

Putnam, R. (2001) *Bowling Alone*. New York: Simon & Schuster Ltd.

Mernissi, F. (1975) *Beyond the Veil*. Cambridge, MA: Schenkman Publishing Company.

Moghissi, H. (1999) *Feminism and Islamic Fundamentalism*. London: Zed Books.

Rehman, T.F. (2003) Women who choose Islam: Issues, changes, and challenges in providing ethnic-diverse practice, *International Journal of Mental Health*, 32(3): 31–49.

Scheper Hughes, N. (1992) *Death Without Weeping: The Violence of Everyday Life in Brazil*. Berkeley: University of California Press.

Sherwood, H. (2017) Most women in UK who have Islamic wedding miss out on legal rights, *The Guardian*, 20 November. Available from: https://www.theguardian.com/world/2017/nov/20/women-uk-islamic-wedding-legal-rights-civil-ceremony-marriage

Sherwood, H. (2018) English law applies in Islamic marriage, judge rules in divorce case. *The Guardian*, 1 August. Available from: https://www.theguardian.com/law/2018/aug/01/english-law-applies-to-islamic-marriage-judge-rules-in-divorce-case

Siraj, A. (2010) Because I'm the man! I'm the head: British married Muslims and the patriarchal family structure, *Contemporary Islam*, 4(2): 195–214.

Stang Dahl, T. (1997) *The Muslim Family: A Study of Women's Rights in Islam*. Oxford/Oslo: Scandinavian University Press.

Summers, H. (2017) Only 5% of 'honour' crimes reported to CPS. *The Guardian*. Available from: https://www.theguardian.com/society/2017/nov/07/only-5-of-honour-crimes-reported-to-police-are-referred-to-cps

Summers, H. (2018) Woman jailed for duping daughter into forced marriage. *The Guardian*, 23 May. Available from: https://www.theguardian.com/uk-news/2018/may/23/birmingham-woman-jailed-duping-daughter-forced-marriage

Warden, R., Scourfield, J. and Huxley, P. (2016) Islamic social work in the UK: the service user experience, *British Journal of Social Work*, 47(3): 737–754.

Yamani, M. (1996) Introduction. In M. Yamani (ed.) *Feminism and Islam*, New York: New York University Press, pp 1–29.

8

Education and learning in adults: implications for social work

Maggie Hutchings

Introduction

The place and function of education and learning in adults in the context of social work opens a space for a critically informed debate concerning the concepts and purposes of this and related concepts and enactments of continuing education and lifelong learning as relevant to the profession. This chapter will discuss the concepts, theories and models associated with adult education and learning throughout the life course examining the phenomena through social, cultural and politico-economic lenses. The aim is to inform a deeper understanding of the value, strengths and challenges for adult education and learning situated within the complexity of contemporary society and in the light of changes to social work education.

Chapter objectives

- examine the place, form and function that education and learning for adults plays in contemporary social work and society at large;

- distinguish contributions from key thinkers and theorists to our understanding of the strengths and challenges for education and learning in adults;

- identify the essence of learning as a fundamentally social process, recognising how this informs any consideration of adult education policy and provision;

- consider the tensions and challenges to democracy and citizenship where critical liberal approaches to social work education and general adult learning are eroded in favour of technical rational approaches.

Background and context

The history and development of adult education and learning policies and practices, whether enacted within or outside formal post compulsory education provision, distinguishes it from compulsory education for children and young adults. The 1996 UNESCO report of the International Commission on Education for the Twenty-first Century (Delors et al, 1996), concentrated on post-school learning, largely situated in educational institutions, colleges and universities. By contrast, *The Learning through Life* report (Schuller and Watson, 2009), an independent inquiry into the future of lifelong learning in the UK, focused on adults learning at work and in the community (Schuller and Watson, 2015), which in turn resonates with recent social work education trends. These two reports suggest a clear distinction between the *formal* post-compulsory education system and *non-formal* adult education provision aligned more closely with the concept and practice of *lifelong learning*; both of which carry implications for social work in terms of qualifications to practice and pursuing greater expertise as a practitioner.

These two seemingly straightforward policy-focused divisions, conceptualised according to the distinct locus of activity, belie the reality of a far more complex web of relationships affecting the positioning, form and function of adult education and learning, strongly influenced by economic and social factors in contemporary society. These latter factors have always been at the forefront of thinking in social work. We may think here of how the first formalised 'social work' body in the UK, the Charitable Organisation Society, 1869, was established, with a remit to investigate cases of need and support the self-sufficiency capacities of recipients of charity. Today, government focus on the need to rapidly and inexpensively produce qualified social work staff trained in workplace settings can also be viewed as driven by social and economic need.

Returning to policy divisions, this foregrounds debates concerning the importance of appreciating the distinctions and relationships between *education* and *learning*, *liberal* and *vocational* education traditions, and promoting *training* over *education*, towards the most significant question of what functions adult education and learning serve in contemporary society.

REFLECTION POINT 8.1

Think about your own route to qualified social work status. What do you think may be lost or gained through the various choices open to pre-qualified individuals – for example, gaining an honours degree in social work or having a degree in another topic and thinking about work-based training routes like Step-Up, Frontline, Think Ahead, or undertaking an MA in social work? Which did you choose and why?

Key thinkers in adult education

Distinguishing shifts from education to learning in adults

While social work's own educational journey has followed a number of convoluted, evolving paths influencing practice today, it is worth seeing this in a wider policy context of attitudes towards education. Jarvis's (2014) account of the development and changes in the education of adults and adult learning provides a valuable synopsis of the field. Jarvis states that 'education is fundamentally an institutional phenomenon offering learning opportunities to people throughout their lives' (2014, p 52). The institutional systems associated with childhood and youth, represented by the compulsory education period in schools and colleges (raised in the UK from 16 to 17 in 2013 and again in 2015 from 17 to 18), are complemented by other forms of provision such as further and higher education institutions offering academic and vocational courses and the growing number of private providers offering apprenticeships and training courses. Indeed, apprenticeships in social work are now also being added to a mix of qualifying routes open to individuals that are moving towards a more instrumental approach to learning.

It is in the more diverse relationships of adulthood with education that the shift to learning becomes more prominent or perhaps a more convenient placeholder in contemporary neo-liberal society. The shift in conceptualising adult education as *lifelong learning* occurred when it was recognised that a large amount of *vocational learning* was taking place in the *workplace* and 'education' was no longer regarded as 'significant as the term "learning"' (Jarvis, 2014, p 52). Billett (2010) criticises this shift manifest in the *Learning Through Life* 2009 report, which identified the field of adult education as *provisions* 'for, across and beyond working life'. Billett's contention is that these provisions narrowly position *learning* as primarily something that arises through individuals' participation in educational provisions, conceived as 'courses, courses and more courses' (2010, p 410); the multitude of *continuing professional development* (CPD) courses open to qualified practitioners might testify to this.

So why is the distinction between education and learning so significant? Is it that adults learn differently when compared with children? Or, is it that the needs and expectations of individuals and society change over the life course? And, if this is the case, how and in what ways are these individual and societal needs and expectations conceived and enacted? Defining and understanding learning is an essential prerequisite for situating arguments about the form and function of adult education. Peters's (1973) interpretation of education as distinct from learning is helpful here. Education is defined as consisting of three facets, that it is situated 'in schools and universities', focused on 'an organised sequence of learning experiences called the curriculum', with the aim of achieving 'the development of knowledge and understanding' (Peters, 1973, p 5).

Learning, by contrast, can take place outside formal education. Peters's interpretation allows us to distinguish experiences of learning from experiences of formal education and to consider opportunities for learning in different situations both within and outside formal education. This has enormous implications for social work where there has been strong critique by social work academics regarding the 'watering down' of content (Parker, 2019). This has taken place recently, partly through a highly restrictive, standardised social work curriculum that has removed content not seen as directly relevant to direct practice. Government attempts to reduce a more expansive social work education in preference to heavier weighting towards the more instrumental vocational training concept can find some unlikely allies in those promoting evidence-based learning in social work, with its argument that only what is seen to work need to be learned. This might seem valid were it possible to use specific tools and processes on homogeneous, non-differentiated groups or similar disposition and behaviour, but given issues of huge social diversity, such claims are suspect. What may be lost as well as gained through technical, instrumental training programmes precisely requires the discipline of critical thinking promoted by engagement with deeper pedagogy in order to evaluate its relevance and appropriateness.

CASE STUDY 8.1

Jilly has just finished her BA degree in sociology and social policy and is potentially interested in following a social work career. Her cousin, Amy, works in adult social care already would like to become a qualified social worker owing to better career prospects and pay. At a family reunion they discuss their various plans with their aunt, Helen, a retired social worker. Helen tells them about when she was a student at the London School of Economics (LSE) studying for her Certificate of Qualification in Social Work (CQSW) and describes some of her more memorable times at LSE, which pioneered social work education in the UK. Helen recalls that her classes were very varied according to the interests of lecturers with teaching covering a lot of different subjects, including social policy, child development, working with offenders along with all kinds of sociological and psychological theories. Interested in counselling therapy and psychodynamics, which she learned about at the LSE, Helen later went on to do some work at times with the famous Tavistock Institution, a charity that works within a psychoanalytical tradition, as part of her social work role. Jilly says she would like to do this kind of work herself as it sounds so interesting but says that she doesn't think that they offer the same level kind of courses that Helen studied and from her search it seems most social work courses are similar across the country. She says she would also choose to work in mental health but from what she's discovered it seems more focused on safeguarding and risk management than counselling therapy. Fortunately, though at least she is familiar with some of the social science theories from her degree that Helen talks about. Jilly feels that this wider knowledge might help to make her a better social worker. Amy listening in comments it's best to take a practical point of view to education.

She thinks the best thing is to get trained up in the workplace quickly, because at least you still get a salary and are learning about things that your employers want from you, instead of getting frustrated that the things you'd like to learn about or do are not really expected of social work students and practitioners now.

Questions

1. How would you describe the different attitudes portrayed by Jilly, Helen and Amy towards social work education and practice?
2. Do you think there is any difference between the concepts of education and training? If so, what might they be?
3. Do you agree with Amy that it is best to accommodate yourself to employers' expectations of what the social work job entails in today's society?
4. What are the advantages and disadvantages in the different positions taken by the three women?

Discussion

As the preface to this volume indicates there have been many challenging changes that social work has had to adjust to over the decades, most of which have been brought about by government interference in social work services and policies, as well as the education of new generations of social workers. Qualifications have changed over time from the old CQSW, to the updated Diploma in Social Work, to BA Social Work programmes, to workplace training and apprenticeships. If these trends appear to chart an evolution, although that is questionable, condensed workplace training programmes adds a different complexion to education. Employer input into the development of curricula has become commonplace owing to these changes, to the extent that employers have even been involved in the recruitment of social work academics to university positions. This raises many questions for the profession, its practitioners, service users and wider society. This case study touches on a number of such points including practice role restrictions over time, education as opposed to practical training. Readers are also invited to explore who should decide on how social workers should be trained and for what social purpose?

Illeris (2003) argues that learning is not driven by curricula but by skills development and perceived social function and value, something we can identify in our discussion of social work education/training. Illeris (2003, p 170) defines learning as 'all processes that lead to relatively lasting changes in capacity, whether they be of a motor, cognitive, psychodynamic (i.e. emotional, motivational or attitudinal) or social character, and which are not due to genetic-biological maturation'. Thus we can see how educational reinforcement of social work principles and values, a key one being anti-oppressive practice, can become internalised by students over time through the change that is needed to undertake a new social identity, that of the qualified social worker. While this position emphasises 'the *internal psychological process* of acquisition and elaboration, in which new impulses are connected with the results of prior learning', Illeris also acknowledges 'the *external interaction process*' between the learner and environment (2003, p 396). For social work students the external stimuli can clearly come from many sources, including personal experiences, practice placements, connecting perceived social conditions to theoretical knowledge (see also Chapters 1 and 2). Similarly, Jarvis defines learning as a process whereby individuals acquire knowledge and skills (and much more besides) from different sources, 'either intentionally or not' (2014, p 52).

The question of intentionality is key here as is the relationship between the individual and their social context. Bagnall suggests Jarvis's conceptualisation of the lifelong learner provides a view of learning as 'an unavoidable (essential) human property' (Bagnall, 2017, p 62).

While learning may be considered an essentially individual process it is inextricably bound up in relationships with the social order and those relationships between the individual and the social operate at a number of levels. West intimates:

> The sociocultural lies at the heart of who we are and may become; it lies too at the core of our psychological being, and of our self-formation in intimate relationships. (2017, p 129)

This humanist-existentialist focus foregrounds individual learners as holistic beings in dialectical engagement with their cultural contexts – their individual life-worlds (Husserl, 1970; Bagnall, 2017). This gives prominence to intentionality through agency in learning and it is in this way that we can respond to the question of how adults learn differently to children. Knowles (1988) considered differences in life experiences were significant here. He distinguishes a shift from the *pedagogy* of dependency and limited experience in childhood to the *andragogy* of self-direction in adult learners who take responsibility for their own learning and offer a rich resource for themselves and in association with others, based on their life experiences. Indeed, we can see this at work in relation to the difference between moving from unqualified social work or social care practice, and associated status and duties, to undertaking programmes of study as an adult that will lead to qualified status and better opportunities. While the theory has had considerable influence and continuing appeal, it has also been strongly criticised (Elias, 1979; McKenzie, 1979; Hartree, 1984; St. Clair, 2002; Jarvis, 2014). Elias argues that rather than creating two distinct and unconnected approaches that meet the different needs of children and adults, Knowles's approaches to pedagogy and andragogy align with Dewey's much earlier consideration of concepts of *traditional* and *progressive* education.

Dewey (1938) questions how formal education goes about the process of educating individuals. His approach situates learning in a social order by identifying experience at the heart of a philosophy and theory of education. Dewey suggests the problem of interpretation lies with the history of educational theory 'marked by opposition between the idea that education is development from within and that it is formation from without ...' (1938, p 1). This is a distinction that continues to mark out the territory between the psychology and the sociology of education and learning in contemporary society. On the one hand, the focus is towards internalised processes of change associated with behaviourist perspectives on learning from the work of Pavlov and Skinner (Jarvis et al, 2003), Gagné (1977), and Gagné et al (1992) or with cognitive and constructivist approaches such as the work of Piaget (1953) and of Bruner (1966). On the other hand, the focus is on externalised processes contextualised to being in relationship with others and associated with the work of Lave and Wenger (1991) on situated learning and communities of practice (Wenger, 1998).

REFLECTION POINT 8.2

Think of an occasion while undertaking your studies when you have learned about something that you found surprising or intriguing. Did this information tend to support your previous beliefs or challenge them? How far has it since changed your thinking on the issue and why? How may this make you act in the future?

Dewey (1938) contrasts the key principles and oppositions between traditional and progressive education, developed here as a table based on his analysis, to identify implications for both learners and teachers in developing relevant and appropriate education strategies and learning experiences (see Table 8.1).

It is important to recognise that Dewey does not accept either of these domains as the way forward for education and learning. Rather he uses the challenges of these 'Either-Or' beliefs to identify the theory of experience as a way of bridging the gap between formal education and lifelong learning. Incidentally, Knowles subsequently revised his thinking to move from an andragogy versus pedagogy position to representing them on a continuum ranging from teacher-directed to student-directed learning (Merriam, 2001).

Table 8.1: Traditional and progressive education

Traditional education	Progressive education
Imposition from above	Expression and cultivation of individuality
External discipline	Free activity
Learning from texts and teachers	Learning through experience
Acquisition of isolated skills and techniques by drill	Acquisition of skills as a means of attaining ends which make direct vital appeal
Preparation for more or less remote future	Making the most of the opportunities of present life
Static aims and materials	Acquaintance with a changing world

Source: Key oppositions adapted from Dewey, 1938, pp 5–6

Dewey (1938) argues that we must understand the nature of human experience, in order to develop a theory of education. He identifies two key principles necessary for the validation of experience, the concepts of continuity and interaction. Dewey also identifies the principles of interaction as giving equal responsibilities to the educator for adapting the environment and to the individual for adapting the self in a partnership: here we might think of social work CPD training where the learner must take active steps towards initiating or pursuing their own learning objectives, which are normally grounded in the need to maintain or accrue professional recognition. This position highlights the fundamental essence of learning in relationship with others, an essentially social process, which needs to take precedence in any consideration of education opportunities and provision for adults. Dewey's analysis is related to learning situated in formal education but, by identifying learning as transformation through experience, it provides a theory of learning valid in different contexts, both formal and informal. The degree of agency, and hence intentionality that can be exerted by individuals will influence the form and function that learning takes and in turn any learning will be influenced by the social nexus in which individuals are located. Accordingly this brings us back to questions about what we learn and how in the different learning contexts we find in social work. While the formal compulsory education system cannot guarantee outcomes for children and young people, adults may feel they have freedom and choice in the learning projects and pathways they select and where there is a proliferation of training opportunities available in the social work world for individual choice, albeit with differing educational experiences attached.

It is in this respect that it becomes possible to see how Dewey's theory aligns with Archer's (2000) three orders of reality and their respective forms of knowledge, the natural order with embodied knowledge, the practical order with practical knowledge and the social order with discursive or propositional knowledge, all of which are constituted by and interlinked through practical action. While human powers and propensities give access to these three kinds of knowledge, at one and the same time, humans as agents may be constrained by anyone of the three orders of reality. The contention is that no order has precedence; nevertheless, the practical order is pivotal for understanding human activity and the interplay between structure and agency through social interaction, and augmented through reflexivity (Archer, 2000, 2007).

Situating the functions of liberal and vocational education traditions

Merriam's (1977) critical review of the philosophy of education literature set out to identify the aims and objectives of adult education but found little consensus due to varying assumptions about the basic nature of adult education. Two distinct positions were identified, between aims directed to personal fulfilment, offering a consensus perspective for adult education, and aims directed towards social change, providing a conflict perspective. Merriam also recognised that where each educator/philosopher positions themselves on this issue 'seems to determine to a large extent how the learner, the teacher, and the instructional process are conceptualized' (Merriam, 1977, p 201).

Examples provided by Merriam focus, on the one hand, on the structural functionalist benefits for the individual and the society in, for example, fulfilling the American Dream, after Kallen (1962), who described a daylife 'as a producer in society, a worker' and a nightlife in which 'one is able to consume the cultural benefits for which one has worked during the day'. The necessary labours of the daylife are endowed with 'restoration intrinsic to nightlife' (Merriam, 1977, p 197). On the other hand, Merriam identifies the conflict perspective represented in the work of Paulo Freire (1996) whose critical radical position focuses on the pedagogy of the oppressed where the purpose of education is to liberate the oppressed and, concomitantly, to free the oppressor, to make individuals aware of their false consciousness and their social condition.

Both these examples demonstrate the influence of history and context in understanding the functions of adult education and learning, although clearly Freire's work more closely resonates with social work commitments to equality and social justice, which he shares. Kallen's work was influenced by his experiences and location in the US (1882–1974), where interest in adult education was spurred by 'reaction to the propaganda of the First World War; dissatisfaction with the increasing specialisation of higher and children's education; calls for better use of the new leisure; and post War interest in democracy and citizenship' (Rose and O'Neill, 1997). It was in this context that Kallen's liberal tradition, extoling the possibility of liberation through education was situated. The reader could be forgiven for interpreting Kallen's description of the daylife versus the nightlife of 20th-century man as a representation of Marcuse's (1964) *One-Dimensional Man*, in which the concept of 'repressive desublimination' represents the disciplining of the body through entertainment to prevent repressed desire from interfering with capitalist exchange values' at work in the age of mass consumerism and popular culture. Kallen's description certainly resonates with the critical theory of the Frankfurt School concerning the development of the culture industry put forward by Horkheimer and Adorno as a means of pacifying people through superficial meaning and distraction (2002 [1944]). Social work has been used by successive British governments as another form of pacification of the people, by being viewed as a human service sticking plaster to cover superficially the wounds of deeper injuries sustained by trying to survive in an unequal and often highly oppressive society. In fact, Kallen's contribution was more considerable; he identified the potential for education embedded in such diverse activities as labour organising and consumer cooperatives; he saw the purpose of workers' education being worker control over production and warned against restricting workers' education to the applied or the vocational, arguing that a narrow emphasis on training neglected both the liberating and responsible purposes adult education should serve (Rose and O'Neill, 1997). Accordingly, we can here find a telling critique of the narrowness of training models as working against the emancipation of workers (see Case Study 8.1).

By contrast, Freire's work (1921–97) was situated in his experience of Latin America against a background of illiteracy and poverty. Freire (1996) identified the significance of praxis for critical reflection on the situation of oppression, working in synthesis with action as a means for changing that situation. Reflectiveness and praxis are key pedagogic devices used in good social work education where Freire's work holds an established and deeply respected position in social work educational history. He emphasised the development of critical consciousness which enables a purposeful combination of thought and action as the means for reclaiming humanity. Freire described the traditional relationship of teacher and student as the 'banking' concept of education in which the teacher's task is to 'fill' the students as 'receptacles' with contents, 'detached from reality, disconnected from the totality that engendered them and could give them significance' (Freire, 1996, p 52). In this scenario, the teacher is in full control and takes on the role of oppressor, while the student accepts the passive role imposed on them (1996).

REFLECTION POINT 8.3

Role play in the classroom is a case of Marmite, you either enjoy it or loathe it, but it can be a very helpful learning tool in social work. If you have had experience of role play, think about what you learned from taking on different roles. If you have yet to experience role play, what kind of acting scenario would you like to be involved in to stretch you further?

Freire proposed a problem-posing method as an alternative to the banking system. Here, the teacher and student enter a partnership based on critical dialogue for making sense of the world. The teacher and the student learn from each other. Freire points out: 'The unfinished character of human beings and the transformational character of reality necessitate that education be an ongoing activity' (1996, p 65). Freire's work continues to have relevance for liberal community education and community action groups bringing a critical neo-Marxist perspective which recognises that education cannot be viewed as a neutral process (Jarvis, 2014). Indeed, a critical Marxist position continues to have significant relevance to the social work profession in a social context where deep poverty and the impact of austerity ideologies have blighted the lives of so many British families (Parker and Ashencaen Crabtree, 2018).

The liberal perspective of Kallen, focusing on the liberation of self through education and learning, may be set against the more radical perspective of Freire focused on liberating society, where the relevance to the social work profession becomes apparent. These examples appear to place them at opposing junctures along a continuum from a liberal functionalist to a radical conflict perspective on the functions of education and learning. However, the realities of their experiences and the influences of their contexts offer a more nuanced and complex picture where the interplay of social enablements and constraints is central to understanding the different functions and praxis of adult education and learning.

The history of adult education is marked by movements for self-fulfilment, betterment and social change. Smith (2004) explains how the traditions of fellowship and spirituality formed the foundations for adult schools in 18th-century Britain, where discussion and concern with democratic ways of working became important elements in the making of the 'adult education method'. While the early schools focused on literacy for Bible reading and were intended for the instruction of children, adults could also attend. The massive growth of Sunday schooling from the 1780s encouraged adult participation in some areas. Independent adult schools are said to have begun in Nottingham in 1798 to meet the needs of younger women in lace and hosiery factories and subsequently in London to teach reading. These schools were largely associated with the Quaker movement and emphasis was on discussion, fellowship and mutual aid activities such as book and library clubs, saving banks, sick funds and temperance societies (Smith, 2004). The rapid growth and participation in adult schools up to the First World War was followed by a period of decline due to the impact of the war. What followed was the emergence of other adult education organisations such as the Workers Educational Association (WEA) (Smith, 2004).

West (2017) identified the 'liberal', fraternal, self-help traditions which shaped workers' education and states that 'human flourishing and social solidarities depend on strengthening these processes of mutuality' (2017, p 130). He discusses the legacy of Richard Tawney, a Christian socialist and pre-eminent leader of the WEA and of Raymond Williams, who he describes as the ' humanistic Marxist'. West suggests that much of what they offered can speak to contemporary society, reinvigorating democratic forms of education, which uphold the spirit of education as 'determined scholarship forged in relationships of fraternity' and 'struggles for a better and more democratised social order, where students make up their own minds rather than being led to predetermined truths'; and where fundamentalism is opposed in whatever form (2017, p 130).

The challenges to democracy in contemporary society necessitate reclaiming the essential functions of adult education and learning which lead to change for the individual and for society. Built on the critical theory tradition of writers like Freire (1996), Brookfield (2005), Mezirow (1981, 1991) and Jarvis (2004, 2014), these critical perspectives provided the means for promoting and securing critical humanist pedagogy. The humanist existential position of Jarvis identifies 'we as people are never fully developed – always becoming' (2004, p 92). We can see how closely such thinking relates to social work in which social workers view themselves and those with and for whom they work as similarly works-in-progress motivated by a need for self-fulfilment of which autonomy forms a powerful component. In a similar vein, the radical Marxist position of Freire contends that education is a fundamental function for humanity because oppression is dehumanising, both for the oppressed and for the oppressors. Once again, social work experience suggests that this is so: authentic autonomy is fundamentally emancipatory and liberating; while power over others is not only obviously wrong but corrupting and imprisoning to those that wield such power. Education and learning can liberate through adopting a critically reflexive position. Individuals must work their way towards a critical understanding of reality, through praxis which leads to change for the individual and for society. Such individuals are not afraid to confront, to listen, to see the world unveiled, and to meet the people and enter into dialogue with them (Freire, 1996). Dialogue is at its most constructive when the balance of power is not overly weighted in one direction or another. Power differentials between practitioners and service users are therefore an aspect that social workers need to be closely aware of in creating discursive spaces where knowledge is more readily created and exchanged.

Yet, as is apparent in the case of social work, the modern context for adult education and learning continues to be marked by tensions in the relationship between liberal and vocational traditions. Wiltshire (2003) conceptualised adult education in liberal terms, criticising the rise of 'vocationalism' which he saw as threatening the 'Great Tradition' of university extension-based adult education. He identified key characteristics of this tradition, including a particular curriculum devoted to the humane or liberal studies, which he defined as that which 'can reasonably be expected to concern us as men and women, not as technicians, functionaries or examinees'; a focus on understanding 'the great issues of life', demanding what he described as a 'non-vocational attitude' from learners; and a commitment to equality of access (Wiltshire, 2003, cited in Hodge et al, 2017, p 251). This echoes the experiences of Helen in Case Study 8.1, whose social work education indeed incorporated much of the so-called 'liberal studies' Wiltshire (2003) refers to. It demonstrated similarities with the historical development of adult schools and workers' education in employing the Socratic method based on small groups and guided discussion. Wiltshire distinguished between liberal and technical subjects in the curriculum but appreciated that the impact on learners could be influenced as much by the pedagogical method as by the nature of the subject, conceding that literature could be taught 'technologically' (i.e. by drill), while in contrast engineering (a technical subject) could be 'turned into something more than a study of means and skills' (2003, p 95, cited in Hodge et al, 2017, pp 251–252). However, here we can see the danger for social work where the elimination of the wider social sciences, for example, might well reduce the critical capacities of social workers to engage in thinking critically about how social structures shape human lives. By contrast technical-rational instrumental training models focusing on how best to deal with 'faulty' service users can hardly address the much bigger implications of widespread social inequality and structural oppressions, for example.

This critique of adult education anticipates subsequent discussion about the economic functions of adult education and learning in contemporary neo-liberal society and the question of self-direction in terms of the freedom and control that can be exercised by adults in education and learning.

Making it real: applying knowledge to practice

The growing influence of economic considerations and the impacts of globalisation have been identified in contemporary adult education and learning from the 1970s (Jarvis, 2014; Bagnall, 2017; Wright and Sandlin, 2017). Aspin and Chapman (2000) identify three central elements or functions in what they describe as the 'triadic' nature of lifelong learning: for economic progress and development; for personal development and fulfilment; and for social inclusiveness and democratic understanding and activity; and argue that these three facets are intertwined. However, the realities of provision continue to be divided along liberal academic and technical vocational divides with consequent implications for human service professionals negotiating between priorities when faced with questions of resourcing and provision, according to the relative values placed on the different functions of provision, and for individuals making their way through the life course.

By way of illustration, see Case Study 8.2.

CASE STUDY 8.2

I had the privilege to meet a young man in his early 20s attending evening classes at the Working Men's College in Camden, London. Rick had not enjoyed school and had few academic qualifications. He had trained as a plumber and gained considerable practical life experience working on building sites. Brought up in a working-class family with parents who did not have the benefits of education and he married young and had dependent children, which did not bode well for Rick's future life chances when viewed through a Bourdieusian cultural capital perspective (Bourdieu and Wacquant, 1992). Yet, that young man went on to gain the necessary education qualifications to achieve his ambitions – going to university and becoming a teacher. Rick demonstrated agency in his commitment and intentionality to change his life and that agency was strongly influenced by the liberal and fraternal support offered by his peer group and teachers working within the ethos of adult liberal education.

Questions

1. How far do you think Rick's past experiences may have shaped his attitude towards education as an adult?
2. What personal attributes do you think Rick can bring to his work as a teacher?
3. What concepts or theories discussed in this chapter might be relevant to Rick's case?

Discussion

This case study provides important messages for human service professionals encouraging them to hold the vision and enabling powers of liberal-humanist education as a worthy and worthwhile pursuit, nurturing and supporting adults to grow and prosper in directions of their making, encompassing economic

> progression, personal fulfilment and democratic citizenship. The short-term, rational-instrumental objectives of education policies designed to train and fit human resources into prescribed occupations to fuel the hungry fires of economic growth would not have offered the enabling environment that contributed to Rick the plumber becoming Rick the teacher.

Neither adult education nor university education are immune from the growing significance being placed on education's role in supporting economic growth. Education is being positioned as 'the handmaiden of industry taking the raw material of humanity and turning it into the human resources that would drive the world' (Jarvis, 2014, p 46). Arguably, in-house training schemes are a direct consequence of economic drivers in cost-effectively producing qualified staff in concentrated periods of time to meet increasing social need for regulated services (Jarvis, 2014). While adult education in the UK had been regarded as fundamentally knowledge-based, training was about skills development; the former being taught in adult education institutes, university adult education departments, the WEA and the WI (Women's Institutes), and the latter in colleges of further education and the emerging polytechnic sector in the 1960s (Jarvis, 2014, p 46). Where adult liberal education is now associated with community education, universities of the third age and retirement education, it is marginalised and poorly resourced. Jarvis (2014) describes the case of 'adult education beyond the walls', or extra-mural adult education, where classes or a course of study are arranged by a university or other educational establishment for people who are not full-time members. He explains how such non-formal projects, working on the margins of formal education, are at greater risk of being terminated in times of austerity and how 'the advent of neo-liberal economic policies and practices' have curtailed university funds 'to such an extent that they are ceasing to provide such education' (2014, p 50). It is true that universities are no longer permitted to be geared towards assisting the community so much as being viewed as a quasi-businesses in their own right demanding student fees (Ashencaen Crabtree and Shiel, 2018), and therefore contribute to neo-liberal and capitalist discourses about education as about economic returns rather than personal liberation.

On the other side of the divide is vocational training, initially associated with non-university students working as apprentices in employing organisations and attending colleges of further education and polytechnics on a part-time basis; but there was little opportunity to study at degree level until the polytechnic sector was granted awarding powers through the Council for National Academic Awards (CNAA) (Jarvis, 2014). Gradually, universities in the UK began offering short courses in a variety of vocational subjects on an in-service, part-time basis as *continuing professional development* (CPD), of which social work has been one of the main recipients, or recurrent education, and provision continued to expand in support of the knowledge economy with the introduction of part-time higher degrees, Masters and doctoral programmes (Bourner et al, 2001; Usher,

2002; Jarvis, 2014). However, Jarvis argues that 'the focus was on preparing and upskilling the workforce for the good of the employing organisation rather than the benefit of the workers' and points out that 'employing organisations also began to develop their own training courses and employees were regarded as human capital' (Jarvis, 2014, p 51). Indeed, this is precisely what is occurring in contemporary UK social work in a trend towards weighting employer wishes for a competent but compliant workforce, above that of hopefully producing a critically thinking professional able to influence policy and practice whether at micro, meso or macro levels.

By contrast, the foundation of the Open University (OU) (familiar to some readers for its social care course provision) in the UK and the University of the Third Age (U3A) in France presented significant new departures in liberal education. The OU was a catalyst for the development of distance education in the UK and other countries and began to offer vocational courses as well as liberal ones (Jarvis, 2014). The University of the Third Age spread throughout Europe, where it was attached to a local university while, in the UK, it formed 'a separate and almost completely independent local, non-governmental organisation with no formal connection to the university sector' (Jarvis, 2014, p 47).

The refocusing of priorities for adult education on economic progress and development has implications, not only for providers, but also for individuals making their way in the world, where social work students are experiencing their fair share of the dilemmas this is raising. As a result, adult education has become 'increasingly institutionalised in the interests of global competitiveness, with a pronounced focus on employability and competence development' (Field and Schemmann, 2017, p 175).

Various attempts to bridge the gaps between vocational and academic education were introduced in the 1980s, to overcome criticisms of curricula largely centred on academic concerns, narrowly focused, and allegedly out of touch with the needs of individuals and industry requirements (Lea, 2003). These included Youth Training Schemes (YTS), work experience, and GNVQs as a new vocationally oriented alternative to the GCSE/A level. The 1990s saw the introduction of modern apprenticeships and continuing moves towards competence-based education and training. The growth of this new vocationalism has been criticised in promoting a narrow agenda focused on *performativity*. Billett argues that in times of economic uncertainty, 'governments and others reassert the importance of fundamentals (e.g. back to basics) in compulsory education, and a stronger regulation and control' (2010, p 404). We have duly seen the outcome of this government preoccupation with regulatory control in the social work profession, which has become increasingly demoralised and stretched in resources.

Accordingly, we can appreciate the implications of this contemporary neoliberal situation focused on performativity, in the sense that all human endeavour is judged in terms of its *effectivity*, as highlighted by Bagnall (2017, pp 66–67), who describes a cultural context exhibiting 'the erosion of intrinsic value in knowledge, action and metaphysics: value being significantly reduced to *instrumental* value …'

or what Vattimo (1988) termed 'exchange value'. Value is here *'externalised'* and *'privatised'*, with responsibility, performance and risk, 'devolved to successively lower levels of social organisation, from governmental authorities, to organisations and, ultimately, to individuals'.

This devolvement of responsibility to the individual is further evidenced in Lee's analysis of self-help books embodying neo-liberal perspectives of self-managing, self-monitoring, self-regulating and self-disciplining enabling adult learners to take responsibility for their own learning as entrepreneurs of themselves (2017, p 148). Lee warns that this approach in adult education has been 'subverted by its compliance with existing social systems in learning goals and its prescriptive and directed nature in learning processes' (2017, p 146). In defence of lifelong learning in all its forms, formal and informal, Lee reiterates that it is 'neither incidental to living nor instrumental itself – it is an intrinsic part of the process of living' (Lee, 2017, p 146). Brookfield (2005) portrays this technical and bureaucratic rationality as entering into and distorting everyday relationships, including those between social workers and service users and their families, in what Habermas calls the colonisation of the lifeworld by the system. Lee calls for human service professionals to adopt 'vigilant realism' as a 'platform for navigating counter-hegemonic discourses to neoliberal governance' (2017, p 159).

Conclusion

We set out to examine the place, form and function that education and learning for adults plays in contemporary society. We have viewed the inherent tensions in a shift in adult education policy away from a liberal-humanist tradition grounded in critical theory, democracy and citizenship to a more technical-rational and instrumental focus grounded in economic progress and nation state competitiveness in a globalised economy. The wider discussion of education connects closely to the changing face of social work education in which concrete examples can be found to illustrate the conceptual and theoretical arguments offered here. Contemporary society is faced with the economic and social challenges of an ageing population owing to increasing life expectancy, so often framed as a social problem to be managed, usually by social workers, rather than a notable social achievement of improved public health and social environments. The life course, as we know, is more complex and less predictable with more frequent job changes, geographic mobility, and changes in family composition. More people are living longer, entering the 'third age' and spending a larger proportion of their lives in healthy and active retirement (Schuller and Watson, 2015). Billett argues that, where people are living longer and nations are having to cope with ageing populations, 'the promotion and support for adults' learning across the lifespan' has become all the more essential for achieving both 'economic and social goals' (Billett, 2010, p 406). Accordingly. a new remit opens up for social workers to consider in how to promote education as life enhancing, psychosocially and emotionally liberating, and socially critical for healthy, inclusive democratic discourses.

What is needed to reconcile the 'triadic' goals of economic progress, personal development and fulfilment; and social inclusiveness and democratic understanding are multiple approaches for adult education and learning which enable the liberal humanist tradition to be reasserted. This may occur, perhaps through newer providers like the University of the Third Age, working in partnerships and affiliations with higher and further education providers (Aspin and Chapman, 2000) and in this enterprise supported by a progressive, education valuing social work vision. This liberal provision needs to go hand in hand with 'revitalising' economic and social opportunities not narrowly focused on isolating specific skills and content from the providers' perspective but the development of embodied practical knowledge, or know-how, through enabling individuals to function holistically with their senses, emotions and cognitions intertwined and interacting with objects in the world (Archer, 2000). Indeed, we must recall that social work itself has been viewed as a practical vocation that applies common-sense approaches to situations. The UK Department of Education 'Step-Up' programme of condensed workplace training might be viewed as such an example of undertaking a crash course in practical know-how. This theory of learning, following Dewey (1938), is focused on transformation through experience, valid in different contexts, both formal and informal, and recognises and celebrates learning, as not only an essential human property, but an essentially social process in relationship with others.

Such 'revitalising' opportunities then need to be open to all irrespective of age stages and economic and social positions in society, appreciating differences and diversity. Billett (2010) argues that it would be more helpful to have and organise arrangements, experiences and interactions, focusing on five process-focused categories: (1) initial preparation for occupational and societal roles; (2) transitions across social and economic roles; (3) management of disappointments in social and work life; (4) revitalisation (such as professional development); and (5) bases for overcoming bias, albeit gender, ages or racial. Such an approach would not be narrowly circumscribed by terms like training, competence-based curricula and performativity but focused on reinvigorating critical pedagogy for humanising relationships and democracy in contemporary society.

These liberal humanist and revitalising stances support Archer's claim that our sociality does not have to make us into society's creatures (Archer, 2000). Adult education and learning opportunities provide the focus for lifelong learning, but provision needs to give precedence to praxis over content. Carr and Kemmis (1986) argue that thought and action are dialectically related not in a mechanical way but as constant reflection and questioning – a process that social work has traditionally prided itself on and which is a key characteristic of good social work pedagogy.

Reflective questions

1 How is learning different from education? Why is it important to distinguish learning from education in contemporary society?

2 What are some of the most significant challenges for education and learning in adults identified by key thinkers and theorists?

3 In your opinion, what are the key challenges for contemporary social work education?

4 What are the challenges for sustaining critical liberal-humanist approaches to adult education and learning in contemporary society? Why does this approach matter?

Further reading

• Brookfield, S. (2005) *The Power of Critical Theory for Adult Learning and Teaching*. Maidenhead: Open University Press.
  This is a very important book for understanding how critical theory expands our understanding of interactions in the social world and the interface with education as well as with ourselves as learners.

• Jarvis, P. (2010) *Adult Education and Lifelong Learning* (4th edn). London: Routledge.
  What is lifelong learning and what could be its relevance to social work? This useful book is a very good place to start grappling with such important questions.

• Usher, R., Bryant, I. and Johnston, R. (1997) *Adult Education and the Postmodern Challenge: Learning Beyond the Limits*. London: Routledge.
  This book offers a solid grounding in understanding the challenges facing liberal and broad education from narrow, regulated and vocational agendas, such as those that appear to be redefining social work education.

References

Archer, M. (2000) *Being Human: The Problem of Agency*. Cambridge: Cambridge University Press.

Archer, M. (2007) *Making Our Way Through the World: Human Reflexivity and Social Mobility*. Cambridge: Cambridge University Press.

Ashencaen Crabtree, S. and Shiel, C. (2018) Loaded dice: Games playing and the gendered barriers of the academy, *Education and Gender*. Available from: https://www.tandfonline.com/doi/full/10.1080/09540253.2018.1447090

Aspin, D.N. and Chapman, J.D. (2000) Lifelong learning: Concepts and conceptions, *International Journal of Lifelong Education*, 19(1): 2–19.

Bagnall, R.G. (2017) A critique of Peter Jarvis's conceptualisation of the lifelong learner in the contemporary cultural context, *International Journal of Lifelong Education*, 36(1–2): 60–75.

Ball, S. (2012) Performativity, commodification and commitment: An I–Spy guide to the neoliberal university, *British Journal of Educational Studies*, 60: 17–28.

Billett, S. (2010) The perils of confusing lifelong learning with lifelong education, *International Journal of Lifelong Education*, 29(4): 401–413.

Bourdieu, P. and Wacquant, L.J.D. (1992) *An Invitation to Reflexive Sociology*. Oxford: Polity Press.

Bourner, T., Bowden, R. and Laing, S. (2001) Professional doctorates in England, *Studies in Higher Education*, 26(1): 65–83.

Brookfield, S. (2005) *The Power of Critical Theory for Adult Learning and Teaching*. Maidenhead: Open University Press.

Bruner, J.S. (1966) *Toward a Theory of Instruction*. Cambridge, MA: Harvard University Press.

Carr, W. and Kemmis, S. (1986) *Becoming Critical: Education, Knowledge and Action Research*. Abingdon: RoutledgeFalmer.

Delors, J. et al (1996) *Learning: The Treasure Within*. Report to UNESCO of the International Commission on Education for the Twenty-first Century. Paris: UNESCO Publishing.

Dewey, J. (1938) *Experience and Education*. New York: Simon & Schuster.

Elias, J. (1979) Andragogy revisited, *Adult Education*, 29(4): 252–256.

Field, J. and Schemmann, M. (2017) International organisations and the construction of the learning active citizen: an analysis of adult learning policy documents from a Durkheimian perspective, *International Journal of Lifelong Education*, 36(1-2): 164–179.

Freire, P. (1996) *Pedagogy of the Oppressed*. London: Penguin Books (first published by Continuum, 1970).

Gagné, R.M. (1977) *The Conditions of Learning* (3rd edn). London: Holt, Rinehart and Winston.

Gagné, R.M., Briggs, L.J. and Wager, W.W. (1992) *Principles of Instructional Design* (4th edn). Fort Worth, TX: Harcourt Brace College Publishers.

Hartree, A. (1984) Malcolm Knowles theory of andragogy: A critique, *International Journal of Lifelong Education*, 3(3): 203-210.

Hodge, S., Holford, J., Milana, M., Waller, R. and Webb, S. (2017) Vocational education and the field of lifelong education, *International Journal of Lifelong Education*, 36(3): 251–253.

Horkheimer, M. and Adorno, T. (2002) [1944] *Dialectic of Enlightenment: Philosophical Fragments*, Gunzelin Schmid Noerr (ed.) Edmund Jephcott (trans.). Stanford, CA: Stanford University Press.

Husserl, E. (1970) *The Crisis of European Sciences and Transcendental Phenomenology: An Introduction to Phenomenological Philosophy*, D. Carr (trans.). Evanston, IL: Northwestern University Press.

Illeris, K. (2003) Workplace learning and learning theory, *Journal of Workplace Learning*, 15(1): 167–178.

Jarvis, P. (2004) *Adult Education and Lifelong Learning* (3rd edn). London: Routledge.

Jarvis, P. (2014) From adult education to lifelong learning and beyond, *Comparative Education*, 50(1): 45–57.

Jarvis, P., Holford, J. and Griffin, C. (2003) *The Theory and Practice of Learning* (2nd edn). London: Kogan Page.

Kallen, H.M. (1962) *Philosophical Issues in Adult Education*. Springfield: Charles C. Thomas.

Knowles, M.S. (1988) *The Modern Practice of Adult Education: From Pedagogy to Andragogy*. Englewood Cliffs: Cambridge Adult Education.

Lave, J. and Wenger, E. (1991) *Situated Learning: Legitimate Peripheral Participation*. Cambridge: Cambridge University Press.

Lea, J. (2003) Overview: Post-compulsory education in context. In J. Lea, D. Hayes, A. Armitage, L. Lomas and S. Markless (eds), *Working in Post-Compulsory Education*. Maidenhead: McGraw-Hill Education, pp 5–32.

Lee, M. (2017) Decoding the neoliberal subjectivity in self-helping adult learners, *International Journal of Lifelong Education*, 36(102): 145–163.

McKenzie, L. (1979) Andragogy revisited: A response to Elias, *Adult Education*, 29(4): 256–261.

Marcuse, H. (1964) *One-Dimensional Man: Studies in the Ideology of Advanced Industrial Society*. Boston: Beacon Press.

Merriam, S. (1977) Philosophical perspectives on adult education: A critical review of the literature, *Adult Education*, 27(4): 195–208.

Merriam, S. (2001) Andragogy and self-directed learning: Pillars of adult learning theory, *New Directions for Adult & Continuing Education*, 2001(89): 3–13.

Mezirow, J. (1981) A critical theory of adult learning and education, *Adult Education*, 32(1): 3–27.

Mezirow, J. (1991) *Transformative Dimensions of Adult Learning*. San Francisco: Jossey-Bass.

Parker, J. (2019) Descent or dissent? A future of social work education in the UK post-Brexit, *European Journal of Social Work*, first published 12 February 2019. Available from: https://doi.org/10.1080/13691457.2019.1578733

Parker, J. and Ashencaen Crabtree, S. (2018) *Social Work with Disadvantaged and Marginalised Groups*. London: Sage.

Peters, R.S. (1973) Introduction. In R.S. Peters (ed.), *The Philosophy of Education*. Oxford: Oxford University Press, pp 1–7.

Piaget, J. (1953) *The Origin of Intelligence in the Child*. London: Routledge and Kegan Paul.

Rose, A. and O'Neill, L. (1997) Reconciling claims for the individual and the community: Horace Kallen, cultural pluralism, and persistent tensions in adult education, *Adult Education Quarterly*, 47(3/4): 138–152.

St. Clair, R. (2002) *Andragogy Revisited: Theory for the 21st Century? Myths and Realities*. Washington, DC: Office of Educational Research and Improvement. Columbus, OH: ERIC Clearinghouse on Adult, Career, and Vocational Education.

Schuller, T. and Watson, D. (2009) *Learning Through Life: Inquiry into the Future for Lifelong Learning*. Leicester: NIACE.

Schuller, T. and Watson, D. (2015) The treasure within and learning through life: A review and prospectus, *European Journal of Education Research, Development and Policy*, 50(2): 214–224.

Smith, M.K. (2004) Adult schools and the making of adult education. In *The Encyclopedia of Informal Education*. Available from: http://www.infed.org/lifelonglearning/adult_schools.htm

Usher, R. (2002) A diversity of doctorates: Fitness for the knowledge economy?, *Higher Education Research & Development*, 21(2): 143–153.

Vattimo, G. (1988) The end of modernity: Nihilism and hermeneutics in post-modern culture (trans. J.R. Snyder). Cambridge: Polity Press.

Wenger, E. (1998) *Communities of Practice: Learning, Meaning, and Identity*. Cambridge: Cambridge University Press.

West, L. (2017) Resisting the enormous condescension of posterity: Richard Henry Tawney, Raymond Williams and the long struggle for a democratic education, *International Journal of Lifelong Education*, 36(1–2): 129–144.

Wiltshire, H.C. (2003) The great tradition in university adult education. In P. Jarvis and C. Griffin (eds), *Adult and Continuing Education: Major Themes in Education* (Vol. II). London: Routledge, pp 109–118.

Wright, R.R. and Sandlin, J.A. (2017) (Critical) learning in/through everyday life in a global consumer culture, *International Journal of Lifelong Education*, 36(1–2): 77–94.

9

Life course criminology and adults

Richard Heslop and Jonathan Parker

Introduction

Have you ever wondered why some people commit crime and others seemingly do not? Or why is it that children from the same communities or even the same families grow up to be so different? Why is it that some form of delinquent behaviour is a normal part of growing up and adolescence for arguably the majority of teenagers, yet most do not engage in criminal behaviour as adults? Questions such as these are central to the academic study of criminology and in particular a branch of criminology usually referred to as life course criminology, which will be the focus of this chapter. More specifically, the chapter will provide an overview of life course criminology with respect to adults and the application of life course criminology to understanding and working with adults. As former practitioners turned university academics, we, the authors, have been working with adults for all of our professional lives and we have found that an understanding and appreciation of key ideas, concepts and theories from criminology, sociology and other related academic disciplines have helped us to make some sense of the complex and difficult professional situations we have faced. Richard is a former British police sergeant and Jonathan was previously a senior social worker working in England.

Although our aim is not to make the chapter overly theoretical, it will be necessary to explore the background and key features of life course criminology including its leading theorists. Much of this theoretical overview builds in those models and theories that we have introduced in Chapter 9 of the companion volume concerning children and young people. Thus, there will be some repetition but this is to be expected and can help you make links between theories, thinking and, indeed, practice. Throughout the chapter we will refer to case study material to exemplify the use of life course criminology models for understanding issues in the changes and developments experienced and manifested by adults and to demonstrate the complexity and the limitations of such approaches.

For readers new to the discipline of criminology we feel that it will be helpful to begin by discussing some key features of academic criminology, before examining how life course approaches relate to some of its central concerns and debates. We have introduced criminological theory for understanding how children and young people may be drawn into crime and diverted from it in Chapter 9 in the companion volume. It would be useful to read this chapter as many theories and models can be applied across the lifespan.

Chapter objectives

- provide a brief overview of the academic discipline of criminology to set the context;

- introduce life course criminology and key theorists;

- consider how life course approaches relate to the discipline of criminology;

- illustrate the impact of partners, family members, friends, work, organisations and environment on the continuing development of adults throughout their lives;

- explore transitions in and out of crime throughout the life course.

What is criminology?

Criminology is an unusual academic discipline. For a start, it can be argued that, at a basic level, practically everyone these days thinks that they are a criminologist. What we mean by this is that if we find ourselves in, for example, a bar, a restaurant, the street, or in the privacy of people homes around their television sets, we will find that many, if not most people, hold strong views about crime and justice matters, which they will often forcefully express. Should 'we bring back hanging'? Why are so many young people in Britain carrying knives? Are the police racist? And what could possibly have 'gone wrong' in the life of the fictional character Tommy Shelby from the popular BBC television show *Peaky Blinders*, which has turned him from a patriotic war hero to become the leader of a ruthless criminal gang? These and many other conundrums are key criminological questions, but just because we may hold strong opinions on these matters and argue forcefully about them we are not necessarily criminologists.

What separates the arguments of professional criminologist from the proverbial man or woman in the pub is that crime (the central organising concept of criminology) has to be studied *systematically* and to do this requires an *epistemology*. While most people understand the general meaning of what it means to be systematic (to be organised, methodical and work to a clear plan), the word epistemology sounds somewhat scary and indeed mere mention of it sometimes causes some of our first year criminology students to break out into a cold sweat. In formal terms, epistemology is a branch of philosophy concerned with the theory of knowledge, especially with regard to research methods, the validity and scope of it, and the distinction between justified belief and mere opinion.

In more simple terms, epistemology may be defined as: 'how do we know what we know?' For example, if we were to claim that young men who have been brought up in economically deprived areas commit more crimes than similar aged men who have been raised in more affluent areas, then how do know this? On the face of it, such a claim seems like common sense, but a criminologist would set out to distinguish fact from fiction or opinion and this requires taking an epistemological position. As we shall discuss in more detail, the epistemological stance of many early criminologists was based around the 'scientific method' (or what is sometimes referred to as 'positivism'), and this continues to be the case for many contemporary criminologists working within the discipline. We will also see that the development of life course criminology has also been heavily influenced by positivist approaches.

REFLECTION POINT 9.1

When you are reading the following sections on the key life course theories and theorists, think back to this concept of epistemology and consider how the researchers and theorists 'know what they know'. This will help you to reflect on your own opinions and what can be known through evidence (another contested term) and research (a complex and varied activity).

Criminology and crime

A further unusual feature about criminology is that it is something of a 'parasitic' academic discipline. What we mean by this is that criminology or more accurately criminologists tend to borrow and make use of ideas, concepts and theories from other more established academic disciplines, such as: sociology, psychology, biology, psychiatry, law and politics. The British sociologist and criminologist David Downes famously described criminology as a 'rendezvous discipline' (Young, 2003). What he meant by this is that criminology has become a meeting place (or rendezvous point) for ideas, concepts and theories from a range of disciplines as applied to the problem of *crime*. For at the most fundamental level, criminology is concerned with the systematic study of crime and its causes. If we set aside for the time being the 'deceptively simple' yet 'highly contestable and problematic question' of what we mean by crime (Newburn, 2017, p 6), we may deduce from this definition that the key challenges in criminology include attempting to explain two things. Firstly, why is it that some individuals or groups of people commit crimes? And, secondly, why is it that others seemingly do not? This is something we explored in respect of children and young people (Chapter 9 in the companion volume).

The final unusual feature we wish to draw your attention to about criminology is that, when compared with other academic disciplines, the systematic study of crime and offending (the academic discipline of criminology) is a relatively recent intellectual endeavour. Most modern criminology textbooks date the emergence of criminological thinking to an era between the late 17th and early 18th centuries (see, for example, Chamberlain, 2015; Newburn, 2017). What scholars usually refer to as 'classical criminology' emerged through the writings of 18th-century philosophers of social reform, most notably, Jeremy Bentham and Cesare Beccaria. As part of the broader Enlightenment movement, classical criminologists began to reject longstanding religious interpretations of individual behaviour, 'hold[ing] that the causes of crime are not a result of inherent sinfulness of the individual. Rather, they are the natural outcome of the rational application by the individual of a cost-benefit analysis of their situation so they can maximise pleasure and minimise pain' (Chamberlain, 2015, p 27). These ideas about the 'rational subject' and a social contract led to new legal and criminal justice systems under which punishment should be proportionate to crime (Bowling, 2013). Allowing that history is not the central feature of this chapter, it is interesting to note that changing ideas about crime and its causes lead to social changes towards those who commit crime as well as knowledge about what constitutes crime. This is important for you, as social workers or professionals working in criminal justice settings, because it provides a perspective on why you might be thinking or acting in certain ways when faced with aspects of crime and criminality. Keep this in mind as we explore a little about later changes in thinking.

By the mid-1800s, this philosophical approach to the problem of crime was subsequently challenged by the so-called 'positivist' criminologists. The primary idea behind positivist criminology is that criminals are born and not made, in other words it is the nature of the person, not nurture which results in criminal behaviour. Most well-known, if somewhat notorious, in developing a positivist critique was the Italian physician and psychiatrist Cesare Lombroso (1835–1909). He studied the cadavers of soldiers and executed criminals to determine 'scientifically' the bio-physiological reasons underlying 'criminal' and 'non-criminal' behaviour. Lombroso believed that a person's criminal behaviour and tendencies were inherited. He published research which claimed to show that the inherited facial features of criminals included, for example, large jaws and bloodshot eyes. You may have heard the phrase 'his eyes are too close together' being used, probably somewhat jokingly, to describe a person who appears a little suspicious. This phrase stems from Lombroso's studies and reinforces how embedded such thinking became. Although Lombroso's ideas were subsequently discredited, he was one of the first people in history to use a systematic scientific method to study crime and contemporary criminologist owe much to this turn.

The early criminologists, as we discussed in Chapter 9 of the companion volume, the study of criminology has grown and developed methodologically. It has also become attractive as a programme of study in universities and among the general public through media and popular culture (Loader and Sparks, 2012). A wide range of theoretical developments have occurred during this period that are drawn from mainstream sociology and other disciplines depending on the approach taken by those developing them.

REFLECTION POINT 9.2

Think of as many different theoretical approaches to or models of criminal behaviour that you can and consider which disciplinary background they most fit. As a social worker it would be useful to reflect critically on the meanings that each theory or model suggests to you, to the general public or to a person who might be the focus of it. Some theoretical perspectives may make it more likely that certain people are negatively labelled.

Although it has already been mentioned that crude forms of positivism have long since been discredited, many scholars and commentators still insist on an experimental and 'scientific' approach to criminality. Given the breadth of theoretical and epistemological approaches to crime and criminality we would argue that it is more important to be flexible and to use an approach that best fits the questions you want to answer. With this in mind we may now turn to an examination of life course criminology.

REFLECTION POINT 9.3

Think of a crime or case that you have read about or seen on TV. What do you think might be some of the reasons behind the crime? Compare your thoughts with the brief journey we have just taken through the development of criminology and criminological thought.

Life course criminology

The term life course perspective relates to a wide-ranging approach which may be used in a variety of disciplines such as history, biology and human geography. However, from a specifically criminological perspective it is set apart from other subject matters by its conceptual focus on crime and offending behaviour across an individual's lifespan. It does not suggest a static approach and diverges from earlier positivist approaches by recognises that an individual's relationship with crime may change over time and life stage (McAra and McVie, 2012). Before discussing the life course approach further, we must make two points that we have covered in more detail in the companion volume.

Firstly, because the focus is on crime and criminal behaviour it represents a highly contested area. As Reiner (2016, p 2) reminds us, 'crime is an example of what has been called an essentially contested concept' – in other words, it involves 'endless disputes' about its meaning. Of course, there are many debates and disputes about all manner of things in all academic disciplines, including the natural sciences – for example, biology (which as we have already noted may also be approached from a life course perspective). But we would suggest that the majority of, if not all, biologists can agree on what biology means, as well as accepting key concepts such as a cell or gene. The same cannot be said within criminology of the concept of crime, especially by those of us who approach criminology from diverse sociological and critical standpoints.

However, even at a straightforward practical level, readers will be aware from their own 'life course' how our ideas about what is and what is not regarded as a crime changes over space and time. For example, when we were growing up parents would sometimes take children out of school for a week or two as part of a family holiday. This was accepted, if somewhat frowned upon, by teachers. On the other hand, this is now something that may result in a fine, which, if not paid, could result in prosecution. When teaching in Frankfurt-am-Main in Germany in the late 1990s, Parker was involved in taking groups of social work students to 'shooting galleries' where heroin users could exchange needles for clean ones and inject safely knowing that there was medical support available should they need it and that they would not face arrest or hassle from police officers. This approach reduced drug-related deaths and ill-health and seemed also to reduce crime associated with drug use. In Britain, such an approach was illegal: anyone visiting such a place would be liable to arrest. Thus, these two examples show how fluid the concept of crime and criminal behaviour is. Dorling et al (2008, p 7) explain this more academically, saying that crime is a 'socially constructed concept' which has 'no ontological reality' – by which they meant crime has no hard and fast reality that can be easily and finally defined.

You may think that some acts or crimes are beyond such contest, for instance, murder. However, even the conception if murder differs from country to country and the planned killing of another person is permitted under certain circumstances. However, the key question arising from this acknowledgement is whether or not it debunks the concept of life course criminology. The concept is predicated on establishing patterns of offending over time, across the life of individuals.

The second point relates to the terminology variously used by writers when discussing the life course approach, but this can be described as: the 'criminal career paradigm'; or 'developmental criminology'; or developmental and life course criminology (DLC), with all four terms being sometimes used interchangeably. As noted earlier, the life course perspective is a wide-ranging longitudinal approach which is used in a range of subject matters, but with the common idea of exploring individual change over time; this change occurs at all points throughout life from childhood to old age. In this chapter on adults, we will predominantly use the term life course criminology or LCC for short.

The core focus of LCC is individual change in offending patterns and behaviours over the course of an adult's life and relating this to an individual's life and environmental circumstances, the twists and turns in that person's life at various stages (Chamberlain, 2015). Life course criminologists are interested in what social, developmental and environmental aspects of a person's life can influence their transition into or away from crime. This provides understanding which can be used to develop interventions to change behaviours and, thereby, the life trajectories of adults involved in crime (Bottoms and McWilliams, 1979; McNeill, 2006).

It is generally assumed in life course criminology that an adult 'criminal career' is commonly preceded by childhood criminality, although the explanatory power of this is left wanting, as not all children and young people who commit crime go on to do so in adulthood. It is recognised, however, that experiences of neglect and other forms of early abuse in childhood, may affect our attitudes and behaviour in adulthood. Thus, it is important to ensure that we acknowledge the structural pressures that help to construct lifestyle behaviours and characteristics (see Chapter 5). However, we are also still left with the question why some adults with complex and difficult backgrounds from childhood and beyond move into criminal behaviour and some do not.

As with many ideas in criminology, they relate to adults as well as children and young people. Indeed, much of the research that is covered in Chapter 9 in the companion volume is equally relevant to considering the passage of adults through the life course.

Although it is difficult to identify precisely the origins of LCC, it is possible to relate much of it back towards 19th-century positivist criminology (Homel and France, 2005; Blokland and Nieuwbeerta, 2010). In methodological terms (that which is concerned with the ways research is conducted and the theosophical reasons underlying those methods), the development of LCC theory has been heavily informed by quantitative and statistical methods. These approaches aim to measure precisely and thereby to quantify and establish associations between life experiences and the development of and changes within patterns of offending behaviour. To an extent, therefore, life course criminology research fits closely to longitudinal study methods which is a research design in which data are repeatedly gathered from or about the same 'subjects' over time, with the aim of establishing correlations between risk factors such as neglect or poverty and offending or other social phenomena.

Sheldon and Eleanor Glueck's work is often seen as seminal in beginning the life course approach and used statistical approaches to study persistent juvenile offenders (Glueck and Glueck, 1930, 1950; Blokland and Nieuwbeerta, 2010; McAra and McVie, 2012). However, their work is important to understanding adult criminality as well. They developed prediction tables and a determinist approach to the development and continuation of criminal behaviour in adulthood (see Chapter 9, the companion volume).

The life course perspective grew in popularity over the course of the 20th century, particularly from the 1970s onwards within US Criminal Justice Studies (McAra and McVie, 2012). The central focus in those early studies concerned young people (Wolfgang et al, 1972). However, this led to other longitudinal studies, including research to follow participants from childhood into middle/late adulthood. Notably, John Laub and Robert Sampson (2003) conducted a qualitative and quantitative analysis of a follow-up of the Gluecks' (1930) study of the criminal careers of the 500 Boston-area male delinquents through to age 70. Laub and Sampson are regarded as two of the leading theorists within life course approach and their decade's long follow up study of the Boston delinquents remains the longest longitudinal study of criminal behaviour in the field. Although the results from their research indicated that there were groups of individuals who demonstrated patterns of involvement in crime over their lives, most groups appeared to be law abiding by late to mid adulthood, with little to no evidence of criminality at age 70. This and other related research led to Laub and Sampson developing their influential 'age graded theory of informal social control' (Sampson and Laub, 1993; Laub and Sampson, 2003). As Blokland and Nieuwbeerta (2010, p 60) summarise:

> The basic argument of their theory is that criminal involvement results from a lack of informal social controls and that what constitute appropriate sources of social control varies throughout life. Important transitions in other life course domains yield changes in the level of informal control and can therefore act as turning points for crime.

These turning points include employment, military service and marriage which arguably provide stability, structure and even discipline (see Farrington et al, 1986; Farrrington, 2003, 2017). What is important to realise about this theory is that it brings together social influences on crime, such as family and employment, with psychological predispositions; in other words, it attempts to take account of both nature and nurture. Arguably, then, this 'social psychological' approach to crime brings together some of the most persuasive features of narrower psychological and sociological approaches, as it acknowledges personal differences in criminal propensity, but it also makes a place for society to counteract, these propensities (Moffitt, 1993; Chamberlain, 2015).

An extended consideration of the work of British criminologist and forensic psychologist David P. Farrington is given in Chapter 9 in the companion volume. However, it is important that précis his contribution in this chapter as well. Farrington's own research included cohort studies designed to investigate whether criminal behaviour persists from childhood into adulthood (Farrington et al, 1998). The study found that persistent criminals are likely to be male, from economically deprived areas and separated families. As a social worker it is important that you develop your thinking about how criminal behaviour may develop as this will help you to identify potential trigger points, structural and personal influences that can be acknowledged and worked on to divert someone from criminal behaviour while recognising that those behaviours are labelled according to social and cultural norms at the time. This will help you in applying your value base and not judging the person or labelling her or him but focusing on the behaviours themselves. Social and environmental factors played a large part in the continuation of criminal behaviour. We can see how these factors may combine in Case Study 9.1.

CASE STUDY 9.1

This case study briefly discusses the 'career' of John McVicar who was a former violent criminal turned author and broadcaster. Although there are certainly many other similar cases we could have examined, unlike the majority of former criminals, McVicar has written about his life in his autobiography, *McVicar by Himself* (McVicar, 2002) as well in other publications. A period of his life which focused especially on his criminal behaviour was also the subject of a powerful film (Clegg, 1980) starring the British rock singer and actor Roger Daltry in the title role. We know from McVicar's autobiography that his early life and relationships were not atypical for a youngster in East London in the 1940s and 1950s. His heavy-drinking father and experiences while growing up did, however, exert an influence on this bright grammar school boy. However, it is perhaps interesting to note that while McVicar wished to protect his own son from making the same mistakes as him, he was not able to do so. He had fathered a child when on the run and living with a bar hostess. When he was rearrested he wrote pieces for the newspaper to provide money for his son to ensure his son was sheltered from crime. However, the boy's mother did not use the money for the child, and in later life McVicar's son was imprisoned himself, for armed robbery. Although no one should claim that his upbringing *made* him a criminal, it seems evident that no one in his family – or what criminologists often term 'the primary agents of socialisation' – had sufficient influence to stop him and this gave him the opportunity for early delinquent activity. McVicar was clearly a tough young boy and wanted to be the best fighter in his school, and by the age of 16 he was accepted into a criminal gang where he and other gang members (or, put more theoretically, 'secondary agents of socialisation') engaged in petty crime and what we now term anti-social behaviour. McVicar's criminal career progressed and he was sentenced to a term of imprisonment after having been involved in violent, armed bank robbery. Prisons have been described as 'criminal universities' and the prison system gave him ample opportunity to associate with other criminals – a term which criminologists refer to as 'differential association'. As very well depicted in the film about this period of his life, the prison institution also gave him opportunity to stay very fit, alert and physically strong, as well as to strengthen his 'criminal values'. In 1968, he managed to escape from prison and Scotland Yard dubbed him 'public enemy no. 1'.

As Hutchings describes, in Chapter 8, education and learning can be lifelong. Just as in the case of relationships, a positive learning experience can open new avenues for people and can deflect people from previous entrenched behaviours.

John McVicar began studying sociology and deviance in the 1960s and was initially taught by the famous sociologist and broadcaster, Laurie Taylor, with whom he established an ongoing friendship. When McVicar escaped prison in 1968, he was on the run for two years and during this time he kept up his reading and studies. When re-imprisoned in 1970, he studied for two A-levels and later for a degree.

On his parole in 1978, he traded his life as an armed criminal for that of a writer, thinker and journalist (McVicar, 2002) and undertook postgraduate studies.

McVicar's change of direction was certainly not sudden. It was a gradual process of learning and inquiry that eventually offered him new directions to pursue. What his story shows is the power of education to change lives and that this can happen at any point in a person's life.

Questions

1. How do you think the various points in his life influenced McVicar?
2. What do you think may have led him into crime?
3. How might this knowledge be used to deflect someone from criminality?

Discussion

It is not necessarily the case that McVicar's earlier experiences led him into crime, although the interpretation of experiences and learning from them can, as we have seen, exert a powerful influence on future decisions and behaviour. It is important to remember, however, that most people who experience adverse family environments and negative attachment experiences do not commit crime. Just as the environment in which adults live, grow and develop is much wider than their family, the structural aspects – quality of accommodation, neighbourhood, poverty, employment prospects – must also be taken into account.

REFLECTION POINT 9.4

Mark Duggan was a 29-year-old man who was shot dead by police in 2011 after reports that he had taken possession of a hand gun and was a gang member. His death exacerbated the already poor relations between community and police and resulted in extensive rioting. Although inquiries into his shooting have judged he was lawfully killed, there have been many questions and criticisms against the inquiry and outcome.

Do a search of the web to find out what you can about Mark Duggan. You will no doubt find some contradictory statements about the extent of his criminal career, his family and his intentions. You will also find a focus on some of the labels that were applied to him, such as 'gangster' or 'father of six'. Think about how Duggan was portrayed and what this says about the media's view of criminal behaviour.

It can often be the case that media stories about criminals tend to demonise, through their explanations, certain groups or individuals who commit crime or who simply challenge the social mores of the time. A critical approach to the structural and environmental factors is avoided in such thinking and therefore it can be politically useful in deflecting attention from governmental or organisational responsibilities to finding effective ways of reducing crime and diverting those who have been involved into more prosocial activities. Stanley Cohen's (1972) recognition of the development of moral panic is useful here. His seminal study of the way media portrayed fighting in the 1960s between rival groups allows us to see how the presentation of events may give rise to an interpretation that is more than it actually is and thereby create the impression that things are worse than they are.

What we do know from research, however, is that secure adult attachments are more likely to lead to positive outcomes and that satisfying relationships can stabilise behaviour and redefine life goals for the partners (see Chapter 6). Hirschi's (1969) theory of the strength and inhibitory power of relationships is useful here. The inhibiting effect of relationships and the growth of responsibilities to entering or maintaining involvement in crime links back to earlier research that helped to develop life course criminology. However, the growth of a sense of responsibility can influence behaviour in other ways too. Consider the actions of Extinction Rebellion protesters in Trafalgar Square in 2019. Many of the protestors were older people, both male and female, with responsible positions or who were grandparents.

When confronted by a change in Metropolitan Police tactics banning all protests in London and making them subject to a public order offence under Section 14 of the Public Order Act 1986, many of these protesters were potentially criminalised. LCC has made a significant contribution to our understanding of the relationship between offending and antisocial behaviour and age and a wide range of factors that vary over the life course but it offers little to explain the behaviour of Extinction Rebellion. The problem here is something that we highlighted earlier on in this chapter. Crime, criminality and criminal behaviour represent social constructions that are mutable and dependent on the social and political conditions of the time. So, for social workers, it is something that we need to keep in mind and to look under the behaviour to the person, their relationships and environment, and the structural conditions in which the behaviours are taking place.

Making it real: applying knowledge to practice

Asking yourself some key questions when working with people who have offended is important. The need to maintain a critically reflective stance should be uppermost in your mind. So, asking how you perceive certain environmental situations, what you think of families, partners and friends in a very honest way can help you identify some of the prejudices you might have that may suggest simplistic cause and effect understandings of these people's lives. Identifying your own biases and prejudices (and we all have them, however unconscious these are!) will allow you to move beyond them to see the young people and the ecological systems which they inhabit. In social work and other human service professions it is crucial to develop your reflexivity. Case Study 9.2 adds a perspective that is beginning to be more understood concerning changes that are out of character with the person someone appeared to be.

CASE STUDY 9.2

Zeinab was in her late 50s. She was the daughter of medics who had moved from Syria to Britain 10 years before she was born. Zeinab was a teacher in a local primary school and involved in the local community in campaigning for area development, leisure activities and play spaces for children. She was well liked and appeared devoted to her husband of 30 years and their two young adult children. Over the last few months, she had been arrested twice for shoplifting. She confided in her husband that she had been doing this for some time and many more occasions than the two for which she was arrested. She said she did not know why she did it.

Questions

1. What do you think you need to know as a social worker?
2. How might your knowledge of adult development help you to understand the situation?
3. How might you work alongside others in helping Zeinab at this time?

Discussion

Of course, a comprehensive assessment is necessary here and it is probably something that needs to include a health and psychological assessment. So, you are likely to be working with both health and possibility criminal justice workers here. A knowledge of how mental health can affect people, how physical changes can manifest in ways that appear inexplicable and an understanding of the impact of social and structural pressures are all important to comprehending the situation and communicating with others involved in it. This will also be important when working alongside her husband and children who are likely, we may assume, to be profoundly affected by Zeinab's change in behaviour. So, not only a knowledge of criminality through the life course but also significant and unexpected changes at points within it form part of the social worker's knowledge.

Conclusion

In general terms, we can see that people develop across the life course depending on different experiences, environmental and personal factors. Understanding the impact that these influences have on people is important in understanding them in their context and offers ways of understanding how they might best be helped. This is where life course criminology, and other theories of crime and criminal behaviour, offer important understandings for social workers to use. It is also important, of course, for working interdisciplinarily with police officers and others in the criminal justice system.

Reflective questions

1 As a social worker, what do you think some of the benefits may be of knowing the theory of life course criminology?

2 What do you think some of the criticisms of life course criminology are when considering adult development?

3 How might you introduce some of the thinking behind life course criminology when working with someone involved in crime?

Further reading

- Farrington, D.P. (2017) *Integrated Developmental and Life-Course Theories of Offending.* London and New York: Routledge.
  This book provides the most comprehensive and rigorous approach to life course criminology. Farrington's work is second to none and for anyone seeking more in-depth knowledge: this is the text to go to.

- Sampson, R.J. and Laub, J. (2005) A life-course view of the development of crime, *The Annals of the American Academy of Political and Social Science,* 602(1): 12–45.
  Sampson and Laub's original research and the development of the Gluecks' work underpins much of what we know about how the life course potentially moulds and changes one's involvement with crime. While the study focused on US juveniles moving through the life course and their criminal behaviour or otherwise, it is still useful for considering adult development, although its context and emphasis on career criminality must be taken into account.

- Winstone, J. (ed.) (2016) *Mental Health, Crime and Criminal Justice: Responses and Reforms.* Basingstoke: Palgrave.
  This book provides a comprehensive overview of the interactions between crime and mental health and mental health and crime. It will help you expand your knowledge of this important area.

References

Blokland, A.A.J. and Nieuwbeerta, P. (2010) Life course criminology. In P. Knepper and S.G. Shoham (eds), *International Handbook of Criminology.* London: CRC Press.

Bottoms, A.E. and McWilliams, W. (1979) A non–treatment paradigm for probation practice, *British Journal of Social Work,* 9(2): 159-202.

Bowling, B. (2013) Epilogue. The borders of punishment: Towards a criminology of mobility. In K.F. Aas and M. Bosworth (eds), *The Borders of Punishment: Migration, Citizenship and Social Exclusion*. Oxford: Oxford University Press, pp 291–306.

Chamberlain, J.M. (2015) *Criminological Theory in Context*. London: Sage.

Clegg, T. (Director) (1980) *McVicar*. Starring Roger Daltry. London: The Who Films/Brent Walker Film Distributors.

Cohen, S. (1972) *Folk Devils and Moral Panics: The Creation of the Mods and the Rockers*. London: MacGibbon and Kee.

Dorling, D., Gordon, D., Hillyard, P., Pantazis, P., Pemberton, S. and Tombes, S. (2008) *Criminal Obsessions: Why Harm Matters More than Crime*. London: Centre for Criminal Justice Studies.

Farrington, D.P. (2003) Developmental and life-course criminology: Key theoretical and empirical issues. The 2002 Sutherland Award address. *Criminology*, 41(2): 221–225.

Farrington, D.P. (2017) *Integrated Developmental and Life-Course Theories of Offending*. London and New York: Routledge.

Farrington, D.P., Lambert, S. and West, D.J. (1998) Criminal careers of two generations of family members in the Cambridge study in delinquent development, *Studies on Crime and Crime Prevention*, 7(1): 85–106.

Farrington, D.P., Gallagher, B., Morley, L., St. Ledger, R.J. and West, D.J. (1986) Unemployment, school leaving and crime, *British Journal of Criminology*, 26(4): 335–356.

Glueck, S. and Gleuck, E. (1930) *500 Criminal Careers*. New York: Knopf.

Glueck, S. and Glueck, E. (1950) *Unravelling Juvenile Delinquency*. Oxford: The Commonwealth Fund.

Hirschi, T. (1969) *The Causes of Delinquency*. Berkeley: University of California Press.

Homel, R. and France, A. (2005) *Youth Justice Dictionary*. Cullompton: Willan.

Laub, J.H. and Sampson, R.J. (2003) *Shared Beginnings, Divergent Lives: Delinquent Boys to Age 70*. Cambridge, MA: Harvard University Press.

Loader, I. and Sparks, R. (2012) Situating criminology: On the production and consumption of knowledge about crime and justice. In M. Maguire, R. Morgan and R. Reiner (eds), *The Oxford Handbook of Criminology* (5th edn). Oxford: Oxford University Press, pp 3–38.

McAra, L. and McVie, S. (2012) Critical debates in developmental and life-course criminology. In M. Maguire, R. Morgan and R. Reiner (eds), *The Oxford Handbook of Criminology*. Oxford: Oxford University Press.

McNeill, F. (2006) A desistance paradigm for offender management, *Criminology and Criminal Justice*, 6(1): 39–62.

McVicar, J. (2002) *McVicar by Himself* (2nd edn). London: Artnik.

Moffitt, T. (1993) Adolescence – limited and life course persistent antisocial behaviour: A developmental taxonomy, *Psychological Review*, 100(4): 674–700.

Newburn, T. (2017) *Criminology* (3rd edn). London: Routledge.

Reiner, R. (2016) *Crime: The Mystery of the Common Concept*. Oxford: Oxford University Press.

Sampson, R.J. and Laub, J. (1993) *Crime in the Making: Pathways and Turning Points through Life*. Cambridge MA: Harvard University Press.

Wolfgang, M.E., Figlio, R.M. and Sellin, T. (1972) *Delinquency in a Birth Cohort*. Chicago: University of Chicago Press.

Young, J. (2003) In praise of dangerous thoughts, *Punishment and Society*, 5(1): 97–107.

10

Health and disability in adults: definitions and models

Vanessa Heaslip

Introduction

Many adults in the world live with a disability. It is, however, a somewhat nebulous term which collectively refers to individuals with different experiences, such as being born with a cognitive impairment or becoming disabled as a result of chronic illness or accident. Irrespective of the type of disability, it is widely accepted that living with a disability can have significant impact upon individuals' lives contributing to health inequity and lack of access to health and social care. This chapter examines current evidence with regards to prevalence of disability as well as contemporary guidelines redefining disability. The chapter develops by examining the historical management of adults with a disability and how this contributes to the different ways in which disability is perceived. Moving on, the chapter presents contemporary challenges that adults living with a disability face in the 21st century and how health and social care professionals can inadvertently perpetuate vulnerability of these individuals.

Chapter objectives

- investigate definitions of disability extending beyond that of individuals born with either an intellectual or physical impairment;

- explore the historical management of adults living with a disability and how this has influenced contemporary discourses regarding disability;

- consider wider social influences and how these impact upon health and well-being of adults living with a disability;

- examine health inequalities of adults living with a disability;

- identify professional practice suggestions to working with adults living with a disability.

Prevalence and definitions

Current estimates of people living with a disability vary, the World Health Organization (WHO, 2019) estimate the figure to be over a billion people, equating to 15 per cent of the world population; whereas Hosseinpoort et al (2016) estimate that the prevalence of adult disability to range between 15.6 and 19.4 per cent. These differences occur due to the complexity of defining what is meant by the term disability. The *World Report on Disability* (WHO, 2011) identifies that rather than being a homogenous group, adults living with a disability are diverse and heterogeneous ranging from individuals who are wheelchair users, individuals born with congenital conditions (such as cerebral palsy, Down's syndrome), individuals who lose a limb due to a traumatic event, individuals living with a chronic debilitating illness (such as arthritis or dementia), individuals living with a specific learning difficulty (such as dyslexia, dyspraxia and so forth). As such, disabilities can be permanent or temporary, visible or hidden, single or multiple events and can have a significant impact upon the individual and their family (WHO, 2011).

One particular group of people who are increasingly finding themselves 'disabled' are adults living with a long-term condition, this is due to both a growth in ageing population and a growth in chronic illnesses (WHO, 2018). Long-term conditions are identified as medical conditions for which there are currently no cure and which are managed by medications and other treatment (George and Martin, 2016) and include conditions such as dementia, arthritis, osteoporosis, chronic obstructive pulmonary disease and chronic heart failure. There is also a significant growth in the numbers of adults living with not just one but multiple chronic conditions, referred to as co- or multi-morbidity, and this has a significant impact not only on financial health-care costs, but also on human costs, such as quality of life (Goodwin et al, 2010). In light of this, it could be argued that every single one of us will, at some point in our adult lives, experience impairment or disability.

Disability has been defined by the World Health Organization (WHO, 2001) as an 'umbrella term for impairments, activity limitations and participation restrictions', referring to the negative aspects of the interaction between the individual (with a health condition) and that individual's contextual factors (environmental and personal factors). Although this definition is now 18 years old, it is still the most commonly used international definition of a disability. Vornholt et al (2018) argue that this definition recognises that people can be disabled not only by their bodies, but also by environmental factors, and that disability is not equal to medical concepts of impairments, but rather to the relationship between the person and their environment.

It is important to note when this chapter refers generically to an adult living with a disability, it is inclusive of all of these particular groups of individuals, exploring the wider health issues related to living with a disability.

Historical overview

In order to understand some of the prevailing discourses surrounding disability, there is a need to explore how adults living with a disability were perceived and treated in the past. What follows is a brief history adapted from Historic England (2018). During the medieval period of 1050–1485, adults with a disability had a highly visible presence in society. Types of disability prevalent during this period included sensory impairments ('blynde', 'deaff', 'dumbe'), intellectual disabilities ('fools'), mental illness ('lunaticks') and physical impairments ('lame', 'creple'), as well as what we would commonly refer to as medical conditions today, such as leprosy ('lepre'). Leprosy (Hansen's disease) is a chronic infectious disease affecting the nerves and skin that was extensive during the medieval period and at that time there were no effective treatments. Perceptions of adults living with a disability were mixed; some perceived that the disability was a punishment from God, while others saw it as a blessing, as the individuals were in fact living in purgatory on Earth and as such their transition to heaven would be smoother. As there was no state provision for support, if adults could not work then they were largely supported by their family, by the local community, by begging or by the church. Many churches provided the first hospital-type care for people living with leprosy, especially in the aftermath of the Black Death, where fears of contagion were widespread, resulting in greater isolation for people living with leprosy. It was also during the medieval period that the first mental institution in England was established to manage adults living with mental illness.

During 1485–1660, the dissolution of monasteries by Henry VIII led to many of the religious hospitals closing and adults living with disabilities found themselves homeless, forced to live on the street. These attacks on the Church and the Catholic faith shifted the focus of care from a religious to a civic duty in towns and local communities, and it is here that hospitals began to be built. Henry VIII's reign also saw an increase in infectious diseases such as the sweat, the plague and smallpox, and this was coupled with an increased fear of contagion, leading to the development of 'pest houses', where people living with contagious diseases were forced to live, isolating themselves and their infection from wider society. Perceptions towards disability were also changing: the introduction of a variety of Poor Laws reflected the very negative societal view of the poor; adults living with a disability were perceived as 'impotent poor', which resulted in them being provided with some charitable financial relief. During 1660–1832, adults living with a disability still largely lived in their own homes and communities and support continued to be based upon charitable and civic duty. However, during this time, there was a real expansion of medicine and with it the development of large hospitals expanding greater knowledge and study of health and illness. Embryonic ideas began to emerge that institutions were the right place for adults living with disabilities; however, it wasn't until the 19th century that there was a real growth in asylums and the introduction of workhouses, where increasing numbers of adults living with a disability found themselves located. These institutions developed largely due to the very negative societal attitudes to the poor and destitute, as such workhouses were designed to root out individuals who did not want to work and live productive lives, resulting in poor living conditions and harsh work environments.

The first half of the 20th century (1914–45) saw the growth in the Eugenics movement, which perceived disability as a defective threat and burden to society. This led to the development of rural communities for people with disabilities, isolating them from wider society. This began to be challenged at the end of the First World War, as many returning soldiers returned home with a physical disability as a result of the conflict, yet, these soldiers had very high societal regard as they had served their duty to their country. This led to advances in science, especially the prosthetic movement, striving to find ways to enable the soldiers to return to work. However, there was also an increasing epidemic of adults living with a disability due to childhood infectious diseases such as skeletal tuberculosis, poliomyelitis and rickets. It wasn't until after the Second World War with the general public's increasing knowledge of the mass killing of disabled people in Germany that the Eugenics movement really subsided. This collapse was supported by more returning soldiers with disabilities, men who had become disabled in their fight to protect the nation, and this led to an increased social awareness of the rights of people with a disability, which culminated in the 1944 Disability Employment Act and, in part, the introduction of the NHS in 1948.

It is evident that some of the prevailing perceptions of adults living with a disability that were prevalent in the UK before the 19th century are still apparent in other parts of the world today. Research by Bunning et al (2017) on perceptions of disability among local communities in Kenya identified that disability occurs due to witchcraft, demons and evil spirits, as well as it being God's will. However, this tends to focus on cognitive and physical disabilities rather than disability as a consequence of old age. Yet, a review by Hosseinpoort et al (2016) of 48 low- to middle-income countries identified a statistically significant likelihood of disability associated with women as well as age; in that one in five people aged 50–59 identified as having a disability, rising to three in five people aged over 80.

Models of disability

As can be seen from the historical overview, the 'medical model' of disability largely developed from the 19th century onwards reflecting society's growing interest and knowledge in science and medicine, as well as the introduction and growth of the number of asylums and larger hospitals. In the medical approach there is a focus on 'pathologising' the disability and in classifying the impairments, with a view that treatments could then focus on helping the patient manage those impairments (Larkin, 2009). Disabled people were therefore seen as 'abnormal' and treatment really relied upon institutional care. The medical model of a disability was the prevailing view until the later part of the 21st century, where the civil rights movement in America inspired many disabled groups to take action against the discrimination and inequity they experienced. This led to the development of a social model of disability arising from the social movement of disabled activists during the 1980s, which is described further in Chapter 12. Activists involved in this movement argued their impairments did not make them disabled, instead it was wider social factors and attitudes which curtailed their opportunities and capabilities resulting in them being disabled from engaging (Larkin, 2009). In part, it can be argued that in order to really understand an individual's experience, there is a need to incorporate both the medical and social needs, as an individual's disability is an interaction between the features of the person and the context in which that person lives (WHO, 2002). The International Classification of Functioning, Disability and Health (Figure 10.1) was developed to provide a universal classification of disability and health in health and health-related sectors (WHO, 2001). This classification incorporates a bio-psycho-social model of disability, recognising an integration of biological, individual and social dimensions in understanding disability.

While this international classification was developed in order to address the challenges of defining disability, there are still numerous issues. Bogart and Lund (2018) identify that not all individuals who would meet the criteria of having a disability under the ICF would self-identify as having a disability. Health-care research by Morris et al (2018) with all new outpatient visits at a clinic asked patients if they were disabled, and those who responded yes were asked to describe

Figure 10.1: Functioning, disability and health

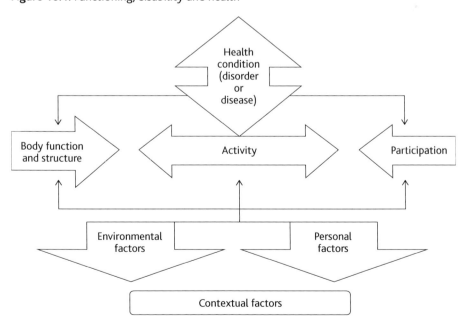

Source: Adapted from the International Classification of Functioning, Disability and Health (WHO, 2001)

their disability. Of the 14,908 participants who identified as having a disability, there was a difference in their categorisation of their disability. Adults tended to describe their disability in terms of activity limitation (56 per cent), whereas children tended to describe a diagnosis (83 per cent). In contrast, research by Eccles et al (2018) in a higher education sector identified that many higher education students also experienced difficulty in identifying what is meant by disability and, as a consequence, did not self-identify as disabled on university application forms. Their difficulties related to three different areas. Firstly, they had normalised their 'disability', seeing it as part of who they were, and therefore did not perceive it as a disability. Secondly, they struggled with identifying the range of impairments together as a disability, often viewing disability in terms of traditional physical impairments, such as being blind or being a wheelchair-user, rather than chronic illnesses. Lastly, the students identified discomfort in identifying a disability to others due to fear of stigmatisation. Not only are the issues with individuals self-identifying as disabled, but a scoping review by Gulley et al (2018) exploring how disability and chronic conditions are defined and measured in health-care access, quality utilisation and costs from a professional perspective identified that disability tended to be assessed through a variety of functional assessments, such as activities of daily living and functional limitations, while chronic illnesses were defined by the existence of a medical diagnosis. What these studies identify is that individuals living with a condition and/or the social workers or health and social care professionals working with them may perceive their disability status differently, and this can influence the degree of support and services received. Moving forwards, Gulley et al (2018) argue that there needs to be more focus on the development of assessment methods which account for both chronic illness and disability.

REFLECTION POINT 10.1

How far do you think can we extend the term 'disability' to include a range of non-visible conditions that may affect people or those they live with? What would the implications be?

Not only are there challenges related to the identification of a disability, the ICF model still largely perceives disability as an issue or challenge to be resolved. This linking of a disability as a negative constraint can result in the person with the disability being perceived as 'less' than other people (Ellis–Hill et al, 2008). Recently, this notion of perceiving disability negatively has been challenged through the introduction of the Affirmative model of a disability. Swain and French (2000, p 569) define this as '… essentially a non-tragic view of disability and impairment which encompasses positive social identities, both individual and collective, for disabled people grounded in the benefits of life style and life experience of being impaired and disabled'. They argue that rather than perceiving disability as a negative tragedy, it could be seen as a blessing which enables individuals to be more fully themselves (Goble, 2010). This affirmative model is developing traction, largely in challenge to the continued negative perceptions of disabilities.

Wider social influences and disability

In order to fully appreciate the wider factors that can influence a person's experience of living with a disability, let's explore the experience of two older people (see Case Studies 10.1 and 10.2).

CASE STUDY 10.1

Peter is an 85-year-old gentleman living with his wife and extended family in an urban area. Peter lives in a four-bedroom house which was the family home; down the road live Peter's children and grandchildren and they regularly visit Peter and his wife. Peter is a retired General Practitioner (GP), who is enjoying an active retirement, playing golf and attending his local sailing club, as well as being an active member of his local church. Peter's wife Mary has become increasingly concerned regarding Peter's health as he has recently lost weight, and has reduced energy levels, resulting in him feeling unable to go out and attend his local groups and activities. Peter has also recently become unsteady on his feet and has fallen. He has been seen by his GP, who has diagnosed Peter to be at risk of falls and frailty.

Questions

1. What factors influence Peter's current ability to remain living at home?
2. What support do you feel that Peter needs?
3. How do we weigh the competing views and needs of different actors in this scenario? That of Peter, Mary and any others directly affected by his abilities?

Discussion

Peter is living in a house where he and his wife brought up their family. In the case study, it is described as having been the family home, with the implied suggestion that somehow it is no longer that – so what has changed? Is it that it is no longer the same 'home' that it once was and if so why? Or is it that Peter has changed over time and so he cannot use it as the same 'home'? Whichever it is, Peter has lived in the house for many years, and probably enjoys the connections that have come with a known and familiar environment that is close to family and friends. Now Peter and Mary appear to be facing some difficult issues, where his increasing frailty will require some adaptions to their life, which could be major changes. These could have some serious implications not only at a practical and financial level, but also at a psychosocial level that must be considered carefully, not to detract from Peter and Mary's life.

CASE STUDY 10.2

Doreen is an 87-year-old widow living alone in a very remote rural community. She lives alone in a three-bedroom house. Doreen admits to feeling isolated at times, as many of her friends from the village have passed away, and she finds is difficult to walk the 10-minute walk into the village. Doreen has two children, but they live around a two-hour drive away, and while they try to visit regularly, they also work full time. Mary used to be a part-time cook in the village school and she will often talk about missing her work, the companionship of the other women and seeing the children at the school. Doreen's next-door-neighbour tries to pop in at least three times a week to check on her. He is concerned that she is not eating and is spending more time in her nightgown and asleep on the sofa. He calls the GP as Doreen had fallen during the night, sustaining a laceration to her lower right leg. The GP visits with the District Nurse; he feels that Doreen is becoming increasingly frail and is at risk of falls.

Questions

1. What factors influence Doreen's current ability to remain living at home?
2. How would you evaluate what her wishes are in this scenario?
3. What support do you feel that Doreen needs?

Discussion

We know that familiar surroundings can be very important to everyone, including ageing people who are becoming frail. We also know that moving such people can be detrimental to their mental health even if it is safer physically. However, this has to be balanced by the issue of loneliness (see Chapter 12, Case Study 12.4) and with that possible depression, which could in part explain why she is not eating. Doreen has become isolated at home as well as frail, and seems to be relying heavily on the goodwill of her neighbour for support and company, which could be a burden or could be beneficial to them both. It is difficult to tell without further investigation of Doreen's needs. How Doreen can best be helped to be physically safe and cared for, socially engaged, meaningfully occupied and perhaps also spiritually supported are important considerations here.

It is evident from reviewing the examples of Peter and Doreen that both have experienced the same symptoms (weight loss, increased tiredness and falls) and could be identified as frail. Frailty is defined as a progressive ageing–related, multi-system clinical state characterised by loss of physiological reserves and diminished capacity to withstand exposure to stressors (Gibson and Crowe, 2018). However, the management of these cases may be very different, in that it is more likely that Peter will remain at home, but it is more likely that Doreen may require additional support. Frailty is an increasing disability experienced in old age. It is these wider personal and environmental factors in the International Classification of Functioning, Disability and Health (WHO, 2001 Figure 10.1) that need to be explored further. Within public health there has been recognition of the wider social factors that impact upon health. While there are numerous models exploring this, the most commonly used is that of Dahlgren and Whitehead 1991 (Public Health England, 2017): see Figure 10.2.

Figure 10.2 consists of five concentric circles. At the heart of the model is personal biological factors such as age, sex and constitutional factors; both Peter and Doreen are of a similar age (85 and 87), an age group where 9 per cent experience frailty, although Doreen, as a woman, is more likely to experience frailty (Clegg et al, 2013). Looking at the individual lifestyle factors, Peter lives with his wife, whereas Doreen lives alone, and admits to feeling socially isolated at times. Research by Gale et al (2018), with 2,187 people aged over 60, highlighted that social isolation was more common in those who were older, less educated and less wealthy, resulting in an increased risk of physical frailty. In aspects of living and working conditions, while considering that both are retired, their working lives would have impacted on their finances in their retirement. For example, there is a significant difference in the wages Doreen would have earned as a part-time school cook compared to Peter as a partner in a GP practice. Part-time work is estimated to result in a 47 per cent reduction in women's pensions (Now Pensions, 2019), so it is more than likely that Doreen has less disposable income to spend on leisure activities, resulting in reduced social contact as well as reduced physical activity, both of which perpetuate frailty. In terms of the social and community

Figure 10.2: Social factors and health

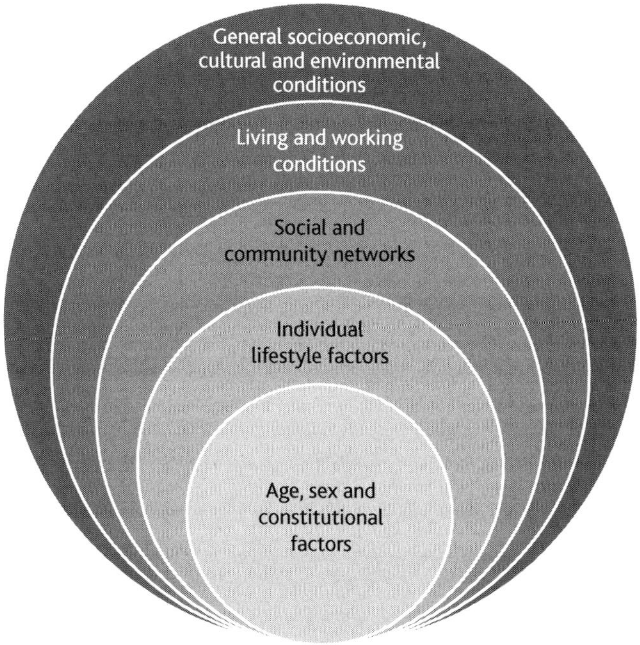

Source: Adapted from Dahlgren and Whitehead, 1991, cited in Public Health England, 2017

networks, not only is Doreen more socially isolated than Peter, but she also lives in a rural area – areas which often have less public transport than urban areas – making it more difficult for her to get out in her local community. Within the general socioeconomic and cultural differences, as well as the financial difference previously mentioned, Peter, as a retired GP, will have a better understanding of navigating health services in comparison to Doreen.

As social workers or health and social care professionals, it is really important that we consider the impact of these wider social factors and how this can influence very different experiences, even though an adult may have the same 'disability'. It is also important that we spend time assessing parents'/carers' knowledge and understanding of statutory services; as health and social care personnel, it is easy to forget how complex the interplay of such services are, and this can result in significant confusion for the lay public. A key aspect of our role is educating and sign-posting to other statutory services.

Discrimination, disability and health inequity

People with disabilities are one of the most socially disadvantaged groups (Bigby et al, 2018; Palad et al, 2016). In order to address this, 2006 saw the introduction of the United Nations Convention on the Rights of Persons with Disabilities (CRPD). This convention promoted full integration of people with disabilities within society and asserted the importance of international collaboration in addressing the rights of persons with disabilities. To date, 177 countries have ratified the CRPD, which carries the force of national law (World Bank, 2018). Within the CRPD, there are eight agreed principles regarding the rights of people with a disability, including:

1. respect for inherent dignity, individual autonomy including the freedom to make one's own choices, and independence of persons;
2. non-discrimination;
3. full and effective participation and inclusion in society;
4. respect for difference and acceptance of persons with disabilities as part of human diversity and humanity;
5. equality of opportunity;
6. accessibility;
7. equality between men and women;
8. respect for the evolving capacities of children with disabilities and respect for the right of children with disabilities to preserve their identities.

In 2014, the Global Disability Action Plan 2014–2021: Better Health for all People with Disability (WHO, 2015) was published; this has an overall goal of achieving health, well-being and human rights for people living with a disability.

In spite of these global action plans, there is a wealth of evidence that people with disabilities experience discrimination and inequity. With regard to education, despite similar educational aspirations between disabled and non-disabled young people (Burchardt, 2005), there are educational attainment gaps in that young people with a disability are less likely to complete secondary-level education than their non-disabled counterparts (Male and Wodon, 2017). This gap in educational attainment of young people with a disability has long-term effects regarding their lives as adults, in that adults with a disability are twice more likely to be unemployed than their non-disabled counterparts (Vornholt et al, 2018). This has significant long-term health implications, as the link between formal education and improved health is well established (Baker et al, 2011), as well as implications for long-term financial security and pensions, identified earlier.

REFLECTION POINT 10.2

You may have heard of the term 'feminisation of poverty', but disability is also heavily implicated in poverty. How far do you think poverty exacerbates the experience of disability?

In health, Article 25 of the CRPD specifically focuses upon the rights of people with a disability to attain the highest standard of health care (United Nations, 2006). Notwithstanding this, people with disabilities are more likely to seek access to health care, yet conversely, report greater unmet health needs (WHO, 2018), resulting in higher morbidity and rates of premature death (Tracy and McDonald, 2015). Sakellariou and Rotarou (2017) highlight that people with a disability experience worse access to health care due to physical and attitudinal barriers (Hanon and Payne, 2017). These have resulted in reduced access to screening for common cancers, including prostate, cervical, breast and bowel (Merten et al, 2015). Not only are there issues with accessing health care, but experiences of care are also worrying. Numerous reports have examined poor care experiences of people living with a disability in health and social care, including *Death by Indifference* (Mencap, 2007), *Six Lives* (Parliamentary and Health Service Ombudsman, 2009) and *Winterbourne View* (Department of Health, 2012); all of these reports highlight significant failures in health and social care which resulted in people with a disability experiencing suffering, abuse and inappropriate care. More recently, a systematic review of exploring hospital experiences of people with an intellectual disability highlighted that, despite 20 years of research and government initiatives, little has changed and that people with a disability still have poor experiences of hospital care (Iacono et al, 2014).

Application to social work professional practice

We have previously explored the recent shift towards the affirmative model of disability promoted by disability writers and activists; however, this has yet to integrate fully into mainstream societal thought. Largely, the predominant perceptions of disability remain negative, perceiving disability as a slowing action, a lack of independence and impairment (Friedman and Owen, 2017) and this perception of a disability can have a direct impact upon social workers' and health professionals' responses to the disability. Focusing upon the negative attributes of a person highlights their vulnerability and in doing so their risk to harm (Heaslip and Hewitt-Taylor, 2014). Professional responses therefore tend to focus on the amelioration of risk and protection of the person, making them safe and making decisions for them. Consequences of this are a reduction in the ability of the individual to self-assess and manage their own risk, a reduction in their personal autonomy and reduction of their citizenship. They become 'something' which must be protected rather than 'someone' with an equal voice. A scoping review of empirical research, published by social work authors in Australia, identified that social work research tends to focus upon the negative attributes of a disability, continuing to describe the problem, drawing attention to the disadvantaged position and service inadequacies, while very few research studies have tested the efficacy of interventions or evaluated service models (Bigby et al, 2018). There is a need to move away from such paternalistic practices towards more inclusive person-centred practices which value and promote the individual's voice. Goble (2010) identified that in order to achieve this, practices must focus on:

1. A dialogue-based approach, drawing on the expertise and experience of individuals in constructing joint narratives about their health.
2. A strengths and abilities focus, focusing on strengths, and capabilities rather than deficit and weakness to create opportunities for engagement.
3. Creating a collaborative culture, focusing on communication which fosters positive inclusive relationships.

In a dialogue-based approach, there is a need to recognise the expertise of individuals who are living with a disability. Examples of this can include the involvement of individuals in the training and education of social workers and, more recently, other health and social care professionals, as this can directly challenge hidden beliefs, values and stereotypes of individuals living with a disability, as the person with the disability is presented as the expert rather than the human service professional. Key to this is the focus and recognition of the need to concentrate upon strengths and capabilities of individuals rather than deficit and weakness and elegantly challenge discriminatory beliefs and values. This serves to create a culture of collaboration; however, here there is a need to focus on positive communication which develops inclusive relationships. This positive communication has to include all individuals living with a disability, so needs to include a variety of communication techniques, such as verbal, non-verbal and appropriate assistive technology, ensuring participation of all parties.

Key to this is both the valuing and the accepting of the other's lifeworld. Ellis-Hill et al (2008) developed a life thread model which can be used to understand the lived experience of a disability. In this model they explain that 'life threads represent the variety of stories that we tell about ourselves. They represent past memories and future plans' (p 152). Some life threads remain consistent, such as roles (e.g. daughter, granddaughter), but others are transient, for example, winning a football match aged 10, while significant then, may not remain so in 59 years' time. It is these life threads which create our sense of identity and our understanding of our current situation, as well as our future possibilities; however, these threads are not fixed, as one's sense of identity is constantly shifting, influenced by societal interactions and life experiences. In this model, we see much more of a holistic picture of the experience of living with a disability. For example, someone living with a disability as a result of a traumatic event can find that their life threads become broken as people find themselves redefining who they are and who they will be in the future (Ellis-Hill et al, 2008). Consider, for example, the fictional story of *Still Alice* (Case Study 10.3)

CASE STUDY 10.3

Still Alice is a movie based upon the book written by Lisa Genova. In this story, Dr Alice Howland, a linguistic university professor at Columbia University, finds herself forgetting words and becoming increasingly disorientated in her daily life. Throughout the film and book you follow Alice's life through her story as she finds herself with a diagnosis of early onset Alzheimer's shortly after her 50th birthday. In this you see how her previous life threads were tied in with her cognitive and linguistic capabilities, her job, her role and the academic papers she has written, yet her life threads shift as she becomes aware of her diagnosis and deteriorating condition; she finds herself having to redefine who she is in the present, as well as coming to terms that this redefinition will also shift as her cognition declines.

Questions

1. Consider yourself and your life threads: how do you define yourself and what is important to you?
2. Consider how you would feel if you found yourself forgetting your words, feeling lost in your own home and losing your sense of who you were.
3. What options do you see for yourself in this scenario?

Discussion

There is no doubt about it, dementia is viewed by most people as a deeply frightening prospect with regard to oneself. It is also altogether too easy to forget that people suffering from dementia may once have enjoyed full, meaningful, busy and intellectually stimulating lives; and if we do remember this, then the losses brought by such diagnosis seem horrifyingly tragic and poignant. It is hard to pull these two pictures together, that of the person who was and that of the person who is, unless we can somehow see them as the same person but in transition, and yet, we must not romanticise the situation, for part of the horror of dementia (at least as seen from the outside) is the existential fear of becoming completely alienated

> from oneself. Yet, the prolific science-fiction writer, Terry Pratchett, produced not only incredibly inventive stories, but eventually, being diagnosed with Alzheimer's disease, openly discussed his condition and became something of a spokesperson for the disease (you can find some of his talks on YouTube). Although Pratchett succumbed to the disease and has now died, he still offers, through his talks, some very important ways by which we can understand the shifting experiences of dementia and how he and therefore we can relate to it.

Ellis–Hill et al (2008) argue that it is vital that we, as health and social care professionals, respond to adjusting life threads by respecting personhood and enabling people to tell their stories. In this we recognise we may not be able to resolve the issues the person is experiencing or indeed make the situation better, yet Ellis-Hill et al (2008, p 156) argue it is equally important that we listen and enable people to tell their stories: in doing so we recognise that 'being with somebody is just as important as doing something for them'.

Conclusion

This chapter has considered wider definitions of disability and examined how some of the current discourses surrounding disability have emerged through society's historical treatment of adults with a disability. It is these wider influences that have resulted in adults living with a disability experiencing health inequities and this is, in part, perpetuated by attitudes towards them. Lastly, different ways in which we as health and social care professionals can strengthen the ways in which we work with adults living with a disability to value them as equal partners have been presented. The reflective questions posed here provide you with an opportunity to consider your personal values, beliefs and practices when working with people with a disability, as well as the service in which you work and how this could be developed to ensure equitable provision.

Reflective questions

1 Consider the words that spring to mind when you think of disability and what does this tell you regarding your definition of a disability and what has influenced this?

2 Reflect upon your experiences of adults with a disability through personal/professional exposure or what you have seen through media, such as television and films. What has been the predominant presentation of the person with a disability?

3 Critically reflect upon the degree to which your assessment process captures the wider determinants of health and how this can influence the experience of the individual. How much of your service actually addresses the wider issues?

4 Consider the service in which you work: what services are in place to ensure that the voices of people with a disability are heard in service development and enhancement? How could you develop this further to include the voices of people who may have a communication difficulty?

Further reading

Read more on the Life Thread Model and explore how this can influence your practice and that of your colleagues:

- Ellis-Hill, C., Payne, S. and Ward, C. (2008) Using stroke to explore the Life Thread Model: An alternative approach to understanding rehabilitation following an acquired disability, *Disability and Rehabilitation*, 30(2): 150–159.
  This is a very useful paper that enables the reader to consider how individuals may experience changes of identity through disability.

Read more about discrimination and disability exploring why people with a disability experience discrimination and the impact it has upon them:

- Temple, J., Kelaher, M. and Williams, R. (2018) Discrimination and avoidance due to disability in Australia: Evidence from a National Cross Sectional Survey, *BMC Public Health*, 18: 1347. Available from: https://doi.org/10.1186/s12889-018-6234-7.

Increasingly, the experiential aspect of individuals, whether in terms of disability, mental health, chronic illness or other human domain of suffering or difference, gives us authentic insights into the key issues, implications and even unexpected benefits and blessings of such lives.

Read the Convention on the Rights of Persons with a Disability and critically question the degree to which this is having an impact on the individual lives of adults living with a disability:

- United Nations (2006) *Convention on the Rights of Persons with Disabilities*. Available from: https://www.un.org/development/desa/disabilities/convention-on-the-rights-of-persons-with-disabilities.html
  It is well worth acquainting yourself with the Convention in order to develop an understanding of overarching international policies relating to disability.

Read the ICF:

- World Health Organization (2001) *The International Classification of Functioning, Disability and Health* (ICF). Geneva: WHO. Available from: http://www.who.int/classifications/icf/en/
  Another useful site that offers definitions and descriptors useful for professional work in this area.

References

Baker, D., Leon, J., Smith Greenway, E., Collins, J. and Movit, M. (2011) The education effect on population health: A reassessment, *Population and Development Review*, 37(2): 307–332.

Bigby, C., Tilbury, C. and Hughes, M. (2018) Social work research in the field of disability in Australia: A scoping review, *Australian Social Work*, 71(1): 18–31.

Bogart, K. and Lund, E. (2018) Disability pride protects self-esteem through the rejection-identification model, *Rehabilitation Psychology*, 63(1): 155–159.

Bunning, K., Gona, J., Newton, C. and Hartley, S. (2017) The perception of disability by community groups: Stories of local understanding, beliefs and challenges in a rural part of Kenya. *PLoS One*, 12(8): e0182214. Available from: https://journals.plos.org/plosone/article?id=10.1371/journal.pone.0182214

Burchardt, T. (2005) *The education and employment of disabled young people*. York: Joseph Rowntree Foundation.

Clegg, A., Young, J., Rikkert, M.O. and Rockwood, K. (2013) Frailty in elderly people, *Lancet*, 2, 381(9868): 752–762. Available from: https://doi.org/10.1016/S0140-6736(12)62167-9.

Department of Health (2012) *Transforming Care: A National Response to Winterbourne View Hospital Department of Health Review: Final Report*. London: Department of Health.

Eccles, S., Heaslip, V., Hutchings, M. and Hunt, C. (2018) Risk and stigma: Students' perceptions and disclosure of 'disability' in higher education, *Widening Participation and Lifelong Learning*, 20(4): 191–208.

Ellis-Hill, C., Payne, S. and Ward, C. (2008) Using stroke to explore the Life Thread Model: An alternative approach to understanding rehabilitation following an acquired disability, *Disability and Rehabilitation*, 30(2): 150–159.

Friedman, C. and Owen, A. (2017) Defining disability: Understandings of and attitudes towards ableism and disability, *Disability Studies Quarterly*, 37(1): 2. Available from: http://dx.doi.org/10.18061/dsq.v37i1

Gale, C., Westbury, L. and Cooper, C. (2018) Social isolation and loneliness as risk factors for the progression of frailty: The English Longitudinal Study of Ageing, *Age Ageing*, 47(3): 392–397.

George, J. and Martin, F. (2016) *Living with Long Term Conditions*. London: British Medical Association.

Gibson, J. and Crowe, S. (2018) Frailty in critical care: Examining implications for clinical practices, *Critical Care Nurse*, 38(3): 29–35.

Goble, C. (2010) Celebrating disability. In C. Gaine (ed.), *Equality and Diversity in Social Work Practice*. Exeter: Learning Matters, ch 5, pp 55–65.

Goodwin, N., Curry, N., Naylor, C., Ross, S. and Duldig, W. (2010) *Managing People with Long-Term Conditions*. London: King's Fund.

Gulley, S., Rasch, E., Bethell, C., Carle, A., Druss, B., Houtrow, A., Reichard, A. and Chan, L. (2018) At the intersection of chronic disease, disability and health services research: A scoping literature review, *Disability and Health Journal*, 11(2): 192–203.

Hanon, E. and Payne, D. (2017) Cervical screening for women with physical disabilities, *Kai Tiaki Nursing New Zealand*, 23(11): 22–44.

Heaslip, V. and Hewitt-Taylor, J. (2014) Vulnerability and risk in children living with a physical disability, *Nursing Children and Young People*, 26(10): 24–29.

Historic England (2018) *A history of disability: from 1050 to the present day*. Available from: https://historicengland.org.uk/research/inclusive-heritage/disability-history/ (accessed 11 October 2018).

Hosseinpoort, A., Bergen, N., Kostanjsek, N., Kowal, P., Officer, A. and Chatterji, S. (2016) Socio-demographic patterns of disability among older adult populations of low-income and middle-income countries: Results from World Health Survey, *International Journal of Public Health*, 61: 337–345.

Iacono, T., Bigby, C., Unsworth, C., Douglas, J. and Fitzpatrick, P. (2014) A systematic review of hospital experiences of people with intellectual disability, *BMC Health Services Research*, 14: 505. Available from: https://doi.org/10.1186/s12913-014-0505-5 (accessed 19 November 2018).

Larkin, M. (2009) *Vulnerable Groups in Health and Social Care*. London: Sage.

Male, C. and Wodon, Q. (2017) *The price of exclusion: Disability and education, disability gaps in educational attainment and literacy*. Global Partnership for Education and the World Bank. Available from: http://documents.worldbank.org/curated/en/396291511988894028/pdf/121762-replacement-PUBLIC-WorldBank-GapsInEdAttainmentLiteracy-Brief-v6.pdf (accessed 17 October 2018).

Mencap (2007) Death by Indifference. Available from: https://www.basw.co.uk/system/files/resources/basw_121542-4_0.pdf

Merten, J., Pomeranz, J., King, J., Moorhouse, M. and Wynn, R. (2015) Barriers to cancer screening for people with disabilities: A literature review, *Disability and Health Journal*, 8(1): 9–16.

Morris, M., Inselman, J., Rogers, J., Halverson, C., Branda, M. and Griffin, J. (2018) How do patients describe their disabilities? A coding system for categorizing patients' descriptions, *Disability and Health Journal*, 11(2): 310–314.

Now Pensions (2019) *Facing an Unequal Future: Closing the Gender Pensions Gap*. London: Now Pensions.

Palad, Y., Barquia, R., Domingo, H., Flores, C., Padilla, L., and Ramel, J. (2016) Scoping review of instruments measuring attitudes toward disability, *Disability and Health Journal*, 9(3): 354–374.

Parliamentary and Health Service Ombudsman (2009) *Six Lives: The Provision of Public Services to People with Learning Disabilities*. London: Stationery Office.

Public Health England (2017) *Health profile for England*. Available from: https://www.gov.uk/government/publications/health-profile-for-england/chapter-6-social-determinants-of-health (accessed 13 October 2018).

Sakellariou, D. and Rotarou, E.S. (2017) Access to healthcare for men and women with disabilities in the UK: Secondary analysis of cross-sectional data, *BMJ Open*, 7: e016614. Available from: https://doi.org/10.1136/bmjopen-2017-016614

Swain, J. and French, S. (2000) Towards an affirmation model of disability, *Disability & Society*, 15(4): 569–582.

Temple, J., Kelaher, M. and Williams, R. (2018) Discrimination and avoidance due to disability in Australia: Evidence from a National Cross Sectional Survey, *BMC Public Health*, 18: 1347. Available from: https://doi.org/10.1186/s12889-018-6234-7

Tracy, J. and McDonald, R. (2015) Health and disability: Partnerships in healthcare, *Journal of Applied Research in Intellectual Disabilities*, 28(1): 22–32.

United Nations (2006) *Convention on the Rights of Persons with Disabilities*. Available from: https://www.un.org/development/desa/disabilities/convention-on-the-rights-of-persons-with-disabilities.html (accessed 11 October 2018).

Vornholt, K., Villotti, P., Muschalla, B., Bauer, J., Colella, A., Zijlstra, F., Van Ruitenbeek, G., Uitdewilligen, S. and Corbiére, M. (2018) Disability and employment – overview and highlights, *European Journal of Work and Organizational Psychology*, 27(1): 40–55.

World Bank (2018) *Disability Inclusion*. Available from: https://www.worldbank.org/en/topic/disability (accessed 11 October 2018).

WHO (World Health Organization) (2001) *The International Classification of Functioning, Disability and Health (ICF)*. Geneva: WHO. Available from: http://www.who.int/classifications/icf/en/ (accessed 11 October 2018).

WHO (World Health Organization) (2002) *Towards a Common Language for Functioning, Disability and Health*. Geneva: WHO.

WHO (World Health Organization) (2011) *World Report on Disability*. Geneva: WHO.

WHO (World Health Organization) (2015) *WHO Global Disability Action Plan 2014–2021: Better Health for all People with Disability*. Available from: https://www.who.int/disabilities/actionplan/en/ (accessed 18 September 2019).

WHO (World Health Organization) (2018) *Disability and Health*. Available from: http://www.who.int/news-room/fact-sheets/detail/disability-and-health (accessed 17 October 2018).

WHO (World Health Organization) (2019) *Disability and Health*. Available from: https://www.who.int/news-room/fact-sheets/detail/disability-and-health (accessed 17 September 2019).

11

Death: a brief social and cultural history

Sam Porter

Introduction

Let me begin bluntly. We are all going to die. Moreover, unlike (most?) other living things, we know that we are going to die. The prospect that our lives will end is something that all human beings have to face. But the capacity of humans to understand that we are finite beings is not the only attribute of our species-being that is at play here. Another human attribute is the almost limitless cultural diversity that we display. Given that death, by definition, renders empirical examination of the self-impossible, it is radically open to the plasticity of human interpretation (Berger and Luckmann, 1966). The incredible diversity of interpretations of the nature and import of death across different times and different cultures should therefore come as no surprise.

This chapter seeks to explore our attitudes to death and how they arose. It is important for social workers and others working in the helping professions to develop such understanding, if we are going to deal sensitively and honestly with people facing death or when bereaved. Therefore, it will be necessary to explore these concerns historically, theoretically and in some depth. I should say at this point that my concentration on the West is very exclusive. Rather than comparing attitudes to death across cultures, my examination is confined to people's attitudes to death in this single meta-culture. Such confinement of analysis is not unproblematic. Its selectivity means that huge swathes of the human experience of death are not considered.

Chapter objectives:

- show the historical importance of Christian attitudes to death in Western societies;

- trace the decline of Christian influence in the West;

- identify modern attitudes to death;

- explore how economic developments have influenced our attitudes;

> - examine whether postmodernist approaches have a significant influence on how death is dealt with.

Background and context

In this chapter, I wish to examine both how our attitudes to death affect how we live our lives, and how we live our lives affects our attitudes to death. In more technical sociological terms, I want to look at the relationship between structure and agency over time. In doing so, I adhere to the precepts of Archer's (1995) morphogenetic approach. Archer accepts that social structures are the products of human agency. However, she reminds us of Comte's observation that 'the majority of actors are dead' (1995, p 696). For Archer, social structures are ontologically different to the actions of the agents that maintain or transform them, not least because of their temporal difference – social and cultural structures are slow to change and rarely do so in ways that social actors expect.

It is my contention that our current attitudes to death have not sprung up out of nowhere but bear the marks of a long history of human confrontation with the problems that it raises. It follows that, if we want to understand where we are now, we need to take into account where we have come from. Understanding approaches to death in the West requires an initial focus on Christendom, the once hegemonic belief system from which Western culture emerged. This will be followed by examination of the era of Christianity's decline in the West – modernity. However, while religious beliefs and institutions will play a large part in our examination, they are only part of the story, which will also include more material facets of modernity and pre-modernity, such as the consequences of changes in the forces and relations of production and of the rise of science and technology.

REFLECTION POINT 11.1

It would be useful at this juncture to spend a few moments thinking about your own understanding of and feelings towards death. This will help you to identify feelings and concerns that you have which, in turn, may help you be more sensitive to those of others.

As noted previously, the focus is on Western perspectives. However, the use of as vague and encompassing descriptor as 'the West' distorts the specificities of approaches to death across the variegated societies of which it is composed. While the West has undergone common structural processes such as industrialisation, the division of labour and urbanisation, these have been responded to in different ways in different countries. National and regional cultural and institutional responses to death and the dead were (and are) similarly diverse (Walter, 2012). Moreover, immigration to the West of both Christians and non-Christians has led to further diversity and may have tended to offset trends towards secularisation associated with modernity (Badcott, 2010).

Comparison of time periods is also an artificial exercise, in that there is never a decisive date of transition between one epoch and another, even if we think in terms of formal control. We might, for example, place the era of Christian dominance from the conversion of the Roman Emperor Constantine in 312 to the execution of the Louis XVI in 1793. But, if we look at the start of this era, the conversion of an emperor does not mean the conversion of a continent. It took a further 11 centuries, until the Christianisation of western Lithuania in 1413, for the whole of Europe to be brought under Christian rule. Moreover, a mere 40 years later, with the fall of Constantinople to the Muslim Ottoman Empire, Christianity once again lost its monopoly of power across the continent and never regained it. Conversely, through the mechanisms of conquest and colonisation that also began in the 15th century, the influence of Christianity began to spread far beyond the bounds of the continent and, in those countries where conquest was accompanied by large-scale European colonisation, such that indigenous cultures were all but eliminated, the Christian 'West' spread not only westward, but also southward across huge land masses.

Just as the institutional rise of Christianity was uneven, so too is its decline. More than two centuries after the divine right of kings was so dramatically curtailed in France, the British monarch remains the 'Supreme Governor' of an established Christian church that continues to wield political power through its automatic right to parliamentary representation in the form of lords spiritual.

Given that such ambiguity and asynchronism surround formal and institutionalised developments, how much more fuzzy must ideological developments be? As we shall see later, this is manifested most obviously in the degree to which Christian approaches to death continue to exert a variable influence throughout the West.

Despite all these codicils, I think that it is important to use this sort of approach to try to understand how death is viewed. As Norbert Elias puts it:

> If we realize that what is decisive for people's relation to death is not simply the biological process of death but the evolving, stage-specific idea of death and the attitude associated with it, the sociological problem of death appears in sharper relief. It becomes easier to perceive at least some of the special features of contemporary societies, and of the associated personality structures, that are responsible for the peculiarity of the death-image. (1985, p 45)

Death in Christendom

Historically, death in Europe was a very visible phenomenon. The average age of death was low, and infant mortality rates high. Infectious diseases, which could kill the infected person very rapidly, were rife, and medical science was relatively ineffective in responding to them or indeed to any other challenge to health (Walter, 1996).

Not only was a lot of dying happening, it was also paid considerable attention. Contemplation of death and the bodily decay consequent to death was part of the medieval Christian mindset. The gruesome realities of life's transience and death's indignities were (from a modern point of view) obsessively interrogated. Perhaps the best way to appreciate this attitude is to consider its expression in the visual arts. There are numerous genres in which it is expressed. These include the 'dance of death' and 'death and the maiden' tropes that reminded their viewers that no matter how rich and powerful or young and beautiful one was, one could not avoid death. Death and the maiden images, such as that of Baldung Grien (1518–20), with their lascivious portrayals of death as a rictus-grinning skeleton sensuously caressing naked young women, are especially unsettling, though the dance of death images, such as those in Holbein's (2016) collection of woodcuts, showing popes, bishops and nobles pirouetting with death to their doom, can hardly have been very comforting to the good and the great. Though this sort of morbid fixation seems grotesque to the modern viewer, we should not be overly complacent. As we shall see when considering modern cultural representations, such grotesqueries remain, but in a far less honest form.

In the face of the ever-present threat of death, it has been argued that Christianity performed important social and psychological functions. From a Durkheimian point of view, its rituals and ceremonies in response to death bound surviving members of society together in a collective reaffirmation of social solidarity. Drawing on the mourning rituals of indigenous groups, Durkheim pushes his argument that it is all about the collective rather than the individual pretty far:

> Mourning is not the natural response of a private sensibility hurt by a cruel loss. It is an obligation imposed by the group. One laments not simply because one is sad but because one is obliged to lament. It is a ritual facade that must be adopted out of respect for custom, but one that is largely independent of the individuals' emotional states. (Durkheim, 1995, pp 400–401)

In contrast, Berger brings individual needs back to centre stage by asserting that a fundamental human imperative is to subscribe meaning to existence. For Berger, the meaning systems that result from the imperative to protect individuals' sense of self from the vagaries of existence are socially constructed. However, in order to provide a robust ontological guard against threats to humans' fragile self-identities, the constructed (and therefore contingent) nature of these shared meaning systems needs to be hidden. As a result, over time they are bestowed with the status of objective social facts. These are in turn internalised by individuals, thus transforming them 'from structures of the objective world into structures of the subjective consciousness' (Berger, 1990, p 4).

Note down some of the ways you think that attitudes towards death has changed throughout history and across cultures. How might you use this understanding when working as a social worker today?

Death, being a crucial challenge to human meaning and identity, is an acute social problem. This makes the shared meaning systems constructed in response to it extremely important. That is where the 'sacred canopy' of religion comes in. Christianity, by positing an ontology that goes beyond the known place and time of the individual into the eternity of the afterlife, while at the same time including the human individual in that expanded ontology, 'appears to the individual as an immensely powerful reality which locates life in an ultimately meaningful order' (Shilling, 2003, p 156).

One of the major criticisms of Berger's thesis is that it is founded on the essentialising assumptions that humans need ultimate meanings and that they need to find them in the laws and mores of society (Beckford, 1989). To the extent that Berger's analysis claims to be trans-historical and trans-cultural, there is some merit in this criticism. However, as a theoretical explanation of the place of Christianity in pre-modern Europe, it has much to commend it. Indeed, there is evidence that Christianity not only claimed to have the solution to the human problems of meaning, identity and dread, but that it also created or at least exacerbated the problems that it claimed to be able to solve.

Using St. Paul's declaration to the Romans that 'by one man sin entered into the world and death by sin: and so death passed upon all men for all have sinned' (5:12), Davies argues that Christianity does not

> regard human death as normal (let alone benign!) and has placed the death of the individual right in the middle of great doom-laden cosmologies and fates, of dread myths of Origin and primal Offence, of the exploding end of worlds and of the small, unique and solitary littleness of each individual man and women. (1996, p 47)

The fates that Davies alludes to are the alternative eternal destinations of hell, purgatory and heaven, the two extremes entailing either eternal bliss or eternal torture. The Protestant Reformation made matters even starker by removing the middle way of time-limited painful purgation.

To the extent that contemplation of being a finite creature on earth was anxiety-provoking, Christianity, with its promise of an everlasting life imbued with profound God-given meaning, provided a very effective sacred canopy to protect believers. While death and the physical consequences of death were candidly acknowledged, their transcendence was also proclaimed.

Take, for example, Albrecht Dürer's (1513) masterpiece engraving, 'Knight, Death and the Devil'. The engraving shows an armoured knight riding up a hill towards his ultimate destination. In front of him, perched on a decrepit nag, is the hideous embodiment of decomposing Death. Death taunts the knight with an hourglass, making the point that, while our hero may currently be a great man of vigour, it is only a matter of time before he is reduced to the same state of decay as the poor wretch that stands before him. But the Knight is nonplussed. He is the ultimate Christian soldier with his eyes on the end of the road – the celestial city that sits on top of Mount Zion. The message of the engraving is that the enemies of piety – the flesh, death and the devil – should be treated as chimera through which the Christian has to pass, protected by his armour of faith on the way to paradise.

Becker (1973) has described this sort of response to death, which involves both a personal and cultural denial of mortality, as a 'hero system'. As we shall see, the rationality of modernity has done great damage to these systems, although they continue to be echoed in the heroics of commercial entertainment.

From the perspective of Christian cosmology, what is real is life everlasting, while what is ephemeral is mortal existence. The promise of Christianity is that, if believers accept this reality and act accordingly, all their problems will be solved. However, if they do not act as they should, then life eternal will work out very differently.

The nature of Christian faith meant that considerable anxiety was caused by the alternative eternal destinations facing humanity. For those who strayed from the straight and narrow path, the payback was gruesome. Given that the Bible says little about heaven and virtually nothing about hell, it fell to the imaginative faculties of theological commentators to construct impressions of what mortals could expect once they had passed into the new realm.

By far the most impressive of these constructions was Dante Alighieri's *Divine Comedy* (Dante, 1984, 1985, 1986). Here, those condemned to hell are doomed to occupy one of nine descending circles. The graver the sin, the deeper the circle, and the more agonising the punishment. Dante identifies three main categories of sin. In descending order, these are incontinence (lack of self-control), violence and fraud. Interestingly, given Christianity's current reputation for obsessing on matters sexual, lust is regarded as the least of the capital vices. The most serious sins involve behaviour that threatens economic (fraud) and political (treachery) integrity. Thus, those who are guilty of heterosexual carnal sins are placed in the second circle of hell, just below limbo, and are doomed to drift helplessly on eternal winds, just as they were swept along by their desires. Homosexuality was a different matter. Regarded as a sin against nature – the God-given sexual function of procreation – it is categorised as violence in the Inferno (although, for reasons obscure, it is upgraded to lust in the Purgatorio). Those condemned for the sin of Sodom wander through the sterile landscape of the seventh circle, perpetually rained upon by the flames of hell. In the deepest circle can be found traitors such as Brutus, whom Dante stuffs into the black mouth of Lucifer himself.

It can be seen that death and its consequences provided an important disciplinary tool in that it functioned to encourage behavioural self-regulation. The price for breaking moral codes was high (and never-ending). Conversely, the temptation to flout those codes was also high – the pleasures of the flesh, be they through the acquisition of material comforts, or the engagement in prohibited sexual activities, beckoned. Hence, the need to reinforce the message. In the visual arts, an example of this moralising propaganda can be found in the 'vanitas' genre (e.g. de Heem, 1659) that used the symbolism of things like skulls, rotten fruit and burnt-out candles to push home the point that earthly goods and pleasurable pursuits are pointless and transitory in the face of death.

The advent of the Protestant Reformation probably increased what Weber (1930) termed salvation anxiety. This resulted from the Calvinist doctrine of predestination whereby it was believed that an omniscient and omnipotent God predestined the fate of humans. The psychological burden of not knowing whether they were among the elect destined for Paradise or were unavoidably doomed to hell (the compromise solution of Purgatory having been eliminated) led believers to look for signs of grace. Given that all life's activities should be oriented to the worship of God, success in earthly activities that added to the good could be regarded as signs of salvation. This encouraged energetic and methodical economic activity, which in turn generated profits that were regarded as signs of God's blessings. However, the ascetic nature of Protestantism meant that these profits could not be used for conspicuous consumption. The solution for the believer was therefore to reinvest them, and so, according to Weber (1978), the cycle of capitalist accumulation was born.

To sum up our survey of attitudes for death during the era of Christian hegemony in the West: it was regarded negatively in that it was seen as the product of sin; it was regarded frankly, in that it was a familiar phenomenon, the physical consequences of which were well understood; it was regarded as a transition to an afterlife rather than the terminus of life; it was used as an ideological weapon of behavioural control, in that people's behaviour was seen as determining their fate after death; and the rituals that surrounded it reinforced collective sentiment and social solidarity. We can see some of these attitudes remaining in our understanding today in Case Study 11.1. These attitudes were fairly universal across Christendom (at least up until the Reformation) because the Church jealously guarded its hegemony and responded fiercely to any heretical challenges. The sacred canopy was both wide and robust.

CASE STUDY 11.1

Camilla, a 48-year-old African-Caribbean woman with two teenage children, has been diagnosed with advanced liver cancer. When talking with you about her fears and concerns for the future, she asked, 'Why has this happened to me? I don't drink, I go to church, I love my family. I don't know why I'm dying, I'm not a bad person.' She then went on to explain that she was worried about the future of her children and how they will cope, and is distressed that she will not see her grandchildren, but will have to wait until they are joined with her again in death.

Questions

1. What do you think Camilla's worries are saying about her and her situation?
2. How might you help her in addressing these concerns?
3. Can you identify the social, historical and cultural foundations to her thinking?

Discussion

Camilla is expressing concern about the reasons for life's changes, a kind of theodicy, or why bad things are allowed to happen. This is common in our culture and we all probably have examples of it that we ourselves have used. However, much of what she is expressing is a concern for those she is responsible for currently, her teenage children, and it is here that you can help in supporting her to find appropriate ways in which her children will be looked after when she dies. It is also important that you listen to her anxieties and anger at her situation. This is where understanding the social, historical and cultural aspects of death becomes important. It is central to your practice that you recognise Camilla will be displaying her concerns in her own way, but a broad understanding of the context is helpful.

Implications for health and social care practice: disenchanting death

With the rise of modernity, this monopolistic interpretation began to be challenged by the increasing replacement of tradition and faith as sources of knowledge by empirical rationality. In Weber's words, 'the fate of our times is characterized by rationalization and intellectualization and, above all, by the "disenchantment of the world"' (1970, p 155). The rational application of empirical strategies to death led to a break with the Christian consensus about the existence of an empirically unamenable afterlife. Atheism, which (somewhat trepidatiously) raised its head in the Scottish (Hume, 1990) and (more brashly) the French (Blom, 2010) Enlightenments, gained considerable philosophical momentum in the 19th century (Nietzsche, 1991; Feuerbach, 1980), and has continued apace (e.g. Dawkins, 2006), to the point where it provides an increasingly influential alternative worldview to traditional perspectives.

The affective consequences of the atheistic dissolution of the sacred canopy and its replacement with the prospect of nothingness following death are contested. We have already noted Berger's thesis about the fundamental need for meaningfulness that the canopy fulfils. A similarly essentialist position is taken by Becker (1973), who argues from a neo-Freudian perspective that the rise of rational interpretations of death has undermined the hero–systems through which death was denied. In doing so, rationalism has opened up humanity to the primordial terrors that its prospect evokes. However, there are alternative interpretations. Thus, for example, absurdists tend to view the tension between the human desire to seek meaning in life and the human inability to do so with a wry perplexity that is well summed up by Samuel Beckett's exquisite Irish bull expressed by a character in Endgame on discovering the absence of God: 'The bastard! He doesn't exist!' (Beckett, 2006, p 119). Many advocates of atheism have taken an even more sanguine view of how the realisation of our finitude will affect us. Thus, for example, Feuerbach makes the comforting observation that 'Death is death only for the living' (1980, p 165).

Whether or not it leads to existential terror, there is no denying the profound significance of the decline in religious influence. As Berger puts it,

> probably for the first time in history, the religious legitimations of the world have lost their plausibility not only for a few intellectuals and other marginal individuals, but for broad masses of entire societies. This opened up an acute crisis not only for the nomization of the large social institutions but for that of individual biographies. (1973, p 130)

While doubtless the process of disenchantment has affected our attitude to death, the nature of death makes our conceptualisation of it more resistant to rationalisation and intellectualisation than other phenomena. While death itself is an empirically verifiable event, claims to the continuation of some form of existence on another plane after death are not. While, on the one hand, those unverifiable claims may appear far-fetched; on the other hand, they may provide their adherents with considerable comfort. Kierkegaard noted that while biological death is a relatively straightforward phenomenon, 'subjective death' is anything but: 'the living individual is absolutely excluded from the possibility of approaching death in any sense whatever' (1941, p 147).

REFLECTION POINT 11.3

How do you think that changes in our attitudes towards religion, whatever our own personal views might be, have influenced our approaches to death and dying, and what does this mean for your practice as a social worker?

The conception of history as flowing unproblematically away from reliance on faith is challenged by the empirical evidence concerning faith's resilience. Thus, in the US (admittedly an exceptionalist redoubt of religion in the West), in 2014, 89 per cent of people still asserted their belief in God (Pew Research Center, 2015). Even in the more secular UK, it was only in 2017 that, for the first time, a majority of people professed that they had no religion. The British Social Attitudes Survey reported that 41 per cent of respondents reported an adherence to Christianity. While we should not exaggerate the degree of disenchantment with religion and its claims concerning the perpetuation of life after death, notwithstanding the fact that whether we see ourselves as a person of religious faith or not, that does not mean that we look on death and the afterlife in the same way as someone who lived in 13th-century Europe did. Social existence in the modern world encourages a different approach to death than was held in times when Christianity had an ideological monopoly.

One of the most significant social processes that has altered people's perspectives on death is the rise of individualism. This had its seeds in Protestantism, which tended 'to particularize death in terms of its concern with the individual's confrontation with death … The symbolic boundaries through which death was organized gradually shifted from the social body to the individual body' (Shilling, 2003, p 164). This process of individualisation has become ever more marked over the course of the modern era.

The implications of this individualism for social workers and others in the helping professions is that they should take nothing for granted when faced with clients faced with life-limiting circumstances or their close others. Because of this diversity, it is important to establish in each case what people's responses are to the challenges confronting them, and that means listening very closely. We can see this in Case Study 11.2.

CASE STUDY 11.2

Melanie, aged 72, was concerned for her son Jacob who was 35 years old, who lived with her and had no partner. Melanie had been admitted into a local hospice having been told she had about two weeks to live. She told the social worker about her worries. The social worker went to see Jacob, who said he felt somewhat confused about the situation, believing that he ought to feel grief and sadness, but he was actually relieved and happy in a way because he felt he could now live his life freely.

Questions

1. Imagine you were the social worker. How might this reaction make you feel and why?
2. How do you think you should you respond as a social worker?
3. How does a broad understanding of history and culture help you to work in this context?

Discussion

How you respond will differ from person to person and if you were to discuss this with your colleagues it would show you the different experiences and the individuality of these among the group. This is partly down to a celebration of the individual and diminution of the group, but also rests on interpretations of experiences (see Chapter 2). As a social worker it is important that you remain an impartial, but warm, listening ear for Jacob, and help him to explore his reactions and feelings in ways that are comfortable for him. Whatever your own background and beliefs, the broad understanding of how the West has developed will help you attune your responses and to understand why people may be thinking and feeling what they do.

The modern individual

The modern division of labour has also greatly encouraged the rise of individualism. Durkheim (1984) argued that what he termed the 'collective consciousness' was shaped by social structures. A society where labour was structured in a homogenous manner, and where everybody lived a very similar existence led to a homogenous collective consciousness that was characterised by an all-embracing consensus, in which values and beliefs were tightly controlled. In contrast, the increasing division of labour led to a looser form of social solidarity in which collectively held values, and beliefs became less important. In their place arises the morality of individualism. For Durkheim, the danger of the rise of individualism was the potential breakdown of social norms and moral obligations, and the spread of a pervasive sense of *anomie*.

The problem in relation to death is that individualism leads people to think of themselves as 'fundamentally independent individual beings, as windowless monads, as isolated "subjects", to whom the whole world, including all other people, stands in the relationship of an "external world"' (Elias, 1985, p 52). The main consequences of this state of affairs is the rise of what Elias terms 'personal and relatively private fantasies about immortality' (1985, p 35) in place of 'institutionalized collective fantasies', by which he refers to established religious eschatology, and the loss of a sense of meaning that comes from the loss of common bonds. Both of these consequences of individualism lead to emotional isolation in the face of challenges such as death.

Giddens (1990) has argued that in late modernity, where all traditional forms of order have been swept away in an unprecedented fashion, the issue of individualism is further exacerbated. Rather than being characterised by a stable core, self-identity has become a continuous process of developing 'reflexively organized projects' (1991) that are built up from the myriad of choices that confront the individual. By means of these projects, individuals attempt to maintain a sense of control and meaning in the careening juggernaut that is late modernity. This precarious stability is constantly in danger of being overwhelmed by 'fateful moments', and death, with its inevitability, unknowability and uncontrollability, is the ultimate fateful moment. Our consciousness of it is 'associated with anxieties of an utterly fundamental sort' (1991, p 50).

If the prospect of death (or the experience of the death of a close other) does overwhelm someone's precarious existential stability, it often falls to members of social work and other helping professions to care for them during this troubled time. Often, the priority of providing physical comfort means they are less able to support people with the psychological challenges that death and dying raise as Case Study 11.3 shows.

CASE STUDY 11.3

Monica, a 47-year-old married teacher, stopped eating unless physically prompted when her father died. She had a close relationship with her father and still lived nearby, no more than a 15-minute drive. He was just 70 when he died, and his death was unexpected. Monica's husband, who had also been close to his father-in-law, was at his wits end trying to help Monica and asked the bereavement support social worker to help.

Questions

1. How might you as a social worker help in this situation?
2. What social and cultural factors might help you understand this situation?

Discussion

As a social worker you will be able to consider what physical and domiciliary supports might help alleviate the strain on Monica's husband. You will also be able to offer a sympathetic and listening approach for the family, as social system. The case study is deliberately devoid of detail. You would want to know more about Monica's family, background and culture; what their expectations and assumptions are in these situations. With that degree of knowledge, it is more likely that you will be able to offer appropriate help.

Capitalist death

The effects of modernity upon our perspectives on death are not confined to the new ideas that it has fostered. The material conditions that have developed in its wake have also been profoundly influential, not least the radical shift in the means and relations of production that were entailed in the unprecedented economic engine of capitalism. As Marx put it, 'it is not the consciousness of men that determines their being, but, on the contrary, their social being that determines their consciousness' (1980, p 160).

While in its early stages, capitalism was highly deleterious to the health of the proletariat upon whose labour it depended (Engels, 2009), by the end of the 19th century, the 'urban penalty' began to disappear, mortality rates went into steep decline, and life expectancy began to rise, largely due to reductions in infectious disease. This was the result of a number of factors, including improved nutrition and living conditions, and public health measures such as the supply of clean water (Cutler and Miller, 2005).

The increased likelihood of us living out a full lifespan is not just to do with improvements in nutrition and environmental hygiene. It is also related to 'the relatively high degree of internal pacification' (Elias, 1985, pp 47–48) in contemporary Western societies. Death by violence has become something exceptional and criminal, and peaceful death in bed has become the expected norm. Of course, this process has to be qualified by recognition of the carnage that resulted from two world wars and genocidal programmes in the 20th century. It also ignores the carnage that the West has visited upon other areas of the globe as part of its imperialist and neo-imperialist ventures. Nonetheless, people in the West are considerably less likely to be killed by violence than their ancestors were.

One of the consequences of falling mortality rates, and especially infant mortality rates, was that death increasingly became a phenomenon of old age. As a result, in modern Western societies the death of a close relative is far less frequently experienced by people over the course of their lives. This makes death seem a longer way off for many. As Elias puts it, 'In a society with an average life expectancy of seventy-five, death for a person of twenty or even thirty is considerably more remote than in a society with an average life expectancy of forty' (1985, p 45). Related to this is an increased perception that death comes most commonly at the final stage of a natural process. We can feel relatively secure about the unlikelihood of our demise occurring in youth or middle age. Taking this security for granted enables us to consign death to the background of our consciousness for much of our lives. While people are aware at an intellectual level that death will come, the knowledge that it will occur at the end of a natural process makes its prospect less concerning.

REFLECTION POINT 11.4

Think about when you might be likely to work with someone who is dying or someone who has been bereaved. What age might these people be? How, therefore, might it make you feel or influence your practice when confronted with someone dying much younger in adulthood?

The avoidance of contemplation of death has been strongly reinforced by popular culture.

> Any film-going American adult can point to ... scenes in which heroic characters metaphorically 'give the finger' to death. Cinematic death may be grotesque and extreme, but our heroes can retaliate, escape, shrug, or laugh off death's best shots and survive for the kiss in the final scene. These outlandish cinematic death rituals set a public context for denial of death, repression of emotion and avoidance of authentic death concerns. (Schultz and Huet, 2000–01, p 147)

The replacement of the reality of death in the household by the hyperreality of it in the mass media (Baudrillard, 2017) demonstrates the Janus-faced approach we now have. On the one hand, death and its aftermath have been disenchanted by the empirical thrust of modernity. On the other hand, the grotesque honesty of pre-modern cultural products such as the death and the maiden trope have been replaced with equally grotesque fantasies that would make even the most outlandish medieval theologian blush. Dürer's stoic knight has been replaced by cardboard cut-out warriors who blithely dismiss the indismissible.

This unfamiliarity with, and indeed denial of death means that, when confronted with its realty, people are often ill-equipped to cope with its consequences. This makes the supportive role of the nurses, social workers and bereavement counsellors all the more important. However, looked at from another perspective, increasing reliance on professional 'support' has not been an unambiguously positive development.

Professionalism in health and social care, and death

This reduction in the visibility of death was reinforced by the increasing division of labour that was a core part of modern capitalism (Durkheim, 1984). Durkheim noted that in pre-industrialised societies, the tasks people perform and the types of lives they lead were very similar. They made their own clothes, grew their own food and so forth. In contrast, people in industrialised societies tend to specialise in one type of task, for which they get paid. They then use their wages to buy products and services from other specialised workers.

The death industry is no different from others in this respect. Instead of looking after our dying relatives at home, we transfer that task to health-care specialists in hospitals and hospices. The management of dying became a technical matter to be dealt with by the medical profession (Glaser and Strauss, 1968; Giddens, 1991). Instead of preparing the dead body for disposal, we delegate that task to funereal specialists; and in many Western countries (with the notable exception of Ireland, where it is usual for the body to be brought home and waked), we also delegate pre-interment storage of the body to these funereal professionals as well. The organisation of funeral rites has been professionalised (Huntington and Metcalf, 1979). In short, the growth of occupational specialities for dealing with death means that we no longer need to have very much to do with it. It becomes a thing apart from our personal experience. In Giddens's (1991, p 156) words, death has been sequestered from the public space.

The power of medicine

The sequestration of death from the public sphere into the relatively closed environment of hospitals and hospices has been reinforced by people's confidence in the capacity of health care to ward off death. While the efficacy of medicine in curing disease is a far more recent (and generally overestimated) phenomenon than is usually realised (Porter, 1999), it has had a profound influence on the way we think about death, which has come to be seen as something that can be warded off by the application of medical science. Never before in the history of humanity have so many resources been invested in the prolongation of life. The discourse about the capacity of science to keep death at bay is both pervasive and ambiguous. Medicine's capacity to improve survival rates of specific diseases has fuelled this discourse, which has led to often unrealistic expectations of what health care can and cannot do:

> The dream of the elixir of life and of the fountain of youth is very ancient. But it is only in our day that it has taken on scientific, or pseudo-scientific, form. The knowledge that death is inevitable is overlaid by the endeavour to postpone it more and more with the aid of medicine and insurance, and by the hope that this might succeed.
> (Elias, 1985, p 47)

The significance of the rise of scientific medicine in shaping the modern approach to death cannot be underestimated. Walter argues that the key change between traditional and modern death is the transfer of authority from the priest to the doctor; from theology to medicine. One of the consequences of the great investment of trust in this expertise is that the dying person and their family have 'little authority and even less knowledge' (1996, p 196).

For many commentators, professional takeover of death by health and social care professionals and institutions and its consequent removal from the public gaze is the most significant aspect of the modernisation of death. Thus, in addition to Giddens's identification of the sequestration of death, Elias refers to 'the social repression of death' (1985, p 45), which in turn echoes closely Ariès's assertion that the 20th century has seen 'the removal of death from society' (1974, p 575). However, things are not quite so simple.

Late-modern choice?

While death may be sequestered from public space, the amount of both popular and academic discourse about it demonstrates that it is neither a forbidden nor a forgotten subject (Mellor, 1993). If there was any taboo surrounding talking about death, the death café movement (Miles and Corr, 2015) has done much to bring the topic out of the closet (although such honesty is counterbalanced by the continuing facile treatment of the subject in popular media such as film).

Walter (1996) has argued that the changes occurring in our approach to death are not just about discourse but also about practice. He contends that the modern way of death characterised by professional medical dominance is being supplanted by a postmodern approach that replaces such assumed expertise with personal choice and the doctor and hospital by the individual self and their family. Postmodern modes of death and dying can be seen, for example, in people's increasing involvement in treatment decisions as is evidenced by things like advance care directives, the growth of individualised life-centred funerals, and the return of death at home as a choice. In the 20 years since Walter identified postmodern death, the shift in the balance of power between the laity and professionals, such as health-care or social workers, has been substantial but partial.

The issue of whether control over dying lies with health and social care professionals or with dying people and their families is major dynamic that is currently being played out in late modern societies. Social workers have an important role to play in this dynamic, whose trajectory will at least partially depend on the degree to which they are prepared to encourage and empower people to be more deeply involved in decisions and actions relating to the ending of life. This is explored further in Case Study 11.4.

CASE STUDY 11.4

Jemima, a white British agnostic, has always said to her daughter she would 'take matters into her own hands' if suffering a debilitating illness that she felt was taking away her dignity. Her illness has prevented her actively making a trip abroad to end her life which she was keen to do, and she is demanding that she be assisted to die before her illness incapacitates her further.

Questions

1. How might you help in this situation as a social worker?
2. How might you look after yourself as a social worker?

Discussion

You are in a position of negotiation and brokering as a social worker. Of course, you are bound by the law of the land and cannot simply fulfil Jemima's wishes, but you can explore options of no further treatment that may extend life and ensure her wish not to be resuscitated is known, recorded and acted upon. You can listen to her and her daughter and ensure that her views are known and respected as far as they can be.

You are working in an emotionally demanding area and need appropriate support and supervision as a social worker or nurse. It is important that you have this as it is easy to burnout or become hard and insensitive in your work without processing the experiences you have.

Conclusion

This chapter has provided a deeply theorised and historical overview of death and dying in a Western context. It has been important to do so in order that you are equipped to deal with delicate areas of life and to work as a social worker with the knowledge and awareness necessary to make a positive difference in people's lives.

Reflective questions

1 How psychologically healthy are modern approaches to death and dying?

2 Who are best placed to look after dying people?

3 Is it better to die at home or in a hospital?

Further reading

• Cohen, J. and Deliens, L. (2012) *A Public Health Perspective on End of Life Care*. Oxford: Oxford University Press.
While this is written for the health professions, public health in particular, end-of-life care straddles the social care and social work professions too. This book provides a useful introduction to ways in which we might as multidisciplinary professionals respond well to sensitive matters.

• Elias, N. (1985) *The Loneliness of the Dying*. Oxford: Blackwell.
Elias's work provides a robust sociological understanding of death and dying. It is important as social workers to be able to grapple with the underpinning theories to your work.

• Parker, J. (ed.) (2005) *Aspects of Social Work and Palliative Care*. London: Quay Books.
This book covers a range of aspects of working in palliative care that social workers might find useful in their practice.

• Walter, T. (1996) Facing death without tradition. In G. Howarth and P.C. Jupp (eds), *Contemporary Issues in the Sociology of Death, Dying and Disposal*. London: Macmillan, pp 193–204.
Changing approaches and attitudes towards death and dying pervade our times and this paper examines some of the novel and different ways we approach it. It will be useful as a way of looking into difference – something important in social work practice.

• Walter, T. (1999) *On Bereavement: The Culture Of Grief*. Buckingham: Open University Press.
Walter explores some of the key changes in the ways we grieve as a late modern society. This is important for you as social workers as there are changes, individualities and cultural variations with which you must grapple.

References

Archer, M. (1995) *Realist Social Theory: The Morphogenetic Approach*. Cambridge: Cambridge University Press.

Ariès, P. (1974) *Western Attitudes Towards Death: From the Middle Ages to the Present*. Baltimore: Johns Hopkins University Press.

Badcott, D. (2010) Assisted dying: The influence of public opinion in an increasingly diverse society, *Medicine, Health and Philosophy*, 13(4): 389–397.

Baldung Grien, H. (1518–20) *Death and the Maiden*. Web Gallery of Art. Available from: https://www.wga.hu/html_m/b/baldung/1/061death.html

Baudrillard, J. (2017) *Symbolic Exchange and Death* (revised edn). London: Sage.

Becker, E. (1973) *The Denial of Death*. New York: Simon & Schuster.

Beckett, S. (2006) *The Complete Dramatic Works*. London: Faber & Faber.

Beckford, J. (1989) *Religion and Advanced Industrial Society*. London: Unwin Hyman.

Berger, P.L. (1973) *The Social Reality of Religion*. Harmondsworth: Penguin.

Berger, P.L. (1990) *The Sacred Canopy: Elements of a Sociological Theory of Religion*. New York: Anchor Books.

Berger, P.L. and Luckmann, T. (1966) *The Social Construction of Reality: A Treatise in the Sociology of Knowledge*. Harmondsworth: Penguin.

Blom, P. (2010) *A Wicked Company: The Forgotten Radicalism of the European Enlightenment*. New York: Basic Books.

British Social Attitudes Survey (2017) Record number of Brits with no religion. Available from: http://www.natcen.ac.uk/news-media/press-releases/2017/september/british-social-attitudes-record-number-of-brits-with-no-religion/

Cutler, D. and Miller, G. (2005) The role of public health improvements in health advances: The twentieth-century United States, *Demography*, 42(1): 1–22.

Dante (1984) *The Divine Comedy,* Vol. I, *Inferno*, M. Musa (trans.). Harmondworth: Penguin.

Dante (1985) *The Divine Comedy*, Vol. I, *Purgatory*, M. Musa (trans.). Harmondworth: Penguin.

Dante (1986) *The Divine Comedy*, Vol. III, *Paradise*, M. Musa (trans.). Harmondworth: Penguin.

Dawkins, R. (2006) *The God Delusion*. London: Bantam.

Davies, J. (1996) Vile bodies and mass media chantries. In G. Howarth and P.C. Jupp (eds), *Contemporary Issues in the Sociology of Death, Dying and Disposal*. London: Macmillan, pp 47–59.

Dürer, A. (1513) *Knight, Death and the Devil*. Web Gallery of Art. Available from: https://www.wga.hu/html_m/d/durer/2/13/4/071.html

Durkheim, É. (1984) *The Division of Labor in Society*. New York: Free Press.

Durkheim, É. (1995) *The Elementary Forms of Religious Life*. New York: Free Press.

Elias, N. (1985) *The Loneliness of the Dying*. Oxford: Blackwell.

Engels, F. (2009) *The Condition of the English Working Class*. Oxford: Oxford World Classics.

Feuerbach, L. (1980) *Thoughts on Death and Immortality*. Berkeley: University of California Press.

Giddens, A. (1990) *The Consequences of Modernity*. Cambridge: Polity.

Giddens, A. (1991) *Modernity and Self-Identity*. Cambridge: Polity.

Glaser, B. and Strauss, A. (1968) *Time for Dying*. Chicago: Aldine.

Heem, C. de (1659) *Vanitas Still-Life with a Skull and an Écorché*. Web museum of Art. Available from: https://www.wga.hu/html_m/h/heem/cornelis/vanitas1. html

Holbein, H. (2016) *The Dance of Death*. London: Penguin.

Hume, D. (1990) *Dialogues Concerning Natural Religion*. Harmondsworth: Penguin.

Huntington, R. and Metcalf, P. (1979) *Celebrations of Death*. Cambridge: Cambridge University Press.

Kierkegaard, S. (1941) *Concluding Unscientific Postscript*. Princeton: Princeton University Press.

Marx, K. (1980) From a contribution to the critique of political economy. In E. Kamenka (ed.), *The Portable Karl Marx*. Harmondsworth: Penguin.

Mellor, P.A. (1993) Death in high modernity: The contemporary presence and absence of death. In D. Clark (ed.), *The Sociology of Death: Theory, Culture, Practice*. Oxford: Blackwell, pp 11–30.

Miles, L. and Corr, C.A. (2015) Death cafe: What is it and what can we learn from it? *Omega: Journal of Death and Dying*, 75(2): 151–165.

Nietzsche, F. (1991) *The Gay Science*. New York: Random House.

Pew Research Center (2015) *Religious Landscape Study*. Available from: http://www.pewforum.org/religious-landscape-study/

Porter, R. (1999) *The Greatest Benefit to Mankind: A Medical History of Humanity*. London: Fontana.

Schultz, N.W. and Huet, L.M. (2000–2001) Sensational! Violent! Popular! Death in American movies, *Omega: Journal of Death and Dying*, 42: 137–149.

Shilling, C. (2003) *The Body and Social Theory*. London: Sage.

Walter, T. (1996) Facing death without tradition. In G. Howarth and P.C. Jupp (eds), *Contemporary Issues in the Sociology of Death, Dying and Disposal*. London: Macmillan, pp 193–204.

Walter, T. (2012) Why different countries manage death differently: A comparative analysis of modern urban societies, *British Journal of Sociology*, 63(1): 123–145.

Weber, M. (1930) *The Protestant Ethic and the Spirit of Capitalism*. London: Unwin.

Weber, M. (1970) Science as a vocation. In H.H. Gerth, and C.W. Mills (eds), *From Max Weber: Essays in Sociology*. London: Routledge and Kegan Paul, pp 129–158.

Weber, M. (1978) *Economy and Society*. Berkeley, CA: University of California Press.

12

Working with adults with disabilities

Rachel Fyson

Introduction

This chapter will briefly explore some of the disadvantages which adults with disabilities frequently experience before giving an overview of some key ways of theorising disability. It complements Chapter 10, which discusses historical, definitional and theoretical concepts relating to disability, to focus more on contemporary social work theories and working practice. The chapter will also consider how the experience of disability may affect human growth and development and what the implications of this are for those who work with and for people with disabilities.

Chapter objectives

Understand that the term *people with disabilities* is used to refer to people with a wide range of impairments including:

- physical impairments, such as an inability to use a part of the body;

- sensory impairments, meaning loss of sight or hearing;

- cognitive impairments, including intellectual disability,[1] brain injury and dementia.

Consider how people may be born with an impairment or may acquire an impairment as a child or adult as a result of an accident or the effects of an illness:

- explore how the individual impact of an impairment may be hugely varied, depending on both the nature of the impairment, the point in the lifecycle at which it occurred and the individual's personal, cultural and social circumstances;

- reflect on how people with disabilities face multiple disadvantages and their needs are often overlooked by those who provide services.

Background and context

In the UK, a person is legally categorised as disabled if they have a physical or mental impairment, which has a substantial and long-term adverse effect on their ability to carry out normal day-to-day activities (Equality Act, 2010). Legislation provides further detail about how the terms 'substantial', 'long term' and 'adverse' should be interpreted, but whether or not any particular person is disabled is recognised to be highly subjective. This is to say that it will depend on the person's individual experiences of how their impairment impacts upon their day-to-day life.

The international definition of disability, found within the United Nation's *Convention on the Rights of Persons with Disabilities* (CRPD), is broader and includes both a description of disability and a description of the impact disability has on individuals:

> Persons with disabilities include those who have long-term physical, mental, intellectual or sensory impairments which in interaction with various barriers may hinder their full and effective participation in society on an equal basis with others. (United Nations, CRPD, 2006)

When thinking about disability, it is important to bear in mind that this is a term which covers a wide range of individual bodily differences, situations and experiences. What unites this diverse group of people is that, as a result of their impairment, they are likely to be prevented – to a greater or lesser extent – from participating in society on an equally basis. As a result, people with disabilities have reduced opportunities throughout their life.

Government statistics show that around 22 per cent of the UK population is disabled (Department of Work and Pensions, 2018). However, disability is not spread evenly amongst the population, and women (23 per cent) are more likely than men (20 per cent) to be disabled. This gender disparity in prevalence of disability is linked to the fact that, on average, women live longer than men. The older a person is, the more likely they are to be disabled (see Case Study 12.1) and the proportion of disabled people in the population tends to increase the overall population ages.

In the UK, 8 per cent of children are disabled; 19 per cent of working-age adults are disabled; 45 per cent of adults aged 65 and over are disabled; and 61 per cent of people aged over 80 are disabled (Department of Work and Pensions, 2018). Statistics from other industrialised nations show similar trends. For example, the proportion of the US population who are disabled rises from 6 per cent amongst 18–35-year-olds to 50 per cent amongst those aged over 75 (Pew Research Center, 2017). Similarly, in Australia, just under a fifth (18 per cent) of the population is disabled, and the percentage of people with disabilities rises from 7 per cent of girls and 12 per cent of boys aged five to 14 to 68 per cent of women aged over 90 (Australian Bureau of Statistics, 2016). What these figures demonstrate is that although some people are born with disabilities, many more become disabled during their life course due to accident, injury or the effects of illness. By old age, most people have some degree of disability. This has led some disability campaigners to use the acronym TAB (standing for 'Temporarily Able Bodied') to refer to people without disabilities. The use of the term TAB serves as a reminder that we may all experience disability at some point in our lives.

CASE STUDY 12.1

Dorothea is 87 years old and lives alone, though has lots of friends in her local community as well as two daughters who live nearby. She helps out two days a week at a lunch club for 'the aged' (many of whom are younger than she is). Dorothea suffers from a number of health conditions, including high blood pressure, age-related macular degeneration and severe osteoporosis which has resulted in damage to her spine. She walks with a stoop and needs the support of two sticks, but remains fiercely independent and does not identify as being disabled. Dorothea continues to drive despite her deteriorating eyesight. Her daughters have tried to persuade her to hand in her driving licence, but she refuses to do this, saying that she only drives short distances in the local community, on routes she knows well, and that if she handed in her licence she would lose her independence.

Questions
1. Why do you think that Dorothea rejects the idea that she is disabled?
2. Would there be any benefits to Dorothea if she self-identified as disabled?
3. Should Dorothea continue to drive? Who should decide this?

Discussion
Dorothea and her daughters appear to be approaching her situation from very different positions. Dorothea's deteriorating health condition presents a danger to herself, and if she continues to drive, to others as well. In this respect the daughters' attempts to remove her ability to drive can easily be construed as concern for her, but also clearly one of social responsibly that is mindful of the law. Dorothea regards this, however, as a clear threat to her ability to manage her own life, which is already jeopardised and restricted by her physical conditions. There is also the issue of social connections that are maintained by mobility, where we know that frail, elderly and housebound people are some of the loneliest in the country (along with young people) and that loneliness itself is implicated in serious illness and decline. How these points of view can be resolved without resulting in further detriment of Dorothea's life is the challenge.

The impact of disability upon individuals and families is significant and stretches beyond the immediate effects of limiting a person's ability to undertake ordinary daily activities. The impacts of disability include:

- Physical impacts: an impairment may limit a person's ability to do certain things either as a direct consequence of the disability or due to aggravating factors such as pain, discomfort and tiredness.
- Impact on employment: disabled people are less likely to be in paid employment than non-disabled people and, if they do work, are likely to earn less; this means that disabled adults are more likely than others to be living in poverty (Department of Work and Pensions, 2018; EHRC, 2017; Pew Research Center, 2017).
- Impact on family life: parents of disabled children (particularly mothers) are less likely than other parents to work because of the child's higher care needs; this contributes to the fact that these families are more likely than other families to be living in poverty (Hope et al, 2017; Shaw et al, 2016).
- Impact on poverty: households which include a disabled adult or a disabled child are more likely to experience poverty than other households; this holds true across all age groups (EHRC, 2017; Tinson et al, 2016).
- Social impact: people with disabilities are more likely to be socially isolated; they are more likely than other people to be victims of bullying or hate crime including physical assault, verbal insults and threats (Rickard and Donkin, 2018; EHRC, 2017).
- Child abuse: disabled children are more likely than other children to experience abuse; there are multiple reasons for this including disabled children being more dependent on others for care, being less able to speak out about abuse (where communication difficulties are present), being less likely to understand that they are being abused (where intellectual disabilities are present) and because 'challenging behaviours' are often misinterpreted as a part of the child's disability, rather than recognised as a potential sign of abuse (Taylor et al, 2016).

The cumulative effect of these disadvantages and adverse life experiences can be substantial.

In the UK, it has been shown that people with intellectual disabilities not only die 15 to 20 years earlier than other people, but that the reduced life expectancy of people with intellectual disabilities is caused by negative life experiences and not by the impacts of their disability (Rickard and Donkin, 2018). This study summarised its findings as being that people with intellectual disabilities 'are more likely than the general population to experience some of the worst of what society has to offer – low incomes, no work, poor housing, social isolation and loneliness, bullying and abuse' (Rickard and Donkin, 2018, p 3). Other types of impairment may have different impacts, but people with disabilities of any kind are disadvantaged in comparison to those without disabilities.

REFLECTION POINT 12.1

Think back over any media reports regarding 'hate crimes' towards adults: were any of these victims described as disabled?

Historical considerations

Within most societies, people with disabilities are treated differently from, and less favourably than, non-disabled people. While this remains true today, historically the differences in life experiences between disabled and non-disabled people were even more extreme as discussed in more detail in Chapter 10. In the UK, as the Industrial Revolution advanced in the 18th and 19th centuries, people with disabilities began to be increasingly visible within society. This was both because some disabilities made it difficult for individuals to engage in new industrial (factory) jobs and because industrialisation (particularly coal mining) led to a high number of industrial injuries (Historic England, 2018). At the same time, the 'science' of eugenics led to a belief that disabled people should be prevented from having children in order to preserve the 'purity' and 'health' of the population (Wright, 2011). While these ideas have now been comprehensively discredited, the institutions and social attitudes which were established during this era have proved harder to dislodge.

The 19th century saw the creation of many large-scale institutions, in the UK and elsewhere, which were used to segregate disabled people from the rest of society. While, in some cases, these institutions began as places of sanctuary, they soon became places where society hid those who were perceived as 'different' and 'less able' (Wright, 2011). These establishments were used to house both children and adults with a range of physical and intellectual disabilities; men and women were made to live separately, and many people living there were sterilised. Conditions were poor, staff had little training and abuse was commonplace.

The creation of the welfare state in the UK, after the Second World War (1936–45), saw these institutions become a part of the newly created National Health Service and renamed long-stay hospitals, but, despite this, conditions did not show any immediate improvement. Things began to change – slowly – from the 1960s onwards, after journalists exposed regimes of abuse in a number of hospitals (Fyson et al, 2004; Atkinson et al, 1998). From this point onwards, it was government policy to support people with disabilities to live in the community, but the closure of long-stay hospitals has taken many decades. At the time of writing, Calderstones Hospital on Merseyside is the last long-stay hospital in England for people with intellectual disabilities. Its planned closure was announced in 2016 (NHE, 2016), but has not yet happened.

However, despite the continuing existence of long-stay hospitals, life for most disabled people has changed considerably over the past half century. This is due largely to the pressure for change put on politicians, policymakers and providers of services by people with disabilities, their friends, families and supporters. This work has included challenging the power of professionals; working to secure the human rights of people with disabilities; and campaigning under the slogan '*Nothing About Us Without Us*' as a way of emphasising that policies which affect people with disabilities need to be created with the involvement of people with disabilities. Alongside direct action and political campaigning, changing the way in which disability is theorised has been key to the successes of the disability movement.

Physical and sensory impairment: the social model of disability

The origins of the social model of disability can be found in the work of UPIAS (Union of the Physically Impaired Against Segregation). This group fought to eliminate segregated services for people with disabilities; to ensure that disability organisations were shaped by disabled people; and to establish the right of disabled people to have control over their own lives. One of the ways in which the group sought to achieve these aims was by developing a new way of theorising disability and this was encapsulated in an early statement:

> In our view, it is society which disables physically impaired people. Disability is something imposed on top of our impairments by the way we are unnecessarily isolated and excluded from participation in society. (UPIAS, 1976, p 3)

At the time this statement was made, it was a radical departure from mainstream thinking about disability. Half a century ago, most services for people with disabilities were provided in segregated settings, disabled people had very little say over their lives and many had limited access to education or employment. Disability was predominantly regarded as a 'personal tragedy' for an individual and their family. The policy response to people with disabilities at that time, other than to provide medical services to 'cure' disability, was largely to ignore them by shutting them away from the rest of society.

The ideas set out by UPIAS have been developed over time by disability activists and academics. The expression 'social model of disability' was first coined in 1983 by UK academic and disability activist, Mike Oliver (Oliver, 1983). The social model of disability is not a static theory and it has continued to be developed, critiqued and refined over time by a many different groups and individuals (see, in particular: Swain et al, 2013; Shakespeare, 2007, 2013; Goodley, 2011). However, there is broad agreement about the key elements which together constitute the social model of disability and these are set out in Box 12.1.

Box 12.1: The social model of disability

An *impairment* is a limitation in the way that a person's body is able to function.

Disability is something which is imposed on people with impaired bodies by a society which does not take account of their needs and which denies their human rights.

Disability is created by *physical barriers* and by negative *social attitudes*.

A *social approach to disability* would result in a society which removed the physical and social barriers which prevent people with disabilities from being fully included in mainstream society.

The *social model of disability*, which emphasises the *rights* of disabled people and the need for societal change, is often contrasted with the *medical model of disability*, which does not distinguish between disability and impairment and which sees disability as an individual 'problem' which can be 'cured' by medical intervention.

The social model of disability is an approach which advocates for change to our physical, social and cultural environments in order to make them more accessible for and inclusive of people with disabilities. A key practical demand is that politicians, policy makers and service providers all need to adopt approaches which remove the barriers to participation which disadvantage people with impairments. However, while some of these barriers may be easy to identify and remove, others are more complex. Some examples of impairments, barriers and possible ways of removing the disabling barriers are shown in Table 12.1, using the example of travelling by bus.

It should be noted that removing the barriers to inclusion may require a range of different approaches. Most physical barriers (within man–made environments) can be overcome by ensuring that the needs of people with impairments are considered when transport, buildings or other systems are designed. However, social and cultural barriers require other solutions which rest primarily on population–level education about disability and impairment, so that people modify their behaviours in order to take account of the needs of people with impairments (as in the

Table 12.1: Impairments, barriers and solutions (bus travel)

Impairment	Barriers to inclusion	Ways of removing the barriers to inclusion
Spinal cord fracture – unable to walk	Buses that are inaccessible to wheelchairs	Buses which 'kneel' to allow level access between pavement and floor of bus; spaces on bus designed for wheelchair users
Blind or partially sighted	Buses that do not stop; not knowing when to alight from the bus	White stick indicates that driver must stop even if person does not hold out their hand; automated announcements of each stop
Parkinson's disease	Limited seating	Designated seating for people with disabilities; social norm that able-bodied people vacate these seats if required to do so
Down Syndrome	Unable to read bus destination or number	Support staff/personal assistant to help the person with their journey

example of giving up a seat on the bus). It has been argued that some barriers may ultimately be impossible to entirely eradicate: physical barriers because they occur in the natural world (mountains are usually not wheelchair-accessible) and social or cultural barriers because they require population-level education and behavioural change. Social and cultural barriers can be most readily understood as the unthinking expectations which the average member of the public may have about disability. So, for example, if non-disabled people believe that people with disabilities are weak, stupid, lazy, benefit scroungers and so on, this will affect the way they treat any person with a disability that they meet (Ryan, 2019). Social and cultural issues create particularly complex barriers to inclusion.

REFLECTION POINT 12.2

Not all disabilities are visible. Some may be invisible and yet impair people's ability to manage quite significantly. Many affected people are reluctant to reveal these hidden disabilities publicly. List some that come to mind and reflect on why people may not wish to disclose them.

The social model of disability was initially developed by and for people with physical and sensory impairments, but its use has since been broadened to include people with intellectual disabilities and people experiencing mental distress (Goodley, 2011). However, there are ongoing debates about how well the social model of disability fits with or explains the experiences of people with cognitive impairments, particularly whether the barriers to inclusion can be removed. For example, it has been argued that:

> Short of a global catastrophe which returned western society to medieval levels of economic and social organisation, it would be impossible to recreate a world in which literacy and numeracy were not important attributes for economic independence and advancement. (Shakespeare, 2007, p 49)

It is beyond the scope of this chapter to do justice to the full range of arguments about whether intellectual disability is socially constructed or grounded in physical biology (that is, an impairment of the brain). However, it is important to understand that, because people with cognitive impairments such as intellectual disability often also have additional physical and/or sensory impairments, the barriers to inclusion that they experience are likely to have physical, social and cultural aspects (see Case Study 12.2). This is not least because the history of segregated services has resulted in the public having limited contact with, and therefore limited opportunities to develop an understanding of, people with intellectual disabilities. For this reason, and others, it is useful to consider another theory when thinking about intellectual disability.

CASE STUDY 12.2

Gordon is 62 years old and lives in a group home for adults with intellectual disabilities; he also lacks confidence and often experiences low mood. At the age of three, doctors told Gordon's mother that he was 'educationally subnormal' and advised that he should be placed permanently in a 'mental handicap' hospital. Gordon spent the next 34 years in a long-stay institution, receiving limited education and experiencing a range of physical and psychological abuse. He eventually moved back into the community in 1990, by which time he had lost contact with his family. Gordon shares his home with three other adults with intellectual disabilities, aged 27, 31 and 34. The other residents enjoy a range of community-based activities, but Gordon often declines invitations to join in. Staff are concerned that Gordon is becoming increasingly withdrawn, spending large amounts of time alone in his room.

Questions

1. How have Gordon's life experiences differed from those of the other people he lives with?
2. How may this be affecting him?
3. What are the physical, social and cultural barriers to inclusion for Gordon and how might these be overcome?

Discussion

It is apparent that there is quite an age difference between Gordon and the other residents, but he has been placed within this home owing to commonalities of disability rather than through an appreciation of what he may have in common with others. While large institutions were often settings where abuse took place, they were also contexts in which people could and did form relationships of friendship, 'family'-type relations, intimate and supportive and caring ones. In addition to losing his original family, Gordon will have lost yet more connections with others through his move to the new home. Gordon may find the ethos and expectations of the new home difficult to comprehend as it will be quite unlike the large institutions he grew up in. What can be done to help Gordon fit into his new environment and to enjoy its benefits will be the question on caregivers' minds.

Intellectual disability: social role valorisation

It is important to understand that social role valorisation is not an alternative to the social model of disability: it is a different theory, which tries to understand a different aspect of disablement. Social role valorisation theory focuses specifically on people with intellectual disability and not on disabled people more broadly; it does not aim to theorise what intellectual disability is, or how it may be socially created. Instead, social role valorisation provides a way of thinking about how support services for people with intellectual disability should be organised in order to maximise their social integration and acceptance. Just as it was relevant to understand the context from which the social model of disability emerged, in order to fully understand social role valorisation it is necessary to have an awareness of how it developed.

Social role valorisation is a renaming and extension of the theory of 'normalisation' (Nirje, 1969; Wolfensberger, 1972), which was developed at a time when, across Europe and North America, government provision for people with intellectual disability consisted of large-scale segregated 'hospitals'. These institutions separated children and adults with intellectual disability from wider society, as well as separating men from women. They were 'total institutions' (Goffman, 1961), meaning that people did *everything* (lived, ate, slept, made friends, died) within the walls of the institution (Atkinson et al, 1998). As a result of both the separation from mainstream society and the abuse which was rife in such settings (Fyson et al, 2004), people with intellectual disabilities who lived in long-stay hospitals often behaved very differently from other people. Some argued that the behaviours seen in institutions were an inevitable consequence of intellectual disability. However, in the 1950s and 1960s, a pioneering project in the UK, known as the Brooklands experiment, showed that intellectually disabled children who were taken out of long-stay hospitals and cared for in family-like environments displayed measurable improvements not only in behaviour, but also in intelligence (King et al, 1971).

These findings from the Brooklands experiment encouraged psychologists working in segregated institutions in other countries, particularly Scandinavia and North America, to consider whether adults with intellectual disabilities might also benefit from improvements to their environment. From this, the 'principle of Normalization' was developed (Nirje, 1969; Wolfensberger, 1972). It proposed a way of re-organising the environment within segregated institutions so that they more closely followed the patterns and rhythms of life in wider society – for example, by having hours of work or other purposeful activity and hours of leisure; by having different activities for children and adults; and by having cultural activities that were in line with wider norms, such as (in Europe) celebration of birthdays and Christmas.

At the start, normalisation was about improving the way in which care was provided within institutions rather than about trying to bring about the closure of institutions. However, the theory laid a pathway towards deinstitutionalisation and was one of the drivers towards the closure of long-stay hospitals:

> The normalisation principle means making available to all mentally retarded [sic] people patterns of life and conditions of everyday living which are as close as possible to the regular circumstances and ways of life as society. (Nirje, 1980, p 33)

It was soon noted how the term 'normalisation' was frequently misunderstood as meaning that people with intellectual disabilities had to be 'made to be normal', rather than understood as it being the institutional environment which needed to be normalised (see Case Study 12.3). For this reason, when the theory was redeveloped with a focus on non–institutional settings it was renamed 'social role valorisation' (Wolfensberger, 1983).

Like normalisation, the purpose of social role valorisation was to provide a theory to underpin the development and delivery of improved services for people with intellectual disabilities. Social role valorisation starts from the position that people with intellectual disability are devalued within society, in part because of the history of segregation. It proposes that, in order to become more valued within society, people with intellectual disabilities need to not only live alongside other people, but also to be supported to take on roles and engage in activities which are socially valued by others. The theory is that if people with intellectual disabilities are seen undertaking socially valued roles (such as being part of a family, having friends, working, shopping, using mainstream health, transport and leisure facilities), then they will become socially valued. In other words, social integration coupled with skilled support staff can be the start of a virtuous circle through which people with intellectual disabilities gradually become less socially excluded and more socially valued.

CASE STUDY 12.3: SOCIAL ROLE VALORISATION

Josh is young man with intellectual disabilities and autism who lives in his own flat, with daily support from a supported living team. Josh's support workers have attended social role valorisation training and are keen to ensure that they support the development of skills and behaviours which will help Josh be accepted in his local community. Josh can find social situations difficult, particularly situations involving unfamiliar people and/or high noise levels; this includes everyday situations such as supermarkets or public transport. When he feels overwhelmed, Josh reacts by running away from the noise and the people; this can result in unsafe situations. Josh finds it comforting to carry a small metal fire engine, which he has had since childhood. He self-sooths by running the toy fire engine across any available surfaces, with full sound effects. The staff who support Josh are concerned that the fire engine is not 'age-appropriate' and causes people to stare and laugh at Josh, reducing his standing in the eyes of others.

Questions

1. How does the fire engine affect the way Josh is viewed by others?
2. How does the fire engine support Josh leading an ordinary life?
3. How might these two positions be reconciled?

Discussion

A casual observer might say that there is a difference between the supported independence Josh has achieved so far and his seeming regression to childish comforts during times of stress – but that this may be understandable given his level of disability. While the staff have clearly embraced the idea of social role valorisation it would seem that this requires Josh to behave in ways that are viewed as less socially incongruous, but these are not likely to help Josh to move towards greater self-reliance. It suggest the risk that the staff are leaning towards the values of conformity, whereby what might be socially expected of a 'grown man' might be of greater importance than that individual's (non-harmful) repertoire of behaviours as a way of coping with an often stressful and uncertain world. If so, the suggestion is that Josh's way of being is currently unacceptable, and does not contribute to a socially valorised role in society carries large and worrying implications about disability, diversity and social norms, which tends to undermine the notion of valorisation.

Although developed in Scandinavia and North America, social role valorisation has heavily influenced policy and practice in the UK – particularly through the work of John and Connie O'Brien, who in 1981 published *The Five Accomplishments*. At a time when long-stay hospitals were being closed, this set out what community-based services should aspire to provide for people with intellectual disabilities. The 'accomplishments' drew explicitly on social role valorisation, including an appeal to *encourage valued social roles* (O'Brien and O'Brien, 1981). They also helped to embed notions of social role valorisation into UK government policy, particularly through the *Valuing People* white papers (Department of Health, 2001, 2009). *Valuing People* is government statutory guidance on how health and social care services should be provided for people with intellectual disabilities. As Table 12.2 shows, there are clear overlaps and continuities between the O'Briens' five accomplishments and the principles set out in the *Valuing People* white papers.

While social role valorisation and the social model of disability are different theories developed for different reasons, *Valuing People* is evidence of the synergy between them. Social role valorisation can be clearly seen in the principles which underpin the policy and the social model of disability is implicit throughout (Burton and Kagan, 2006). The social model of disability is also explicitly evident in the fact that *Valuing People* was the first government policy in England to have been developed with the active participation of people with disabilities:

> *Nothing About Us Without Us*: For the first time, people with learning disabilities have played a direct part in formulating Government policy. The members of the Service Users Advisory Group conducted a series of visits to local groups of learning disabled people. Listening to what people with learning disabilities had to tell us about their lives has helped us to understand the need for change. (Department of Health, 2001, p 11)

Table 12.2: Mapping the O'Briens' 'five accomplishments' against the four principles of *Valuing People*

The O'Briens' *Five Accomplishments* (O'Brien and O'Brien, 1981)	The principles of *Valuing People* (Department of Health, 2001, pp 23–24)
Community Presence: how can we increase the presence of a person in local community life?	**Inclusion**: enabling people with learning disabilities to do ... ordinary things, make use of mainstream services and be fully included in the local community.
Community Participation: how can we expand and deepen people's relationships?	**Inclusion**: (see previous section)
Encouraging Valued Social Roles: how can we enhance the reputation people have and increase the number of valued ways people can contribute?	**Independence**: while people's individual needs will differ, the starting presumption should be one of independence, rather than dependence, with public services providing the support to maximise this. Independence in this context does not mean doing everything unaided.
Promoting Choice: how can we help people have more control and choice in life?	**Choice**: everyone should be able to make choices. This includes people with severe and profound disabilities.
Supporting Contribution: how can we assist people to develop more competencies?	**Legal and Civil Rights**: ... for disabled people in order to eradicate discrimination in society. People with learning disabilities have the right to a decent education, to grow up to vote, to marry and have a family, and to express their opinions, with help and support to do so where necessary.

Practice relevance

Given that neither the social model of disability nor social role valorisation provides blueprints for people working in health and social care settings, how are these theories relevant to practice? The answer is that they should inform our thinking, both about the experiences of individual people with disabilities and about how services further impact – positively or negatively – on people's lives. These theories can also aid awareness of the ways in which disability impacts on human growth and development. For people working in social work and social care, knowing about these theories can help us to understand how having an impairment will have affected a person's life experiences, and how these life experiences, in turn, uniquely shape each person with disabilities. In order to explore this more fully, it is helpful to consider how impairment can affect all aspects of an adult's life, including personal, cultural and socio-economic domains.

The impact of disability on human growth and development

As explained in the Introduction to this chapter, people with disabilities are likely to experience a range of disadvantages compared to people without disabilities. For those who are born with physical, sensory or cognitive impairments, these factors will impact on their growth and development (see the companion volume). Although some impairments may affect physical growth and development (for example, people with the genetic condition achondroplasia[2] will always be of short stature as an adult), for most people the more profound impacts with be on their social and/or psychological growth and development. This section will therefore explore the personal, cultural and socio-economic impacts of disability, in each case giving consideration to how disability shapes this aspect of human growth and development. It is important to note that the domains are not separate phenomena, but rather each interacts with the others, and together they create barriers to inclusion for people with disabilities.

The first domain: personal impacts of disability

Impairment causes individual differences in physical, sensory and/or cognitive abilities which impact on growth and development. For example, some impairments cause ongoing pain and discomfort; others may cause fatigue. Living with chronic pain or fatigue can shape what a person is are able to do, the risks they are willing or able to take and their ability to act spontaneously. Cumulatively, the impacts of pain, discomfort and fatigue may lead to fewer opportunities to enjoy activities and experiences which other people take for granted and for some people this will be a cause of low mood (depression). Another example is that some impairments may require medical interventions, including prescription drugs and surgical or other procedures. Adults with these impairments may have spent long periods in hospital during their childhood and may have missed out on education, with consequent impacts on educational attainment and employment opportunities. Those who require frequent and/or long-term medical interventions in adulthood may find it harder to maintain paid employment.

These direct, personal impacts of disability shape individual opportunities for human growth and development. This is because of the complex way in which these impairment effects influence opportunities for engagement in culturally normative activities. Exclusion from activities such as friendships, education, employment at any point in the life cycle will create disabling barriers. The impact of these barriers is likely to be more disabling for those with more severe impairments and those whose impairments were present from birth.

The second domain: cultural impacts of disability

As outlined previously, people with impairments have many life experiences which are different to those of people without impairments, this will have an impact on growth and development because people's day-to-day experiences will be different from people who lives are otherwise culturally similar. However, the biggest difference in life experiences between the people with and without disabilities is arguably the fact that disabled people have to contend with the disablist attitudes of the able-bodied. This may take many forms, including being pitied, bullied, abused, ignored, underestimated or assumed to be incapable. Less commonly, it may be being assumed to have special powers or abilities.[3] The key thing is that many/most people with disabilities are treated differently by others because of their impairment. Different treatment lies at the core of the social barriers which disabled people face.

One example of different treatment is in relation to bullying and abuse. Adults with disabilities are more likely than other adults to have experienced abuse of all kinds (physical, sexual, neglect) during childhood and these childhood experiences of old abuse are known to be associated with mental distress/mental ill health in adulthood (Read et al, 2005). Adults with disabilities may therefore experience higher rates of mental distress/mental ill-health than adults without disabilities. Mental distress may be further exacerbated by the social stigma associated with some impairments and the withdrawal and social isolation which may result from this.

Bandura's *social learning theory* (Crain, 2017) suggests that a key element of human development (see the companion volume) is learning through copying the behaviour of caregivers. Some impairments may make this type of learning more difficult (for example, a person with a visual impairment will be unable to see what a caregiver is doing), but in other cases the difficulty will arise because caregivers treat those with impairments differently. This means that disabled adults may have missed out on ordinary learning. For example, the parents of a young adult with intellectual disability may understandably want to protect them from bullies and other risks, but this may result in the loss of opportunities to develop friendships.

Younger disabled adults will have grown up in a world in which the social model of disability has begun to change both government policy and public attitudes towards disability, with consequent improved access to mainstream activities and services. By contrast, older adults with lifelong disabilities are likely to have experienced segregated education and segregated care. These intergenerational differences will affect disabled adults' understanding of, and attitudes towards, their own impairment and what they expect to be able to achieve in life. Older adults, who have become disabled later in life, are likely to have grown up with a more individualistic/medical understanding of disability which may affect their attitude towards their own disability. This may include a reduced confidence in challenging disablist attitudes.

Adults who have a hidden disability may or may not identify as disabled. Hidden disabilities are impairments which are not immediately perceptible when you first meet somebody and include conditions such as HIV/AIDS, diabetes, Crohn's disease, back pain and many others. Some people may not wish to identify as being disabled because being disabled is not a valued social role; this can be a barrier to the individual receiving peer support; to employers making allowances (known legally as 'reasonable adjustment') for the impact of disability; or to the person receiving the welfare benefits to which they may be entitled (Ryan, 2019). Negative cultural attitudes towards disability not only deter people from identifying as disabled, they also impact on the life chances of all people with disabilities.

The third domain: socio-economic impacts of disability

The majority of working-age adults are not disabled and, for the most part, the world is designed to meet the needs of this majority. Able minds and able bodies are taken as the norm, and adults whose physical, sensory or intellectual abilities do not fit normative expectations are systematically disadvantaged. Building upon the personal and cultural impacts of disability, the socio-economic impacts of disability can be seen in the lower educational attainment, lower rates of employment and increased chances of living in poverty which adults with disabilities experience. Research shows that educational opportunities, employment prospects and poverty are inextricably intertwined:

> There is a strong link between poverty and special educational needs and disability (SEND). Children from low-income families are more likely than their peers to be born with inherited SEND, are more likely to develop some forms of SEND in childhood, and are less likely to move out of SEND categories while at school. At the same time, children with SEND are more likely than their peers to be born into poverty, and also more likely to experience poverty as they grow up. (Bart et al, 2016, p 4)

In other words, adults with life-long disabilities are more likely than the non-disabled to have been born into poverty and their childhood poverty will have affected their educational outcomes, which in turn will have affected their employment prospects and means that they are more likely to remain poor as adults. Socio-economic disadvantages affect all aspects of people's lives – health, education, social networks (see Case Study 12.4). Poverty contributes to the barriers to inclusion faced by disabled people, who may be unable to afford to engage in the leisure and cultural activities enjoyed by others (Ryan, 2019).

CASE STUDY 12.4

Muneeba was born with spina bifida. She lives with her mum who is unable to work due to severe and enduring mental health difficulties. Muneeba has to self-catheterise to pass urine and recently started using an electric wheelchair because of loss of sensation in her legs. Her condition frequently causes her both pain and fatigue. Despite these challenges, Muneeba attended mainstream school, achieved high A-level grades, and graduated with a 2:1 degree from her local university. However, as Muneeba continued to live at home while attending university, she made few friends. Since graduating a year ago, she has applied for over 200 jobs and has had 11 interviews, but no job offers. Muneeba is struggling to survive on welfare benefits, anxious about how she is perceived by potential employers, and losing confidence that she will ever get a job.

Questions

1. What are the personal, cultural and socio-economic impacts of disability for Muneeba?
2. To what extent is Muneeba's situation the same as or different from other young women of her age?
3. What might help Muneeba to build confidence and reduce her social isolation?

Discussion

Muneeba is coping with a lot: not only does she manage her own painful and difficult condition, but she also offers companionship and probably care to her severely ill mother. She has already achieved a lot by remaining in formal education to degree level and is now seeking career opportunities. Apparently a very capable and determined young woman, Muneeba's life is constrained by, not only her own physical capacities, but more seriously by her social and family circumstances and the perceptions of others towards people with disabilities. Here, it might be useful to think of intersectional oppressions (see Chapter 15) where Muneeba is a woman + young (less experienced) + disabilities + limited income (or actual poverty) + possibly of minority ethnic background + possibly with few resources: friends, helpful relatives and other social networks to help her, in a context where it is often through wider social networks and word-of-mouth that jobs may be found.

In addition to these three interlinked domains, disability may also intersect at an individual level with other factors such as gender, ethnicity, age and sexuality. So, for example, men and women with the same impairment may experience different disabling factors due to assumptions made on the basis of gender – for example, a young woman who speaks with a lisp might be regarded as sounding 'cute', while a man with a similar speech impediment might be regarded as effeminate. Likewise, ethnicity is likely to affect a person's experience of impairment. This is not only because of varying cultural attitudes towards disability within different ethnic minority communities, but also because disabled people from ethnic minority communities face 'double discrimination' – that is, discrimination on the grounds of both ethnicity and disability. Although it is beyond the scope of this chapter to explore these intersectional dynamics in depth, it is important to recognise their existence.

Implications for social work practice

All social work and social care professionals, whatever the particular focus of their role, will work with people with disabilities. This is not only because people with disabilities mostly use the same services as everybody else, but also because most people will experience disability at some point in their lives. Because of this, everybody working in the sector needs to understand the basics of disability: the interplay between impairment and disability; how disability is created/exacerbated by the way in which society is organised; how disability affects individual growth and development; and how it impacts upon socio-economic outcomes.

In the UK and elsewhere, including Australasia, North America and Scandinavia, the social model of disability has reshaped many health and social care services. This has included ensuring better access to mainstream services and providing fewer segregated services for people with disabilities. At the same time, personalisation policy and person-centred approaches to practice (Glasby and Littlechild, 2016) have emphasised the need for support which puts individuals with disability in control of decision making about their own lives and which respects each person's unique needs and abilities (see Case Study 12.5). Such approaches inherently reflect a social model of disability and implicitly call for services which promote social role valorisation.

CASE STUDY 12.5: TRANSITION

Sally-Ann, who has intellectual disabilities and needs a walking frame to move around, lives at home with her parents. She is an only child. Her father works long hours, but her mother gave up work after Sally-Ann was born in order to become her carer, and together they enjoy painting, cross-stitch and origami. Sally-Ann is 19 and in her last term at special school, having transferred there in Year 9, after her mum felt that she was being bullied in a mainstream secondary school. Sally-Ann will be leaving school soon and, as part of her transition plan, it has been suggested that she enrols on a life-skills programme at the local college of further education. The course will involve learning skills such as cooking, budgeting and use of public transport. This course is only available at college, where students are unsupervised during lunch breaks. Sally-Ann's parents want her to attend a local church centre, which provides craft activities, as they say she will be safer and happier there.

Questions
1. What part may gender be playing in this family dynamic?
2. What are the longer-term developmental implications of either option?
3. Which option will be more likely to keep Sally-Ann safe, both in the short and longer term?

Discussion

Sally-Ann is a lucky young woman to have such devoted and loving parents looking after her. They have worked hard to create a very safe and protective environment for Sally-Ann and given their personal sacrifices and knowledge of their daughter, their views of what is best for her should be respectfully listened to and their cooperation enlisted. However, at the same time, some loving families can find it very hard and frightening to relinquish some of that protection in order to enable their children to experience life more fully. Maybe it was all for the best to remove Sally-Ann from mainstream school, especially if she was being bullied, so a trade-off is made: she will experience a different childhood from other children and have a more limited social experience, but it will constitute less of a risk to her. Now a similar situation is arising, but Sally-Ann is older, she has different needs and abilities, and her future could take a potentially very different turn from that her parents may visualise for her: it may be better or it may be worse at times, but at least it will be a new adventure where Sally-Ann will have new experiences. Should this new road be tried?

Conclusion

While it may not be possible to entirely remove all barriers to inclusion faced by people with disabilities, those working in health and social services have an important role to play in minimising these barriers. This can be achieved in a number of ways including involving people with disabilities in planning and management of services; considering the needs of people with disabilities when mainstream policies and services are developed; and each professional taking personal responsibility for educating themselves about the impact of disability on human growth and development.

Reflective questions

1 What is the difference between impairment and disability? How are they connected?

2 Would it be possible to create a world in which having a physical/sensory/cognitive impairment did not result in any disability? What would this world be like?

3 Now that people with intellectual disabilities live in the community rather than in hospitals, have they become more socially valued? If not, what else needs to change?

4 How do personal, cultural and socio-economic influences combine to disable people who are born with or acquire physical, sensory or cognitive impairments? How do these effects differ for people with different types of impairment?

Further reading

- Priestley, M. (2003) *Disability: A Life Course Approach.* Cambridge: Polity Press.
  This book offers a useful overview of how disability affects individuals across the lifespan from childhood to old age.

- Shakespeare, T. (2013) *Disability Rights and Wrongs Revisited.* London: Routledge.
  This important book explores the strengths and limitations of the social model of disability.

- Swain, J., French, S., Barnes, C. and Thomas, C. (eds) (2013) *Disabling Barriers – Enabling Environments* (3rd edn). London: Sage.
  This classic edited volume offers a number of essays exploring social disability in society.

Notes

[1]   This chapter uses the term 'intellectual disability' in preference to alternatives such as 'learning disability' or 'learning difficulty'. This is because the term intellectual disability is more widely used and understood internationally and because it is less likely to create confusion with specific learning difficulties such as dyslexia or dyspraxia. In the context of this chapter, intellectual disability is referring to those who: *have a significantly reduced ability to understand new or complex information or to learn new skills (impaired intelligence)* **and** *a reduced ability to cope independently (impaired social functioning), which started before adulthood and with a lasting effect on development* (Department of Health, 2001).

[2]   Achondroplasia is also sometimes referred to a 'dwarfism'; the average height of adults with this genetic condition is around four feet or 1.2 metres.

[3]   For example, a common misperception is that people on the autistic spectrum all have one area of extraordinary skill, such as an amazing memory or an incredible artistic ability. While this can happen, it is extremely rare.

References

Australian Bureau of Statistics (2016) Disability, Ageing and Carers, Australia 2015. Available from: http://www.abs.gov.au/ausstats/abs@.nsf/Latestproducts/4430.0Main%20Features202015?opendocumentandtabname=Summaryandprodno=4430.0andissue=2015andnum=andview=

Atkinson, D., Jackson, M. and Walmsley, J. (eds) (1998) *Forgotten Lives: Exploring the History of Learning Disability.* Kidderminster: BILD.

Bart, S., Bernardes, E., Trethewey, A. and Menzies, L. (2016) *Special Educational Needs and their Links to Poverty.* York: Joseph Rowntree Foundation. Available from: www.jrf.org.uk

Burton, M. and Kagan, C. (2006) Decoding valuing people, *Disability and Society,* 21(4): 299–313.

Crain, W. (2017) *Theories of Development: Concepts and Applications* (6th edn). London: Routledge.

Department of Health (2001) *Valuing People: A New Strategy for Learning Disability for the 21st Century.* London: The Stationery Office.

Department of Health (2009) *Valuing People Now: A New Three-Year Strategy for People with Learning Disabilities 'Making it Happen For Everyone'.* London: Department of Health.

Department of Work and Pensions (2018) *Family Resources Survey 2016/17.* Available from: https://assets.publishing.service.gov.uk/government/uploads/system/uploads/attachment_data/file/692771/family-resources-survey-2016-17.pdf

Equality Act (2010) https://www.legislation.gov.uk/ukpga/2010/15/contents

EHRC (Equality and Human Rights Commission) (2017) *Being Disabled in Britain: A Journey Less Equal.* Available from: https://www.equalityhumanrights.com/sites/default/files/being-disabled-in-britain.pdf

Fyson, R., Kitson, D. and Corbett, A. (2004) Learning disability, abuse and inquiry. In N. Stanley and J. Manthorpe (eds), *The Age of The Inquiry: Learning and Blaming In Health and Social Care.* London: Routledge.

Glasby, J. and Littlechild, R. (2016) Direct payments and personal budgets. In *Putting Personalisation into Practice* (3rd edn). Bristol: Policy Press.

Goffman, E. (1961) *Asylums: Essays on the Social Situation of Mental Patients and Other Inmates.* New York: Doubleday.

Goodley, D. (2011) *Disability Studies: An Interdisciplinary Introduction.* London: Sage.

Historic England (2018) *Disability in the 19th Century.* Available from: https://historicengland.org.uk/research/inclusive-heritage/disability-history/1832-1914/

Hope, S., Pearce, A., Whitehead, M. and Law, C. (2017) Effects of child long-term illness on maternal employment: Longitudinal findings from the UK Millennium Cohort Study, *European Journal of Public Health,* 27(1): 48–52.

King, R.D., Raynes, N.V. and Tizard, J. (1971) *Patterns of Residential Care. Sociological Studies in Institutions for Handicapped Children.* London: Routledge.

NHE (National Health Executive) (2016) *NHS England set to close last long-stay learning disability hospital.* Available from: http://www.nationalhealthexecutive.com/Health-Care-News/nhs-england-set-to-close-last-long-stay-learning-disability-hospital

Nirje, B. (1969) The normalization principle and its human management implications. In R. Kugel and W. Wolfensberger (eds), *Changing Patterns in Residential Services for the Mentally Retarded.* Washington, DC: President's Committee on Mental Retardation.

Nirje, B. (1980) The normalization principle. In R. Flynn and K.E. Nitsch (eds), *Normalization, Social Integration and Community Services.* Baltimore: University Park Press.

O'Brien, J. and O'Brien, C.L. (1981) *The Five Accomplishments.* Available from: http://www.inclusionwa.org.au/download/OBrien_Five_Accomplishments.pdf

Oliver, M. (1983) *Social Work with Disabled People.* Basingstoke: Macmillan.

Pew Research Center (2017) *7 Facts About Americans with Disabilities*. Available from: http://www.pewresearch.org/fact-tank/2017/07/27/7-facts-about-americans-with-disabilities/

Read, J., van Os, J., Morrison, A.P. and Ross, C.A. (2005) Childhood trauma, psychosis and schizophrenia: A literature review with theoretical and clinical implications, *Acta Psychiatrica Scandinavica*, 112(5): 330–350.

Ryan, F. (2019) *Crippled: Austerity and the Demonization of Disabled People*. London: Verso.

Shakespeare, T. (2007) *Disability Rights and Wrongs*. London: Routledge.

Shakespeare, T. (2013) *Disability Rights and Wrongs Revisited*. London: Routledge.

Shaw, B., Bernardes, E., Trethewey, A. and Menzies, L. (2016) Special educational needs and their links to poverty. York: Joseph Rowntreee Foundation. Available from: https://www.jrf.org.uk/report/special-educational-needs-and-their-links-poverty

Swain, J., French, S., Barnes, C. and Thomas, C. (eds) (2013) *Disabling Barriers – Enabling Environments* (3rd edn). London: Sage.

Rickard, W. and Donkin, A. (2018) *A Fair, Supportive Society: A Social Determinants of Health Approach to Improving the Lives of People with Learning Disabilities*. London: Institute of Health Equity. Available from: http://www.instituteofhealthequity.org/resources-reports/a-fair-supportive-society-summary-report/a-fair-supportive-society-summary-report.pdf

Taylor, J., Stalker, K. and Stewart, A. (2016) Disabled children and the child protection system: A cause for concern, *Child Abuse Review*, 25(1): 3–79.

Tinson, A., Aldridge, H., Born, T.B. and Hughes, C. (2016) *Disability and Poverty*. London: New Policy Institute. Available from: https://www.npi.org.uk/publications/income-and-poverty/disability-and-poverty/

United Nations (2006) Convention on the Rights of Persons with Disabilities (CRPD). Available from: http://www.un.org/disabilities/documents/convention/convoptprot-e.pdf

UPIAS (Union of the Physically Impaired against Segregation) (1976) *Fundamental Principles of Disability*. London: UPIAS. Available from: http://www.disability.co.uk/fundamental-principles-disability

Wolfensberger, W. (1972) *The Principle of Normalization in Human Services*. Toronto: National Institute on Mental Retardation.

Wolfensberger, W. (1983) Social role valorization: A proposed new term for the principle of normalization, *Mental Retardation*, 21(6): 234–239.

Wright, D. (2011) *Downs: The History of a Disability*. Oxford: Oxford University Press.

PART III

Professional practice

The third part of the book explores the importance of theory and models for social work practice, and considers how these understandings help the range of human service professionals, including social workers, to negotiate the messy and complex worlds of people at different life stages and experiencing different life events. In Part III authors take a social work practice perspective in the main, although mental health nursing, social care and sociological approaches are also included.

Chapter 12 offers a social work view of working with disabled people, exploring the complex issues and worlds affecting adults with a range of disabilities. Then in Chapter 13, we move to explore mental health and mental ill-health. This chapter draws from mental health nursing and is helpful to social workers by introducing known concepts and practices from a different but allied profession with whom social workers work on a frequent basis. In Chapter 14 we consider the still relatively new focus on adults, and especially elders, who experience abuse and neglect. The chapter focuses on social work in the UK but draws on international research and perspectives. Parenting is often a hidden or assumed part of adulthood. In Chapter 15, parenting is considered in tandem with the differences and diversities that influence parenting types and expectations. This is important when practising as a social worker as you become attuned to the centrality of diversities and questioning unspoken assumptions. The final chapter, Chapter 16, looks at dementia, an increasingly common condition affecting millions of people worldwide. The chapter offers an optimistic approach for practitioners by introducing the concept of resilience.

Part III objectives

- bring together aspects of the first two parts of the book;

- demonstrate the practical utility of the theoretical models explored earlier or introduced here;

- consider the advantages and disadvantages of the model and theories and to promote an approach that focuses on the person.

13

Mental health and ill-health in adults

Steve Tee

Introduction

Mental ill-health, or mental illness (you will come across both terms which are used synonymously), in adults is a common phenomenon, with statistics suggesting one in four adults will experience mental health problems, typically at critical stages in their psychosocial development (McManus et al, 2016). This chapter presents a conceptual framework for understanding adult mental health and ill-health. Aimed at social work students and those working in the field, its purpose is to inform and enable people in the helping professions, to appreciate the everyday challenges and taboos that have an impact on the daily lives of adults who experience changes in their mental health and to employ practice that promotes recovery.

Chapter objectives

- appreciate why the concepts of mental health and ill-health are controversial;

- understand the value of the bio-psycho-social-spiritual (BPSS) framework of mental health and ill-health in adults;

- critically appraise the biological/medical model of mental disorder;

- evaluate the impact of stigma and labelling on the mental health and well-being of individuals;

- examine the role practitioners can play in helping those experiencing problems in mental health.

Understanding mental health

Mental health is considered a positive concept that describes an individual's emotional well-being. While the concept, to some extent, remains culturally defined, typically mental health refers to one's enjoyment of life, the ability to cope with stresses and strains, the achievement of one's goals and potential, and a sense of connectedness to others in society. The World Health Organization's (2014, p 1) definition of mental health is:

> [A] state of well-being in which the individual realises his or her own abilities, can cope with the normal stresses of life, can work productively and fruitfully and is able to make a contribution to his or her community. (WHO, 2014, p 1)

However, the term is often misunderstood and interpreted as referring to mental ill-health. Mainly as a consequence of the many perspectives on what constitutes mental ill-health, it remains hotly contested with ongoing debates about the origins, causes, treatments and explanations of mental ill-health.

In order to help piece together the myriad of theories and explanations, this chapter will adopt a bio-psycho-social-spiritual (BPSS) perspective. The original BPS model (Engel, 1977) was seen as a holistic model of mental health, bringing together biological, psychological and social dimensions. However, more recently, researchers have argued that the model should be expanded, to include the relevance of spiritual and religious beliefs and their interactions with other dimensions, for fully understanding mental health outcomes (Katerndahl, 2008; Sulmasy, 2002).

The BPSS framework will enable the reader to take a critical view of the various discourses that seek to explain mental health and in turn mental ill-health. The BPSS framework refers to biological, psychological, social and spiritual explanations as to the origins, causes, manifestations and treatments of mental health and ill-health.

Employing a BPSS framework, the chapter will consider the ways in which adults experience the world and are affected by life changes in respect of developing mental health problems. It will also consider cultural, sociological, spiritual and gendered nuances that are often marginalised.

The purpose is to help social work practitioners appreciate and critically analyse the ways in which these concepts are understood and applied in a health and social care context and to explore the tools employed by the questioning practitioner.

Impacts of mental health and ill-health

When we think of our own mental health, we may think of characteristics such as feeling happy, having productive relationships, being able to work and being emotionally stable. The Mental Health Foundation (2017) suggests that positive mental health enables the individual to make the most of their potential, cope with life and play a full and productive role in their family, workplace, community and among friends. However, this can change when our mental health deteriorates.

Mental ill-health (illness) reflects health changes involving our thinking, emotions and/or behaviour. A mental illness, which refers to a specific type of mental ill-health, can be associated with many different levels of distress and can affect people's functioning in their social lives, spiritual lives, work lives or family activities and relationships.

In the UK, according to the Mental Health Foundation (2017), mental health problems are among the main causes of the overall disease burden worldwide, with mental health and behavioural problems (e.g. depression and anxiety) being the primary causes of disability; if we add this up it would constitute 40 million years of disability in 20- to 29-year-olds. Mental disorders, such as major depression, are also a major contributor to the burden of suicide and ischaemic heart disease.

According to US statistics, in any given year, 19 per cent of adults will experience some form of mental illness, with 4 per cent having one that is considered serious, and 8.5 per cent misusing substances (American Psychological Association, 2017). Whereas, in the UK, it is estimated that one in six people will have experienced a mental health problem in the last week alone (McManus et al, 2016).

While it is evident that mental ill-health is very common and likely to affect many of us, even in the 21st century, there remains serious stigma attached to mental health problems. This results in people feeling uncomfortable and avoiding talking about their experiences, which in turn, increases isolation.

REFLECTION POINT 13.1

Using search techniques including online search engines, reviewing local paper small adverts, service directories, dropping into GP surgeries, etc., produce a list of local services for people experiencing mental health problems and identify whether they are provided by state-funded public sector organisations, charities, private providers or some other organisation. What are your reflections on the range and diversity of services?

Life changes and how we experience the world

As we live our lives, we will experience ups and downs. Life changes and events are inevitable and unavoidable. Some events can be completely life-changing and cause us to re-evaluate our priorities. For example, Helen Keller, the American author, activist and campaigner, throughout the 20th century, overcame the dual disabilities of deafness and blindness. She was the first deaf-blind person to attain a bachelor's degree and went on to become an influential campaigner for disability rights issues. In her book published in 1940, she wrote:

> … [L]ife is either a daring adventure or nothing. (Keller, 1940, p 51)

Of course, we never know what we will encounter in life and what trials we will have to overcome. While we may choose to hide away, unexpected things will inevitably happen. Even in a comparably uneventful life, we will be required to navigate milestones such as growing up, going to school, making friends, getting a job, travelling, possibly meeting a life partner and perhaps having children. But on top of what might be considered 'routine' experiences, we are very likely to encounter some major life events such as births and deaths, marriage and divorce, employment and redundancy, injury and illness, and so on.

Research into mental health has shown that how we respond individually to these experiences will depend on a whole host of factors including our genetics, personality characteristics, developmental experiences, social support, spiritual beliefs, physical and mental health, age, gender, worldview and economic status (Mind, 2013). In other words, individuals will differ significantly in their response to a life event, problem or stressor. All these factors will determine our cognitive appraisal of the situation and the coping abilities on which we draw and reinforce for later use. It is therefore helpful to consider health and illness being determined by the dynamic interplay between biological, psychological and social factors. The bio-psycho-social-spiritual (BPSS) model (Engel, 1977; Katerndahl, 2008; Sulmasy, 2002) proposes that a particular outcome (health or illness) is determined by the interrelation between these four factors, and that each component on its own is insufficient to definitively lead to either health or illness. This helps to explain why two people facing the same struggle in life may respond in different ways.

Bio-psycho-social perspectives on mental ill-health

The bio-psycho-social (BPS) framework of health and illness was developed by George Engel in 1977, and suggests that it is the interactions between biological, psychological, and social factors that determine the cause, manifestation and outcome of health and disease. In other words, one factor is insufficient and that it is the interaction between an individual's genetic make-up (biology), their personality and behaviour (psychology) and their social and cultural context (social) that determine all health–related outcomes, but in particular mental health. Additionally, writers such as Hatala (2013) have argued that the BPS model has marginalised the important role of spirituality. They site empirical evidence that link health outcomes with spiritual or religious beliefs, emphasising that the majority of people from diverse cultural systems typically look to a 'higher power' or faith system during times of ill-health.

Therefore, with the inclusion of spirituality, the BPSS model takes a holistic (seeing the whole system), rather than a reductionist (looking at one piece of the system) view of mental health problems. It raises awareness of and is inclusive of diverse perspectives, where social and behavioural factors such as living conditions, family influences, spiritual beliefs and personal habits, are major influences on mental health and that a reductionist biological/medical approach, often used in the diagnosis and treatment of health problems, does not help in fully understanding these phenomena (Engel, 1977).

For human service professions, such as nurses, social workers, counsellors and occupational therapists, the BPSS model is a helpful framework for understanding health and illness. However, it does have its critics. In its attempts to be holistic and inclusive some argue that this has led to an unscientific, pluralistic approach. For a full account of the limitations of the model we suggest reading Nassir Ghaemi (2009). While acknowledging the critics' arguments, BPSS does at least raise practitioners' awareness of the fact that the causes, manifestation and outcomes of mental ill-health require a multi-dimensional approach. We now consider each dimension in more detail.

Understanding the biological/medical view of mental illness

The biological/medical view of mental ill-health is that mental disorders arise from faults in our biology. In other words, the biological or medical perspective of mental illness takes a disease focus and uses various tools to define and categorise mental illness (disorder).

The most commonly used are the ICD 10 which is the International Classification of Disease (WHO, 2016) typically used in the UK, or the DSM V, which is the Diagnostic and Statistical Manual of Mental Disorders 5 (American Psychiatric Association, 2013) and the handbook used by health-care and social work professionals in the US. These tools are used to categorise the symptoms of mental illness so that clinicians have a common language to diagnose, treat and research mental illness. Typical terminology used to describe mental illness is 'Mental Disorder' or 'Severe Mental Disorder', which is illness that can affect the thoughts, feelings and behaviours of an individual and can prevent them leading happy, healthy and productive lives (Mind, 2016). Common modern diagnostic terms include depression, anxiety, anorexia nervosa and schizophrenia, with each diagnosis being assigned in the presence of a collection of symptoms.

The biomedical approach is an attempt to see mental disorder in the same way as any other human disease process, with clear categorisation of separate disease processes, that can be treated and researched in a consistent way. As a consequence there has been a significant expansion of treatments available, particularly pharmaceutical, which brings welcome relief for many sufferers. This is a great step forward, as historically individuals displaying what were considered unusual symptoms or behaviours or mental disorder, were thought to be possessed by demons and often subject to all sorts of humiliating and dehumanising interventions.

While our understanding and compassion for mental disorder has moved on as a result of biomedical research, sadly, negative and judgmental attitudes still prevail in some communities, which can result in an individual feeling shame or disapproval (Corrigan and Watson, 2002) or being isolated, ignored or rejected by those around them. Indeed, a medical diagnosis of mental disorder should not be applied lightly; because of the judgements of others, there can be significant secondary social deficits such as the inability to find housing, a job, life or health insurance, treatment or social opportunities. This will be discussed in more detail later.

Despite the potential drawbacks and limitations of a diagnosis of mental disorder, the two diagnostic frameworks described earlier are utilised widely and according to the ICD 10 (WHO, 2016) there are now over 200 classified forms of mental disorder. The five major categories are:

- anxiety disorders
- mood disorders
- psychotic disorders
- dementias (see Chapter 16)
- eating disorders

In order to understand these categories, the characteristics of each are briefly considered, but see also NHS Choices (2016a).

Anxiety disorders

Anxiety is a common feeling experienced by all of us and a perfectly normal response to something we perceive as threatening to our safety or well-being. It is the feeling of unease triggered by a stressful situation or change to our usual routines such as making a speech, taking a driving test or starting a new job. It may affect our sleep or appetite or concentration, but the anxiety is generally limited to the time leading up to or during that situation and usually stops once the event is over.

An acute stress or panic reaction is commonly known as the 'fight or flight' response. The reaction occurs in our brain, specifically the hypothalamus, which tells the sympathetic nervous system to respond and the body reacts by speeding and tensing up in order to become more alert. Physiological changes then occur, including increases in heart rate and blood pressure, dilating pupils and distributing more blood to major muscle groups. Consequently the muscles will tense up and other non-essential systems like digestion will shut down in order to enable more energy to be directed to where it is needed, the emergency systems.

Such a reaction is, of course, ideal when faced with an emergency situation such as encountering a wild dog or burglar in the home. But such a reaction becomes problematic when the feelings are sustained unnecessarily or triggered by real or imagined threats that cannot be controlled. This may suggest a more serious underlying anxiety disorder that needs treatment.

In terms of impact, anxiety disorders can make a person feel out of control, causing lowered self-esteem and poor self-image, which in turn may contribute to a lack of confidence and nervousness in normal situations for no apparent reason. Further reactions can include anger, confusion and fear, with the problem moving from an acute issue to a chronic long-lasting disorder, affecting quality of life and the wider ability to engage in situations that others find perfectly manageable, thus contributing to further self-esteem issues.

Stress

Stress differs from anxiety in that it is the general pressures we encounter and experience in everyday life, arising from the demands made on our minds and bodies. NHS Choices (2016i) suggests that although stress might arise from prolonged anxiety, it is more likely to emerge from being asked to do things that are out of our comfort zone or that we are unhappy with. It can also arise from seeing or being told things that are upsetting or from significant life changes. As with anxiety, stress can have its uses in that it helps us to adapt and learn new skills but when prolonged, stress can become a problem.

If we apply this to a health-care and social work practice context, we know from research that victims of childhood abuse may go onto experience anxiety disorders as adults. The reasons for this are complex and are likely linked to the type of abuse suffered but typically involve fear of repeated abuse and flash backs to traumatic events. Survivors of abuse may experience such overwhelming feelings of stress and anxiety and feelings that they are unable to cope.

Anxiety disorders can affect anyone in any walk of life and encouragingly more people in the public eye are talking about their experiences in order to spread the word and help normalise their experiences. One example is Marcus Trescothick (2015), the English Cricketer who describes his experiences and his support for the Anxiety UK campaign:

> People often don't understand how debilitating anxiety disorders can be, and the devastating effect that they have on the lives of sufferers and their families, … I am joining with Anxiety UK to reduce the stigma attached to these conditions, so others don't have to feel the shame and embarrassment that I did. There are many treatments and therapies which can help, and I would advise other sufferers to get help sooner rather than later.

Mood disorders

Depression

Many of us go through life experiencing regular changes to our moods in response to day-to-day events. We may feel elated in response to a promotion at work or the birth of a child and feel sad in response to a sudden loss. This is perfectly usual when within normal limits, however, clinical depression involves more persistent levels of sadness that may last for weeks and months. The symptoms may manifest themselves in complex ways but typically are characterised by intense sadness, hopelessness, helplessness and a general loss of enjoyment. Symptoms, which can be psychological, physical or social, will often persist for weeks or months and interfere with work, social and family life.

The common psychological symptoms can be found on the NHS Choices website (2016b) and have been helpfully listed under the BPS headings. Gilbert (2009) provides a helpful guide on overcoming depression.

The English actor and comedian Stephen Fry (2017) famously said of his experiences of depression:

> If you know someone who's depressed, please resolve never to ask them why. Depression isn't a straightforward response to a bad situation; depression just is, like the weather.
>
> Try to understand the blackness, lethargy, hopelessness, and loneliness they're going through. Be there for them when they come through the other side. It's hard to be a friend to someone who's depressed, but it is one of the kindest, noblest, and best things you will ever do.

Suicide

For both the sufferer and those seeking to help, one of the most distressing and disturbing symptoms of mood disorders are the suicidal feelings and consequent attempts to take one's own life. In fact, suicide is one of the leading causes of death in the UK and worldwide. According to NHS Choices (2016c), 90 per cent of those who take their own life have subsequently been found to have a mental illness such as depression (see Case Study 13.3).

Suicidal behaviour is particularly linked to feelings of hopelessness, helplessness and worthlessness and while there is no single cause, research suggests that a person's vulnerability to suicide can be linked to several common factors:

- deterioration in a person's mental health – including a diagnosis of a serious mental health problem such as schizophrenia or bipolar disorder – which are discussed later;
- a history of traumatic life events – this may involve sexual or physical abuse or parental neglect in childhood;
- drug and/or alcohol misuse;
- unemployment or poor job or employment prospects;
- social isolation or being a victim of abuse/bullying;
- genetic links.

As practitioners, it is important to note that the presence of any or all of these factors will not automatically mean the person will exhibit suicidal behaviour. However, these factors combined with a sudden life event such as loss of a significant relationship or job or something that others might perceive as trivial, such as a minor argument, can lead the person towards displaying suicidal behaviour. Therefore, the astute practitioner will be alert to the risk factors and consider these carefully in the context of what else is going on.

There are of course many more obvious indications of suicidal intent. These can include spoken or written threats to harm or kill themselves or overt efforts to seek out methods to kill themselves, such as stockpiling hazardous materials. Access to the means is an important risk factor here for those with easy access to firearms, drugs and chemicals are proportionately at higher risk.

There are also less obvious indictors of suicidal risk, including complaints of feeling hopeless and helpless and that life is not worth living. There may be rapid changes to the mood such as rage and anger accompanied by reckless behaviours. The person may not be able to see any solutions to their problems or believe life has become purposeless. They may display acts of self-harm, actively withdrawing from social contact and experiencing sleep disturbance, loss of interest and starting to put their affairs in order as if preparing for death.

Self-harm

Self-harming behaviour is very different to suicidal behaviour in significant ways, although unfortunately sometimes an act of self-harm can lead either intentionally or unintentionally to a suicidal outcome. In fact, as NHS Choices (2016d) point out, over 50 per cent of those who die by suicide are found to have a history of self-harm.

Self-harm is the intention to injure or damage one's own body and is often used as a means for coping with and/or communicating significant emotional distress. There are many types of self-harm but typically involve cutting the skin, hitting oneself, self-poisoning, using drugs or harmful chemicals, and intentional starvation (see Case Study 13.1).

It is surprisingly common with estimates suggesting around 10 per cent of young people using self-harm as a mechanism for coping with overwhelming emotional problems. This can arise from incidents of bullying, sexual identity issues, sexual abuse, significant loss or in some cases thoughts or internal 'voices' that instruct them to harm themselves.

The pattern of behaviour will often involve a build-up of intense and uncomfortable feelings, including anger, guilt and self-hatred. The individual may experience feelings of isolation and use self-harm to express their discomfort and release the build-up of tension. In some cases, antisocial behaviour may be displayed resulting in the attention of the police or school.

As previously indicated, while the underlying dynamics and motives leading to suicide or self-harm are different, there is an association, with most not wishing to kill themselves, but using self-harm as in important coping strategy thus avoiding the need to end their lives. For more information see NHS Choices (2016c, 2016d).

Bipolar disorder

The condition formerly known as manic–depression is now known as bipolar disorder. It is a condition involving extreme changes in mood, energy levels and behaviour. Typically this involves cyclical episodes of depression, with low mood and lethargy, followed by mania, with extreme feelings of elation and over–activity. Less severe mania is known as hypomania. A really interesting account of what it is like to live with bipolar disorder is published by Mind (2015).

The experience of depression is as described above, but mania is a complete contrast, with the person feeling 'high' and having lots of energy, often accompanied by ambitious plans and ideas. This can involve spending large amounts of money on things they cannot afford and would not normally want. As a consequence of an overactive mind and preoccupation with plans, there will be loss of appetite and sleep, with a short attention span and irritation when plans are thwarted. Bipolar disorder is primarily a mood disorder but can also involve psychotic features as described in the section on psychosis to follow. For more information, see NHS Choices (2016e).

CASE STUDY 13.1

Amelia is a 20-year-old university student, who has become increasingly low in mood, with episodes of anxiety and panic attacks for no apparent reason. Her friends have reported that she has become increasingly withdrawn and uncommunicative and is not eating, and they have observed her cutting and scratching her arms.

Her university tutor has observed this behaviour and suggested she see the counsellor for some support and the opportunity to talk about the difficulties she is having in her life.

This case study may be familiar to you or a friend or relative, as many of us experience changes in our mental health at key points in our lives. This is quite normal and may be resolved by having the opportunity for someone to talk to. Counsellors provide an important confidential and safe space to share and allow the person to work through their difficulties without the need for further treatment.

Questions

1. What might be the reactions of other family members to Amelia's situation?
2. Counsellors often talk about 'boundaries' within the counselling relationship. What are the key characteristics of 'boundaries' in a helping relationship and why are they important?
3. Social media is seen to play an increasingly significant role in people's mental well-being. What 'boundary' issues might be at play?

Discussion

Many students experience mental health problems at university and increasingly students are arriving at university with such a history. University student support systems are often insufficient to cope with demand, while most academics will not have the training or a workload able to supplement suitable services. While these deficits relate to the infrastructural and funding problems associated with insufficient service delivery, cases like Amelia's still require urgent support given that she is clearly distressed and self-harming through cutting and starvation.

Psychotic disorders

Most of what are described as severe and enduring mental health disorders come under the heading of psychotic disorders. One definition is any form of severe mental disorder in which the individual's contact with reality becomes highly distorted.

Psychosis

A person experiencing psychosis may judge external reality differently to those around them, they may wrongly evaluate the accuracy of their thoughts and perceptions and, despite evidence to the contrary, may continue to believe these errors of judgement.

These thoughts will often be accompanied by auditory hallucinations (voices) and delusions (fixed false beliefs). The voices may act as a commentary on their behaviour or urge them to take actions; the delusional beliefs can be paranoid in nature causing fear and anxiety. This, in turn, results in unusual behaviours or moods that appear to others out of context with the situation. Due to the unpredictable nature of the condition, this may cause concern among those around them, such as family and friends. Treatment is typically by medication, which may be life-long.

The UK charity Rethink Mental Illness (2016) provides some excellent evidence-based resources on understanding the nature of psychosis and how it affects people.

For more information, see also NHS Choices (2016f).

Schizophrenia

The diagnosis of schizophrenia, while still in common use, is a controversial label covering a range of psychotic disorders characterised by cognitive, emotional and behavioural symptoms. The controversy derives from the stigma surrounding the label and its connotations. The controversy is discussed in detail by Lasalvia et al (2015), who argue for a change of name in order to improve care and services.

The most common characteristics include an insidious deterioration from previous levels of social, cognitive and behavioural functioning. The onset of the condition is before the age of 45, with a duration of at least six months. The features typically include those described under psychosis – namely disturbed thought, delusional ideas, hallucinations and a loss of effective reality testing. For more information, see NHS Choices (2016g).

Eating disorders

The category of conditions known as eating disorders are mental health problems that can affect physical, psychological and social functioning. The most common eating disorders are anorexia nervosa, bulimia and binge eating disorder.

- Anorexia nervosa involves a person seeking to keep their weight as low as possible by starving themselves or through excessive exercise.
- Bulimia involves episodes of binge eating and then inducing vomiting or taking laxatives to empty the bowel, in order to control their weight.
- Binge eating disorder (BED) involves a person feeling compelled to overeat large volumes of food in a short space of time.

It is also possible to receive a diagnosis of an 'eating disorder not otherwise specified' (EDNOS) where some, but not all, symptoms are present. For more information, see NHS Choices (2016h).

REFLECTION POINT 13.2

Most people will have experienced times of emotional distress that affects their mental well-being, if only temporarily. Think back to a time when you became aware of this in yourself or someone else. What did you feel was happening to yourself or the other person?

Critique of the biological medical model of mental health

While the medical model is well-meaning and aimed at curing disease, there are a number of serious concerns about the biological/medical approach. For a full discussion of these, see McLeod (2016), from the University of Manchester, who writes on the Simply Psychology site: https://www.simplypsychology.org/. However, the key arguments are summarised here:

- There are serious questions about the research evidence that purportedly demonstrates that psychiatric drugs address the assumed chemical imbalance that causes mental illness.
- Common treatments such as drugs and ECT have very severe and disabling side-effects which can become what has been described as a 'chemical straight-jacket'.
- Genetic and neurochemical explanations for diagnoses such as schizophrenia remain inconclusive.
- The secondary social deficits of diagnosing people with mental disorders can lead to homelessness, unemployment, isolation and poverty.
- Psychiatric manuals such as ICD 10 and DSM V are not works of objective science but should be considered works of culture.

While the biological/medical approach does alleviate distressing symptoms and can provide relief from significant distress, it should not be seen as a panacea for mental ill-health problems, hence the emphasis on a more holistic BPS model.

Despite these criticisms it should be stressed that there has been promising research into the genetic origins of mental disorder. For example, in a study published in 2013 a Cross-Disorder Group of the Psychiatric Genomics Consortium looked at the genetic relationship between five psychiatric disorders (Cross-Disorder Group of the Psychiatric Genomics Consortium, 2013). They found that five of the most common psychiatric disorders (schizophrenia, clinical depression, bipolar disorder, attention deficit hyperactivity disorder and autism) are genetically linked. This, it is argued, could have important implications for diagnostics, treatment and research, although further research is needed.

Psychological perspectives on mental health

Throughout the 20th century, a number of what are known as 'grand psychological theories' emerged that sought to explain human mental health development and disorder. These psychological perspectives can broadly be divided into four categories:

- behaviourism
- analytic/psychodynamic
- humanistic
- cognitive

For more detailed discussion on each of these theories, see McLeod's (2016) Simply Psychology site: https://www.simplypsychology.org. However, a brief summary of each theory is outlined here.

Behaviourism

Behaviourism places a great focus on learning, emphasising the role of environmental factors influencing our behaviour, to the near exclusion of innate inherited factors. This theory suggests we learn new behaviour through classical or operant conditioning, with chief theorists being Watson, Skinner and Pavlov.

These theorists would argue that psychology should be seen as a science, to be studied in a scientific manner with behaviourism being primarily concerned with observable behaviour, as opposed to internal events like thinking. Our behaviour is therefore the result of a basic stimulus – response. In other words, all our behaviour, whatever the complexity, can be reduced to a simple stimulus – response – and is largely determined by the environment through conditioning (Cherry, 2014).

In terms of the treatment of mental disorder, the focus is on unlearning unhelpful, self-destructive or unhealthy behaviours and replacing these with healthier and helpful alternatives (see Parrish, Chapter 2 in this volume).

Psychodynamic

Psychodynamic theory stems from the work of Freud, Jung, Erikson and Kohlberg (Cherry, 2014) and proposes that our behaviour and feelings are powerfully influenced by unconscious motives, with resulting psychological problems being firmly rooted in our childhood experiences.

It is further suggested, particularly by Freud, that our personality is made up of three interrelated parts (Id, Ego and Super-ego), with behaviour being motivated by two drives, Eros (sex and life) and Thanatos (aggression and death) that are derived from the Id. The unconscious mind (Id and Super-ego) is in conflict with our conscious mind (Ego) and it is this conflict that creates the anxiety, dealt with by defence mechanisms. Consequently, our personality is shaped by the resulting conflicts at different times in our childhood psychosexual development.

The purpose of treatment using the psychodynamic approach is to explore the unconscious content of a client's psyche in an effort to alleviate conflict, tension and distress.

Humanistic

The humanistic theory, also known as a phenomenological approach, considers the study of the whole person with humanistic psychologists looking at behaviour from the perspective of the observer and the person displaying the behaviour. Key theorists are Rogers and Maslow.

Humanists suggest the personality should be studied through subjective experience and perception of the world and events. This was an approach developed by Carl Rogers (2003a), as described in the book *On Becoming a Person*, first published in 1961. For a first-hand account of the approach, see *Client Centred Therapy: Its Current Practice, Implications and Theory* (Rogers, 2003b)

The aims and benefits of the humanistic approach to therapy in mental health are to encourage both self-awareness and mindfulness that enable the individual to understand their responses and behaviours in life and to develop healthier and more productive alternatives based on greater self-awareness and reflexive actions.

Cognitive approaches

The cognitive approach to psychology involves scientific methods largely based on laboratory experiments (Cherry, 2014). The key theorists are Tolman, Piaget and Chomsky, who argue that behaviour can largely be explained by how information is processed by the brain. Thus, the brain is seen as similar to the input, storage and retrieval of a computer.

The cognitive approach is typically combined with behaviourism in the form of Cognitive Behavioural Therapy (CBT). CBT is talking therapy that helps individuals address mental health problems by changing the way they think (cognitions) and behave. It's most commonly used to treat anxiety and depression (see earlier sections), but is also used in a wide range of other mental and physical health problems, including the treatment of psychotic symptoms. Davey et al's (2014) text provides a useful guide to a cognitive–behavioural treatment approach to anxiety.

Social perspectives on mental health

Peter Beresford, Mary Nettle and Rebecca Perring in 2010 wrote a report entitled *Towards a Social Model of Madness and Distress – Exploring What Service Users Say*. They described the origins of the social model of disability being derived from the disabled people's movement, transforming understandings of disability. The previous deficit laden and medicalised view of disability was challenged and replaced by viewing disability as negative societal reactions. Disability thus becomes understood as a discriminatory and oppressive societal response to individuals who are seen as having an impairment, rather than a characteristic attached to the individual. This shifted blame and responsibility from the individual to society and gives important insights into the postmodern approach to mental health.

The social construction of mental illness

To understand this discriminatory and oppressive response in the context of mental health, we need to draw on social construction theory. Having presented the various diagnostic categories according to the bio-medical model it might be assumed that once diagnosed the successful treatment of the disorder would naturally progress. But unlike the diagnosis and treatment of physical health problems such as diabetes or arthritis, the situation for many of the more serious mental health problems is more complex.

A critical perspective suggests that the social construction of mental ill–health through the use of diagnostic labels and categories has potentially detrimental effects on those on the receiving end. To illustrate this more clearly, Walker (2006) takes the perspective of linguistics to argue that questionable categories only exist through consensus and that such a pathologising approach and deficit–laden vocabulary is of little use in helping people to improve the quality of their lives.

Walker argues that words like mental disorder, schizophrenia and bipolar disorder, which are defined by groups of symptoms, are abstractions used as a communication shorthand by nurses, psychiatrists and other health professionals for the purposes of treatment, but which also communicates a detrimental 'hierarchical role relationship'. Such categories, Walker suggests, are fundamentally flawed as they not only denigrate a person's identity but also fail to improve outcomes. Walker quotes Paula Caplan (1995), former consultant to the creators of the DSM, to emphasise the disparity between diagnosis and treatment outcome:

> The professionals most concerned with labelling claim that they assign people to categories of mental illness so that they will know how to help them. If such assignments to categories really did help very much, that would indeed be encouraging, but treatment of emotional problems and conflicts is very different from medical or surgical treatment. If I broke a limb, I would want to be properly diagnosed as having a broken arm so that the surgeon would not mistakenly set and put a cast on my leg. But diagnosing individuals as mentally ill has not been shown to do much to alleviate their anguish and indeed often makes it worse. (p 12)

REFLECTION POINT 13.3

Review a couple of newspapers, television programmes or films to find depictions of people experiencing mental ill-health. Having read the previous sections on social construction and discrimination, what are your observations on how mental health problems are depicted in the media?

Listening to the voice of the service user in mental health

To appreciate the impact of the medicalisation of mental health issues one only needs to listen to those that use services. The narrative in much of the mental health clinical literature on the treatment and symptom relief of disease processes, are seen by some as hegemonic. In other words, they are dominated by medical/ disease perspectives and therefore at odds with the needs and views of a great number of people who use mental health services, many of whom choose not to define their experiences using a medical model or diagnosis. One powerful example where the voice of service users is being used to challenge this hegemony is outlined in Case Study 13.2.

CASE STUDY 13.2

James, who is now 26, developed a psychotic disorder when he was aged 18 and at university studying to be a school teacher. He received a diagnosis of schizophrenia resulting in a period of hospitalisation and treatment. He heard voices and experienced paranoid thoughts, believing he was under the surveillance of the CIA. He has spent the last 18 months at home and could not continue with his university degree, although does want to return to his studies at some point in the future.

The mental health services are helping James to gain work and to establish a network of friends. However, James would also like to use his experiences of mental ill-health and his skills in teaching to contribute to the training of the next generation of mental health practitioners. Service user voices, like James's, are routinely used to bring about significant change in the recruitment, preparation and training of health care and social work professional practitioners, such as the Bournemouth University Public Involvement in Education and Research (BUPIER, 2017).

Questions

1. The psychiatric diagnosis of 'schizophrenia' is considered contentious. Why do you think this is the case?
2. What are the key arguments on both sides of the debate?
3. People with serious mental health problems often face discrimination. Consider the following section on anti-discriminatory practice and explore how might you support James in this regard.

Discussion

Service user experiences offer important insights into what it is like to suffer from a particular condition, which adds a new domain to, say, a biomedical understanding of the disease and its prognosis. James's journey through mental illness and his access to mental health services may not only help health-care and social work professionals to understand service users better but may help James to come to terms with not only his history of mental health problem but all the disruptions and disappointments that this has caused to his life plans over time, while providing him with a new outlet for his talents and abilities.

The medical model is rooted in the medicalisation of individual experience and consequently implies that all 'mental illness', and its care and treatment, can be studied using methods common in the study of natural science with consequent services and policy being built on this same flawed premise. Barnes and Bowl (2001) have argued that this maintains medicine's power over individuals' lives and, in many cases, leads to secondary social deficits.

Although writing about mental health and psychiatry over 50 years ago, Foucault's (1961) views on mental health and psychiatric practice still resonates. He argued that the hegemonic practice of the psychiatrist, and those that subscribe to this view, remain too secretive and unaccountable. Over time, Foucault argues, the 'patient' begins to see the doctor as '*a magician*' (p 261).

To explain this view further, Cooper (2001), introducing Foucault's *Madness and Civilisation*, argued that clinical psychiatry devalues certain aspects of human experience, through the process of diagnosis and what Cooper described as '*pseudo-medical classification*' and '*quasi-academic compartmentalisation*' (p ix) into illness categories, which through this process can be cured. Furthermore, Foucault (1961), reflecting particularly on Western society, argued that institutions, such as hospitals, are expressions of this medical power exerted over people in marginalised groups by the dominant group.

Although it could be argued that with the push towards community care provision, the closure of major psychiatric hospitals particularly in the UK and safeguards in mental health legislation, the landscape has sufficiently changed to reflect a more inclusive and empowering discourse. However, the reality is that many working today in psychiatry continue to embrace the prevailing discourse and accept the dominant position of psychiatry despite its limitations. Consequently, this has meant that the practice of many in the field remains too narrowly focused on symptom relief, surveillance and monitoring rather than active involvement and attendance to other important psychosocial aspects discussed previously.

Implications for professional social work and health care practice

Enlightened social work practitioners who want to take a broader holistic approach could feel professionally compromised, on the one hand attempting to work co-operatively within a multi-professional team and deliver intervention which is both sound and evidence-based while, at the same time, being required to work in structures which may actually be doing more harm, due to the imbalance in power between service user and the service provider.

To understand the origins of this power imbalance it is worth revisiting the work of Guggenbuhl-Craig (1971), who argued that the roots of the prevailing culture of health care and social work emanate from the Enlightenment and still drive many aspects of our work. Consequently, the values communicated through our practice, albeit well-meaning, result in efforts to enforce what the practitioner considers right for the individual. Guggenbuhl-Craig (1971) adds that in doing so, services:

> ... [F]requently force a certain view of life upon others whether they agree to it or not. We do not choose to acknowledge a right to sickness, neurosis, unhealthy familial relations, social degeneracy, and eccentricity. (p 3)

Guggenbuhl-Craig (1971) further suggested that there is an underlying assumption that because practitioners intend to benefit clients, their decision making actually does do so. In the current context, it has been argued that the professionalisation of mental health practice has resulted in a shift away from the fundamentals of caring towards 'transactional' relationships characterised by interventions that follow strict guidelines rather than something that is tailored to individual need. As an example, when practice protocols suggest one course of action in a particular situation, but the service user disagrees about the nature of the problem and the possible solutions, then significant ethical issues must be addressed.

For practitioners who aspire to adopt emancipatory stances in the process of working with clients, then they will need to constantly examine the values that inform their practice. This may mean adopting a more questioning and objective position in relation to the medical approach. Thus, the effective practitioner becomes someone who can manage the inconsistencies between what the service user might report and other interpretations of that experience:

> ... [A]ccess[ing] the experiential knowledge of people experiencing psychological distress in order to develop alternative models of explaining, understanding and hence responding to such experiences. (Barnes and Bowl, 2001, p 51)

Being able to achieve this degree of access will be highly dependent on the person-centred nature of the helping relationship established (Tee, 2016). This means overcoming the barriers that may prevent authentic relationships being established and finding ways to ensure full participation in decisions about all aspects of the care.

The ability of a client to engage with the practitioner, and the depth of that engagement, will be influenced by the client's life experiences of trusting relationships, separation, loss, intimacy and maintenance of relational boundaries. In other words, building a working relationship with a client is a very individualised thing, requiring sensitivity to the specific needs and characteristics of the client, demanding patience, compassion and sometimes perseverance to build rapport and a working relationship with someone who finds trusting someone else difficult. It will also require an understanding of the values of that individual, which have often been developed early in life, and will influence their attitude and behaviour, providing a broad set of internal 'rules' for their decision making.

This shift away from purely health care or social work values to the values of the service user, is already enshrined within much of the consumerist discourse within the policy objectives of the five year forward view (NHS England, 2014). However, translating these aspirations into the day-to-day practice that overcomes stigmatisation and marginalisation requires a whole variety of strategies to facilitate real change. The first step is to think very carefully about how we operate as practitioners to avoid doing further harm by adopting the principles of anti-discriminatory practice.

Anti-discriminatory practice

Drawing on the work undertaken in the preparation of social workers, anti-discriminatory practice has a significant contribution to make. Thompson (2016) suggests it is about overcoming oppressive behaviour that disempowers or marginalises other people because oppression is the use of power to dominate, disempower or marginalise others. Therefore, oppression represents a denial of citizenship.

The Anti-Oppression Network (2015) uses the term Kyriarchy, which is derived from the Greek words meaning 'master' and 'rule' and was first used by feminist writer Elizabeth Schussler Fiorenza (1992) to illustrate her theory of oppression. Fiorenza argued that society has interconnected and adapting systems that lead to domination and submission. At an individual level, a person may simultaneously find themselves being oppressed in some relationships but privileged in others.

The important point is that it is not a hierarchical system of domination, but one in which multiple sources of oppression interrelate and create entities that reflect the intersection of many forms of discrimination. According to Hill Collins (2015), the term intersectionality refers to the theory of how our social and group identities and sources of oppression cut across each other to create new entities that may differ significantly to the component parts.

REFLECTION POINT 13.4

Using an intersectional analysis, consider your own characteristics (gender, ethnicity, faith identity, class, (dis)abilities, etc.) How have these intersected to shape you and your experiences and attitudes towards times when you have felt vulnerable in terms of illness, disability or any other challenging life event?

As our individual structural position in this system is assigned at birth (e.g. gender, race, religion, class), where particular positions are privileged, for example, being male, other relationships are experienced from that position. This suggests individually we are all oppressed and we are also all oppressors. We may be members of a marginalised group but also a member of a group that oppresses others.

When applied in practice the anti-discriminatory approach seeks to adopt a set of principles/values drawn from critical, feminist, post-structural and post-modern theories focusing on structures of power and oppression within marginalised groups and service provision (Payne, 2014). Consequently, practice becomes focused on challenging structural inequalities, empowering individuals to understand their rights and supporting them to progress towards greater citizenship.

In relation to mental health anti-discriminatory practitioners, attempts to conceptualise client problems within a broader social context and in so doing distance themselves from notions of expertness in practice which may be oppressive (Pollack, 2004). In this way, there is an attempt to embrace and value user experience and recognise the individual's coping and their stand against oppression and discrimination.

For those embarking on developing such practice, there is a need through supervision within your team to create a working environment where the nature of anti-discriminatory practice can be explored to examine deeply their role and consider how the various positions, values and beliefs interact, relate and affect relationships and to introduce new and more enlightened narratives that challenge the prevailing narrow medical paradigm.

One outcome of this process is to support systems which are led by service users themselves in order to confront inequalities, where practitioners work openly alongside service users in an atmosphere of partnership and co-operation. In other words, sharing power in all aspects of decision making. A first step might be to look carefully at the medicalised language used to define a person's experience. The problem in mental health is that the language of diagnosis and treatment positions the practitioner as expert, with the terms used leading to alienation, causing the client to feel different and abnormal.

As mentioned previously, the disability and consumerist movement have long realised and challenged the use of medicalised language and terminology and seen it as the focus of its fight against oppression. Similar struggles can be seen among other oppressed people including women, LGBT and minority ethnic groups, and is a struggle that practitioners could get behind and lend their support.

Application in a health and social work context

A model of practice commonly adopted in mental health is that derived from the recovery-oriented model. It is primarily based on the concept of hope and is an approach that seeks to give people primary control over decisions about their own care.

The recovery model seeks to challenge the professionalised position by being client-centred (humanism), being positive about helping clients to overcome barriers and get what they want and to make a meaningful contribution to society through a vocational approach and community integration (see Case Study 13.3).

CASE STUDY 13.3

Jean is a 53-year-old factory worker who had been employed for 40 years up until she was made redundant. She struggled to find work and began to doubt her ability, becoming increasingly low in mood, with intense feelings of hopelessness and suicidal ideation. At one point, she made a plan to jump in front of a train, but following a chance encounter with someone on the station platform, who showed her some concern, she decided not to go through with the plan, but instead rang the Samaritans and then went to see her GP. The GP provided some medication but also referred her to a mental health team who have provided ongoing rehabilitative support. Following a person-centred assessment of her individual needs, Jean was introduced to the local Mind centre, which has a project that she might be interested to attend.

The project is a partnership between a garden centre for people with mental health needs and the local council who are working to transform outdoor spaces on local estates and improve people's well-being. This project has given Jean's life some new meaning: she feels she is able to make a valuable contribution and has also extended her social contacts, both of which have boosted her confidence. For an example of this type of project, see SolentMind (2017).

Questions

1. Why do you think making a meaningful contribution to society is so important to mental health?
2. What other activities might make a positive contribution to a person's mental health and well-being?
3. It is said that 'normalising' mental health conditions can help challenge assumptions. What is normalisation and how is it helpful?

Discussion

Gardening is being seen as the new way to treat a variety of health conditions that require more than medical expertise and pharmacology, this being 'social therapy' where exposure to green and natural environments is viewed as immensely therapeutic in a concreted, traffic-tangled world where we are losing our daily connections to nature. The social aspect relates to exposure, not just to plants but to peers, with whom one can work side-by-side with a common aim in a friendly and accepting environment. Social gardening provides not only mental respite, but a much-needed creative outlet, sensory delights and the opportunities to socialise in a gentle and normal way rather than in an enforced context.

Working in a recovery-oriented way means acting in a manner that empowers rather than disenfranchises people, being aware of communication techniques and body language to promote positive engagement, respecting cultural differences and avoiding negative behaviours such as talking about people in the third person when they are present.

A key challenge in practice arises when the outcomes desired by the professional team are at odds with those of the individual. To address such situations, an approach known as Values–Based Practice (VBP) was developed by Woodbridge and Fulford (2004). VBP is typically employed when working with people where there are complex and conflicting values in health care. It is seen as a partner to evidence-based practice in support of health care and/or social work judgements focused on the individual.

The aim is to engage with the unique set of values of the individuals involved in coming to a given decision and to adopt a position of mutual respect in the making of the decision. Only when practitioners adopt a truly person-centred, values–based position (Tee, 2016) will they be able to help overcome the huge obstacles faced by people with complex mental health needs.

Conclusion

In this chapter, we set out objectives to examine the controversial concepts of mental health and ill-health and to understand why a more holistic bio-psycho-social (BPS) framework is needed to challenge the prevailing biological/medical model of mental disorders. We have also looked at the impact of stigma and discrimination on the mental health and well-being of individuals within the context of wider systems that has the potential to oppress, while, importantly, examining the essential role social work practitioners can play in helping to challenge discrimination in all its forms.

Mental health and mental ill-health remain complex and contested concepts which are fraught with multiple and often contradictory ideas. Mental ill-health is a common experience among the general population, often arising as a reaction to life changes and significant personal events. It is the interaction between biological, psychological and social factors that cause and maintain many mental health problems, but the narrow medicalisation of that experience can limit individual life chances and opportunities due to the fear and discrimination that such labels evoke.

The negativity surrounding the deficit model of disability has motivated a growing social disability movement who convincingly argue that many of the 'problems' faced by people with mental ill-health, arise from society and its institutions and not the individual, and that it is up to society to adapt to ensure greater inclusivity and integration. Thus, health care and social work practice has a dual individual and societal focus to empower, support and be active in overcoming the barriers to full engagement. Working alongside people with mental health problems requires the social work practitioner to be aware of their own values, the potential for the misuse of power arising from inappropriate language and communication and the need to adopt a position of hope and positivity.

As Walker (2006) points out, wherever possible, we should seek to promote emancipation and inclusion and limit the negative influence of the medical and psychological vocabularies. It is only through an anti-discriminatory stance that challenges the inequalities and negative attitudes in society and negotiating decisions by employing a person-centred, values-based approach that we will avoid further disempowerment and support greater engagement and integration for those who experience mental ill-health.

Reflective questions

1 What can you do to reduce the stigma of mental health in our communities?

2 What can you do to help people with mental health problems overcome the barriers they face getting into work?

3 How would you maintain compassion, kindness, dignity and respect when practising with someone experiencing mental ill-health?

Further reading

- Golightley, M. and Goemans, R. (2020) *Social Work and Mental Health* (7th edn). London: Sage.

  Golightley and Goemans outline the key elements of social work practice with people who are experiencing mental health problems. The book covers a wide range of practice settings, laws and policies influencing practice and it a good place to start in developing your knowledge base.

- Gould, N. (2016) *Mental Health Social Work in Context*. Abingdon: Routledge.

  A very useful introductory text to mental health issues for social workers.

- NHS Choices – http://www.nhs.uk/livewell/mentalhealth/Pages/Mentalhealthhome.aspx
- Mind – www.mind.org.uk
- Rethink Mental Illness – https://www.rethink.org
- Mental Health Foundation – https://www.mentalhealth.org.uk

  These four websites are easily accessible and offer a range of useful information regarding mental illness, mental health services and thinking through what we mean by both.

- Tee, S. (2016) *Person-Centred Approaches in Healthcare*. Maidenhead: Open University Press and McGraw-Hill Education.

  An important text that is applicable to a range of multidisciplinary professionals, including social workers.

References

American Psychiatric Association (2013) *Diagnostic and Statistical Manual of Mental Disorders (DSM–5)*. Available from: https://www.psychiatry.org/psychiatrists/practice/dsm/educational-resources/dsm-5-fact-sheets

American Psychological Association (2017) *Data on Behavioral Health in the United States*. Available from: http://www.apa.org/helpcenter/data-behavioral-health.aspx

Anti-Oppression Network (2015) *What is anti-oppression?*. Available from: https://theantioppressionnetwork.wordpress.com/what-is-anti-oppression/

Barnes, M. and Bowl, R. (2001) *Taking Over the Asylum: Empowerment and Mental Health*. New York, NY: Palgrave.

BUPIER (2017) *Bournemouth University Public Involvement in Education and Research*. Bournemouth: Bournemouth University. Available from: https://www1.bournemouth.ac.uk/about/our-faculties/faculty-health-social-sciences/public-involvement-education-research

Beresford, P., Nettle, M. and Perring, R. (2010) *Towards a Social Model of Madness and Distress – Exploring What Service Users Say*. York: Joseph Rowntree Foundation. Available from: https://www.jrf.org.uk/report/towards-social-model-madness-and-distress-exploring-what-service-users-say

Caplan, P. (1995) *They Say You're Crazy: How the World's Most Powerful Psychiatrists Decide Who's Normal?* New York, NY: Addison Wesley.

Cherry, K. (2014) *Psychology Theories*. Available from: http://psychology.about.com/od/psychology101/u/psychology-theories.htm

Cooper, D. (2001) Introduction. In M. Foucault, *Madness and Civilisation*. London: Routledge.

Corrigan, P.W. and Watson, A.C. (2002) Understanding the impact of stigma on people with mental illness, *World Psychiatry*, 1(1): 16–20.

Cross-Disorder Group of the Psychiatric Genomics Consortium (2013) Genetic relationship between five psychiatric disorders estimated from genome-wide SNPs, *Nature Genetics*, 45(9): 984–994.

Davey, G.C., Cananagh, K., Jones, F., Turner, L. and Whittington, A. (2014) *Managing Anxiety with CBT for Dummies*. Chichester: John Wiley.

Engel, G.L. (1977) The need for a new medical model: A challenge for biomedicine, *Science*, 196: 129–136. Available from: https://doi.org/10.1126/science.847460

Fiorenza, E.S. (1992) *But She Said: Feminist Practices of Biblical Interpretation*. Boston, MA: Beacon Press.

Foucault, M. (1961) *Madness and Civilisation*. London: Routledge

Fry, S. (2017) *Stephen Fry at 60: The Polymath's Wisest and Wittiest Quotes*. 24 August. Available from: http://www.telegraph.co.uk/men/thinking-man/stephen-frys-best-quotes/stephen-fry-quotes17/

Gilbert, P. (2009) *Overcoming Depression: A Self-Help Guide Using Cognitive Behavioural Techniques*. London: Robinson.

Guggenbuhl-Craig, A. (1971) *Power in the Helping Professions*. Putnam, CT: Spring Publications.

Hatala, A.R. (2013) Towards a biopsychosocial–spiritual approach in health psychology: Exploring theoretical orientations and future directions, *Journal of Spirituality in Mental Health*, 15(4): 256–276.

Hill Collins, P. (2015) Intersectionality's definitional dilemmas, *Annual Review of Sociology*, 41: 1–20. Available from: https://doi.org/10.1146/annurev-soc-073014-112142

Katerndahl, D.A. (2008) Impact of spiritual symptoms and their interactions on health services and life satisfaction, *Annals of Family Medicine*, 6(5): 412–420.

Keller, H. (1940) *Let Us Have Faith*. London: Doubleday and Company Inc.

Lasalvia, A., Penta, E., Sartorious, N. and Henderson, S. (2015) Should the label 'schizophrenia' be abandoned?, *Schizophrenia Research*, 162(1–3): 276–284. DOI: 10.1016/j.schres.2015.01.031

McLeod, S. (2016) *Simply Psychology*. Manchester: University of Manchester Press. Available from: https://www.simplypsychology.org/

McManus, S., Bebbington, P., Jenkins, R. and Brugha, T. (eds) (2016) *Mental Health and Wellbeing in England: Adult Psychiatric Morbidity Survey 2014*. Leeds: NHS digital.

Mental Health Foundation (2017) *How to Look After Your Mental Health*. Available from: https://www.mentalhealth.org.uk/publications/how-to-mental-health

Mind (2013) *Mental Health Problems – An Introduction*. London: Mind.

Mind (2015) *Bipolar Disorder*. London: Mind. Available from: https://www.mind. org.uk/information-support/types-of-mental-health-problems/bipolar-disord er/?gclid=CKXsq4iXhtQCFYYV0wodb0IAOg#.WSRBApMrI6g

Mind (2016) *Understanding Mental Health Problems*. London: Mind.

Nassir Ghaemi, S.N. (2009) The rise and fall of the biopsychosocial model, *The British Journal of Psychiatry*, 19: 3–4. Available from: https://doi.org/10.1192/ bjp.bp.109.063859

NHS Choices (2016a) *Mental Health*. England: National Health Service. Available from: https://www.nhs.uk/livewell/mentalhealth/Pages/Mentalhealthhome. aspx

NHS Choices (2016b) *NHS Conditions and Treatments – Clinical Depression*. England: National Health Service. Available from: http://www.nhs.uk/ Conditions/Depression/Pages/Symptoms.aspx

NHS Choices (2016c) *NHS Conditions and Treatments – Suicide*. Available from: http://www.nhs.uk/conditions/suicide/pages/introduction.aspx.

NHS Choices (2016d) *Conditions and Treatment – Self-Injury*. England: National Health Service. Available from: http://www.nhs.uk/Conditions/Self-injury/ Pages/Treatment.aspx

NHS Choices (2016e) *NHS Conditions and Treatment – Bipolar Disorder*. England: National Health Service. Available from: http://www.nhs.uk/conditions/ Bipolar-disorder/Pages/Introduction.aspx

NHS Choices (2016f) *NHS Conditions and Treatment – Schizophrenia*. England: National Health Service. Available from: http://www.nhs.uk/Conditions/ Schizophrenia/Pages/Introduction.aspx

NHS Choices (2016g) *NHS Conditions and Treatment – Psychosis*. England: National Health Service. Available from: http://www.nhs.uk/conditions/ psychosis/pages/introduction.aspx

NHS Choices (2016h) *Conditions and Treatment – Eating Disorders*. England: National Health Service. Available from: http://www.nhs.uk/conditions/ Eating-disorders/Pages/Introduction.aspx

NHS Choices (2016i) *Moodzone – Stress, Anxiety and Depression*. Available from: https://www.nhs.uk/conditions/stress-anxiety-depression/Pages/low-mood- stress-anxiety.aspx

NHS England (2014) *Five Year Forward View*. England: National Health Service. Available from: https://www.england.nhs.uk/five-year-forward-view/

Payne, M. (2014) *Modern Social Work Theory* (4th edn). London: Palgrave Macmillan.

Pollack, S. (2004) Anti-oppressive social work practice with women in prison: Discursive reconstructions and alternative practices, *British Journal of Social Work*, 34(5): 693–707.

Rethink Mental Illness (2016) Psychosis. Available from: https://www.rethink. org/diagnosis-treatment/conditions/psychosis

Rogers, C. (2003a) *On Becoming a Person – A Therapist's View of Psychotherapy*. London: Little Brown Book Group.

Rogers, C. (2003b) *Client Centred Therapy: Its Current Practice, Implications and Theory*. London: Robinson.

SolentMind (2017) *New Gardening Partnership Aims to Transform Lives and Council Estates*. Available from: http://www.solentmind.org.uk/content/new-gardening-partnership-aims-transform-lives-and-council-estates

Sulmasy, D.P. (2002) A biopsychosocial-spiritual model for the care of patients at the end of life, *Gerontologist*, 42: 24–33.

Tee, S. (2016) *Person Centred Approaches in Healthcare*. Maidenhead, UK: Open University Press and McGraw-Hill Education.

Thompson, N. (2016) *Anti-Discriminatory Practice: Equality, Diversity and Social Justice* (Practical Social Work Series) (6th edn). London: Palgrave/Macmillan.

Trescothick, M. (2015) *Celebrity, Patrons and Ambassadors Anxiety UK*. Available from: https://www.anxietyuk.org.uk/about-us/whos-who/celebrity-patrons/

Walker, M.T. (2006) The social construction of mental illness and its implications for the recovery model, *International Journal of Psychosocial Rehabilitation*, 10(1): 71–87.

WHO (World Health Organization) (2014) *Mental Health: A State of Well-Being*. Geneva: WHO. Available from: http://www.who.int/features/factfiles/mental_health/en/

WHO (World Health Organization) (2016) *International Statistical Classification of Diseases and Related Health Problems* (10th revision). Geneva: WHO. Available from: http://apps.who.int/classifications/icd10/browse/2016/en

Woodbridge, K. and Fulford, K.W.M. (2004) *'Whose Values?' A Workbook for Values-Based Practice in Mental Health Care*. London: The Sainsbury Centre for Mental Health.

14

Adults at risk of abuse

Bridget Penhale and Jonathan Parker

Introduction

'Safeguarding is everybody's business' as guidance in the Care Act 2014 states. This chapter will consider the impact that experiencing abuse and witnessing the abuse of others may have on people in social and professional settings. An historical excursus into adult protection, including elder abuse and domestic abuse will be offered showing the development of this issue through social problem construction. In this vein moves towards the concept of 'safeguarding' in the UK will also be analysed. This will be further critiqued through the lens of cultural and social diversity leading to a range of questions social workers should ask when working in these complex and often emotionally challenging areas.

> ## Chapter objectives
>
> - provide an overview of abuse of adults at risk of harm, with a particular focus on the UK;
>
> - consider the problems of definition and identification of abuse or the risk of harm;
>
> - introduce some of the complexities of working in this area.

There has been increasing global recognition of the abuse and neglect of adults as a social problem in need of attention. The UK was one of the first European countries to undertake work on policy and practice development in this area and to undertake research. However, despite recognising the phenomenon from the late 1970s onwards, the identification of abuse as a safeguarding issue remains problematic. Also, defining abuse remains difficult, and especially so when the abuse occurs within an institutional setting, although scandals within such have been repeatedly shown (Parker and Ashencaen Crabtree, 2014). Studies of how we might intervene with people who have experienced abuse and, indeed, those who abuse are in comparatively early stages of development. In recent years, however, there has been some progress in the development of policies and procedures for health and social care professionals and social workers, especially within the UK, but, also, throughout Europe and the rest of the world (Penhale, 2020). A number of national and international organisations have been established to respond to abuse and abusive situations; there are also differences between different nations of the UK in how abuse is responded to. Various research and educational initiatives are underway.

Background and context

There has been an increasing emphasis on dealing with situations of violence and abuse in many countries. In the UK, after an initial focus on child abuse in the 1970s and domestic violence in the 1980s, the abuse and neglect of older people began to be raised as a concern from the early 1990s. At the same time, some concern was developing over adults with learning disabilities, in particular relating to sexual abuse. However, these two foci were treated very much as distinct and separate entities. In relation to older people, the principal focus initially was on abuse and neglect in the domestic setting, although increasingly there has been consideration of abuse and neglect in institutional settings (Glendenning and Kingston, 1999; Stanley et al, 1999).

Elder abuse and neglect are not new phenomena (Stearns, 1986); the existence of literary and historical documents confirms this. However, in the UK, it is effectively only since 1988 that the problem has really begun to be identified and explored as a serious concern, despite the fact that the phenomena were initially recognised by English doctors in the mid-1970s (Baker, 1975; Burston, 1977). The prompt for the initial early focus on elder abuse that developed in England appears largely due to a national conference organised by the British Geriatrics Society (a group of physicians concerned with older people), which was held in London in 1988, and at which issues concerning elder abuse and neglect were raised and the need for responses was promoted. Likewise, in relation to abuse of adults with disabilities of different types, initial attention was paid to the issue of sexual abuse of adults with learning disabilities in the early 1990s and was raised by organisations working with adults with such disabilities (ARC/NAPSAC, 1993); this was followed by attention paid to physical and other forms of harm towards disabled adults, although for some areas, such as adults with mental health difficulties, there has been a relative lack of attention until recent years.

Since these early beginnings, the amount of research and material published about the topic of abuse of adults who might be at risk of violence and harm in the UK has been steadily increasing. Yet, in a number of ways, it is still relatively early in the recognition of the problem and the development of ways to deal with it. For instance, it was not until 1993 that there was any clear sign from the UK government that elder abuse was acknowledged as a problem in need of attention (DoH, 1993). Recognition of similar issues in relation to adults with disabilities came at around the same time but was treated as a separate phenomenon. Since that time, there has, however, been a consistent, if somewhat slow response from successive governments (DoH, 1999, 2000; WAG, 2000), leading to the development of framework legislation in this area embedded within the Care Act 2014 (Cooper and White, 2017). In general, the abuse of adults living in institutions is an area where there has been even less research and attention paid. Despite a long history across the UK, particularly of scandals within institutional care of older people and adults with learning disabilities, these tend to have been investigated and treated as separate inquiries into standards and quality of care, rather than as specific concerns relating to abuse and abusive and harmful situations that have occurred within institutional settings.

Abuse and neglect are complex and sensitive areas to examine. In relation to older people, there has been a development of terminology from an initial focus on 'granny bashing' or 'granny battering' (used in the writings of medical doctors in the 1970s referred to previously), to old age abuse (Eastman, 1984), to elder abuse (following US research, in the 1990s), to adult protection (DoH, 1999, 2000) and then to adult safeguarding, or safeguarding adults (ADASS, 2011).

It has also been difficult to theorise the social problem of elder abuse for a range of reasons. These include a lack of agreement concerning definitions of abuse itself and particularly of elder abuse, and also difficulties in researching the topic resulting from conceptual inconsistencies (Ogg and Munn-Giddings, 1993; Penhale, 1999, 2008). While many previous taboos associated with violence and abuse have been challenged, and over time reduced, making it easier to report and know about it, in some areas, such as the sexual abuse of older people, the taboo is still very apparent in Western societies and others.

REFLECTION POINT 14.1

Why do you think that it has been so difficult to define and theorise abuse and violence?

What do you think the effects of these difficulties have been to both research and practice in the area?

It is likely that there are deep-seated aversions to discussing the abuse of and violence towards older people and adults because it arouses powerful feelings of shock and disgust. There is also a human reaction not to mention things, as a means of hoping they will quietly go away. Of course, that is not the case and there has been a developing awareness that allows increased attention from social workers, health professionals and the police.

Some of the reasons for this increasing recognition and concern about adult safeguarding include the following:

- systems of de-institutionalisation of care and care provided in the community for adults in need of support;
- demography and an ageing population;
- medical advances, technology and improvements in public health leading to more people living longer, even with complex health conditions/disabilities;
- a comparatively recent focus on advocacy and rights (human and citizenship rights);
- changing social structures, for instance patterns of mobility and changes in family structures and support systems for those in need of care and support.

It is important here to recognise the significance of social work, health care and criminal justice service recognition of the issue of abuse of adults and adult safeguarding as a problem area and one in need of attention. However, it was activists in the feminist movement in the 1970s who first drew attention to violence and abuse directed towards (younger) women, specifically in relation to domestic and intimate partner violence. This resulted in a more political 'grass-roots' approach to the apparent problem, that directed attention towards the issue and the development of responses in this area reflecting this type of identification. Moreover, concerning elder abuse and neglect, and abuse of adults with learning disabilities/intellectual disabilities, it was not until the late 1980s, within a European context, that social workers began to draw attention to the phenomenon, although this recognition had occurred some years earlier in the North American region. Recognition of these processes of identification is important, as this has had an influence on the development of responses to the issues associated with these problems and is also related to the comparative lack of awareness by the wider public of the issue (Penhale, 2008).

Additionally, it is difficult to accurately compare the results of research studies in this area, largely because of variations in research designs and methods used. Definitions and concepts of violence, mistreatment, and abuse used; measurements, together with sample sizes, time periods for prevalence, and age limits used may all vary between studies (Bonnie and Wallace, 2003; De Donder et al, 2011; Nerenberg, 2007). Therefore, there is a wide range of results concerning the nature and scope of the problem across the different types of situations that may occur; this then means that generalisability of findings is almost impossible.

Some important considerations

There has been no agreement on a universal or standardised definition. Different stakeholders, for example legal and policymakers, practitioners and researchers, may use different definitions, although ideally these should be explicit and acknowledged by the different stakeholders involved (Penhale, 1993). However, there is still some debate about definitions, indicators of mistreatment and, in particular, different aspects of neglect. Yet, despite the lack of consensus, it is reassuring that most people involved in the issue agree on the different types of abuse that can occur. The most usual types of abuse that are included are:

- physical abuse;
- sexual abuse;
- neglect;
- financial abuse (including exploitation and misappropriation of an individual's property and possessions);
- psychological and emotional abuse (including verbal abuse).

In England and Wales, the category of discriminatory abuse was added in the policy guidance that was issued at the beginning of the century (DoH, 2000; WAG, 2000). Institutional abuse is also usually included within policy documents produced at the local level, and considerations of societal level abuse may also appear in such documents. In the more recently introduced consolidating legislation, the Care Act (2014), the typology was expanded to include a number of other types of violence and harm, as will be seen.

In many countries, there is also a general lack of awareness of abuse and this can lead to difficulties in detection and identification of abuse and neglect – for practitioners as well as the wider public and older people themselves. The concept of abuse and neglect is both under-developed and under-researched.

At a national level, in the UK, charities such as Action on Elder Abuse (see http://www.elderabuse.org.uk) and the Ann Craft Trust relating to the abuse of children and adults with disabilities (see http://www.anncrafttrust.org.uk) have undertaken much work to raise awareness of the general public and of relevant professionals, such as social workers, nurses and doctors, about the mistreatment of adults at risk. However, there is still an important need for more education, training and awareness-raising at a range of different levels: for the general public, as well as for practitioners and students in the fields of health and care.

When considering the term vulnerability, there is a need to acknowledge that there are issues that relate to visibility and invisibility in terms of what is recognised as mistreatment or not, as well as such aspects as marginalisation and exclusion of those who may be considered vulnerable, or at risk of mistreatment and harm. From current understanding, vulnerability appears to be largely situational; it is not solely the characteristics of a person that results in assignment of the status 'vulnerable', but it is, rather, the interaction with other, situational and circumstantial factors that lead to a vulnerable state developing for the individual (Penhale and Parker, 2008). It also seems that those individuals who are most at risk of harm from abuse and/or neglect are likely to be people who are acknowledged to be from 'hard to reach' or 'seldom heard' groups, and who may experience life on the margins of society because of a number of reasons. This marginalisation and social exclusion will likely have adverse effects on individuals' health and well-being, but we must recognise that this is not just in relation to physical health but also states of mental well-being (Parker and

Ashencaen Crabtree, 2018). Individuals who have impairments, either due to a physical or cognitive related illness or disability (or even more complex conditions, combining both aspects), may also be 'hard to reach' as their needs may mean that they are not fully addressed by current service structures – we can see this in Case Study 14.1. This may be particularly relevant in relation to such individuals' experiences of abuse and violence, as existing provision may not adequately serve intersectional interests.

CASE STUDY 14.1

As a small child, Giuliana came to the UK with her mother from Italy after the end of the Second World War to be reunited with her father who had been a prisoner of war. She spoke mainly Italian as she was growing up, although quickly learned English at school. Now widowed and in her early 80s, she found herself increasingly isolated as her mobility decreased. She had recently been befriended by a young woman in her 20s with whom she could speak Italian and enjoy company. Her neighbours were concerned that her young friend may be taking advantage of her financially, seeing Giuliana give her money at times. A social worker visited but Giuliana did not wish to talk with her and would not let her in to the house. She said she likes to speak Italian and her friend is a good companion.

Questions

1. What do you think might be going on in this situation?
2. Do you think Giuliana *may* be being abused and what, as a social worker, would you seek to do?
3. How might Giuliana's Italian background influence your practice?

Discussion

These are not easy questions to answer and we must always work from a position of trusting the person. Giuliana has a right to have who she wishes in her house and, indeed, not those whom she does not want. What we do know is that Giuliana's wish for company and speaking Italian is a deep wish, and it may be something that a social worker could attend to as part of relationship building. Recognising important aspects of her life and the meaning she gives to it is central to good practice (see also Chapter 3). In the pressured rush of contemporary social work it is this central aspect, building a relationship, that can often be overlooked. So, rather than make assumptions that she is fine or that she is potentially being abused, it is incumbent on the social worker to take time to build a relationship before a true assessment can be made.

The nature of public policy and service provision and the changing nature of relationships between the individual and the state, and perhaps particularly the welfare state (and the residualisation of welfare) in many countries, need further exploration in relation to mistreatment. This is especially relevant, regardless of whether a situation consists of violence, abuse, neglect or exploitation or indeed combinations of these – mistreatment is the term used to encompass these aspects, as suggested by O'Keeffe et al (2007), albeit specifically in relation to elder abuse, but relevant to the broader field of adult safeguarding.

A number of additional issues appear to be linked with family relations and familial matters. During the last century, there were a number of changes to family structures, particularly in Western and more industrialised countries. As a result of such changes, family types and patterns have changed and developed; such as the rise in levels of lone parenting and increases in the number and extent of re-constituted families following divorce and separation. In many countries, there have also been increases in multi-generational families, some of whom share accommodation and family life; this is due at least in part to the demographic changes already referred to in the list earlier in this chapter, and the rising number of people living into late old age (Antonucci, 2007). Socio-demographic factors such as gender, marital status, education and income have also resulted in substantial changes. There have been significant effects from these and other factors on patterns of familial relationships in the 21st century, and on the nature of care-giving, perhaps particularly for older people, but also in relation to care for adults with disabilities.

Within this field, however, it is important that various forms of differentiation occur. It is necessary, for example, to differentiate between the different types of mistreatment (abuse, neglect and exploitation) that exist. However, in certain societal contexts, there may be differences in the typologies that have been developed and are used. For example, in France, societal abuse exists as a distinct category, whereas in England due to recent changes instigated by the Care Act, 2014, several additional types have been included, as indicated previously, although societal abuse is not one of them. Importantly, however, this revised framework, introduced in England from April 2015, includes self-neglect as a distinct category of adult safeguarding and those who may be at risk of harm. Other categories that have been included in the revised policy framework are domestic violence and abuse, which includes situations of honour-based violence, organisational abuse (also referred to institutional abuse in some countries) and modern slavery, which includes human trafficking, domestic servitude and forced labour. Coercive and controlling behaviour has also recently been included as important to consider and that needs to be taken into account (see Box 14.1).

Box 14.1: Coercive and controlling behaviour

Coercive and controlling behaviour represents a single act or a pattern of acts of assault, threat, humiliation or intimidation that are specifically designed to harm, punish or induce fear. Section 76 of the Serious Crime Act 2015 made this a criminal offence for offences occurring after its implementation at the end of December 2015. This is important when considering human growth and development because it indicates that an offence has been committed if it has a serious effect on the person and the perpetrator knows this or ought to know it. The law only relates to those who are personally connected, that is, they are in or have been in an intimate relationship, live together or are part of the same family.

The impact of controlling and coercive behaviour can be profound and cumulative and may result in drug or alcohol use, detachment, anger and guilt, depending on the ecological context inhabited by a person. It is important to bear this in mind when working with a person who has experienced domestic abuse, or domestic violence and not to jump to immediate conclusions about a person because of their reactions and behaviours (Curry et al, 2001). As the Crown Prosecution Service (CPS) guidance indicates, increasing a person's safety represents the key responsibility of the helping professions, it may be difficult to achieve this or, indeed, may even be resisted, because of the impact the behaviour has had on them (CPS, 2017).

There are also different levels at which mistreatment may arise: at individual, community and societal levels (micro, meso and macro levels: Bennett et al, 1997). This differentiation also relates to ecological frameworks that have been developed at international level (see, for example: WHO, 2002 and Dahlberg and Krug, 2002). The framework has previously been used in consideration of risk factors for elder abuse (Schiamberg and Gans, 1999).

Use of an ecological framework allows for a broader exploration of the associated risk factors as it suggests that violence can be understood as a result of human behaviour on individual, relational, community and societal levels, and the impact this may have on an individual's development in respect of those levels. A combination of characteristics at individual, relational and community levels can be employed to identify the most important factors for increased likelihood of victimisation from violence. This then allows for the development of appropriate interventions on a societal level that goes beyond a normative design of interventions at the individual (micro) level.

There are a number of different locations and settings in which abuse may happen. For instance, domestic and familial settings, as well as a variety of institutional and community settings. There are a number of possible different participants in abusive situations; not just 'victim' and 'abuser', but also potential witnesses, who may provide valuable assessment information, but who may also be emotionally affected by such situations.

Theories and theoretical perspectives

We have noted some of the difficulties of theorising in this area, but theoretical or conceptual frameworks, causative factors or indicators of risk for individuals, need to be taken into account when discussing abusive and harmful situations. While some aspects of theories relating to family violence may be of use when developing a theoretical framework of elder mistreatment (or other forms relating to adult safeguarding), it is important to recognise that the phenomenon of elder abuse is not just a sub-type of family violence. As observed earlier in this chapter, abuse does not just occur in familial or domestic settings. Within the continuum of abuse, neglect and mistreatment are found many different types of behaviours, actions and lack of actions.

> ## REFLECTION POINT 14.2
>
> Consider the potential impacts on an older person's emotional, psychological and spiritual well-being of recognising that mistreatment may be embedded or 'institutionalised' in society.

From the evidence to date, abuse relating to adults at risk appears to be a complex and multi-causal phenomenon. However, a number of the causal factors that have been suggested as relevant seem to focus more on micro, individual factors. This means that the macro, structural factors are not fully taken into account and that, in addition, there often appears to be an ascription of pathology to individuals, perhaps particularly those with some form of visible disability, whether this is physical or mental in nature. For example, when an older person who is dependent on others for care and support is seen as a source of stress and therefore in some way held responsible for abuse. Such perceptions of pathology have a tendency towards confirmation of some existing societal views of older people as dependent and powerless, which is not helpful. And despite attempts to disseminate the social model of disability as widely as possible across societies, this is comparable to existing and quite prevalent societal perceptions of disabled people as helpless and dependent and unable to care for themselves or to live independently. Thus, individuals who are both disabled and older may actually be more likely to be perceived in this way and to experience an increase in vulnerability, due to this intersectionality (Parker and Ashencaen Crabtree, 2018). Such situational vulnerability, compounded by intersectionality, also includes exposure to violence, abuse and neglect so that older disabled individuals (perhaps in particular women) are more likely to experience violence in their daily lives. However, such positioning (of older and disabled people as dependent and powerless) also fails to take account of the potential role of other factors (for example, such as neighbourhood and community, Buffel et al, 2009) in acting as protective factors against the development of abusive situations.

It is unlikely that any one theoretical perspective can account for every type of mistreatment that happens to adults at risk. Indeed, there is a history of different theoretical perspectives in this field (Phillips, 1986; Pillemer, 1993; Steinmetz, 1993). The aim is surely to more accurately reflect what is likely to be: 'A complex and multi-layered structure' (Sprey and Matthews, 1989, p 57). If this is so, then a variety of different conceptual frameworks and explanations will likely be necessary in order to develop a theoretical model that accounts for specific but different phenomena that constitute the continuum (of violence, abuse and mistreatment) as a whole. This is especially so in considering the intersectional issues of age, disability, violence and gender raised previously and ensuring that these are included in the frameworks that are developed in future. Developing the concept of intersectionality in order to locate older individuals who are disabled and have been abused alongside alliances of oppression, discrimination and power, relevant to other marginalised individuals and groups (particularly relating to a disability focus) will highlight the complex nature of such abuse experiences for individuals and emphasise the inadequacy of the responses which have been developing (both professional and lay), that in particular tend to leave women with specific needs without sufficient support and protection where this is needed. Moreover, in general terms, the whole area of theoretical frameworks and development has been viewed as difficult and problematic. However, in addition, such perceptions also have a bearing on the development and implementation of interventions and responses to mistreatment.

Risk factors

A number of issues are relevant in considering risk factors including mental health problems, alcohol and/or substance misuse, a past history of violence or abuse (within the family), dependency, stress and isolation are important factors to take account of when exploring allegations and situations in which abuse (and/or neglect) may occur. In relation to social isolation, it would seem that there are significant risks arising from being socially isolated from welfare agencies or other forms of community support, as well as from wider family, relatives and friends. Overall, such risk factors should be considered in any comprehensive assessment of a potentially abusive situation and may contribute to both the development and maintenance of abuse. However, it is important to take note that it is not possible for social workers, health-care practitioners and others to predict or determine levels of risk of abuse with any certainty simply on the basis of identifying such factors. While such an identification could suggest the possibility that mistreatment may be occurring, other additional assessments would need to take place in order to confirm (or refute) the existence of such harm(s).

In addition to the more established knowledge about risk factors, there are a series of points that have emerged from both the work of Lachs et al (1997) and the National Center on Elder Abuse (1998). Lachs et al suggest that:

> In summary, poverty, minority status, functional disability, and worsening cognitive impairment were risk factors for reported elder mistreatment. (1997, p 474)

The National Center on Elder Abuse study (1998) also determined the issue of worsening cognitive ability and the development of impairment as factors of relevance. Comparable to the risk from dependency, this factor has been reiterated in more recent studies (for example, Görgen et al, 2009; Iborra, 2008). As stated previously, older people who are disabled, whether this is physical, intellectual or incorporates a mental health component – or indeed those who may have complex health conditions combining a number of impairments – are more vulnerable to risk of violence or neglect. Although an early paper indicates younger age as a variable increasing the likelihood of intimate partner violence, since gender and disability also feature as variables of relevance it is important to investigate intersectional conjunctions further in order to extend understanding of this area (Smith, 2007).

Therefore, risk of mistreatment should be assessed at a range of different levels. Structural factors, including environmental issues and social factors and divisions need to be taken into account, together with particular family histories and relationships as well as individual characteristics. Consideration of micro, meso and macro levels of risk would also seem to be necessary within any comprehensive assessment of an individual and their situation.

In developing interventions and responses to abusive situations, we must take into account societal, social, relational and cultural contexts concerning situations that occur (Penhale and Parker, 2008). The phenomena of abuse and mistreatment are socially constructed, so it is imperative that the meanings and understandings that are ascribed to situations by individuals are fully considered (Biggs et al, 1995). However, we also need to develop our knowledge and understanding of issues relating to both gender and power relations (Brandl et al, 2003; Whittaker, 1995, 1996) and their respective roles in both the development and maintenance of abuse and abusive situations. The conjunctions that occur and inter–relate between age, disability and violence are also of increasing interest and concern and to these further intersections of gender and race might also be usefully added.

Within the continuum of adult mistreatment, it is evident that there is a range of actions and behaviours (including some lack of actions and some failures to act) that need to be considered as indicative of abuse. In relation to interpersonal abuse, family members living together and relationships between health status and dependency (including poor health – of the caregiver, both physical and mental health) also appear to be pertinent. However, when considering the spectrum of mistreatment, it is also apparent that it is not just familial and interpersonal relationships and violence that are relevant, but as previously stated, other aspects, such as institutional forms of mistreatment are of importance and need to be taken into account (Stanley et al, 1999). This is of particular concern when considering the individuals who are most likely to be at risk of such harms: for example, older disabled women, or younger adults with conditions in which behaviour that challenges is a prominent feature – who are also more likely to be admitted to institutional care.

The overall context in which mistreatment of older people occurs is one of societal ageism. This structural context is the backdrop in which, mistreatment of older adults is both accepted and somehow seen as behaviour that is permitted within society. To this degree, this structural oppression appears to act as a 'master category' in the power relationships that affect older people (Penhale et al, 2000). The situation would appear likely to be similar in relation to adults with disabilities, who experience high levels of disablism within society. Thus, we can see that other intersectional interests such as gender and disability are also of significance and need to be taken into account, particularly when considering mistreatment of adults in a more general sense and the associated disablism and othering that exists within society. This interplay can be seen in Case Study 14.2.

CASE STUDY 14.2

Jeremiah is an African Caribbean naturalised British man of 82 years old. He has lived with his son and daughter-in-law since he had a stroke five years ago. The stroke has left him slurred in speech and having a swaggering gait, both of which lead to unwanted attention when he goes out.

Jeremiah had been attending a local day centre to give him some outside company and interests. However, he came home one day very upset and saying he could not return. When his son asked him why he told him that he had made a good friend at the day centre and had asked him out for a drink. He had put his hand on his new friend's knee, but his friend George moved it and said he was just a friend. The supervisor at the day centre saw this and berated Jeremiah, calling him a 'dirty old poof' and said, 'No-one in their right mind could fancy him anyway because he slobbers everywhere'.

Jeremiah's son challenged the supervisor but was told firmly that it was his level of disability that meant he could not be accommodated at the day centre and it was no doubt his over-active imagination that anything like he said was actually said to him. The day centre was difficult to access, and local transport was erratic.

Questions
1. What are your reactions to this case?
2. How would you deal with this as a social worker?
3. How do you ensure your own emotional safety in situations like these?

Discussion
It appears in this case that structural and discriminatory aspects are at work – structural in respect of the day centre and its accessibility. It was geared towards the majority and did not make reasonable adjustments to accommodate people with disabilities. In this case it is likely that serious questions would be asked about its appropriateness as this reinforces the message that some older people are worth more than others. The prejudicial and discriminatory aspects are ones you might not expect to find in someone working in a caring profession, or that you would see in other professionals as a social worker. However, this can happen and as a social worker it is important to have a thorough theoretical underpinning to rely on

> as well as one developed from your value base. The third question asks something important. Social workers often forget about or dismiss their own needs. This can be counterproductive and ensuring you have adequate supervision at work – both formal and informal – and protective leisure time allows you to continue to support people in difficult situations while maintaining your own health.

In general, the links between disability and violence have been under-examined until relatively recently and this has led in particular to the marginalisation of disabled women who experience violence. Several years ago it was identified that this side-lining occurred across the spheres of politics, theory and practice (Thiara et al, 2011). This is even more apparent in the context of the topic(s) covered by this chapter and emphasises the evident need for intersectional approaches that cover the nexus of age, disability, gender and violence, together with ethnicity and race.

Issues in responding to mistreatment

In determining decisions about responding to mistreatment, there are several additional aspects to consider. Firstly, are elder abuse and neglect issues only related to ageing? From what is known so far, this would seem unlikely to be the case. For example, domestic violence that occurs in later life may be a continuation of very long-standing problems within a relationship (Brandl and Horan, 2002; Fisher and Regan, 2006; Sev'er, 2009), rather than something that only occurs due to the ageing process or in later life. Risk of violence and mistreatment relating to disability and impairment is also germane in this respect, with risk appearing to relate more to perceived dependency (due to disability) than to age itself. It is also apparent, however, that there are several different forms of elder mistreatment, and some of these, for example neglect, may be more related to ageing processes than others.

Secondly, does mistreatment principally arise as a complication of care-giving? Since it is clear that situations of abuse and neglect can happen beyond a care-giving context, this also does not appear to provide a satisfactory answer. Further, there does not seem to be any direct causal link between caring and mistreatment. If this were the case, then all care-giving situations would likely be abusive, and as work on the satisfactions of care-giving and relational aspects of caring demonstrate, this is evidently not the case (Nolan, 1997; Ward-Griffin et al, 2012).

If we take a family violence perspective, which is relevant in much of this area in terms of interpersonal and familial-type relationships (Gelles, 1987; Browne, 1989; Browne and Herbert, 1997; Lowenstein, 2009), then our focus for interventions may be on systems of prevention, protection and punishment. Yet, even within this situation, it seems that there are some apparent tensions between service and welfare perspectives on the one hand and an orientation towards justice and criminalisation, on the other. The implication of this is that an orientation towards prevention of mistreatment occurring may be quite different from one that is premised on either protection or punishment. The latter of these perspectives may mean that there is an emphasis on criminal justice approaches rather than on the provision of welfare, care and treatment, which may be more likely to be found in systems that are concerned with prevention (or at times also some non-legalistic or judicial forms of protection). In addition, it seems evident that the types of interventions that have been developing in relation to mistreatment of adults at risk need to take into account different types of violence, abuse and neglect that may happen.

Decisions concerning which intervention(s) to use will depend on the context, the situation and the type of mistreatment that has taken place. For example, provision of practical assistance to support the individuals involved may be used effectively in situations in which the abuse and/or neglect is due to caregiver stress, but this type of intervention may not work in situations related to financial abuse and exploitation, or sexual abuse. Furthermore, we do not know enough yet about which strategies of intervention work best and are most effective for which situation to be able to state categorically that a specific intervention is best for a particular type of mistreatment. This is particularly likely to be the case in under-researched areas like the abuse of older disabled women, and work in this area also needs to include determining the perspectives of individuals on their situations, incorporating their views about the impacts of mistreatment. Such aspects as these are likely to require much greater attention in future. Clearly, the intersections between age, disability, gender and abuse are crucial here, and ascertaining which perspective(s), preventive strategies and interventions will best meet the needs and situations of individuals whose needs fall within these intersections is fundamental to this endeavour.

Conclusion

At this time, we do not know or understand enough about abuse and neglect of adults at risk of harm in the UK, irrespective of the setting in which this occurs. It is clear that more needs to happen to improve the identification of such situations and some of the causes and factors involved, and also to increase our understanding about which approaches to prevention and intervention are most successful and effective within different types of situation. There needs to be recognition and acknowledgement of both social work standards, and also, to an extent, personal values, of individuals working in such situations, and these areas also require more exploration and development, perhaps particularly concerning the support that social workers and health-care practitioners need to remain effective in their roles when working with individuals who have been harmed by experience(s) of mistreatment – of whatever type and regardless of the setting in which it occurred. The possibility of secondary trauma, affecting individual practitioners vicariously, is one that must be acknowledged, and systems put in place to deal with this when it occurs. Just as trauma-informed responses must be developed for individuals who have experienced various harms from mistreatment, trauma-informed support needs to be developed to support practitioners and to enable them to continue working in this complicated and multi-faceted area and to retain appropriate levels of empathy.

It is also essential that work on determining effective systems of public accountability is continued. This needs to include the development of distinct and well-understood lines of support for individuals, as well as clear expectations of what is required of social workers, doctors, nurse, criminal justice workers and para-professionals working in this area. Interventions need to be relevant and sensitively tailored in order to meet the needs of the individuals involved as fully and effectively as possible and to reduce risk of harm where possible. The different levels at which prevention may be targeted in the UK context need to be further explored and developed, together with thorough evaluation of approaches used, using methods established in the field of public health, in order to establish what works best, for whom and in which circumstances.

Coupled with this is an important need to increase awareness and knowledge about this problem, including at the level of the general public, where this is still very much needed. Public awareness campaigns form one obvious element of this and the continued development of World Elder Abuse Awareness Day, which achieved UN recognition (since November 2011) will also assist here, together with the promotion of Safeguarding weeks and campaigns at local/regional levels. However, to really attain increased knowledge and awareness of the issue, systems and approaches to education and training must be developed further and ideally this would consist of a more integrated approach to such provision. Such an approach would then act as the framework from which appropriate and effective responses to prevention can further develop. In addition, more research in this whole area is necessary so that there can be much needed improvement in our knowledge and comprehension of abuse, neglect and mistreatment, and ultimately, there will be increased understanding of how best to prevent it. These factors are key elements to ensure continuing progress will be made in this most complex of areas.

Reflective questions

1 Why do you think women are more at risk of experiencing abuse and violence and individuals with disabilities experience higher levels of risk of harm from childhood onwards?

2 How do societal and structural factors affect the ways in which mistreatment is defined and acted upon?

3 Different strategies for prevention and intervention are likely to be needed for different types of abuse and the settings in which abuse occurs. The use of trauma-informed

approaches to tailor responsive interventions for individuals affected by mistreatment needs to be further developed. What things do you need to know in order to intervene appropriately?

4 What support and supervision do you need to deal with the vicissitudes of relational work in instances of abuse, violence and mistreatment?

Further reading

• Cooper, A. and White, E. (eds) (2017) *Safeguarding Adults under the Care Act 2014: Understanding Good Practice*. London: Jessica Kingsley Publishers.
This edited collection presents the thoughts and reflection of academics and practitioners working in these areas. As such they present useful material that concerns practice in England and Wales under current legislation. However, the chapters translate well to other contexts given that they concern practical ways of working.

• Penhale, B. (2020) Elder abuse and adult safeguarding in UK. In M. Shankardass (eds), *International Handbook of Elder Abuse and Mistreatment*. Singapore: Springer.
This chapter presents a comprehensive tour through current elder abuse practice, providing a history and an up-to-date set of reflections.

• Penhale, B. and Parker, J. (2008) *Working with Vulnerable Adults*. London: Routledge.
In this book we explore underlying concepts, issues and theories for working with people at risk of abuse, exploitation and mistreatment which can be used within diverse contexts. The knowledge presented underpins practice and shows how it is important to have a broad understanding of the issues.

References

ADASS (2011) *Safeguarding Adults – Briefing Note*. London: Association of Directors of Adult Social Services (ADASS).

Antonucci, T. (2007) *Elder Abuse and Family Structures*. Presentation at Third World Elder Abuse Awareness Day Conference. Geneva: WHO.

ARC/NAPSAC (1993) *It Could Never Happen Here*. Bradford: Thornton & Pearson.

Baker, A.A. (1975) Granny battering, *Modern Geriatrics*, 5(8): 20–24.

Bennett, G., Kingston, P. and Penhale, B. (1997) *The Dimensions of Elder Abuse: Perspectives for Practitioners*. Basingstoke: Macmillan.

Biggs, S., Phillipson, C. and Kingston, P. (1995) *Elder Abuse in Perspective*. Buckingham: Open University Press.

Bonnie, R.J. and Wallace, R.B. (eds) (2003) *Elder Mistreatment: Abuse, Neglect, and Exploitation in an Aging America*. Washington, DC: National Academies Press.

Brandl, B. and Horan, D. (2002) Domestic violence in later life: An overview for health providers, *Women and Health*, 35(2–3): 41–54.

Brandl, B., Hebert, M., Rozwadowski, J. and Spangler, D. (2003) Feeling safe, feeling strong: Support groups for older abused women, *Violence Against Women*, 9(12): 1490–1503.

Browne, K. (1989) Family violence: Elder and spouse abuse. In K. Howells and C.R. Hollins (eds), *Clinical Approaches to Violence*. Chichester: John Wiley and Sons.

Browne, K. and Herbert, M. (1997) *Preventing Family Violence*. Chichester: John Wiley and Sons.

Buffel, T., Verte, D., De Donder, L., Dury, S. and De Witte, N. (2009) *Conceptualizing the Neighbourhood as a Dynamic Social Space: Recognizing Older People as Actors in Placemaking*. Lisbon: European Sociological Association Conference.

Burston, G.R. (1977) Granny bashing, *British Medical Journal*, 3(5983): 592.

Cooper, A. and White, E. (2017) *Safeguarding Adults under the Care Act, 2014: Understanding Good Practice*. London: Jessica Kingsley.

CPS (Crown Prosecution Service) (2017) *Controlling or Coercive Behaviour in an Intimate or Family Relationship*. Available from: https://www.cps.gov.uk/legal-guidance/controlling-or-coercive-behaviour-intimate-or-family-relationship

Curry, M., Hassouneh-Phillips, D. and Johnston-Silverberg, A. (2001) Abuse of women with disabilities: An ecological model and review, *Violence Against Women*, 7(1): 60–79.

Dahlberg, L.L. and Krug, E.G. (2002) Violence – a global public health problem. In E. Krug, L.L. Dahlberg, J.A. Mercy, A.B. Zwi and R. Lozano (eds), *World Report on Violence and Health*. Geneva: World Health Organization.

De Donder, L., Luoma, M.L., Penhale, B., Lang, G., Alves, J -F., Santos, A.J., Tamutiene, I., Koivusilter, M., Enzenhoffer, E., Perttu, S., Savola, T. and Verté, D. (2011) European map of prevalence rate of elder abuse and its impact for future research, *European Journal of Ageing*, 8(2): 129–143.

DoH (Department of Health) (1993) *No Longer Afraid: The Safeguard of Older People in Domestic Settings*. London: HM Stationery Office.

DoH (1999) *No Secrets: The Protection of Vulnerable Adults – Guidance on the Development and Implementation of Multi-Agency Policies and Procedures*. London: HM Stationery Office (consultation document).

DoH (2000) *No Secrets: Guidance on the Development and Implementation of Multi-Agency Policies and Procedures*. London: HM Stationery Office.

Eastman, M. (1984) *Old Age Abuse*. London: Age Concern.

Fisher, B. and Regan, S. (2006) The extent and frequency of abuse in the lives of older women and their relationship with health outcomes, *The Gerontologist*, 46(2): 200–209.

Gelles, R.J. (1987) *Family Violence* (2nd edn). Sage Library of Social Research, No. 84; Beverly Hills, CA: Sage.

Glendenning, F. and Kingston, P. (1999) *Elder Abuse and Neglect in Residential Settings: Different National Backgrounds and Similar Responses*. New York, NY: Haworth Press.

Görgen, T., Herbst, S., Kotlenga, S., Nagele, B. and Rabold, S. (2009) *Kriminalitäts- und Gewaltgefährdungen im Leben älterer Menschen – Zusammenfassung wesentlicher Ergebnisse einer Studie zu Gefährdungen älterer und pflegebedürftiger Menschen.* [Experiences of crime and violence in older people's lives: Summary of key results of a study on hazards to older people and care recipients]. Berlin: Bundesministerium für Familie, Senioren, Frauen und Jugend.

Iborra, I. (2008) *Elder Abuse in the Family in Spain.* Valencia: Queen Sofia Centre.

Lachs, M.S., Williams, C., O'Brien, S., Hurst, L. and Horwitz, R. (1997) Risk factors for reported elder abuse and neglect: A nine-year observational cohort study, *The Gerontologist*, 37(4): 469–474.

Lowenstein, A. (2009) Elder abuse and neglect – 'old phenomenon': New directions for research, legislation, and service developments, *Journal of Elder Abuse and Neglect*, 21(3): 278–287.

National Center on Elder Abuse (1998) The National Elder Abuse Incidence Study. Available from: http://www.aoa.gov/abuse/report/default.html (accessed March 2018).

Nerenberg, L. (2007) *Elder Abuse Prevention: Emerging Trends and Promising Strategies.* New York, NY: Springer.

Nolan, M. (1997) Sustaining meaning: A key concept in understanding elder abuse. In P. Decalmer and F. Glendenning (eds), *The Mistreatment of Elderly People* (2nd edn). London: Sage.

O'Keeffe, M., Hills, A., Doyle, M., McCreadie, C., Scholes, S., Constantine, R., Tinker, A., Manthorpe, J., Biggs, S. and Erens, B. (2007) *The UK Study of Abuse and Neglect of Older People.* London: National Centre for Social Research, p 1305.

Ogg, J. and Munn-Giddings, C. (1993) Researching elder abuse, *Ageing and Society*, 13(3): 389–414.

Parker, J. and Ashencaen Crabtree, S. (2014) Covert research and adult protection and safeguarding: An ethical dilemma, *Journal of Adult Protection*, 16(1): 29–40.

Parker, J. and Ashencaen Crabtree, S. (2018) *Social Work with Disadvantaged and Marginalised People.* London: Sage.

Penhale, B. (1993) The abuse of elderly people: Considerations for practice, *British Journal of Social Work*, 23(2): 95–112.

Penhale, B. (1999) Research on elder abuse: Lessons for practice. In M. Eastman and P. Slater, (eds), *Elder Abuse: Critical Issues in Policy and Practice.* London: Age Concern Books.

Penhale, B. (2008) Elder abuse in the UK, *Journal of Elder Abuse and Neglect*, 20(2): 151–168.

Penhale, B. (2020) Elder abuse and adult safeguarding in the UK. In M. Shankardass (ed.), *International Handbook of Elder Abuse and Mistreatment.* Singapore: Springer.

Penhale, B. and Parker, J. (2008) *Working with Vulnerable Adults.* London: Routledge.

Penhale, B. and Parker, J. with Kingston, P. (2000) *Elder Abuse.* Birmingham: Venture Press.

Phillips, L.R. (1986) Theoretical explanations of elder abuse: Competing hypotheses and unresolved issues. In K.A. Pillemer and R.S. Wolf (eds), *Elder Abuse: Conflict in the Family*. Dover, MA: Auburn House.

Pillemer, K. (1993) The abused offspring are dependent: Abuse is caused by the deviance and dependence of abusive caregivers. In R.J. Gelles and D.R. Loseke (eds), *Current Controversies in Family Violence*. Newbury Park, CA: Sage

Schiamberg, L.B. and Gans, D. (1999) An ecological framework for contextual risk factors in elder abuse by adult children, *Journal of Elder Abuse and Neglect*, 11: 79–104.

Sev'er, A. (2009) More than wife abuse that has gone old: Violence against the aged, *Journal of Comparative Family Studies*, 40(2): 279–292.

Smith, D. (2007) Disability, gender and intimate partner violence: Relationships from the behavioral risk factor surveillance system, *Sexuality and Disability*, 26(1): 15–28.

Sprey, J. and Matthews, S.H. (1989) The perils of drawing policy implications from research: The case of elder mistreatment. In R. Filinson and S.R. Ingman (eds), *Elder Abuse: Practice and Policy*. New York, NY: Human Sciences Press.

Stanley, N., Manthorpe, J. and Penhale, B. (1999) *Institutional Abuse: Perspectives Across the Life Course*. London: Routledge.

Stearns, P. (1986) Old age family conflict: The perspective of the past. In K.A. Pillemer and R.S. Wolf (eds), *Elder Abuse: Conflict in the Family*. Dover, MA: Auburn House Publishing Co.

Steinmetz, S.K. (1993) The abused elderly are dependent: Abuse is caused by the perception of stress caused by providing care. In R.J. Gelles and D.R. Loseke (eds), *Current Controversies in Family Violence*. Newbury Park, CA: Sage.

Thiara, R., Hague, G. and Mullender, A. (2011) Losing out on both counts: Disabled women and domestic violence, *Disability & Society*, 26(6): 757–771.

WAG (Welsh Assembly Government) (2000) *In Safe Hands: Implementing Adult Protection Procedures in Wales*. Cardiff: WAG.

Ward-Griffin, C., McWilliam, C.L. and Oudshoorn, A. (2012) Relational experiences of family caregivers providing home-based end-of-life care, *Journal of Family Nursing*, 18(4): 491–516.

Whittaker, T. (1995) Violence, gender and elder abuse: Towards a feminist analysis and practice, *Journal of Gender Studies*, 4(1): 35–45.

Whittaker, T. (1996) Elder abuse. In B. Fawcett, B. Featherstone, J. Hearn and C. Toft (eds), *Violence and Gender Relations: Theories and Interventions*. London: Sage.

WHO (World Health Organization) (2002) Violence Prevention Alliance: The Ecological Framework. Available from: http://www.who.int/violenceprevention/approach/ecology/en/ (accessed September 2018).

15

Parenting and care in adulthood: an intersectional framework for support

Hyun-Joo Lim and Mastoureh Fathi

Introduction

A significant part of many adults' lives relates to parenting children, and, increasingly, extends to caring for grandchildren. This can be further compounded by care-giving responsibilities for ageing parents and/or partners with the multiple losses one endures during adulthood. There is an increasing need for social work involvement in providing support to those who may see themselves unable to cope with different types of pressures. This demanding and nurturing support draws on the learned resources of adults and creates opportunities for new learning and behaviours.

Chapter objectives

- challenge human developmental perspectives by highlighting the multidimensional characteristics of parenting and care in adulthood;

- provide a platform for social workers to reflect and engage more meaningfully with the needs of their service users using case examples and transnational research;

- illuminate the usefulness of an intersectional framework in offering appropriate services for those who are in need of social work support.

Background and context

This chapter explores several aspects of nurturing support important to social workers: firstly, when such help and support may be necessary; secondly, what forms it may take and what questions should be asked; and, thirdly, we consider at what stages people start caring for others as well as who they care for, together with the distance between care providers and receivers.

The following section begins with a brief outline of Erik Erikson's theory of human development, first introduced in Chapter 1, and discusses its limitations in exploring the lives of individuals who have care responsibilities. This will be followed by the examination of existing publications on parenting and care in adulthood both in the UK and transnational settings. In this section, we also draw our own research on the experiences of East Asian and Iranian migrant mothers in Britain. Founded on these, we will offer some recommendations for social workers and health-care professionals.

Problematising Erikson's theory of human development

Human development perspectives treat individual lives as comprised of different developmental stages that can be represented by typical characteristics. In particular, Erikson's theory has been highly influential in studying human life and identity development. Building on Freudian psychoanalytic theory, Erikson (1980, 1982) develops eight psychosocial stages of identity development that cover the life span. His eight stages of development begin with the 'first year' during which consistent and stable care are regarded as necessary to develop a sense of security (Miller, 2002). This 'first year' is followed by 'second and third years', 'fourth and fifth years', 'age six to eleven' and 'adolescence'. His last three stages are comprised of three different periods of adulthood. His fifth stage refers to 'young adulthood', during which young adults begin to search for a coherent personal and vocational identity. 'Middle adulthood' is described as a developmental stage where individuals seek to be productive and creative and to contribute to society. 'Late adulthood' is depicted as a stage where individuals reflect upon and evaluate what they have accomplished (Erikson, 1980, 1982). His work has been influential and continues to inspire scholars to work on his theory and expand it further.

> ### REFLECTION POINT 15.1
> How does Erikson's theory fit with your own observations of the ageing process in your family or among those you know well?

While we recognise the valuable contributions Erikson's theory and other developmental studies have made, we question the premise of such theorisations, because human lives are multifaceted rather than linear. Social lives are intersectional. It means that we do not just live with one form of identity, but are located in the intersection of multiple identities, influenced by factors such as gender, class, ability, sexuality and ethnicity. These social categories have a significant influence on constructing individuals' lives and how people understand themselves and others (Anthias and Yuval-Davis, 1983). Erikson's developmental life stages suggest our lives follow the trajectory of 'progress' as we move onto different stages of life. In particular, his last two stages demand further interrogation. According to Erikson (1980, 1982), 'middle adulthood' is represented as the most productive and creative period for individuals in terms of their employment and contribution to society. Although this might be the case for many middle-aged adults, it does not necessarily reflect upon those whose participation in economic activities or creativity is limited or curtailed due to care responsibilities, who are largely made up of women (Carmichael and Charles, 2003; Heitmueller and Inglis, 2007; van Houtven et al, 2013).

In this regard, Erikson's theory has multiple substantial flaws: firstly, it is male-centred, overlooking the gendered experiences of women and how their sense of self develops differently from that of men. Secondly, the fact that each stage has typical and fixed characteristics that can be completed before moving to the next step is problematic, as it views life cycles in a rather linear and simplistic way. Additionally, changes in (post)modern models of parenting such as parenting in later stages of life means that many people who become parents are in their late 30s and 40s. This trend has significant implications for individuals' productivity, creativity, identity, mental and physical well-being. Moreover, his proposition of the last stage of adulthood as a time of reflection and evaluation of life does not appropriately represent the societal changes that have occurred in recent times. For instance, an ageing population has brought significant changes in the way and stages that adults have become involved in care. More adults in their 60s and 70s are involved in the care of their partners and ill relatives, as well as grandchildren (Timonen, 2008), rather than spending their last stage quietly reflecting on life. Simultaneously, increasing numbers of middle-aged adults in their 40s and 50s are caring for ill parents and their relatives as life expectancy rises. Further to this, globalisation and technological development have engendered profound shifts in the way people construct relations, intimacies and connection with their families and relatives as more and more people's lives are shaped through their migration to another country (Urry, 2007). Thus, individual lives in many developing and developed societies are constructed through the complex networks of relationships that cross different geographical, economic, political and socio-cultural boundaries (Baldassar and Merla, 2014). These characteristics have transformed the nature of care in adulthood in both developed and developing countries. Hence, in order to understand these diverse and multifaceted characteristics, adults who are involved in various forms of care should not be confined to those who provide care within national boundaries. Our contention is that applying an intersectional framework will be more useful in understanding these complexities and delivering more meaningful and satisfactory services to people with care duties.

National and transnational contexts of parenting and care

As parenting and care provision are important aspects of adulthood, there is an abundance of research addressing different aspects of parenting and caring.

Parenting

Sharon Hays's seminal piece (1996) on 'intensive motherhood' examines the historical development of different parenting beliefs and practices and how 'intensive motherhood' has gained cultural dominance in developed Western societies. Hays (1996) defines 'intensive motherhood' as the beliefs and practices of mothering that are labour-intensive, expert-driven and expensive, which requires mothers' dedication to rearing their children, putting aside their own needs and desires. This concept clearly indicates the highly gendered characteristics of parenting in many Western societies, where women are expected to take the brunt of care responsibilities despite gender equality acts and progressive policies that facilitate women's social participation. Although her work was written over two decades ago, it continues to have resonance and more recent research has demonstrated the persistent impact of 'intensive motherhood' in many countries (Damaske, 2013; Faircloth, 2013; Harmony and Henderson, 2014; Harsha, 2016; Henderson et al, 2016; Murray, 2017). These works have elucidated the significant impact of this dominant ideology on women's identity and well-being.

Alongside this body of literature, Furedi's (2008) book on contemporary parenting in developed Western contexts, such as the UK, provides an important platform for debates over parenting, the changing landscape of parenting culture and its subsequent impact on children and parents. Consistent with Hays, Furedi (2008) argues that the changing meanings of childhood have been directly associated with the shifting demands and expectations on parents throughout history. Furedi also points out how changes in societal expectations towards parents have significant implications on not only the practices of raising children but also the well-being and identity of parents. He argues that today parents are expected to do much more than what they used to be; child-centred parenting requires parents to respond to their children's needs and wants on cue. In addition, the idea of children as being vulnerable and thus needing the constant intervention of parents undermines children's resilience and ability to solve problems while also putting untenable pressure on parents. Moreover, since children are seen as the direct reflection of parenting, parents' identity has become closely associated with childrearing (see Faircloth, 2013, for her work on breastfeeding and mothers' identity). Furthermore, Furedi (2008) suggests we are living in a culture of parent-blaming, where parent-bashing has become normalised. Undoubtedly this has a detrimental effect on parents' confidence and sense of self-worth. All of these suggest parents today face more pressure from society, constantly judged about their parenting styles. Inevitably this has direct and indirect ramifications for those who care for young children, which leads to more scope for social workers' roles in supporting them.

While Furedi's work aptly makes a critical point of the undue pressure and challenges contemporary parents face, his largely blanket use of the term 'parenting' throughout his book disregards the highly gendered aspect of childcare. Although there is evidence of a growing participation rate of men in childcare in the UK and some Asian countries, such as Japan and South Korea (Sullivan and Gershuny, 2001; Ishii-Kuntz et al, 2004; Shwalb et al, 2004; Ruppanner, 2010; Altintas and Sullivan, 2016), it is unequivocal that mothers continue to take the majority of childcare responsibility globally (Chan, 2006; van Hooff, 2011; Miller and Carlson, 2016; Nitsche and Grunow, 2016). This has significant repercussions for many women in terms of their identity, well-being, earnings and career progression, having long-term effects in their old age (Carmichael and Charles, 2003; Heitmueller and Inglis, 2007; Le and Miller, 2010; Dex and Bukodi, 2012; van Houtven et al, 2013; Abendroth et al, 2014). Evidence suggests that while many women cherish their motherhood and 'choose' to give up their work or reduce their working hours to look after their children, they also express a loss of identity, freedom and adult interaction (Vincent et al, 2004; Johnston and Swanson, 2006). Women often suffer from depression and the cultural expectations and pressure that are placed on them to be the 'sacred Madonna' leaves little room for them to be able to express such feelings (Thurer, 1994).

REFLECTION POINT 15.2

In Western societies how is expressed ambivalence towards motherhood likely to be received and understood? Think of any examples you have heard or read about in reflecting on this point.

Caring

Alongside parenting, many people spend a significant proportion of their adulthood looking after other family members, such as ageing parents, partners and grandchildren. The 2003 report of the European Observatory on Ageing and Older People stated that families provide a large share of care in all Western European countries, except Denmark (Timonen, 2008). Johnson (2005) maintains that a substantial reduction in premature death and increasing life expectancy has brought 'the stretch of life span', which demands reshaping and rethinking of the life course. The dramatic shift in demography as a consequence of an ageing population and delayed first births have meant that adults with childcare responsibilities also care for their old parents who suffer from debilitating ill health (Evans et al, 2016). In conjunction with these demographic changes, the decline in the birth rate in many countries has also resulted in the growing importance of spousal care in old age (Timonen, 2008). In addition, adulthood is facing dramatic changes as a result of the elongated dependency period due to longer stay in education and later commencement of employment, late childbearing and incidents of adult children returning to their parents' home due to factors such as divorce and financial hardships (Harper, 2006). Hooyiman and Kiyak (2011) also note the challenges faced by elder parents who care for adult children with physical disabilities or developmental disabilities or chronic mental health issues.

According to these authors, improved life expectancy for people with such conditions might put an extra burden on elderly parents struggling with their own ageing and debilitating health conditions. All these responsibilities directly and indirectly impinge on people's experiences of care.

In addition to the outlined care responsibilities previously mentioned, a high proportion of adults also provide care for their grandchildren. In the UK, childcare costs are the second most expensive in the world (Hill and Adams, 2015; Rutter, 2015), which has necessitated the help of grandparents to ameliorate the financial burden of childcare and many young couples with children are relying on their parents' support (Wheelock and Jones, 2002; Age UK, 2017). Furthermore, some grandparents provide primary care to their grandchildren as a consequence of absent adult children who are not in positions to look after their own children because of drugs and alcohol addiction, imprisonment and mental illness (Hooyiman and Kiyak, 2011). Custodial grandparents often experience financial hardship primarily because they are more likely to be unemployed, live with limited income or are in poverty (Park, 2006). Furthermore, their care needs might force them to reduce working hours, aggravating their financial situations, which can worsen other stress related diseases, such as depression and anxiety. Plus, increasing divorce rates have significant reverberations in the lives of some adults.

Maternal grandparents might function as a safety net when fathers of their grandchildren are absent due to separation. Consistent with the highly gendered feature of childcare, patterns of informal care for elderly parents, spouses and grandchildren are also marked by gender. Not surprisingly, women constitute the majority of care providers as wives, daughters and grandmothers (Harper, 2006). For instance, Grigoryeva (2017), examining the elderly parent care among adult children in the US, highlights that daughters provided twice as much care to their elderly parents compared to the sons. Daughters were involved in slightly more care provision if they had brothers while the latter did slightly less care if they had sisters. According to Grigoryeva, not only did daughters provide more care but they also did kinds of care provision that differed between daughters and sons: the former provided more routine and hands–on care while the latter provided instrumental and sporadic tasks, such as financial management and house maintenance.

Similar to findings regarding the impact of childcare on women, informal care providers for the elderly are negatively affected by their care responsibility in their careers, as well as well-being (Heitmueller and Inglis, 2007; Leigh, 2010; van den Berg et al, 2014; Loken et al, 2017). Plus, those who care for elderly partners or spouses experience more difficulties with their own health problems and feelings of grief, especially those who look after partners with dementia or Alzheimer's disease or brain injury. Although care giving by families has positive effects and benefits, such as a sense of fulfilment and connection, there are several negative consequences. These include: firstly, physical and mental health outcomes, such as increased chance of mortality. Poor physical health is also related to poor emotional state. For instance, Casnnuscio et al (2002) found that women who care for spouses with chronic illnesses for over six years suffer from depression and/or anxiety, compared to those who had no care responsibilities. Relating to the first outcome, emotional suffering is another consequence, which entails depression, anxiety, anger, loneliness, a sense of isolation and low self-esteem, and feeling overwhelmed (see Case Study 15.1). Thirdly, for those who work, care responsibility can create work–related stress and increased incidents of absenteeism because carers have to balance both demands of work and care. Working in a care–unfriendly place could therefore aggravate the abilities of care providers to effectively deal with their multiple demands.

CASE STUDY 15.1

Shirley is a carer in her mid-60s. She looks after her husband who was diagnosed with Alzheimer's disease three years ago when he just turned 70. Since both Shirley and her husband worked in low-skilled jobs, neither earned enough to save nor invested in secure pension funds. Shirley used to work as a shop assistant on a zero-hour contract but had to stop since the diagnosis of her husband's illness. With her husband's condition deteriorating at a fast rate, she finds looking after him emotionally and physically draining. He frequently does not recognise who she is, which makes her deeply sad and upset. On top of caring for her husband, Shirley also tries to help with the childcare needs of her daughter, who has two children, aged two and three, and suffers from depression as a result of an abusive relationship with her ex-husband, from whom she has recently divorced. Shirley often feels overwhelmed by the whole situation and has started to develop sleeping problems due to anxiety. Shirley is worried about her daughter's condition as well as her own future after her husband dies as she has no secure income to look after herself and she would be too old to find paid work.

Questions

1. What are the gendered characteristics of Shirley's experiences?
2. How does the intersection between her gender and class affect Shirley's life?
3. What would be the best steps to help Shirley's situation?

Discussion

Shirley represents the assumption of society that women are the main, and often unpaid, carers of sick, disabled or elderly relatives. She cares for both her husband suffering from Alzheimer's disease but also her mentally ill daughter and toddler grandchildren, and yet is of an age when she could rightfully expect to be leading an easier life and one perhaps more devoted to her own needs. Shirley embodies the concept of the feminisation of poverty, in which women are often employed in low-income jobs with few prospects, to the degree that she has had few chances to build her own savings and has no financial buffer against an uncertain personal future. Feelings of being overwhelmed would appear to be entirely justified in this scenario, which is itself unsustainable in view of the toll that is being taken on Shirley's physical and psychological well-being.

Care in migration

Care provision continues for those who migrate to another country whether it is to look after their children or their relatives. Existing works on motherhood of migrants suggest ethnic minority women encounter challenges that are different from native mothers, due to the language and cultural barriers (Liamputtong, 2010). Also, women from different ethnic backgrounds have heterogeneous understandings of 'good' mothering and mothers' participation in the labour market (Duncan and Edwards, 1999; Lim, 2018). These studies have suggested the vitality of cultural scripts in shaping women's experiences of motherhood. Lim's (2018) research on East Asian mothers in Britain illuminates a number of issues that are pertinent to mothers who have crossed different boundaries. For instance, her work (2018) highlights that women's beliefs and decisions around childcare and employment are significantly influenced by their national cultural heritage. Thus, mothers from China and Korea have notable divergent patterns of behaviour towards what they support as 'good motherhood' and subsequent decisions towards employment. However, the motherhood ideology these women hold, as influenced by their cultural heritage, is not the only factor that affects their motherhood, but it also concurrently intersects with their husband's gendered beliefs, as originated from their culture and the geographic location of their settlement. Thus, those who have settled in a tight ethnic enclave area tend to maintain what they perceive as the typical cultural tradition of their 'home' country. By contrast, those who live in a multi-ethnic cosmopolitan environment and who have married white British men tend to diverge from what they regard as the conventional gender norm of their 'home' culture. In this regard, social workers and others who work with migrant women and men need cultural understanding of the potential environmental and personal factors that are likely to affect the experiences of carers.

In addition to the experiences of migrant mothers who provide care in close proximity, social workers also need to understand the experiences of those who practise care across different nation-states. Transnationalism delineates 'a range of practices, activities and institutions through which migrant individuals maintain multiple connections and interactions with people and organisations in their homelands and/or across borders of other nation-states' (Lim, forthcoming, p 3; Vertovec, 2009). Linking to this concept, transnational care refers to the provision of care from afar, across different national and cultural boundaries. Globalisation, technological development and growing inequalities between countries in Southern and Northern hemispheres have driven a growing number of parents in poor countries to migrate to wealthier nations for economic reasons, leaving their children behind. In this context there have been profound shifts in the practices of care and forging intimate relations among extended family members. Scholars working in the field of transnational families have identified that the practices of care from afar are highly gendered: although both men and women migrate to support children financially, mothers are expected to provide emotional care, unlike fathers, and their physical absence often creates dissatisfaction of children (Parrenas, 2005; Carling et al, 2012). In addition, shifts in the demands from wealthy countries have encouraged the feminisation of migration, which has generated the emergence of 'transnational motherhood' (Hondagneu-Stelo and Avila, 1997) while dealing with similar pressures of mothering and caring from afar (Chib et al, 2014). One of the central challenges of transnational care is maintaining connection and social participation without having physical presence (Carling et al, 2012; see also Chib et al, 2014). Transnational mothering involves women taking a wide array of strategies to compensate for their absence, sending remittances, and regular conversations via phone or Skype (Fresnoza-Flot, 2009; Chib et al, 2014). The stereotypical expectations of motherhood can be challenging for transnational women who leave their children in the hands of other people within the context where the mother, especially the biological one, is expected to be the primary care provider. Such a move that often involves challenging the existing gender norms has ramifications for women, such as undergoing stigma, criticisms from others and guilt; it also engenders them to worry about the detrimental effect of their absence on children, as well as experiencing a sense of loss through not having direct interaction and contact with families (Hondagneu-Stelo and Avila, 1997). Akesson et al (2012) additionally point out the difficulties some mothers face in re-arranging foster childcare from a distance in case of the dissolution of existing arrangements due to ill health of old relatives, such as grandmothers, or migration of the current carer to another country.

Madziva and Zontini (2012) elucidate the different kinds of challenges faced by Zimbabwean female asylum seekers in the UK who were forced to leave their country without their children. Through this study, the authors stress the importance of the context of departure and argue that forced migrants encounter different challenges from those who are economic migrants. Often forced migrants do not have time to plan their departure and arrange childcare appropriately, which makes them riddled with guilt and anxiety. Also, Madziva and Zontini stress the importance of migration and the asylum policy of the host society, which has a direct impact on women's experiences of childcare. Uncertainty connected with their legal limbo hinders women's ability to practise 'appropriate' transnational mothering and aggravates women's sense of guilt and failure as mothers.

What we have examined in this section underscores the multifaceted dimensions of care and caring in adulthood. Hooyiman and Kiyak (2011, p 395) astutely state that 'the complexity and diversity of family support vary by geographic proximity, gender, race, social class, sexual orientation, family structure, and the history and nature of the relationship between care provider and care recipient'. Thus, social workers and others who work with care providers should be able and willing to fathom complex issues that have arisen through the intersection of multiple structural and individual factors.

> **REFLECTION POINT 15.3**
>
> Working together with a colleague on your social work course, role-play being a service user in a difficult situation and a social worker who tries to help the user to ameliorate the situation.
>
> 1. Create a scenario in which the client is facing difficulties as a result of the intersection of multiple marginalisations (gender, class, racial group, disability, etc.).
> 2. Act out how the social worker considers these nuanced positions before their assessment. List at least three considerations.
> 3. Based on the three criteria that the social worker has taken into account, what would be appropriate advice to provide for the problem presented by the service user?
> 4. Swap roles and this time imagine a different scenario and repeat the same three steps.
>
> After this, discuss how each other dealt with the situation and explore whether there might be better ways to improve social work and other helping approaches to social problems.

Intersectionality

The term 'intersectionality' refers to interlocking relations between different social categories, such as gender, ethnicity and class. The term 'intersectionality' was coined by Kimberlé Crenshaw (1991) to refer to the complex, dynamic and interlocking categories of identity that constitute each other. In her seminal article 'Mapping the Margins', Crenshaw stresses the salience of recognising the interconnection of various forms of domination, such as sexism and racism, by using the examples of anti-racist and feminist movements but emphasising how one particular example i.e. violence against women of colour has been missed due to the lack of an intersectional approach. She argues that the category 'race' was missed in feminism because of its emphasis on 'womanhood' and womanhood was missed in the anti-racist movements. Hill Collins and Bilge (2016, p 2) describe intersectionality as:

> A way of understanding and analysing the complexity in the world, in people, and in human experiences. The events and conditions of social and political life and the self can seldom be understood as shaped by one factor. They are generally shaped by many factors in diverse

and mutually influencing ways. When it comes to social inequality, people's lives and the organisation of power in a given society are better understood as being shaped not by a single axis of social division, be it race or gender or class, but by many axes that work together and influence each other. Intersectionality as an analytic tool gives people better access to the complexity of the world and themselves.

According to Hill Collins (1990), the intersectional approach shifts the focus of analysis from simply describing similarities and differences to the ways in which they interact with each other. Andersen and Hill Collins (2004) argue that this encourages social researchers to pay attention to the structural links between different axes of social inequality and the complicated configurations of social categories that structure every individual life in society. No wonder the framework was embraced by Gender and Women Studies scholars, as it has offered a new framework to the study of inequality in its multifaceted form (McCall, 2005). It has been suggested that intersectionality moves away from the 'additive approach' that was proposed in the 'multiple identities' model in which categories are mechanically added to each other (Yuval-Davis, 2006). Such an approach fosters hierarchical views about inequality, placing those who are cumulatively privileged at the top and those who are additively underprivileged at the bottom. This attitude to inequality misses the complex interrelation between categories such as the relationship between gender and race, or gender and class. More importantly, it also undermines the intricate and complex identity formation within categories such as middle-class and working-class experiences among women. Although intersectionality as a framework was coined as a term in 1990s, some, like Anthias and Yuval-Davis (1983, pp 62–63), pointed out this problem in sociological frameworks well beforehand and wrote: 'race, gender, and class cannot be tagged onto each other mechanically for, as concrete social relations, they are enmeshed in each other and the particular intersections involved produce specific effects'. The exponential development and popularity of intersectionality has witnessed its wider application beyond academic disciplines but also national and international policy, such as the UK's Equality Act 2010 and the UN's Equality and Human Rights Commission 2010. Intersectionality is a useful framework particularly for exploring the relationships within the family to analyse the different forms of care, support and gender role, but also their intersections with race and class. As such, the framework is useful for social workers to make sense of the experiences of their service users and provide well-thought-out support.

Using intersectionality in migrant families

The studies of Lim (2018) and Fathi (2018) highlight the importance of intersectionality in unpacking the complex experiences of those whose lives are situated cross-nationally. The number of works on national and transnational parenting and care has demonstrated that individual lives are not structured by a singular matrix but by the multiple intersections, as examined previously. Lim's research (2018) on East Asian mothers in Britain proposes employing a broader conceptualisation and application of intersectionality that goes beyond identity categories, such as gender, sexuality, class and ethnicity, by including, for example, the locality of settlement for migrant women as part of analyses. Whether migrants have settled in ethnic enclaves or not can have a significant impact on individuals, as living in tight ethnic communities can reinforce their perceived national/ethnic cultural beliefs and practices. Moreover, various policy measures of the host society, such as immigration policy (Madziva and Zontini, 2012; Akesson et al, 2012) and labour market policy towards immigrants (Lim, 2018), should be taken into consideration when studying the lived experiences of migrants because it directly affects their experiences of care. On the other hand, Fathi (2017, 2018) focuses on the complex micro formation of classed identities in diasporic settings. Iranian families that she includes in her research see themselves belonging to an in-between class category.

Although on one hand the parents are highly educated and earn higher than average salaries in the UK, on the other hand, their migration history intersects with their class identity and they do not feel valued in the British context. The application of an intersectional framework in the analysis of the experiences of migrant women illuminates that intersectionality can highlight the relationship between social categories, neither just the existence of such categories in their ontological basis (Yuval-Davis, 2011) nor proving the increase or decrease of one factor in relation to another as is the case in quantitative research. Such relationships between and within categories are pertinent to different individuals in different contexts when addressing complexity in their lives and the care and ultimately the support they need. Think of how you could help your service users in Case Study 15.2:

CASE STUDY 15.2

Consider the case of Isola, a care worker from Zanzibar who is a single mother in her mid-40s. The father of her children has minimal contact with them. Isola came to Britain two years ago. She has left her three children, aged 13, 8 and 5, back in Zanzibar in the care of her mother, who suffers from arthritis, in order to be able to provide a better life for them. Isola makes regular contact with her children as well as her mother, using telephone calls and Skype. However, she is constantly worried about her children, especially the youngest one, as he cries every time she talks to him and she has been told by her mother that his behaviour at school has become disruptive and violent towards other children. She is also very concerned about her mother's debilitating health condition and its impact on her mother's ability to look after herself as well as her children. Additionally, Isola struggles financially in Britain due to low wages and high living costs. After sending remittance to her family back home, Isola is left with a small amount of money, which is just enough to cover her rent and a minimum standard of food plus phone bills. Isola does not have friends she can talk to in Britain. Although she has made a conscious and difficult decision to leave her children and come to Britain to improve their lives, she has begun to question her decision and feels depressed.

Questions

1. In what ways have Isola's caring experiences been affected by her status as a transnational migrant?
2. How does this responsibility intersect with her single motherhood status, class and ethnicity?
3. What would be the best strategy to help her deal with her difficulties?

Discussion

Isola's situation is not an uncommon one in countries which depend on economic migrants financially supporting their relatives from afar. Leaving children in the care of grandparents to seek work abroad is a familiar family model in some countries (such as the Philippines) and does not denote a lack of concern for offspring or ageing parents, but rather is viewed as essential for the life prospects of families inter-generationally. Yet, for such economic migrants, while wages may be higher in the host country on average, this does not take into account the higher cost of living in conjunction with the low wages these jobs offer. Accordingly, what may seem to be a sensible family decision initially can carry unintended consequences of exacerbating poverty, deprivation and family disruption across continents, in which the main breadwinner is too remote geographically to offer more support to family members and may in turn be feeling disorientated, isolated and exploited in the new context.

Conclusion

Drawing on our examination so far, first we suggest that offering a safe place to express and validate carers' views is an important way of supporting those who face challenges. This is especially pertinent to many women whose voices have been silenced and undervalued who are involved in care work (Näre, 2012). Secondly, having cultural sensitivity and awareness is vital and social workers should respect the values of their clients' culture and develop cultural competence. For those who experience loneliness, isolation and cultural loss, social workers may also provide support for them to create and develop a community with people sharing similar cultural values (Falicov, 2007). Evans et al (2016) propose helping care providers to set up or join a community where they can share and learn from people with similar experiences. For instance, for those who are migrants, women from similar situations would find it helpful to learn their experiences are not isolated but also being empowered by being connected with others. Moreover, social workers should provide help for struggling carers to identify what matters to them most, such as religion and creativity, and working in partnerships with relevant organisations, such as churches and temples. Furthermore, those who work with care providers should respect carers' sense of self-care and the way they feel about their own readiness and manageability and help them to set up realistic and sustainable goals. Further to this, social workers should encourage carers to reframe their role expectations, so they do not suffer from a sense of overwhelming guilt while focusing on the strengths of the clients and help with 'resilience building' (Shallcross, 2015).

Additionally, it is vital to gain awareness of a potential impact of care responsibility on carers' career, finance and well-being. Reinhard et al (2008) suggest that social workers should refer their service users to other relevant experts if they experience specific issues. For those who undergo financial difficulties, social workers and others in the helping professions should help them to navigate the governmental support available as well as referring them to local financial experts, such as planners and ageing life care consultants. Carers who are employed should be strongly encouraged to familiarise themselves with workplace policy around care providers, such as flexible working, long-term financial support and back-up care (Gautun and Hagen, 2010).

Additionally, care experiences between men and women differ and thus their needs are likely to be divergent. Understanding this gendered dimension of care is crucial for social workers. It could be the case that for women, loneliness could be tolerated in a different way to men as well as across different social classes. Finally, understanding complexity is the key for social workers so an intersectional awareness would help them to offer appropriate services to people with care responsibilities. As Yuval-Davis (2006) suggests, certain social categories are more important than others in a particular historical and cultural context. In this sense, the first step of social workers would involve identifying such categories on a case-by-case basis through deep conversations with their clients while also paying close attention to other intersecting factors that concurrently shape their experiences.

Reflective questions

1 Think of a family you know and ask yourself if there any intersecting factors you have not previously considered that might affect their life experiences in a significant way, such as their local community, religion, sexuality or other protected characteristics? Project your thinking to social work practice and identify things you may not notice and that your service users may not tell you.

2 In what ways might your subject position (e.g. gender, class and ethnicity) influence the way you deal with a client's situation? If so, what can you do differently to improve the quality of life for the service user?

3 What strategies would best provide the next steps to help your client?

Further reading

- Glenn, E.N., Chang, G., and Forcey, L.R. (eds) (1994) *Mothering: Ideology, Experience, and Agency*. New York, NY: Routledge.
  This thought-provoking book offers insights into how motherhood is a social construction that defines and controls women's reproduction and childcare experiences across ethnicity and class.

- Grant, V. and Hothersall, S. (2018) *Working with Family Carers: Early Intervention, Prevention and Support*. St. Albans: Critical Publishing.
  A valuable text that explores how care-giving of children in the UK is practised and how professionals can best support parents and other care-givers.

- Handcock, A.-M. (2016) *Intersectionality: An Intellectual History*. New York, NY: Oxford University Press.
- Mattesson, T. (2013) Intersectionality as a useful tool: Anti-oppressive social work and critical reflection, *Affilia*, 29(1): 8–17.
  Both Handcock's book and Matterson's article explore the idea of intersectionality, which expands Crenshaw's (see References) original conception of multiple, overlapping oppressions.

References

Abendroth, A.-K., Huffman, M.L. and Treas, J. (2014) The parity penalty in life course perspective: Motherhood and occupational status in 13 European countries, *American Sociological Review*, 79(5): 993–1014.

Age UK (2017) 5 million grandparents take on childcare responsibilities, 29 September. Available from: https://www.ageuk.org.uk/latest-news/articles/2017/september/five-million-grandparents-take-on-childcare-responsibilities/ (accessed 26 April 2018).

Akesson, L., Carling, J. and Drotbohm, H. (2012) Mobility, moralities and motherhood: Navigating the contingencies of Cape Verdean lives, *Journal of Ethnic and Migration Studies*, 38(2): 237–260.

Altintas, E. and Sullivan, O. (2016) Fifty years of change updated: Cross-national gender convergence in housework, *Demographic Research*, 35(16): 455–470.

Andersen, M.L. and Hill Collins, P. (eds) (2004) *Race, Class and Gender: An Anthology* (5th edn). London: Thomson Learning.

Anthias, F. and Yuval-Davis, N. (1983) Contextualising feminism: Gender, ethnic and class divisions, *Feminist Review*, 15(1): 62–75.

Baldassar, L. and Merla, L. (2014) Locating transnational care circulation in migration and family studies. In L. Baldassar and L. Merla (eds), *Transnational Families, Migration and the Circulation of Care: Understanding Mobility and Absence in Family Life*. London: Routledge, pp 25–58.

Carling, J., Menjivar, C. and Schmalzbauer, L. (2012) Central themes in the study of transnational parenthood, *Journal of Ethnic and Migration Studies*, 38(2): 191–217.

Carmichael, F. and Charles, S. (2003) The opportunity costs of informal care: Does gender matter?, *Journal of Health Economics*, 22(5): 781–803.

Cannuscio, C.C., Jones, C., Kawachi, I., Colditz, G.A., Berkman, L. and Rimm, E. (2002) Reverberations of family illness: a longitudinal assessment of informal caregiving and mental health status in the nurses' health study, *American Journal of Public Health*, 92(8): 1305–1311.

Chan, A.H. (2006) The effects of full-time domestic workers on married women's economic activity status in Hong Kong, 1981–2001, *International Sociology*, 21(1): 133–159.

Chib, A., Malik, S., Aricat, R.G. and Kadir, S.Z. (2014) Migrant mothering and mobile phones: Negotiations of transnational identity, *Mobile Media & Communication*, 2(1): 73–93.

Crenshaw, K. (1991) Mapping the margins: Intersectionality, identity politics, and violence against women of color, *Stanford Law Review*, 43(6): 1241–1299.

Damaske, S. (2013) Work, family, and accounts of mothers' lives using discourse to navigate intensive mothering ideals, *Sociology Compass*, 7(6): 436–444.

Dex, S. and Bukodi, E. (2012) The effects of part-time work on women's occupational mobility in Britain: Evidence from the 1985 birth cohort study, *National Institute Economic Review*, 222(October): R20–R36.

Duncan, S. and Edwards, R. (1999) *Lone Mothers, Paid Work and Gendered Moral Rationalities*. Basingstoke: Palgrave Macmillan.

Erikson, E.H. (1980) *Identity and Life Cycle*. New York: W.W. Norton.

Erikson, E.H. (1982) *Life Cycle Completed*. New York: W.W. Norton.

Evans, K.L., Millsteed, J., Richmond, J.E., Falkmer, M., Falkmer, T. and Girdler, S.J. (2016) Working sandwich generation women utilise strategies within and between roles to achieve role balance, *PLOS ONE*, 11(6): 1–23.

Faircloth, C. (2013) *Militant Lactivism? Attachment Parenting and Intensive Motherhood in the UK and France*. Oxford: Berghahn Books.

Falicov, C. (2007) Working with transnational immigrants: Expanding meanings of family, community, and culture, *Family Process*, 46(2): 157–171.

Fathi, M. (2017) *Intersectionality, Class and Migration: Narratives of Iranian Women Migrants in the UK*. New York, NY: Palgrave Macmillan.

Fathi, M. (2018) Becoming a woman doctor in Iran: The formation of classed and gendered selves, *Gender and Education*, 30(1): 59–73.

Fresnoza-Flot, A. (2009) Migration status and transnational mothering: The case of Filipino migrants in France, *Global Networks*, 9(2): 252–270.

Furedi, F. (2008) *Paranoid Parenting: Why Ignoring the Experts May be Best for Your Child*. London: Continuum.

Gautun, H. and Hagen, K. (2010) How do middle-aged employees combine work with caring for elderly parents? *Community, Work & Family*, 13(4): 393–409.

Grigoryeva, A. (2017) Own gender, sibling's gender, parent's gender: The division of elderly parent care among adult children, *American Sociological Review*, 82(1): 116–146.

Harmony, N. and Henderson, A. (2014) The modern mystique: Institutional mediation of hegemonic motherhood, *Sociological Inquiry*, 84(1): 472–491.

Harper, S. (2006) *Ageing Societies: Myths, Challenges and Opportunities*. London: Hodder Education.

Harsha, J.D. (2016) Discouraging discourse: Mommy war rhetoric in the digital age. PhD thesis. Arnes, IA: Iowa State University.

Hays, S. (1996) *The Cultural Contradictions of Motherhood*. London: Yale University Press.

Heitmueller, A. and Inglis, K. (2007) The earnings of informal carers: Wage differentials and opportunity costs, *Journal of Health Economics*, 26(4): 821–841.

Henderson, A., Harmon, S. and Newman, H. (2016) The price mothers pay, even when they are not buying it: Mental health consequences of idealised motherhood, *Sex Roles*, 74(11–12): 512–526.

Hill, A. and Adams, R. (2015) Cost of childcare so high that it does not pay UK families to work, *The Guardian*, 19 February. Available from: https://www.theguardian.com/money/2015/feb/19/cost-childcare-high-uk-families-work-family-childcare-trust-nursery (accessed 23 January 2018).

Hill Collins, P. (1990) *Black Feminist Thought: Knowledge, Consciousness, and the Politics of Empowerment*. London: Routledge.

Hill Collins, P. and Bilge, S. (2016) *Intersectionality*. Cambridge: Polity Press.

Hondagneu-Sotelo, P. and Avila, E. (1997) 'I'm here, but I'm there': the meanings of Latina transnational motherhood, *Gender & Society*, 11(5): 548–571.

Hooyiman, N.R. and Kiyak, H.A. (2011) *Social Gerontology: A Multidisciplinary Perspective* (9th edn). New York: Pearson.

Ishii-Kuntz, M., Makino, K., Kato, K. and Tsuchiya, M. (2004) Japanese fathers of preschoolers and their involvement in child care, *Journal of Marriage and Family*, 66(3): 779–791.

Johnson, M. (ed.) (2005) *The Cambridge Handbook of Age and Ageing*. Cambridge: Cambridge University Press.

Johnston, D.D. and Swanson, H.D. (2006) Constructing the 'good mother': The experience of mothering ideologies by work status, *Sex Roles*, 54(7–8): 509–519.

Leigh, A. (2010) Informal care and labour market participation, *Labour Economics*, 17(1): 140–149.

Le, A.T. and Miller, P.W. (2010) Glass ceiling and double disadvantage effects: Women in the US labour market, *Applied Economics*, 42: 603–613.

Liamputtong, P. (2010) Life as mothers in a new land: The experience of motherhood among Thai women in Australia, *Health Care for Women International*, 24(7): 650–668.

Lim, H.-J. (2018) *East Asian Mothers in Britain: An Intersectional Exploration of Motherhood and Employment*. Basingstoke: Palgrave Macmillan.

Lim, H.-J. (forthcoming) 'Traversing': Familial challenges for escaped North Koreans, *Journal of Ethnic and Migration Studies*.

Loken, K.V., Lundberg, S. and Riise, J. (2017) Lifting the burden: Formal care of the elderly and labour supply of adult children, *Journal of Human Resources*, 52(1): 247–271.

Madziva, R. and Zontini, E. (2012) Transnational mothering and forced migration: Understanding the experiences of Zimbabwean mothers in the UK, *European Journal of Women's Studies*, 19(4): 428–443.

McCall, L. (2005) The complexity of intersectionality, *Signs*, 30(3): 1771–1800.

Miller, P.H. (2002) *Theories of Developmental Psychology* (4th edn). New York, NY: Worth Publishers.

Miller, A.J. and Carlson, D.L. (2016) Great expectations? Working- and middle-class cohabiters' expected and actual divisions of housework, *Journal of Marriage and Family*, 78: 346–363.

Murray, K. (2017) Intensive mothering on the homefront: An analysis of army mothers, *Sociological Spectrum*, 37(1): 1–17.

Näre, L. (2012) Migrancy, gender and social class in domestic labour and social care in Italy: An intersectional analysis of demand, *Journal of Ethnic and Migration Studies*, 39(4): 601–623.

Nitsche, N. and Grunow, D. (2016) Housework over the course of relationships: Gender ideology, resources, and the division of housework from a growth curve perspective, *Advances in Life Course Research*, 29: 80–94.

Park, H-O.H. (2006) The economic well-being of households headed by a grandmother as caregiver, *Social Service Review*, 80(2): 264–296.

Parrenas, R. (2005) Long distance intimacy: Class, gender and intergenerational relations between mothers and children in Filipino transnational families, *Global Networks*, 5(4): 317–336.

Reinhard, S., Given, B., Petlick, N.H., and Bemis, A. (2008) Supporting family caregivers providing care. In R.G. Hughes (ed.), *Patient Safety and Quality: An Evidence-Based Handbook for Nurses*. Rockville, MD: Agency for Healthcare Research and Quality, pp 341–404.

Ruppanner, L.E. (2010) Cross-national reports of housework: An investigation of the gender empowerment measure, *Social Science Research*, 39(6): 963–975.

Rutter, J. (2015) Childcare costs survey 2015. Family and Childcare Trust.

Shallcross, L. (2015) Multiple stressors take a bite out of the sandwich generation, *Counselling Today*, 20 November: 32–39. Available from: https://ct.counseling.org/2015/10/multiple-stressors-take-a-bite-out-of-the-sandwich-generation/#

Shwalb, D.W., Nakazawa, J., Yamamoto, T. and Hyun, J.-H. (2004) Fathering in Japanese, Chinese and Korean culture: A review of the research literature. In M.E. Lamb (ed.), *The Role of the Father in Child Development*. Hoboken, NJ: John Wiley & Sons, Inc., pp 146–181.

Sullivan, O. and Gershuny, J. (2001) Cross-national changes in time-use: Some sociological (hi)stories re-examined, *British Journal of Sociology*, 52(2): 331–347.

Thurer, S. (1994) *The Myths of Motherhood: How Culture Reinvents the Good Mother.* New York, NY: Houghton Mifflin Company.

Timonen, V. (2008) *Ageing Societies: A Comparative Introduction.* Maidenhead: Open University Press.

Urry, J. (2007) *Mobilities.* Cambridge: Polity Press.

Van den Berg, B., D.G. Fiebig and J. Hall (2014) Well-being losses due to caregiving, *Journal of Health Economics*, 35: 123–131.

van Hooff, J.H. (2011) Rationalising inequality: Heterosexual couples' explanations and justifications for the division of housework along traditionally gendered lines, *Journal of Gender Studies*, 20(1): 19–30.

Van Houtven, C.H., Coe, N.B. and Skira, M.M. (2013) The effect of informal care on work and wages, *Journal of Health Economics*, 32(1): 240–252.

Vertovec, S. (2009) *Transnationalism.* London: Routledge.

Vincent, C., Ball, S.J. and Pietkainen, S. (2004) Metropolitan mothers: Mothers, mothering and paid work, *Women's Studies International Forum*, 27(5–6): 571–587.

Wheelock, J. and Jones, K. (2002) 'Grandparents are the next best thing': Informal childcare for working parents in urban Britain, *Journal of Social Policy*, 31(3): 441–463.

Yuval-Davis, N. (2006) Intersectionality and feminist politics, *European Journal of Women's Studies*, 13(3): 193–209.

Yuval-Davis, N. (2011) *The Politics of Belonging: Intersectional Contestations.* London: Sage.

16

Dementia care practices, complexities and mythologies

Julie Christie

Introduction

There has been a growing call for the human rights of people with dementia to be recognised, moving discussions from person-centred care to citizenship. To do this in a meaningful way, the person has to be recognised within their unique sociological and developmental space. In this chapter we will explore the different paradigms that can be used to understand dementia, and in turn, the person with dementia. In particular, we will consider the applicability of resilience in the lives of people with dementia, that promotes dignity and a continuing subjective quality of life although we will not overtly focus on these aspects. This provides a solid foundation for relationship-based social work practice which helps us appreciate the complexity and richness of people's lives and the range of resources we can call on to respond to situations of need and risk.

> ### Chapter objectives
>
> - address our current understanding of dementia;
> - consider new ways of thinking about dementia;
> - introduce the subject of resilience;
> - consider resilience as a new approach in the care and support of people living with dementia.

What is dementia?

The focus of this chapter concerns dementia. Much has been written about dementia; however, the literature to date has tended to focus on the expected increase in the numbers of people who will develop the condition and the increasing costs associated with each person's care and support. Prince et al estimated in 2015 that there were approximately 46.8 million people with dementia worldwide, with numbers projected to almost double every 20 years. Although the risk of dementia increases with age the incidence of dementia is in fact declining. This is believed to be because of the trend to healthier lifestyles and improved cardiovascular health. According to Ahmadi–Abhari et al (2017), the number of people with dementia in England and Wales, for example, is likely to increase by 57 per cent from 2016 to 2040, which is far below previous predictions. Current costs of dementia to the UK economy are estimated at £23bn annually (Knapp et al, 2007). This has implications for present and future health, social care and housing provision, as well as wider infrastructure as we consider how best to support people with dementia and their families especially in time of austerity.

With respect to life span, dementia is often associated with ageing. However, little has been written about the potential of the person to continue to grow and develop. In addition, older age is often discussed as a time of self-reflection, adjustment and acceptance of one's circumstances. What does this mean for people who are considered by some to be in the process of 'losing self' where they are ageing with dementia? Political, economic, social and cultural influences are therefore essential in discussions about the subject of lifespan development and dementia. Attitudes to dementia are changing as people who have dementia take a more visible role in society. TV campaigns, peer support and encouraging people to continue with their routines, relationships, lifestyles and activities for as long as possible, are all playing a part in changing the experience of dementia and challenging the stereotypes of 'the vulnerable older person'. However, organisational responses to dementia remain relatively unchanged. As a result there is now an urgent need for those working with people with dementia to adopt new ways that recognise the complexity of the experience of dementia. In this chapter we will critique understandings of dementia and using the concept of resilience and its potential for working with people living with dementia.

Dementia can be understood as an umbrella term for the signs and symptoms that indicate there may be changes occurring in the brain. The most common symptoms are changes to memory, thinking, behaviour and the ability to perform everyday tasks (Prince et al, 2014). It is recognised as a specific disease process and is defined in the World Health Organization International Statistical Classification of Diseases and Related Health Problems (ICD-10) as:

> [A] syndrome due to disease of the brain, usually of a chronic or progressive nature, in which there is disturbance of multiple higher cortical functions, including memory, thinking, orientation, comprehension, calculation, learning capacity, language and judgement. Consciousness is not clouded. The impairments of cognitive function are commonly accompanied and occasionally preceded by deterioration in emotional control, social behaviour or motivation. (WHO, 1992)

Dementia is not, however, the result of a single brain pathology according to the biomedical model. There are many underlying pathologies such as Alzheimer's disease, vascular dementia, dementia with Lewy Bodies and frontotemporal dementia (Prince et al, 2014). Alzheimer's disease affects approximately 62 per cent of people with dementia. Vascular dementia affects approximately 17 per cent and around 10 per cent of the population will have a combination of both Alzheimer's disease and vascular dementia (Alzheimer's Society, 2014).

There is much debate about the nature of dementia and where expertise in the subject is best located. However, there is scope to understand dementia from a whole person perspective even where a predominant biomedical model is adopted. Scottish dementia policy, for example, placed an equal emphasis on diagnosis, treatment and support to live well in what could be described as a bio-psycho-social approach (Scottish Government, 2010). Such approaches have been developed because previous narrow neuropsychiatric discourses have resulted in the person with dementia being perceived as changed, or diminished, as a direct result of their dementia (Downs et al, 2006). This leaves no room for recognising that the person may influence the disease trajectory and the discourse can focus on loss, suffering and burden (Hughes et al, 2005). Critics of the neuropathology approach began to highlight the lack of evidence between the changes occurring in the brain and the symptoms assumed to be representative of dementia (Kitwood, 1987; Lyman, 1989; Snowden, 1997). These criticisms led to a call for a wider consideration of dementia, which would also incorporate both environmental factors and the experience of living with dementia through acknowledging the personhood of each individual (Kitwood, 1990).

New ways of thinking about dementia

Over the past ten years citizenship as a means of understanding the experience of dementia has grown in interest. Bartlett and O'Connor (2007) believe that citizenship is central as it moves personal experiences of discrimination into a political discourse. Citizenship can be considered as a political and philosophical ideal where all persons enjoy certain rights and freedoms within society, but this is not necessarily realised in real life. Inclusion in citizenship processes such as political discourse and asserting resistance can be difficult for those with dementia to achieve without support. Resistance is often viewed as a negative if demonstrated by those with dementia, where in others it could be seen as an assertion of rights (Ward et al, 2016; Sabat et al, 2004). Kelly (2010) suggested that people with dementia were often labelled as aggressive or challenging where they demonstrated resistance within care interactions. Labels within assessments and reports can therefore work to actively deny citizenship status and rights.

Evolving models of citizenship place an emphasis on agency of the person with dementia who is engaged in everyday relationships with the people and places in their life. This has can be referred to as an 'ecopsychosocial' approach (Zeisel et al, 2016) to dementia. This recognition of the *mundane* (Ward et al, 2016) can reveal important information about identity, sense of self and purpose; that is, citizenship now compels us to create opportunities for the agentic person with dementia to emerge (Poland and Birt, 2016). This offers a new perspective on the role of human service professionals working with people who are living with dementia, as facilitators of agency and purpose.

The role of social workers and allied human service professionals

There are many professionals from a range of disciplines who work with people living with dementia and their carers. Some of these are social workers but the roles undertaken may frequently overlap. Therefore, in this section we will explore some of the ways in which people work with people with dementia rather than distinguishing specific tasks and activities. Traditionally, much of social work with people who have dementia has focused on the assessment of need and the provision of resource. Increasingly, however, both social workers and other human service professionals are now asking searching questions about the ways in which organisations and services respond to referrals. This reflects a blend of human rights and advocacy against a context of resource rationing, risk management and increasing care needs. People with dementia can experience preconceptions of dependence, loss of self and diminishing capacity based on ageist attitudes and social stigma. The predominant discourse on dementia remains one where the person gradually diminishes. As a result, the *label* of dementia itself can be the barrier to inclusive and more creative health and social care relationships. Denying our identification with people who have dementia is a means of protecting ourselves from the potential indignities of old age and ill-health, as the condition represents both the ageing and the disease process: a symbolic rejection of ageing and disease.

Dementia has the potential to disrupt communication and stories of self and can make relationship-based practice more difficult. However, we are always engaged in communication with the other people in our lives overtly or subconsciously. Society is built on relationships with the people that we encounter every day and the meanings that we give to these interactions. Sabat (2001) explored identity through the social construction theory of '*selfhood*' and discussed identity as *the self*, suggesting that identity can be manifested on three levels: Self 1, 2 and 3. Sabat defined Self 1 as 'the self of personal identity which is experienced as the continuity of one's own singular point of view from which one perceives, and acts in, in the world' (2001, p 17). Simply put, we are always the central character in the story of our lives. Self 2 consists of mental and physical attributes, characteristics and qualities which a person thinks makes them unique, for example, tall, intellectual, independent, caring and so on. Self 3 is the public self that we project into the world.

This best version of our selves relies on others, our neighbours, friends the people we meet responding to and validating the person we wish to be recognised as. However, the other in the relationship may see something different, such as a vulnerable person with dementia with Self 3 attributes hidden from view. So, we need to ask, 'what are we communicating and what do we see when we look at a person with dementia and their life?' Why do we think this way? Does this limit the support and opportunities that we bring to the table in finding solutions for people? What are we trying to achieve in our work with people living with dementia, their families and carers?

REFLECTION POINT 16.1

Wishing others to recognise and validate ourselves or those we love is common to us all but sometimes all other people, including social workers, see is a vulnerable or damaged person with dementia. This can raise issues and tensions. Note some that might come to mind as a social worker getting to know someone with a diagnosis of dementia and their family.

Dementia is a global health priority (Prince et al, 2015). There is an international focus on prevention through: healthy lifestyles which promote cardiovascular and brain health; timely diagnosis; and post-diagnostic support and anticipatory care planning. At the same time, policy trends that promote self-management, the mobilisation of community assets and the co-production of support plans appear to have had little impact on the experience of people with dementia in need of support (Österholm and Hydén, 2016). The reason for this might be that because dementia is a progressive condition it is often assumed that there is nothing that can be done, that creative practice is either not possible or not recommended as the person must be kept safe from harm. People with dementia are not thought of as independent, autonomous or as able to make judgements on their own safety or that of other people. I would argue, however, that human service professionals are ideally placed to recognise the individuality of the person concerned and to create space for new ways of being through sensitive and innovative practice. If everyday activities are, in fact, the important foundations of maintaining a sense of self for the person, health and social care practitioners are then ideally placed to change the prevailing discourse of the diminished life of the person with dementia and present a new vision. Research by Giebel and Sutcliffe (2018) highlighted that most studies into everyday activities and dementia focus on what a person can no longer do; losses of functioning. However, they found that where the person with dementia can initiate activities of daily living this can significantly improve well-being and reduce carer stress. Continuing with hobbies and interests was also important in maintaining well-being. Thinking differently about mundane, everyday issues can disrupt the trend to 'hopelessness' I suggest that the concept of resilience might hold the key to achieving this.

What is resilience?

Aburn et al (2016) undertook an integrative review of the empirical literature on resilience in nursing practice and research from 2000 to 2015 and concluded that there was no universal definition that could be applied. Resilience is a 'dynamic process encompassing positive adaptation within the context of significant adversity' (Luthar et al, 2000, p 543). The two elements considered as essential for resilience to develop are exposure to adversity and the achievement of positive adaptation to adversity (Luthar et al, 2000). It is a specific process of adjustment or adaptation as a person faces threats in their life not the absence of problems, hardiness or invulnerability. Growing older with dementia can be viewed as a life adversity (or as a series of adversities), where individuals risk the loss of self as a result of the symptoms of dementia, the attitudes of others and wider society. Loss of self or sense of self occurs through stigma, self-stigma and ageism. Therefore, the preservation of self and identity, in the face of dementia, could be viewed as an outcome of a resilience process.

There is a very small literature dealing with the subject of resilience and dementia. However, interesting debates are emerging around a person's reserve capacity or what I call *resilience reserve* (Christie, 2016) which focus on the skills and resources that people acquire over their lifetime in order to mitigate and respond creatively to challenges in the present. The resilience process is supported by a resilience reserve, a personal bank of skills, experiences, knowledge and resources (see Figure 16.1) which may act as a buffer and facilitate adjustments in situations of adversity or risk.

This occurs within a wider context where the public identities of people ageing with dementia can be framed around vulnerability and the need for protection; and, in turn, the identities of human service professionals are framed around the role of protectors who need to consider the possibility that resilience might apply to those who are perceived to be most frail. This is explored in more detail in Case Study 16.1.

CASE STUDY 16.1

Fay was a 77-year-old widow who lived alone. She had a son and a daughter. Her parents died when she was a young girl and she grew up in boarding school in Ireland. Fay was involved in charity work with young people affected by alcohol which included opening her home to people in need, some of whom had a history of involvement with the police. Fay was referred to the health and social care team as her family were concerned about her safety and her ability to manage at home. They were aware that dementia was a progressive condition and felt that things would just get worse over time. Her son, Jim, was finding it hard to see his mother in such difficulty as she had always been such a capable woman. As a result he found himself visiting less and less.

Questions

1. In what ways might dementia have an impact on Fay and her preferred life choices?
2. What assumptions might Jim be making about his mother and how can he be supported at this time?
3. How might your understanding of dementia and human development over the life span help you as a social worker in this situation?

Discussion

As a social worker, you will focus on values for practice as part of your learning. In this case the importance of seeing the person not the condition and maintaining her life story for those who know her is going to be important. This will help as her condition progresses. In the next section you will be introduced to some of the implications and what this might mean for people living with dementia.

Figure 16.1: The resilience reserve

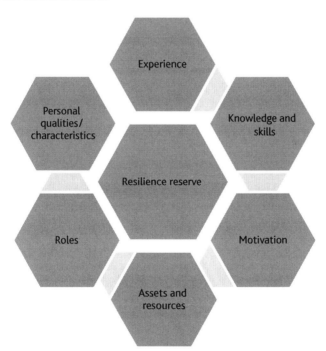

Implications for the person with dementia

Thinking about people with dementia differently and not seeing them as victims of disease but as citizens with the capacity for resilience could facilitate an exploration of the impact of power and inequality on the experience of ageing with dementia, in both everyday relationships and situations, as well as in wider society. I therefore suggest that resilience in the context of dementia could be defined as:

> Adjustment in the face of the threats to personal and public identity experienced when ageing with dementia. (Christie, 2016, p 92)

The interplay between resilience, life experience, previous knowledge and skills and social factors, including networks and access to resources, is not well understood. There is a research focus on resilience in early stage dementia with the aim of providing evidence to support better functioning or a longer period of independence but presently there is insufficient evidence to support the early positive findings in this area. There is also a growing unease that a focus on the individual as resilient or not places an onus on the person themselves to be a better version of themselves, a kind of victim blaming in which dependency could be viewed as a personal failure. This would seem to be a hidden consequence of the 'living well' with dementia narrative (Clare et al, 2011). A focus on what is achieved through adjustment is required, rather than externally imposed measures of what resilience looks like which may be incongruent with the realities of living with the physical and mental health changes of dementia. In order to explore this Case Study 16.2 builds on Fay's story from the perspective of her social worker Lorna.

CASE STUDY 16.2

Lorna was a social worker with the integrated care team. Lorna found that Fay's home was cluttered and untidy and that her personal appearance and hygiene did not appear to have been attended to. Fay's initial referral to the health and social work team focused on those things that she was unable to do and the current risks in her domestic environment. As a result, the local authority came to the decision that because of her dementia Fay was potentially at risk of harm and should be treated as a vulnerable adult. Lorna was concerned about the emphasis on protecting Fay as a move to a care home was being discussed.

Questions

1. What are the implications of Fay being identified as a vulnerable adult?
2. What actions should Lorna take to understand more about Fay's situation?
3. How might Lorna's own experiences affect the way she practises?

Discussion

The questions are those that face both professionals and family and friends when dealing with a person living with dementia. The following discussion points concerning 'surviving' dementia and developing 'resilience' will help you to think about the questions in more depth. It is important, for instance, to maintain connections to the family or community for the person living with dementia and for their carers. It is also important to develop opportunities for individuals to use and practise the repertoire of skills they have built over their lifetime. The chapter will then move on to consider how these issues might affect professionals.

Surviving dementia

In order to address these challenges we could think about the resilient person with dementia as surviving the experience of dementia. Lifton (1993) advised that a survivor is one who has encountered death, literally or figuratively. This can result in feelings of separation from individuals, communities and principles; of disintegration (of falling apart, or the fear of falling apart); and of paralysis stasis or immobility, which the person must adjust to or overcome. People with dementia have advised that the feel increasingly disconnected and isolated as their dementia progresses. Many people disengage from their communities, families and friends for fear of losing face or find that the people that they know avoid their company. Family roles can be eroded as relationships change along with the dementia trajectory. Each person with dementia could then potentially be engaged in a process of continual adjustments, no matter how small, where they adjust to these changes and their life with dementia, even where they are unable to remember or communicate the details of this life. The importance of the everyday is again visible here. For example, Bartlett (2016) raised the importance of the relationships that people with dementia have within their households and families, referring to this as the domestic sphere of citizenship. What occurs within the home is as important as what takes place in the larger social spaces that people with dementia inhabit (Bartlett, 2016) if the person with dementia is to be respected as a person of agency with the potential to continue to grow and develop.

Potential and resilience

Using a model of resilience reserve could re-frame people with dementia as having the potential for resilience, and to be supported in the development of resilience strategies. This changes the current discourse on dementia and decline offering positive, personalised choices to people with dementia in new ways. The opportunity to visualise resilience and resilience reserve offers a powerful tool for people with dementia to use to communicate their needs to others. This approach can also be used with people ageing with dementia where there are communication difficulties to support the storytelling process. There are also opportunities to promote visualisations of resilience using new technologies and applications (apps), which could be more responsive to changing reflections of resilience.

Resilience can be understood as the accumulation of a bank of skills, experiences, knowledge, including personal, familial, social, financial and political resources built over the life course – a resilience reserve. Despite the distress and adversity faced by many with dementia, it is possible that this reserve could facilitate adaptation and/or adjustments in certain situations of adversity. Where dementia threatens a person's sense of self, this reserve could be used to compensate and preserve aspects of personal and public identity which are important to each individual living with dementia. Listening to the experiences and stories of people with dementia could reveal their unique personal and social assets and open up new opportunities for creative practice.

Implications for staff

If conditions such as dementia are seen to confirm the medicalisation of old age and inevitable vulnerability, then by default such people are considered as having no resilience resources. This can result in therapeutic nihilism and residual care. Equally, it can be argued that, although not everyone living with dementia will be resilient, the possibility of resilience could exist despite dementia. However, unless this *possibility* of resilience is acknowledged and staff are equipped with the knowledge and tools to *recognise* resilience, it might never be realised.

Assessment and support planning could reveal the factors at play in realising the resilience of the person ageing with dementia. Practice theories, definitions and models are influenced and constructed through social policy and politics, whether in support of or as a challenge to the policies of the day. The current roles of practitioners in this field have been shaped by modernisation reforms in health and social care (Moriarty and Manthorpe, 2016). For example, many local authorities in the UK have implemented eligibility criteria in order to deliver services to those assessed most at need as they manage reduced budgets. Such practice can be both disempowering and uninteresting for staff, where prescriptive support plans are approved by senior managers, with little space for practitioner autonomy, nor differentiation between situations in relation to organisational response.

Assessment

Opportunities for identifying resilience sit within the broader framework of interpretation or finding meaning. The assessment process is used to identify needs, risks, aspirations and strengths, the outcome of which is, usually, to produce a written assessment record with the purpose of care or support planning (O'Connor et al, 2006). However, as assessment is so closely aligned with resource allocation it can often be approached as a checklist simply focussing on need and risk, or treatment options. If assessments are approached as checklists for resources then the results could be the recording of deficits and risks, over and above strengths. The stories of people living with dementia, however seemingly confused, have the potential to reveal important information about character, themes and personal values. Stories can often also offer an insight into the person's sense of self at the point of the interaction. Biography is also a way of finding out about important relationships, attachments and discovering stories of resilience and survival.

A resilience framework could assist human service professionals to critically analyse their assessments and possibly arrive at new decisions which focus on the facilitation of agency and resilience. Interventions which focus on promoting protective factors and identifying vulnerabilities in the preservation of identity may then be realised. A focus on the stories of people living with dementia could promote narrative based practice, as an alternative to care management models, which could result in more creative practice which keeps the person with dementia at the heart of the process.

Risk and protection

Other important areas such as risk assessment and adult support and protection practice can benefit from resilience perspectives. There can be a focus on risk that encourages people rather than restricts capacities (Barry, 2007). Robinson et al (2007) found that professionals focus on the physical domain of risk such as harm, whereas people with dementia focus on the biographical domain such as loss of identity. Continuing to engage in everyday activities is, therefore, important to each person with dementia and, as a result, is important in our support planning and risk–enablement practice. This then opens up a new perspective on risk management as a building block in the continuity of self, placing care and support workers at the heart of this through their practice relationships and responsibilities. This work could facilitate a re-focus on theories of the role of human service professionals, in the context of older people with dementia.

A case for resilience

I will now bring the discussion points of this chapter together by exploring the interaction between Fay and her social worker Lorna (as described in Case Studies 16.1 and 16.2), describing the ways in which they could use resilience to work differently.

Applying your knowledge of resilience in dementia care

Lorna's assessment included an in-depth analysis of Fay, the subject of Case Studies 16.1 and 16.2, and of the things that mattered to her and why. She identified past experiences and skills and considered the ways in which these things could contribute to the way in which Fay responded to the new problems she was facing; in other words, Fay's personal resilience reserve. Working in this way enables practitioners to identify and categorise resilience reserve. This is where the resilience reserve model is used (Figure 16.1). Taking each of the domains in turn we can populate each with reference to information gathered from our assessments and interactions with the people that we are working with. A focus on the stories shared between human service professionals and the person with dementia, in relation to content but also the story purpose, can reveal the importance of the most routine conversations. Sometimes, the discussions we have every day, about the everyday can be the most significant. Table 16.1 provides a summary of experiences, knowledge and skills that Lorna recorded that could contribute to Fay's personal resilience reserve.

Fay had been considered vulnerable by the local authority adult protection process because of her volunteering role. However, Lorna instead stated the case that it was exactly this experience that empowered Fay. Crucially, Lorna also pinpointed that there was a potential threat to Fay's personal identity if she was denied the opportunity to assess risks for herself and to help others. Lorna challenged the taken for granted narrative of the 'vulnerable person with dementia' and instead re-framed Fay as 'streetwise' and informed in the management of these specific risks due to her unique knowledge and experiences, in this area. In fact, Fay had more experience in this area than her social worker. This is an example of the context specific application of resilience by Lorna in her consideration of Fay's circumstances. Lorna reflected on how Fay maintained an emotional connection with others despite her memory impairment. Lorna also discussed resilience within the context of relationships, role and interactions with others, situating the resilience of the person with dementia in the present or

Table 16.1: Fay's personal resilience record

Fay's unique resilience reserve	Lorna's notes
Fay's experiences	• Previous experience of coping with adversity – death of parents • Adapting to change • Managing on own – moving to Scotland • Positive experience of education and learning • Strong female role models • Supporting others in need • Organising charity work • Happy family life and marriage • Being part of a community
Fay's knowledge and skills	• Good listener/communication skills • Organisational skills • Approachable • Person centred/value-based interactions • Educated • Supporting others • Articulate • Knowledge of adversity in other people's lives through charity work

within the moment of contact with others. Lorna then used this information to populate the resilience reserve domains which focus on roles, personal qualities and characteristics, detailed in Table 16.2.

Table 16.2: Fay's personal qualities and characteristics

Fay's unique resilience reserve	Lorna's notes
Fay's personal qualities and characteristics	• Reflective • Available for others • Self-reliant • Supportive • Empathic • Determined • Caring • Educated • Sense of humour • Sociable
Fay's roles	• Mother • Counsellor/supports others • Manager • Student • Wife • Friend

Using resilience in practice with people living with dementia helps us to refocus on what constitutes *a problem* for those living with dementia. This places issues of identity and loss of recognition for each person at the centre of practice responses. In the case of Fay, the problem to be addressed could be re-framed as to how Fay could continue to contribute to her charity interests, while, at the same time addressing her family's need to know she is not taking unnecessary risks. This utilises information from Fay's resilience reserve as to her preferred roles and importantly Fay's motivations. Motivation is not something that health and care practitioners usually include in assessment and support planning but understanding what drives people can explain much about human behaviour. Lorna has detailed Fay's motivations in Table 16.3.

Table 16.3: Motivating factors for Fay

Fay's unique resilience reserve	Lorna's notes
Fay's motivations	• To try new things • To look after self • To stay socially active • To not be a source of ridicule • To not move into a care setting • To not be viewed as a 'frail' older person or as a dependent person with dementia

The interaction between Fay, her family and her vocational work could be viewed as relational, with changes occurring as Fay experiences new challenges as a result of living with dementia. Removing her vocational work does not therefore resolve the problems that Fay may experience as this absence impacts negatively on her personal ecosystem. Using such a visualisation would have provided Fay's social worker with a platform on which to help Fay negotiate between competing risk perspectives. The role of the human service professional could then instead be to demonstrate Fay's resilience potential and to arrive at a professional consideration as to how Fay could be supported in developing resilience strategies to self-manage elements of risk and lifestyle within her personal network.

Problem-solving approaches to the daily challenges of living with dementia can also be employed. For example, although Fay was reluctant to speak about any problems as a result of dementia, support could focus on the experiences day to day of adjusting to her changing roles. A focus on the challenges of adjusting to living with memory loss through practical support could be approached alongside the emotional impact. This approach could then make use of elements of the resilience reserve to respond to feelings of self-stigma that such perceived losses could generate. This can then address the need for practical and personal support alongside feelings of embarrassment or unhappiness at having to accept (or tolerate) such support. Support can also be mobilised from the person's existing networks through a focus on assets. Table 16.4 lists the assets and resources in Fay's life.

With reference to empowerment, approaches that focus on the stories told by people living with dementia could realise resilience in practice. Empowerment practice in the context of dementia could then be re-framed as promoting the preservation of identity. A focus on identity, threats to identity and responses would then follow. A resilience focussed approach would then involve working with the person with dementia to recognise resilience reserve, building on those areas that can contribute to adjusting to loss of recognition. Stories can therefore provide the context for empowering approaches, placing each person within a situation, and providing a basis from which the people can realise resilience in action. An understanding of these factors can then empower the individual concerned, promoting practice responses which mitigate vulnerability factors

Table 16.4: Fay's networks and resources

Fay's unique resilience reserve	Lorna's notes
Fay's assets and resources	• Home • Family • Dog • Friends and neighbours • Financial security • Social support within the community • Support to manage dementia where it is defined by Fay

and promote protective factors. This can then contribute to a dynamic model of resilience-based social work practice with people ageing with dementia. For example, Fay's resilience reserve content revealed her experience and knowledge as a leader in her voluntary work, supporting others and making day-to-day decisions. Being considered as the person in need of support could potentially be difficult for Fay to accept. However, Fay had a wealth of knowledge, revealed through her resilience reserve, that her social worker could access in order to help Fay explore experiences of living with dementia. Using Fay's knowledge of the charity sector could reveal alternative roles within her area of interest. Instead of visitors arriving at Fay's home, could Fay instead provide support by mail, phone or social media with assistance? By recognising Fay's knowledge she could be empowered to continue to support other people, and in this way maintain her vocational interests, social networks and community recognition.

Empowerment can also be achieved through the creation and sharing of the resilience reserve data itself. Creating a visual record of resilience for the person to refer to and to share with others could potentially be very powerful for the person concerned. Empowerment focussed practice could also look at those areas where a person's resilience could be strengthened through targeted interventions. Fay would appear to be at risk from negative messages about ageing which could contribute to self-stigma. Empowerment practice could then focus on addressing the source of these opinions and fears, in order to lessen the potential impact on Fay as she continues to age, achieving what her social worker described as letting go, such as concerns about the future, residential care and so forth.

Resilience also demonstrates the knowledge, skills and experience that Fay still has access to in order to manage interactions in her day-to-day life. Using Fay's knowledge of the charity sector, new roles could be explored within her area of interest. Fay could be supported to play a role in changing social attitudes to either those individuals that she dedicated her working life to, or indeed people who are living with dementia. Although Fay did not want to be recognised publicly as a person with dementia, and this is important, her influence through other community roles could change the perceptions of other people about what a person with dementia can continue to do. For example, Fay could be encouraged to record her achievements over her life, her ongoing work and importantly her unrealised ambitions or future plans in a continued citizenship role. Lorna concluded that Fay is resilient in experiencing the here and now, that she has an ability to absorb things that are difficult.

In summary, resilience is a powerful concept. It facilitates the visualisation of the person with dementia's experiences, skills, knowledge, assets and roles. All of which is information that we gather for assessment purposes in our day-to-day work with people living with dementia, their families and carers. The resilience reserve facilitates the ordering of this information. Alongside information about the motivations of the person we are engaged with, this provides us with detailed evidence of strengths and assets which can be built on in practice.

Where do we go from here?

Resilience is context specific and, I suggest, is an important aspect in the preservation of identity for people with dementia in relationships with others. Resilience is not static and is influenced by the complex interaction of vulnerability and protective factors in a person's life. I have found that practitioners do not have a current framework that facilitates their use of resilience in work with people ageing with dementia. However, I suggest that a re-framing of theories of what the purpose of our work as human service professionals is with people living with dementia, could promote opportunities to use our knowledge and practice to realise the resilience of the person with dementia. Practice and research, with people ageing with dementia, can then take place within a new model of citizenship that recognises the contributions that people with dementia make to their own lives and to those of other people.

The importance of the everyday in providing the context for knowing oneself cannot be underestimated. Human service professional often come into people's lives at points of transition, upset and crisis. Restoring the everyday for the people that we work with is essentially the focus of our work. Facilitating adjustments to changes in health, circumstances and roles, in a way that respects the person's own sense of identity. Sometimes our work involves helping people to adjust to new identities but importantly we cannot allow stereotypes of people, for example with dementia, to shape our own thinking as to what this identity is. Rather, we must listen and learn from the individual people that we work with, employing our skills, knowledge and expertise in such a way that supports individual expression; and challenges restrictive views from individuals and organisations. Resilience can help us to do this. It is a way of making visible how these support tasks contribute to the whole support plan, contribute to resilience promotion, and in turn, this could result in more rewarding practice for those engaged in this work.

More rewarding practice is also possible through the value that we place on the stories told by people with dementia. The everyday conversations we share are the building blocks of our identity. The stories told by people with dementia can be dismissed as non-factual or superficial, assumed to have no substance or purpose. However, I found that the stories told by people with dementia can in fact be rich repositories of information. In particular, stories can reveal insights on aspirations, quality of life and what might constitute a better than expected outcome for that particular individual, and without that story, these important aspects of life can remain hidden from view. So, although assessment is the bedrock of our practice and support planning, don't dismiss the conversations before or after as simply the prelude to assessment or closing discussions. Sensitivity and respect will reveal lots of important details that can populate the domains of each person's individual resilience reserve.

REFLECTION POINT 16.2

As a beginning social worker, consider how you might look after yourself and use a model of resilience to do so. Write down some ideas and check back throughout the chapter if you need ideas.

Conclusion

It is important to remember that not everyone who is living with dementia will be 'resilient' and not everyone is resilient in every situation. Resilience is a fluid concept. However, following this model will help human service professionals to navigate some of the issues in this area. People living with dementia are individuals with different lives, different life experiences and varying and various skills, knowledge and expertise. Because of stereotypes about dementia, vulnerability and dependence resilience is not considered applicable to people living with dementia. However, if resilience is considered as the process of adjusting to the threats experienced when living with dementia, we can start to see people's responses to the condition in a new light, even if we don't understand exactly what is happening at that time.

Reflective questions

1 What assumptions do I make when I meet a person with dementia in need of support?

2 What am I basing these assumptions on?

3 In what way does thinking about resilience challenge this?

4 How can I use the concept in resilience in my own practice?

5 What are the challenges and opportunities for using resilience in the work place?

Further reading

- Barnes, M. (2012) *Care in Everyday Life. An Ethic of Care in Everyday Practice.* Bristol: Policy Press.
  The contested but extremely importance concept of care – especially when we are talking about social work with people living with dementia – is explored in this book. It makes a claim for a thorough ethic of care.

- Bartlett, R. and O'Connor, D. (2007) From personhood to citizenship: Broadening the lens for dementia practice and research, *Journal of Aging Studies,* 21: 107–118.
  The language of personhood has grown in dementia care. It provides an important way of seeing and valuing people who are living with dementia. This article takes forward the notion and applies it to both research and practice.

- Christie, J. (2018). Social work with older people. In V. Cree and M. Smith (eds), *Social Work in a Changing Scotland*. Oxford: Routledge.
  This chapter provides a specific Scottish focus.

- Christie, J. (2020). *Promoting Resilience in Dementia Care: A Person-Centred Framework for Assessment and Support Planning*. London: Jessica Kingsley.
  The model of resilience on which this chapter is based is developed comprehensively in this book.

References

Aburn, G., Gott, M. and Hoare, K. (2016) What is resilience? An integrative review of the empirical literature, *Journal of Advanced Nursing*, 72(5): 980–1000. Available from https://doi.org/10.1111/jan.12888

Ahmadi-Abhari, S., Guzman-Castillo, M., Bandosz, P., Shipley, M.J., Muniz-Terrera, G., Singh-Manoux, A., Kiyimaki, M., Steptoe, A., Capewell., S., O'Flaherty, M. and Brunner, E.J. (2017) Temporal trend in dementia incidence since 2002 and projections for prevalence in England and Wales to 2040: Modelling study, *British Medical Journal*, 358. Available from: https://doi.org/10.1136/bmj.j2856 (accessed July 2017).

Alzheimer's Society (2014) *Dementia UK Update*. Available from: https://www.alzheimers.org.uk/site/scripts/download.php?type=downloads&fileID=2323 (accessed April 2016).

Barry, M. (2007) *Effective Approaches to Risk Assessment in Social Work: An International Literature Review*. Social Research Findings No. 31. Edinburgh: Scottish Executive Education Department.

Bartlett, R. (2016) Scanning the conceptual horizons of citizenship, *Dementia*, 15(3): 453–461.

Bartlett, R. and O'Connor, D. (2007) From personhood to citizenship: Broadening the lens for dementia practice and research, *Journal of Aging Studies*, 21(2): 107–118.

Christie, J. (2016) 'I try to forget about the dementia': Realising the resilience of the person with dementia in social work practice. PhD thesis. Stirling: University of Stirling. Available from: http://hdl.handle.net/1893/24422

Clare, L., Kinsella, G.J., Logsdon, R., Whitlatch, C. and Zarit, S.H. (2011) Building resilience in mild cognitive impairment and early-stage dementia: Innovative approaches to intervention and outcome evaluation. In B. Resnick, L.O. Gwyther and K. Roberto (eds), *Resilience in Aging: Concepts, Research and Outcomes*. New York, NY: Springer.

Downs, M., Clare, L. and MacKenzie, J. (2006) Understandings of dementia: Explanatory models and their implications for the person with dementia and therapeutic effort. In J.C. Hughes, S.J. Louw and S.R. Sabat (eds), *Dementia: Mind, Meaning and the Person*. Oxford: Oxford University Press.

Giebel, C.M. and Sutcliffe, C. (2018) Initiating activities of daily living contributes to well-being in people with dementia and their carers. *Geriatric Psychiatry*, 33(1): 94–102.

Hughes, J. Louw, S. and Sabat, S.R. (2005) *Dementia, Mind, Meaning and the Person*. Oxford: Oxford University Press.

Kelly, F. (2010) Abusive interaction: Research into locked wards for people with dementia, *Social Policy and Society*, 9(2): 267–277.

Kitwood, T. (1987) Explaining senile dementia: The limits of neuropathological research, *Free Associations*, 10(1): 177–196.

Kitwood, T. (1990) The dialectics of dementia; with particular reference to Alzheimer's disease, *Ageing and Society*, 10(2): 177–196.

Knapp, M., Prince, M., Albanese, E., Banerjee, S., Dhanasiri, S., Plotka, J.L.F., Ferri, C., McCrone, P., Snell, T. and Stewart, R. (2007) A report into the prevalence and cost of dementia prepared by the Personal Social Services Unit (PSSRU) at the London School of Economics and the Institute of Psychiatry at King's College London, for the Alzheimer's Society. Dementia UK.

Lifton, R.J. (1993) *The Protean Self: Human Resilience in an Age of Fragmentation*. New York, NY: Basic Books.

Luthar, S.S., Cicchetti, D. and Becker, B. (2000) The construct of resilience: A critical evaluation and guidelines for future work, *Child Development*, 71(3): 543–562.

Lyman, K.A. (1989) Bringing the social back in: A critique of the bio-medicalisation of dementia, *The Gerontologist*, 29(5): 597–604.

Moriarty, J. and Manthorpe, J. (2016) *The Effectiveness of Social Work with Adults. A Scoping Review*. London: Social Care Workforce Research Unit. King's College, London. Available from: http://www.kcl.ac.uk/sspp/policy-institute/scwru/pubs/2016/reports/Moriarty-&-Manthorpe-2016-Effectiveness-of-social-work-with-adults.pdf (accessed March 2016).

O'Connor, I., Hughes, M., Turney, D., Wilson, J. and Setterland, D. (2006) *Social Work and Social Care Practice*. London: Sage.

Österholm, J.H. and Hydén, L-C. (2016) Autobiographical occasions in assessment meetings involving persons with dementia, *Qualitative Social Work*, 1–24. Available from: https://doi.org/10.1177/1473325016653466 (accessed January 2020).

Poland, F. and Birt, L. (2016) The agentic person: Shifting the focus of care, *Aging and Mental Health*. Available from: https://doi.org/10.1080/13607863.2016.1146873 (accessed February 2016).

Prince, M., Albanese, E., Guerchet, M. and Prina, M. (2014) *Alzheimer Disease International World Alzheimer Report. Dementia and Risk Reduction: An Analysis of Protective and Modifiable Factors*. London: Alzheimer Disease International.

Prince, M., Wimo, A., Guerchet, M., Ali, G.C., Wu, Y.T. and Prina, M. (2015) *Alzheimer Disease International World Alzheimer Report. The Global Impact of Dementia*. Available from: http://www.alz.co.uk/research/WorldAlzheimerReport2015.pdf (accessed July 2015).

Robinson, L., Hutchings, D., Corner, L., Finch, T., Hughes, J., Brittain, K. and Bond, J. (2007) Balancing rights and risks: Conflicting perspectives in the management of wandering in dementia, *Health, Risk and Society*, 9(4): 389–406.

Sabat, S.R. (2001) *The Experience of Alzheimer's Disease: Life through a Tangled Veil*. Oxford: Blackwell.

Sabat, S.R., Napolitano, L. and Faith, H. (2004) Barriers to the construction of a valued social identity: A case study of Alzheimer's disease, *American Journal of Alzheimer's Disease and Other Dementias*, 19(3): 177–185.

Scottish Government (2010) *Scotland's National Dementia Strategy*. Available from: http://www.scotland.gov.uk/Publications/2010/09/10151751/0 (accessed January 2011).

Snowden, D. (1997) Ageing and Alzheimer's disease: Lessons from the nun study, *Gerontologist*, 37(2): 150–156.

Ward, R., Campbell, S. and Keady, J. (2016) 'Gonna make yer gorgeous': Everyday transformation, resistance and belonging in the care-based salon, *Dementia*, 15(3): 395–143.

WHO (World Health Organization) (1992) *ICD-10 Classification of Mental and Behavioural Disorders. Clinical Descriptors and Diagnostic Guidelines*. Geneva: WHO.

Zeisel, J., Reisberg, B., Whitehouse, P., Woods., R. and Verheul, A. (2016) Ecopsychosocial interventions in cognitive decline and dementia: A new terminology and a new paradigm, *American Journal of Alzheimer's Disease & Other Dementias*, 31(6). Available from: https://doi.org/10.1177/1533317516650806

Index